This Special Edition of *Blood in the Streets* is
Number **26** of 1,000 copies.

BLOOD *in*

INVESTMENT PROFITS

the STREETS

IN A WORLD GONE MAD

James Dale Davidson

in collaboration with

Sir William Rees-Mogg

SUMMIT BOOKS   NEW YORK

To our indispensable friends

Library of Congress Cataloging in Publication Data
Davidson, James Dale.
    Blood in the streets.
    1. Investments. 2. World politics. 3. Economic history. I. Rees-Mogg, William.
II. Title.
HG4516.D38   1987   332.6   87-9935
ISBN 0-671-62735-X

CONTENTS

Contents

flation in the 1920s • How the money supply shrank • 27 parallels between the 1920s and the 1980s • Can deflation be avoided? • Bailing out a bankrupt world • The importance of expectations • After the coming crisis

The inevitability of cycles • Product cycles and innovation • "Creative destruction" in the nineteenth and twentieth centuries • Competition and the product cycle • What next for the American economy? • Military costs and declining innovation • Product cycles and stock markets • Paths America may take • Declining scale economies and investment prospects • Wider income gaps • Higher profits for small business • Enhanced demand for luxury goods • Higher savings rates and increasingly private investment • Fewer checkpoints on innovation • Falling scale and the severity of depression • America's remaining advantage in information • Major breakthroughs on the horizon • The decline of raw materials • The information revolution and employment • Beyond bulk technology • The strange economics of material plenty • The prospect for living standards in the future

Six storm clouds over real estate • Understanding international influences on real estate prices • The difficulty of thinking clearly about real estate • The farm depression • The glut of commercial space • The impact of tax change on prices • The Savings & Loan crisis and real estate • The weakness of the mortgage security market • The inflation premium and the private home • Condos look especially weak • Profiting from distress sales

Investing as a skill to be learned • Taking stock of your investment needs and skills • Making a financial inventory • How to match investments to your own temperament • Conservative investment becomes more difficult • More accurate information a key to higher profits • Cultivate an investment frame of mind • Learn to update expectations • Information sources you should not trust • "Plagiarism" as an investment skill • Learn to read the newspaper • The bigger the event, the longer it takes to happen • Practice updating expectations • Exploiting market imperfections • Competition and compound interest • Time and you • Four investment virtues • Rules for managing debt • Twenty-three investment implications of this analysis

Contents

ACKNOWLEDGMENTS

Every book is far more a collaboration than its authors may imagine. In this case, Sir William and I know that we have been largely collating the good work of others. They did the heavy lifting. They prepared the research which is cited on practically every page of our story. Bearing in mind T. S. Eliot's comment that bad writers borrow while great writers steal, we hope we have struck the delicate balance needed to make this book both good and honest. That is to say, we hope that the thoughts of others, gathered from far and wide, have become our thoughts. Perhaps in investment books, as in investment, possession can be nine-tenths of the law. In any event, here are the good people whose help, in some cases inadvertent, contributed to this volume: Angela Drennan and Bea Westerfield transcribed many hours of dictation and wrestled with the word processor. Rita Smith, Edie Patterson, and Kathleen Juhl provided logistical backup. For research help and good advice we thank: Fiona Shields, Nancy Savage, Dominic Brewer, Nils Taube, Gilbert de Botton, Tom Schneider, David Hale, Jimmie Rogers, Gary Vernier, Greg Barnhill, Jim Marques, Nancy Lazar, Marc Leland, Mark Hulbert, Bill Bonner, Steve Newby, Allan Meltzer, Gordon Tullock, Caroline Butler, Adrian Day, Amory Lovins, Esther Dyson, Marshall Goldman, Francis A. Freisinger, Sheila Macdonald, David Keating, David Thomas, K. Eric Drexler, Susan Ellis, Mary Penniman, Garrett M. Moran, Helen Sasson, Bill Strauss, John Browne, Lise Hartman, Beth Johnson, Carter Beese, and Thomas R. Goldberg. Joel Wittenberg wrote some of the definitions of investment terms that appear in the glossary and contribute to an earlier version of the chapter on debt default. We owe him a special thanks, along with Theron Raines, who helped sell the idea of this book; Jim Silberman, who bought it; and Arthur Samuelson, who helped whip it into shape. Undoubtedly, we have forgotten to acknowledge someone whose help was useful. If you know who you are, forgive us and accept belated thanks.

Finally, since I wrote most of the words, I accept responsibility for them. The split infinitives are my doing. So are the sentence fragments. As for the ideas, I hope they can be understood and are right. Their accuracy is not guaranteed. You should think through everything we say for yourself. Then the ideas will no longer be ours, nor even those of the good people from whom we lifted them. They will be yours. I hope you can put them to good use.

James Dale Davidson

The best time to buy is when blood is running in the streets.
—Nathan M. Rothschild

INTRODUCTION

The trouble about man is twofold. He cannot learn truths that are too complicated; he forgets truths that are too simple.

—Rebecca West

On June 18, 1815, one of history's decisive battles was being fought at a Belgian village called Waterloo. On one side were 75,000 British troops under the command of the Duke of Wellington. Pitted against them were 100,000 French troops under Napoleon. Somewhere in the distance were 125,000 German soldiers marching to join the British.

The battle of Waterloo is usually remembered more by military historians than investors. The tactics of the opposing sides have been rehashed and memorized late at night by cadets hoping to be generals themselves someday. The battle and its aftermath have not been hot items of attention for aspiring investors. They should be. No other episode of modern history provides so stark an illustration of the dangers and profit potential of investing under "blood in the streets" conditions.

In those brief days, when the eyes of Europe turned to the scene of the fighting, ordinarily obscure relationships came into focus. Even the dullest of investors saw that the security of his holdings is ultimately connected to the way the power is exercised in the world.

At stake was control over Europe for the foreseeable future. A French victory would mean a radical change in the power equation. No longer would Britain and British commercial interests be predominant. Important investments would turn, as it were, on the flip of a coin. Governments allied with Britain might default on their debts. Traders could be cut off from their markets. The British East India Company's lucrative trade with India and the Orient could be threatened. Even the internal security of Britain itself could be endangered. Investors in London had one eye over their shoulders at recent uprisings centered in

15

Nottinghamshire. Rioters had organized around the frightening cry, "Bread or blood."

As investors in the London market awaited news of Waterloo, they grew more jittery. Early reports told of French victories. The main German army, commanded by Marshal Gebhard von Blücher, was still some way from the scene of the fighting. No one knew how far. Wellington's position looked grim.

Many among the more conservative investors sold into a weak market. Few were ready to increase their stake upon British victory. One exception was Nathan Rothschild, baron of the Austrian Empire and head of the Rothschild banking house in London. However glum the news and rumors became, Rothschild bought.

Communications in 1815 were torturously slow. In those days, of course, there were no radio or TV news bulletins. Information worked its way along a cumbersome relay system until dispatches could be printed in newspapers or shouted out by criers at the corner. No investor with substantial holdings wished to be the last to hear that the battle had gone against the British and allied forces. The market was literally resting on a hair trigger.

Eager to get the jump on one another, traders looked for any clue to discover when news of the battle had reached London. Knowing that they knew too little, they concluded that their best strategy lay in imitation. Like schoolchildren taking an especially difficult exam, they resolved to look over the shoulder of someone likely to get the answer right. It was well known that Nathan Rothschild had bet heavily upon a British victory. It was also known that Rothschild had invested considerable sums to develop a private intelligence system to learn about important events before they were generally known. Many people correctly assumed that Rothschild would be among the first to learn the fortunes of battle. If Rothschild bought, everyone would buy. If Rothschild sold, everyone would take it as an indication that Britain had been defeated.

Nathan Rothschild was in fact the first in London to learn that the Duke of Wellington had triumphed over Napoleon. Realizing the whole market was geared to respond to his actions, Rothschild did not rush to buy. He sold. The result: The London market collapsed. Only after panic selling drove already depressed prices to fire-sale levels did Rothschild step in and buy. Within hours, the news of Wellington's victory sent the market skyrocketing. Rothschild's maneuver earned him one of the great trading profits in history. He made about a million pounds—a fantastic sum in 1815.

MORE THAN A TRADING PRINCIPLE

This story illustrates the Rothschild principle from which the title of this book is taken: "The best time to buy is when blood is running in the streets." It is a principle that is true today. The greatest profits can always be had by buying when prices are most depressed by pessimism. "Blood in the streets," however, is more than just the name for an investment principle. It is also a prediction about the world to come. As you will see, we believe that the world is now in the twilight of a major phase of economic history. The danger you face is practically as great as the threat posed to British investors at Waterloo. In a sense, it may even be more treacherous, because today's is a hidden danger that almost no one sees or recognizes.

The coming years will be a bad time to be ill advised. A time fraught with snares for anyone who is unprepared. We could be on the verge of financial upheaval when blood will, indeed, "run in the streets." Many people will suffer staggering losses. Others, who take the right investment steps, at the right time, will earn handsome profits.

ANOTHER GREAT DEPRESSION?

No economic upheaval of the magnitude we expect has been seen in the world since the Great Depression. That event, now fading into history, was largely unintelligible as it occurred. No one wanted it. Almost no one predicted it. And even those who noticed symptoms of trouble—symptoms ominously similar to characteristics of today's economy—did not draw accurate conclusions, or only gave warnings focusing on narrow aspects of the problem. One economic historian, writing in 1932, concluded: "I know of no competent student who anticipated a world depression of such cataclysmic magnitude as the years actually brought."

Even Lord Keynes, whose economic theories about the depression were later tremendously influential, was no better able than anyone else to see what events of the day meant. He mistook the collapse of the U.S. stock market in October 1929 for "a bull point for world prosperity." He could hardly have been more wrong. It turned out to be the beginning of the greatest financial crisis in history.

The Great Depression still has not been adequately explained to the public. It is like an unsolved mystery, a crime for which a few politicians, like Herbert Hoover, have been hanged in the court of public opinion. But most people have no real conception of what caused the depression. It has been blamed on too much money, too little money, bootleg gin, shoeshine boys buying stocks, new tariffs, recession in the automobile industry, and the usual suspects, Wall Street bankers and the bully boys of high finance. In short, the case has been closed, but not solved.

If you are like 99 percent of the investing public, you are no better prepared to recognize and cope with another upheaval like the depression than you would be had it never happened. You are literally an innocent—trusting to politicians, or your broker, or your luck to pull you through any unexpected trouble. That is like being exposed to a disease or plague that strikes without warning, and whose causes are unknown. If you can not recognize the symptoms, you can hardly protect yourself.

THE LATEST NEWS . . .

But why should you worry? The news is not bad. Even if economic growth has not been all it could be, it has often been worse. Here are some comments that may put the situation in perspective:

"There is little pessimism."

"The basic price situation is notably sound. Commodity markets are free of speculative price inflation."

"As a nation we are living and spending far beyond our income in a manner possible only through a progressive and inflationary expansion of artificial purchasing power."

"Inflation is here."

"[There is] a considerable excess of capacity in many branches of Industry, especially in those producing basic materials or staple commodities."

"The results of a loss of our favorable balance of trade constitute the greatest single threat to American business. . . . Nor is anyone likely to deny the probability that such an excess of imports will impose onerous and possibly dangerous burdens upon those American industries which will most feel the competition."

"The condition of agriculture, the volume of unemployment, the textile trades, coal mining . . . present grave problems."

"[A]ny further great expansion of credit is not warranted under existing conditions. This position is in itself one of the greatest dangers."

"It is quite clear that the general market and speculative situation is quite out of the hands of the Federal Reserve system, just as agricultural credit and land speculation . . . escaped from control."

"America cannot remain prosperous in a world not only impoverished, but overwhelmed by debt."

"We feel that we have an obligation which is paramount . . . to avert any dangerous crisis in the money market." *

Sound familiar? These comments could have been clipped from the business and financial press yesterday. In fact, they all date from the period just before the Great Depression began in 1929. Industrial production turned down in July of that year, but almost no one suspected what was in store until the stock market crashed on October 24. Even then, very few understood what was happening. Widespread optimism returned, and the stock market rose sharply through the early months of 1930.

Major economic upheavals are not easy to recognize. They have not been easy for people in the past. And there is no reason to think that they will be any easier to spot in the future. Unless you are prepared— and know what to look for and how to protect yourself—the coming economic upheaval could catch you as flatfooted as the last Great Depression caught your father or grandfather. But if you understand the powerful forces at work, otherwise puzzling developments will make sense. It will be like seeing color in a color-blind world. What will baffle your neighbors will be understood by you. While they make big losses, you can make big profits. That is what this book is all about— helping you prepare for the new world that is coming.

THE FIVE APPROACHES TO INVESTMENT

As you will see, this book develops a different approach to investment. Although the principles we explore are simple ones, they are manifested in ways that are far from obvious. In fact, for the first several chapters, this may seem more like a history book than an investment guide. As the argument develops, however, you will see that apparently distant and abstract ideas really provide the foundation for practical, money-making decisions. Once you understand them, we believe that you will

* Federal Reserve official.

have a large advantage over investors who don't. You will also be in a better position to make sense of a world running mad.

The novelty of our investment approach rests with the fact that we are analyzing different fundamentals from those noticed by most investors. Very few others have bothered to see and act upon the variables that we think are important. Rothschild did, with fantastic success. Other shrewd investors have as well. But you will see that the approach we explore in *Blood in the Streets* is the least understood and least used of the five basic approaches to investment.

Those approaches are briefly outlined below. They are: 1) random trading, 2) technical trading, 3) fundamental trading on economic information, 4) fundamental trading on political information, and 5) fundamental trading on megapolitical analysis. In practice, most investors use a combination of one or more methods in most of their transactions.

Random Trading

The first of these must be mentioned to be dismissed. It is the random selection method. Some academics have argued unpersuasively that investment selection can be done as effectively by tossing darts as by careful calculation. This is a view that few have believed, and fewer still have put into practice. There never has been, for example, a mutual fund offering purely random stock selection based upon purely random buy and sell signals. While there is undoubtedly a randomness in many investments, this is seldom seen as a virtue. Most people with money to invest are smart enough to look for ways to narrow the odds against their success. They do this by employing information.

Technical Trading

When this information relates solely to price movements and transaction patterns, it is said to be "technical." Technical traders sometimes deny that anything useful can be known about markets other than their transaction histories. Technical traders study price patterns with the idea that certain regularities in the patterns give hints about price movements in the future. We discuss technical trading in more detail later in this book.

Three Levels of Fundamental Information

The most ambitious method of employing information in investment is the "fundamental" approach. This is ours. We believe that it is possible to understand some of the factors that will influence prices in the future. But just what are these factors? And where does one look?

Fundamental investing is usually contrasted with the technical approach as if it were a single way of investing. In fact, there are three basic levels at which fundamental analysis can operate.

Economic Fundamentals

The most common fundamental approach to investment focuses upon economic and demographic factors. Analysts pore over annual reports and cash-flow projections, and sometimes even visit firms to gauge the strength of their top managers. The economic approach may also include an attempt to discover how changing tastes or trends in the population will alter demand for certain goods and services. For example, if the birthrate falls, this implies a declining demand for baby food and Pampers. Those who approach investment decisions by analyzing economic fundamentals take note of such changes.

For many years, the economic fundamentals approach was practically the only one employed on Wall Street. It is still the predominant approach today. Chances are high that your broker, or someone he talks to, uses it in selecting the stocks he recommends that you buy.

Political Fundamentals

Over the past fifteen years, there has been a marked increase in investment analysis that is keyed to political fundamentals. Both investors and the public at large have become more aware that political decisions in Washington or other capitals alter the profitability of investment. The upsurge of inflation in the seventies was a major factor focusing attention on the political environment in which firms operate. Lots of maverick investment advisors cropped up to recommend precious metals as a protection against inflation.

This was something that no one could have understood by referring to balance sheets or by analyzing the quality of a firm's management. Economic fundamentals, as Wall Street had previously understood them, were no longer a sufficient guide to investment profits. As the "gold bugs" pointed out in best-selling books and investment newsletters, the new key to profits was to understand political decisions. First and foremost among these they put the connivance of almost all politicians in inflation and debasement of the currency.

Referring to these fundamentals, many argued that runaway inflation in the 1980s was a certainty. They could foresee no possibility that politicians would behave responsibly, balance the budget, or maintain a steady, modest growth of the money supply. As it turned out, they were correct in their judgment of the politicians, but wrong about what that meant. To almost everyone's surprise, inflation has tumbled during the 1980s. In fact, through mid-1986, the actual increase in the cost of living had fallen below official forecasts for thirteen consecutive semi-annual periods.

Clearly, something of importance had been left out of consideration.

Megapolitical Fundamentals

We believe that the key to many current investment puzzles can be found in fundamental analysis at a deeper and broader level—the mega-political level. It is at this level that news of the battle of Waterloo was important. It is at this level that largely unseen changes are undermining the foundations upon which your investments rest.

A slightly unfair analogy may clarify the distinction between the three basic levels of fundamental analysis. Suppose you were interested in buying a house. You could try to understand the fundamentals by focusing your attention on the house itself. You could check the furnace, find out whether the roof was solid, have tests done for termites, etc. That is more or less equivalent to analysis of economic fundamentals.

A different kind of fundamental approach would be to look at political factors that might influence the outcome of your decision. For example, you might find that though the house you picked was physically a fine specimen, it would be worth a lot less in the future because politicians planned to authorize a freeway to cross through your backyard. That is the kind of information that cannot be turned up by carefully checking the beams or by analyzing soil samples. Yet it might have a major bearing on the success of your investment.

Finally, fundamental information on the deepest level of all is mega-political analysis. This is the equivalent of learning that your house is built upon an earthquake fault line. It is at the megapolitical level that you learn whether your house is more or less likely to be a target of urban terrorists or what the prospects for another depression may be. Unlike political developments, these are matters that are beyond conscious control. You cannot understand them by developing an inside source at the Planning Commission or at the Treasury.

The Secrets of Megapolitics

In our view, you must turn to megapolitics to find the answers to the deepest puzzles of economic and political life. We believe that the worldwide economic collapse that began in 1929 had origins in the hidden workings of megapolitics. We think that megapolitical forces are now at work undermining the basis of today's prosperity.

What exactly is "megapolitics?" It is no good your running to a dictionary to find out. You won't find it listed. We made up the word. We made it up because until now there has not been a fitting word to match the concept we believe is crucial to understanding the way the world works.

"Megapolitics" literally means "politics in the largest sense." It is the study of raw power. It is an attempt to analyze the most basic factors that govern the uses of power in the world. Most of these megapolitical power factors lie far from the spotlight of politics. They have surprisingly little to do with personalities or campaign tactics or ideologies. Instead, megapolitics involves deeper variables that alter the costs of projecting and resisting power. Far more than you may now think, the character and reach of governments, even the way the world economy functions, can be dramatically altered by variables that are more or less beyond conscious control.

The largest of these variables is shifting technology. New weapons and new ways of organizing the use of weapons can sometimes give one group of people an overpowering advantage. With new technology, it can become relatively cheap to deploy force, very costly for anyone to resist. Or vice versa. For months or years or decades, or however long it takes for other groups to copy or defeat the advantage, those at a disadvantage will be like 98-pound weaklings confronting a barrel-chested bully. They will bow to power. Or be forced to bow. And the world will change to reflect the new megapolitical reality. Maps will be rewritten. The terms of trade and finance will alter. Economies will grow or stagnate. Every outcome that power sets will be set wrong or right according to the meanderings of megapolitics.

In coming chapters, we shall tell you some of the startling ways that changing technologies have altered political institutions in the past. We shall also warn you of the hidden dangers posed by up-to-the-minute technologies. If they fragment the modern economy even half as much as we believe they may, the world could face a long period of instability, terrorism, and economic decline.

TECHNOLOGY AND YOU

It is hard to overestimate the powers of technology to change what is important in life. Technology not only helps people work and play, it affects the organization of work. Technology is a factor determining the size of firms. And the size of countries. Technology has an indirect, hidden role to play in the development of political ideologies. It helps change religion. Technology influences our perception of reality itself. In the seventeenth and eighteenth centuries people thought in terms of "a clockwork universe." No one would ever have thought that way without a clock. The key to the hidden workings of history is technological.

Indeed, it is not an exaggeration to say that technology gave man history. The dark centuries in which humans lived with few tools or none, scrounging like animals for food, sleeping in caves or exposed, open spaces, were the time of *pre*history. History began only when people adopted technology. Technology enabled farmers to plant and reap crops. Technology had to be mastered before primitive potters could cast the earthenware whose shards and fragments historians and archeologists would later study. Before carpenters and masons could build the crude shelters that became history's first ruins, they needed technological help. They did not work with their bare hands. The murderous kings who gave history its start would merely have been murderous nobodies without the tools to chisel their names.

Technology is still the driving force that makes history go.

Does it seem as though we give technology too much credit? Think again. *Technology* is just a fancy word for "tools." Tools determine the reach and scope of human behavior. A man's tools can easily alter his mood, his productivity, even his strength and bravery. His tools can affect his realization of the spiritual in life.

A steel-tipped plow can make a dull farmer seem cunning. A sharper blade will make a weak warrior seem strong, and therefore add to his bravery in battle. Remember, weapons are tools, too. In a world where the outcome of war determines who will live and who will die, weapons are in some respects the most important and far-reaching tools of all.

They even help determine the nature of political organization. When Thomas Jefferson declared in the Declaration of Independence that "all men are created equal," he was speaking a contemporary truth. A few centuries earlier, no one could have conceived of such a thought. It simply was not true. A mounted knight in armor was more than the equal of half a village of poorly armed peasants.

FORCES AND INDIVIDUALS IN HISTORY

Man and woman are always whittling away at history with new tools, weakening what seemed strong and redirecting the course of events in ways that are inevitably mysterious and misunderstood. Unraveling these mysteries amounts to both a "who-done-it?" and a "what-done-it?" The strongest forces in history are not the work of a few individuals making decisions for their own private amusement. They are the work of millions of hands employing new tools to do new work—or to do old work in a new way. The invention of industrial machinery that created great numbers of wage-paying jobs altered the landscape of life more thoroughly than the heroic efforts of any individual. The tracks of rural farm boys flocking to factories became new thoroughfares. And the areas around factories became new cities.

At the same time, individuals can play a determining role in megapolitical conditions that will then change the lives of millions. What happened in a scientist's beaker in Delaware has several times in this century toppled governments and turned bright welfare states built upon the export of wool and leather into comic little dictatorships with runaway inflation.

Points of real breakthrough in leading technologies are times when the whole of life is rearranged. Millions of people, operating under new influences, make choices that are as difficult to suppress as the working of the market itself. To speak of these influences as "forces" is only an economy of speech. Like the notion of supply and demand, which seems at first the expression of a mechanical principle, everything that happens in life is really the action of people. People changed from buying wool to rayon. And Uruguay collapsed. Everything is dependent upon everything else.

The purpose of this book is to lay bare these hidden, perplexing interconnections. To tell you where to look for the revolutions to come. To warn you, so you don't invest in the new Uruguay—in the many Uruguays to come. We want to tell you the way the world works. We want to show you the big picture, so you can recognize the patterns in the great jigsaw puzzle of megapolitics, while everyone else is merely feeling around the edges.

We'll tell you why the fate of Iowa is partly in the hands of the genetic engineers whose new seed may make scrubland bloom. And what the scientists do not decide will be determined more by the Politboro in Moscow than the Congress in Washington. We shall explore why what engineers now know about fiber optics dooms every copper mine in

North America . . . why new ceramic processes for fusing sand will overturn what is left of the iron economy of northern Minnesota . . . why improved microtechnology and automation may temporarily halt the rise of mass incomes in the West . . . and much more.

Such is the power of technology. It and other megapolitical variables ultimately determine how power is exercised. Because power sets the rules by which the economy functions, the meanderings of megapolitics can determine whether we have prosperity or depression.

These meanderings involve more than technological change, of course. They also involve changes in relative wealth. Wherever there is a striking disproportion in the control or production of economic resources, power comes into play. Whether it is financial resources, oil, airplanes or silicon chips, control over economic resources is a crucial megapolitical variable.

Changing scale economies in the production process also alters the basic conditions under which power is exercised. When there are large advantages to operating on a grand scale, the power equation reflects this underlying reality. As we shall see, this can have surprisingly far-reaching consequences.

IT SOMETIMES PAYS TO THINK ABSTRACTLY

The secrets of megapolitics have remained secrets to all but a few people because they are largely impersonal. They are at a scale that is not visible from the perspective of day-to-day life. Like the message spelled out by a marching band, they cannot be seen at eye level.

Until now, to see megapolitics you had to stand on a tall stack of history books. And it would have to be the right stack, because most of history, like most of life, is told in personalized terms. That is where the human interest lies. To most people, an abstract accounting of important events is like a drama without characters.

Megapolitics is just such an abstract, impersonal accounting. It is a matter of patterns of behavior. These patterns are influenced by what people think. But they usually have little to do with what people think they are doing. They are more accidental than intentional. These patterns determine the cycles of human affairs. These patterns lead to outbreaks of wars. They seem also to accentuate economic cycles, making for prosperity or depression. They have nothing to do with anyone *wanting* to cause a depression.

Unlike politics, megapolitics has no slogans. It seldom even involves variables that are consciously controlled by anyone to whom a slogan could appeal. No one runs around with a button: "Reduce scale economies in the production process." No bumper sticker says: "Invent a weapons system that increases the military importance of the infantry."

WHAT REALLY MATTERS

To study megapolitics is to dig deeply into the ultimate determinants of history. Changing power relations alter patterns of human behavior. As these power relations change, they alter incentives. As people face new incentives, they behave differently. Major market developments and history itself follow the meanderings of changing incentives. Identify changing power relations, then, and you will have a very good idea of how people will behave in the future. Understanding power and the patterns of behavior that are instigated by shifts of power is the key to understanding the way the world works.

The Erosion of Power: Ominous Parallels

Only when one nation has an overwhelming share of economic resources and power does the world economy seem to function smoothly. Only then is there likely to be free trade and open movement of goods, services, people, and capital across borders. The last Great Depression coincided with a significant megapolitical development—the effective collapse of that day's dominant power—Great Britain. A similar erosion of American power is now well advanced. The very foundations of political stability upon which prosperity rests are severely weakened. For fundamental reasons that we shall spell out in this book, those crucial foundations can be expected to erode further. Sometimes slowly. Sometimes rapidly.

If you have been listening, if you have had your ear to the ground, you have already heard and felt the first rumblings of the earthquakes to come: the defeat of the United States in Vietnam. The collapse of fixed exchange rates. The oil shock. The debt crisis. The upheavals in Iran and Lebanon. These were all just preliminary tremors, warning shocks that foretell major earthquakes of world power.

Why Upheavals Are Depressing

Such dramatic changes in the economy occur only rarely. When they do, they are usually remembered as periods of disaster and great losses.

Only a few are lucky enough or shrewd enough to realize the profit potential opened up by upheavals in the investment landscape. Most people do not understand what is happening and are unprepared.

This is what happened during the Great Depression that began in 1929. At that time the collapsing stock market, falling real estate, tumbling commodity prices, and widespread repudiation of debt plunged the world into the greatest economic cataclysm since the Black Death. A great many fortunes were wiped out for every new fortune that was made.

Many of the peculiar aspects of today's economy have much in common with the period immediately preceding the Great Depression. We doubt that this is a coincidence. They include:

1. A surprising absence of price inflation in spite of loose credit conditions
2. Weak or falling commodity prices, including a major collapse of oil prices
3. Collapse of the farm sector
4. Weakness in mining
5. Declining auto sales
6. Record levels of consumer debt
7. A mounting trade deficit pressing U.S. manufacturers
8. A deteriorating international debt situation
9. Protectionist sentiment growing in the Congress
10. Soaring stock market encouraging optimism, in spite of unexpectedly weak business performance

Other Parallels

These are only the most obvious parallels. There are others. Commodity cartels in rubber, coffee, and copper broke down as the Great Depression began. Oil prices tumbled by 80 percent. Oil, tin, and cocoa cartels have broken down now. Then, as now, the American economy had been strongly outperforming Europe, leading to talk of an "economic miracle" in the United States. The superior U.S. performance was usually attributed to "marvelous technical strides" in America. Shades of Silicon Valley.

Developments in the banking system provide yet another ominous parallel. Both periods are marked by the rapid buildup of illiquid assets on the balance sheets of major banks, with bad farm loans and speculative real estate loans well up on the list. Today's problem loans are at a much greater magnitude than those of the twenties. Then, the debt of Latin America had been pawned off into old ladies' bond portfolios. Today, it is piled up on the balance sheets of the world's largest banks. Default then mainly socked the old ladies. Today, it could send the whole world through the wringer. The huge losses posted by the giant Bank America—reducing its capital below regulatory limits—hint at another "day of reckoning." It could happen.

History does repeat itself, though not always in the way we expect. The parallels between today's financial conditions and those leading to the Great Depression are ominously clear—though almost no one seems to have recognized them. And that may be the most ironic parallel of all. Now, as then, the prevalent economic worry is inflation. And inflation is a worry. But from where we sit an equal worry is deflation, a collapse that would place the most severe strains upon your livelihood and investments.

No one can know for certain what the future holds. But events do follow patterns of cause and effect. Reviewing the evidence has convinced us that the danger of collapse is greater than at any time in recent decades. Throughout this book, we will attempt to guide you through the coming crisis, cautiously and soberly. Our purpose is not to prove a point, but to help you make money. To that end, we are neither bulls nor bears; inflationists nor deflationists. We are realists. And you should be too, if you hope to stay ahead of the markets. They can be treacherous in times of upheaval.

> *We were in the mood for magic.*
> —Anne O'Hare McCormick
> on the United States in 1929

We hope that our worries prove to be exaggerations. We hope the experts are right, as Franz Schneider, Jr., was not, who assured readers of the *New York Sun* in 1929 that "analysis of prevailing economic and financial factors reveals no convincing ground for expecting depression. On the contrary, such an analysis encourages the belief in continued prosperity."

> *When we try to pick out anything by itself, we find it hitched to everything else in the universe.*
> —John Muir

Remember, investment markets are not isolated like casinos, separate from the life of society. They are part and parcel of the larger world. There can never be a great upheaval in markets that does not reflect a great upheaval in society. The markets may react first, because they reflect expectations of the future. But upheavals that would threaten your investments will not just threaten your investments alone. They could threaten your livelihood, your plans for retirement, and the hope of a good life for those you love.

We believe that the explanations in this book will repay your effort in reading it—even if you have no investments and do not expect to have any.

WHY WE ARE PUBLISHING THIS ANALYSIS

During times of rapid change and confusion, a better explanation of fundamental relationships can be of significant value. In many circumstances, the value of this understanding will be greater, the fewer persons who share it. The skeptical reader may therefore wonder why we are willing to spell out the thoughts in this book if we truly believe their investment consequences are significant. It is like being willing to share a treasure map. Why would anyone do it? That is a fair question. Even if it had not occurred to you consciously, it may have come to you intuitively as an element of suspicion about what we have to say. If the information is useful, why share it?

The answer has several parts. One part, of course, is that we were paid to write this book. Writing books is usually not a paying proposition. But writers are always optimistic, and we are no exceptions. Beyond that, there are other considerations. Both of the authors have been providing investment advice for some years. By and large, those who have followed our advice have done quite well. Each month we publish an advisory bulletin called *Strategic Investment*. It makes specific portfolio recommendations based upon our view of the world. While not all of our recommendations have been profitable, the overall track record is outstanding. By sheer coincidence, both our Conservative and Speculative portfolios averaged a gain of 62 percent on trades closed out in 1985. As this is written in 1986, the Conservative portfolio was again outperforming practically every blue-chip portfolio of the professional fund managers, while the profit on Speculative trades had averaged 79 percent over an average holding period of just about two months.

Since both of us are quite busy and are able to focus on investment strategy only on a part-time basis, it is reasonable to infer that a large part of our success is attributable to the accuracy of our fundamental understanding of the way the world works. Otherwise, we could not outperform full-time investment professionals.

Not only have our specific investment picks been right, but our forecasts of economic and political developments have included a number of real bull's-eyes. *Strategic Investment* predicted the collapse in oil prices, the fall of the dollar, the unraveling of the OPEC cartel, the low inflation rates of 1985 and 1986, the skyrocketing of bonds, and three successive discount cuts by the Federal Reserve. We've predicted the fall in value of commercial real estate, worsening problems in the farm sector, the Latin American debt difficulties, and the succession of banking crises that have since been played out in the headlines. We could give more examples, but the point should be clear. The perspective from which this book is written has proven more useful and profitable for understanding the 1980s than more conventional views.

If we could hope to hoard this advantage for ourselves and the select number of readers who follow our advice in *Strategic Investment,* we might have been tempted to do so. But we do not believe that advantages can be hoarded for long. If we had not spelled out the secrets of megapolitics in this book, then in six months or a year or sometime soon, someone else would have done so. By explaining these basic relationships ourselves, we have the satisfaction of presenting our ideas while they are novel, rather than waiting for someone else to come along and do it.

BECOMING A BETTER INVESTOR

You can train yourself to be a better investor. It is largely a matter of thinking clearly. In some respects, investment is a game of puzzle solving. Great investors have many of the same skills as great detectives. These are not skills they are born with. They are not magic. They are skills that you can obtain by training your mind to look for the hidden connections between things.

Investing in markets is like solving a mystery that is really four mysteries in one. There are four overlapping puzzles that you have to resolve; four aspects of reality that you must master:

1. You must try to understand the deep puzzles of megapolitics.
2. You must master the mechanical mysteries of markets.

3. You must collect clues to the way other people react to markets.
4. You have to decipher yourself.

This book will help you solve each of these important mysteries of investment.

INVESTMENT IS A REALITY TEST

A famous physicist once wrote that even if a child were to grow up to become a Nobel Prize winner he would have learned half the physics he could ever grasp by the age of four. The same is true of investment. Its basics are more rudimentary than matters of money, of profits gained or lost, of dollars entered on the ledger sheet. They are an expression of the basic reality of life—a reality that you encounter everywhere. You leave a good parking space on the street; somebody will come by and take it. You find a little restaurant where the food is good and the prices are low. Before you know it, you have to wait in line at the door. A football team introduces a new play. It wins a few games. Or even a season. But before long, a counterplay is developed.

THE LAW OF COMPENSATION

Wherever there is something good, nature will compensate by creating a new aspect that is not good. When something goes up, nature will find a way to pull it down. Nature always sends vandals to the building site. If an experience is too exhilarating, or choicer than the rest, nature will compensate by adding consequences that are bitter, depressing, or hazardous. Even the physical pleasures of sex are subject to this counterattack. When it seemed a few years ago that new, effective means of contraception could relieve sex from responsibility and make it a pure recreation, nature went to work inventing new dark linings to the silver cloud—herpes and AIDS. Nature's minions are doing the same coldhearted work everywhere and always.

This is the all-embracing action and reaction of nature, what Emerson called the "law of compensation." What he meant is simply that nature must always keep its accounts in balance. Every plus must also entail a minus. When one end of the magnet attracts, the other end repels. Every force in nature sets in motion some counterforce that works in the opposite direction. That is a basic, proverbial truth that you find as a child on the teeter-totter. When one end goes up, the other must go down.

The same truth comes out in many different forms, as recorded in the proverbs of every nation:

> The more laws, the less justice.
> Hasty climbers have sudden falls.
> The brightest blades grow dim with rust.
> The way to be safe is never to feel secure.
> He that serves everybody is paid by nobody.
> Buying on trust is the way to pay double.
> Tall trees catch much wind.
> He who has the worst cause makes the most noise.
> He that seeks to have many friends never has any.
> Money lent to a friend must be recovered from an enemy.
> What is bought is cheaper than a gift.
> Trees do not grow to the sky.
> Failure teaches success.
> All sunshine makes the desert.
> He that finds faults wants to buy.
> A flatterer is a secret enemy.

These common epigrams are all roundabout ways of saying: "The best time to buy is when blood is running in the streets." They are different expressions of one profound truth.

CYCLES

Up and down. Ebb and flow. This fundamental rhythm of life is the basis of cycles in human affairs, the cycles in markets, as well as the cycles of tides and seasons. These cycles begin, in Emerson's words, with the "action and reaction . . . we meet in every part of nature."

Of course, it would be too simple to believe that everything in life is riding the same teeter-totter. It is not. There is a powerful tendency for a strong action to set in motion a compensating reaction. But not everything that goes down comes back up again. Some companies whose shares crash simply go out of business. The Roman Empire fell. It never picked itself back up. A message washed out to sea in a bottle may simply be lost. Not even everything that goes up must literally come down. Rockets launched to the outer planets will keep sailing right out of the solar system.

Some injustices, too, are remedied in only the most distant, roundabout way, if at all. There is a *tendency* for one force to set in motion an opposite force. But as slaves once knew, this tendency does not exact justice at the level of individual human lives. If the compensating force were always felt immediately, there would never have been slaves. And there would be no dictators now. Unfortunately, the forces of compensation are sometimes roundabout. Sometimes, complex webs of cause and effect intervene to reinforce negative or positive results. At such times, economies can either break down or become much more prosperous than would seem possible.

UNPOPULAR TRUTHS

The key to being a good investor in the years to come lies in drawing careful distinctions. You must see reality as it is, because every investment is ultimately a reality test. Sometimes it is a ruthless test at that.

The story of this book is the story of raw power and the ways of power. It is a story that will disappoint some of the deep hopes of good people. Those who hope that diplomacy and cooperation are key to solving the world's problems will resent the fact that we believe they are likely to be disappointed. We, too, hope for peace. But our study of the way the world works suggests that cooperation works only in limited ways.

Small-minded people will also take issue with our view that the direction of the economy is usually determined internationally. They hope for something less. A local economy. A personal economy. An economy whose forces are contained in horizons they can see and whose parameters can be controlled, if not by themselves, then at least by the local candidate who comes shopping for their votes.

Unfortunately, this is as vain as expecting that we will have "peace in our time" by all joining hands to wish it so. Neither peace nor plenty are easily had. We can hold our politicians prisoners to wishful thinking and through the application of enough pressure teach them, as H. L. Mencken suggested, to cheerfully embrace "polygamy, astrology or cannibalism." But they cannot supersede the laws of cause and effect. The Iowa state legislature can not raise the price of corn. Neither can the Congress of the United States—except in a temporary way that amplifies the eventual strength of forces deflating the price.

Does our view seem pessimistic? If so, it is only because of the convention that has confused blindness to facts with cheerfulness. We are both cheerful. But we are cheerful realists. We believe that you should face reality for what it is and try to make the best of it, not pretend that things are other than they are. For example, if you were riding on a ship that began to take on water, it would not mean that you were a pessimist if you sounded the alarm. It would simply indicate realism on your part. The test of pessimism and optimism would come later. Pessimists would head for the lifeboats, the optimists for the pumps.

With this book, we intend to reveal patterns of reality—not patterns of pessimism or optimism. We will not try to tell you which to be as an investor. That is something you'll have to decide for yourself depending on your own resources and temperament. But before you can decide how to respond to a challenge, you must know what the challenge is. You must have a *realistic* grasp of the patterns of human behavior that produce various outcomes.

Einstein resolved many mysteries with a simple equation, $E = MC^2$. We have no such simple equation because we are not dealing with physical forces but with human beings, whose behavior is subject to choice. You will probably doubt some of our conclusions, as you should. The story we have to tell is not a tidy one. No story involving people ever can be. But we have given you the most honest, uncompromising exposition of the secrets of megapolitics that has ever been published. We have tried not to let wishful thinking, political enthusiasms, or even simple nationalism color our analysis.

We are citizens of two different countries living a continent apart. Nonetheless, we have no illusions that our viewpoint is a universal one. It is definitely Anglo-American. We are more sympathetic than many to the Atlantic powers that have dominated the world for the last century and three-quarters. It is with regret that we see the power of the United States rapidly receding, much as the power of Great Britain receded earlier. Our regret is natural enough. We are two English-speaking white men who have enjoyed more than most the advantages of Anglo-American dominion over the world. But it would be a mistake to conclude that our view of the economy is colored too much by our circumstances. We are not jingoists. Because of what we now understand, we would be just as displeased to see the end of Anglo-American world dominance if we were Zulus, Mexicans, Japanese, Nigerians, Argentines, or Indians. They, no less than we, have a stake in the preservation of world order.

FINALLY . . .

No analysis of human conduct that excludes the spiritual can ever be more than part of the truth. At times in human history there is a new opening of the human spirit, which by its nature produces miracles, not all of them good. Such miracles are not only found in the birth of the great religions of the world, but also in moments of change in religious structures. At such times, men feel intoxicated by this spirit. At other times, in human history as in human life, the spirit seems to withdraw and the soul walks restlessly to a dry place. The spirit is not content with material things, and its own material prosperity can be a danger to nations as well as to individuals. "The dice of God are always loaded."

The simple arithmetic of markets, the inevitability of struggle, the justice of history, the lightning flashes of human spirit are among the most striking recurrent truths of human experience. And they do recur. We may not be able to trace all the cycles of human affairs, economic or political, but we should listen out for the evidence of them, and form an understanding of the patterns of human history that are shaping the ultimate reality in which we live.

1

The Megapolitics of the Pax Britannica

We don't want to fight but by Jingo if we do,
We've got the ships, we've got the men, we've got the money too.
—Nineteenth-century British music hall song

Let us tell you a story.

It concerns an event that took place in Africa in the waning days of the last century. Even though everyone who witnessed it is now dead, it is really a story with a greater moral for the future than the past.

Like any good adventure, it has everything: action (a clash of cultures, menacing natives, savage killings) . . . a colorful cast of characters (including Winston Churchill and a Dervish chief) . . . strategic implications (a demonstration of the way power is exercised in the world) . . . and, naturally, money.

This story, however, has deeper meanings than meet the eye. It is told here to illustrate some important points about the hidden underpinnings of the economy. We want you to see why the instability of power is among the factors contributing to the danger of a worldwide depression. This could be of crucial importance to you in anticipating and surviving the upheavals to come.

The tale we are about to tell you illustrates an extreme in the power equation. It is the tale of walls knocked down. It explains how power was exercised in the world during one of history's most dramatic periods of economic growth. Unlike the Dark Ages and other periods of economic stagnation, this was a time when megapolitical factors made it easy for one dominant group, in this case, the British Empire, to enforce one set of rules to the far corners of the globe. The effect was like joining thousands of stagnant ponds in a larger body of water. Currents and flows were set in motion that soon made it possible to support much more life. People, goods, and capital flowed across continents with more freedom and security than they could have traveled across a county a few centuries before.

The horizons of life expanded because Great Britain enjoyed a great power gap over thousands of other political authorities. This laid the foundations for decades of progress and growth. But as we shall see, the megapolitical conditions that made all this possible could not last long. The unceasing competition for power, the natural rhythm of action and reaction, made stability fleeting. Now the power equation is moving rapidly back the other way—toward devolution, violence, and decline.

As you read the story of the Dervishes and the details that follow, bear in mind that they tell you more about current events than reports of the latest outrage from Libya or Lebanon. By looking back, you gain the advantage of perspective. Among the points that are revealed:

1. Even though raw power is a key hidden factor in the economic life of the world, it is little understood.
2. Trends and developments that have a major effect on investment markets are often set in motion by events far away.
3. The rules of "reality" as people perceive them, can change abruptly—often with staggering costs.
4. The most likely source of dramatic change is technological innovation.

Those are four important morals of the story we are about to tell you. There are others, also important:

5. There are long lags between technological innovations and comprehension of their impact—even in matters of life and death.
6. The slowness of most people to think deeply about the world around them gives a great advantage to people who do think.
7. Most advantages in life are self-limiting rather than self-reinforcing. Therefore, they cannot be hoarded for long.
8. Systems—including international economic arrangements—based upon the exercise of an advantage are unlikely to remain stable for more than a few decades.

These statements may not mean much to you now. But they will. They are all important clues to understanding how the "game" of megapolitics is played. It is a deadly game with high stakes and hidden rules. It is a game almost no one understands. Yet its outcome could be a matter of life or death for millions. It could determine whether you have a livelihood. It could decide what becomes of the value of money. And whether the world plunges into another Great Depression.

A SHOWDOWN IN THE DESERT

In the summer of 1898, the British Empire appeared to be in its heyday. Queen Victoria had celebrated her Diamond Jubilee the year before. London was the undisputed center of world finance and commerce. The British navy ruled the waves. It was twice as large as any two other navies combined. Efforts to consolidate and extend British power were still continuing. Then, as now, Moslem extremists were menacing Egypt—where the British-held Suez Canal was a vital link in world trade. Out in the desert, a force of Islamic true believers was engaged in a *jihad,* or holy war, against whatever Western targets came within their sights. As the threat grew, London dispatched military forces, under the command of Lord Kitchener. Their mission was to enter the Sudan, secure the Upper Nile, and thus protect British interests in Egypt from attack.

Opposing the British was Abud Allah ibn Muhammed, the Khalifa of the Dervishes, an Islamic religious leader who was the nearest nineteenth-century equivalent of the Ayatollah Khomeini. Like Khomeini, the Khalifa was bitterly opposed to Western disruptions of the settled ways of Islamic society. Like many groups in the Middle East today, he held hostages. Several who managed to escape told tales of cruelty, torture, and murder that shocked British opinion.

The Khalifa commanded an army organized by fierce Islamic fighters known as "Dervishes" (as in "whirling dervishes"). Hardened to life in the desert, the Dervish fighters had been taught from childhood to master hand-to-hand combat. They were good at it. They were brave. They were skilled in using knives and muskets. They were also skilled at screaming. Their practice of using noise as a psychological weapon in battle had been widely reported in Europe for many years. As one writer in the 1870s put it, "And now, their guttural chorus audible long before they arrived in sight, came the howling dervishes."

On September 2, 1898, 40,000 Dervishes began to howl as they swarmed across the desert to attack the British Camel Corps. The at-

tack employed a centuries-old tactic that had worked for Dervish armies many times in the past—a mass frontal assault. The first British
troops drew back to the Nile to avoid being overwhelmed.

What happened next? Let Winston Churchill tell you. He was there
at the battle of Omdurman.

> . . . [A]t the critical moment the gun boat arrived on the scene and
> began suddenly to blaze and flame from Maxim guns, quick-firing guns
> and rifles. The range was short; the effect tremendous. The terrible
> machine, floating gracefully on the waters—a beautiful white devil—
> reethed [sic] itself in smoke. The river slopes of the Kerreri Hills,
> crowded with the advancing thousands, sprang up into clouds of dust
> and splinters of rock. The charging Dervishes sank down in tangled
> heaps. . . . The infantry fired steadily and stolidly, without hurry or
> excitement, for the enemy were far away and the officers careful.
> Besides, the soldiers were interested in the work and took great pains.
> But presently the mere physical act became tedious. . . . And all the
> time out on the plain on the other side bullets were sheering [sic]
> through flesh, smashing and splintering bone; blood spouted from ter-
> rible wounds; valiant men were struggling on through a hell of whistling
> metal, exploding shells, and spurting dust—suffering, despairing,
> dying.*

At the end of five hours of battle, the British had lost 20 men killed.
Another 20 Egyptians who accompanied the British were also dead.
The Dervishes lost 11,000 dead.

THE MEGAPOLITICS OF POWER

Why do we tell you about the gruesome deaths of thousands of Africans
in a faraway colonial war? Because those deaths illustrate important
points about the way the world works today—and the way it will work
in the future.

As an investor, you must understand the megapolitics of power.
Power establishes the boundaries of political ecologies. As they move,
they narrow or broaden the horizons of life. They shift the balance in

---

* Winston Churchill, *The River War: An Account of the Reconquest of the Soudan*
(New York, 1933), 274, 279.

the ages-old competition that determines whether we prosper or decline.

In this sense, political ecologies are like bodies of water. They can be any size from a puddle to an ocean. The bigger they are, the more encompassing, the more life they will support. Only the most primitive forms of algae and single-cell animals will survive in a puddle. The ocean is teeming with life. In other words, the larger ecology is richer and more complex.

The same is true of political ecology. When borders contract, economies tend to contract as well. Breaking up larger political units into smaller ones is like breaking up a large body of water. The tides and currents that flow from one area to another, nourishing and sustaining life, are stopped short at borders. The more impervious borders become, and the more they proliferate, the more the system stagnates. On the other hand, when borders and barriers are knocked down, still waters begin to flow. New currents flush away the old residues that have become poisons inhibiting growth. Life becomes more complex and prosperous as interchanges multiply.

Weapons technology is the major megapolitical force that determines the power equation. When it is cheaper and easier to project power from the center to the periphery, the number of political units in the world declines. Those that remain are more encompassing. And economies tend to prosper. When it becomes more costly to project power and cheaper to resist, borders and barriers proliferate. The number of political units in the world multiplies. Economies stagnate.

As little as we like to face it, the economies of the world still rest upon the primitive algebra of force. Not because economic transactions themselves are based upon force. Far from it. They are peaceful in character. But they can only proceed where there is peace.

A MILLION DOLLARS OR A MACHINE GUN?

Peace can be interrupted at any time by power. Peace is always the hostage of anyone with a weapon. In this sense, power is primary. It must be. Wealth cannot buy peace. In a locked-room showdown, which would you prefer, a million dollars? Or a submachine gun?

If you picked the million dollars you made a mistake that no Dervish would have made after the battle of Omdurman. It suggests that you do not understand the extent to which prosperity is threatened by violence.

Economic transactions are always under threat. They proceed safely only when others, like the British Camel Corps or the U.S. Marines, are standing offstage with a machine gun, ready to use it if necessary to protect you.

If such order is enforced, then a million dollars is preferable to a submachine gun. It is preferable many times over. But when no one is standing by to protect you, the person who grabs the gun can create his own rules. And he could then grab the million dollars as well.

THE PAX BRITANNICA

For many decades, including most of the nineteenth century, Great Britain was the force in the background, the police power setting rules. To a surprising extent, as we shall explore below, circumstances conspired to make the rules the British set primarily fair and good ones. They fought to stamp out slavery. They instituted free trade. They stopped all manner of cruelty, including the Indian practice of burning widows on the funeral pyres of their husbands. In places where there had been no rights, no justice, and indeed, no law other than the arbitrary whim of the ruler, the British instituted individual rights. In many cases, they made it possible for the first time for persons to own property and go to court to recover damages for harms done. In short, they brought many of the rudiments of a peaceful society to places where there had been no peace. Almost throughout the globe, Great Britain protected people, goods, and investment from attack.

The basis of these reforms was not calm persuasion. Nor the liberal legal and economic insights of Adam Smith. The same good arguments in other circumstances have come to little. What made the British accomplishments possible was raw power. For much of the nineteenth century, the British Empire exercised smashing power. Overwhelming, irresistible power. Power that gave London an almost magical ability to impose its influence and settle disputes at the far corners of the globe. Not just at Omdurman, but in one remote place after another in Africa and Asia, British forces overwhelmed their opponents at trivial costs. In one battle near Zimbabwe in 1893, 50 British South African police fought 5,000 Ndebele warriors, killing more than 3,000 in an hour and a half. As an African survivor of such a massacre said: "The whites did not seize their enemy as we do by the body, but thundered from afar.

. . . Death raged everywhere—like death vomited forth from the tempest."* Earlier in the century the Celestial Dynasty in China was brought low by British gunboats and a few marines. Without any apparent difficulty, the "barbarians from the sea" swept in and mauled Chinese forces in a war lasting from 1839 to 1842. The expense to Britain for defeating the most populous nation in the world was trivial, one-tenth of one percent of the gross national product. London's military budget actually fell as the fighting progressed. A few years later, a similar war was fought with equally lopsided results. Again, the Chinese were humiliated.

The abracadabra in British military success was technological superiority. Weapons in the hands of British forces were far deadlier than those available to fighters in traditional societies of Asia and Africa. This made it very cheap for the British to project power at great distances, very costly for local peoples to resist. Historian Barton Hacker summarized the situation this way:

. . . Western military technology was beginning to draw on a maturing science to advance at an ever-accelerating rate. The first half of the century witnessed the opening stages of revolutionary transformation of Western military and naval technology. The smoothbore flintlock musket that equipped European armies in 1800, itself a long step beyond the matchlocks still used in the East, had given way by mid-century to the caplock rifled musket. Artillery had become more mobile, and breech-loading rifled ordnance firing explosive shells had begun to replace the older muzzle-loading smoothbores both on land and at sea. Shell guns were but one aspect of a naval revolution whose most important feature, steam propulsion, was already well established by mid-century.†

In 1898, it was cheap for Western powers—and Great Britain in particular—to control peoples at the periphery. As Churchill described the battle of Omdurman, it was

the most signal triumph ever gained by the arms of science over barbarians. Within the space of five hours the strongest and best-armed savage army yet arrayed against a modern European Power had been

* Daniel Headrick, *The Tools of Empire* (New York: Oxford University Press, 1981), 180.

† "The Weapons of the West," *Technology and Culture* 18, no. 1, January 1977, p. 47.

destroyed and dispersed, with hardly any difficulty, comparatively small risk, and insignificant loss to the victors."*

The cost for consolidating control over a restless Middle East was trivial as compared to the cost to native peoples of resisting. Even though native armies were larger, with far better knowledge of local terrain, they were hopelessly outmatched. Britain had modern weapons—gunboats, breech-loading rifles, machine guns, and more. These weapons were immeasurably superior to those available to people in less technologically advanced societies. As a result, all disputes at the periphery were easily settled. Whenever some local faction threatened investment, stood in the way of trade, or got caught up in a strategic conflict, Britain or another metropolitan power dispatched gunboats and soldiers. The locals had no choice but to yield to overwhelming force—or else. Those who resisted were practically wiped out, absorbing absurd casualties while inflicting almost none.

ALWAYS AN INVESTMENT IMPLICATION

When news of the British triumph reached London, headlines trumpeted, "Complete Defeat of the Dervishes."†

The news had an immediate impact—on the stock market. Share prices rose. The next day, the *Times* of London placed developments in the Sudan first among a number of international factors contributing to the stock market gains:

> News from Sudan caused advances in Egyptian stocks and Consols; and the latter were also affected by the easier state of the Money Market, and by the news that satisfactory arrangements had been made between British and German interests in China and that the general state of affairs in the Far East was decidedly more favorable. . . . The report with regard to Delagoa Bay [in Mozambique, where Portuguese troops had completed the conquest of a native kingdom] caused a further sharp increase in Portuguese stock and South African ventures, while the rise in Argentine and Chilean bonds continued, cable advances being received to the effect that differences between the two Republics will shortly be settled or submitted to arbitration."‡

* Churchill, *The River War*, 300.
† *Times*, Monday, September 5, 1898.
‡ Ibid, Tuesday, September 6, 1898.

Directly or indirectly, all these developments share one factor in common: power. The victory of Omdurman was obviously an exercise of power. So, in less obvious ways, were developments in the Far East, Mozambique, and South America.

Even more than the buyers and sellers of shares in 1898 probably realized, however, the character of economic life is arranged and rearranged by the meanderings of power. They knew that a British victory in the Sudan was good news for "Egyptian stocks and Consols." But more was involved. Something deeper. Something far from the headlines. Indeed, if not for the lopsided imbalance of power enjoyed by Britain earlier in the nineteenth century, Britain could not have created the first global empire, and thus the largest and most encompassing free trading area ever put together. Without this power, there would have been no structure in London or anywhere else for investing in far-flung corners of the globe. If not for Britain's (or some other nation's) early head start in developing industrial technology and organizing activity around that technology, there would have been few investments to make.

The modern corporation itself was an invention that came into its own in nineteenth century London as new technology increased the scale of enterprises. The family firm and partnership ceased to be the predominant form of business organization. As industrial progress allowed for commercial operations of greater scale, the amount of money needed to finance a significant company shot up. The international corporation emerged as a solution. Funded through a stock market, this new enterprise was different in character from the old trading company that had once sent ships toward the East in search of spice. The new corporation did not just gather products that the natives of other areas happened to have on hand, like fur pelts, or cacao or ivory. The new enterprise increased the potential for world wealth by *producing* internationally. It extracted raw materials, finished them into products, and sold those products in far-flung locations around the globe.

None of these things could have been achieved without the advantages of predominant power.

It took power to knock down barriers to trade, including high tariffs, so that capital could be invested freely, and raw materials and manufactured goods could be transported cheaply to market. It took power to transform the legal systems of technologically backward societies to forms that allowed for property ownership and investment. Many of these societies, by the way, were not peaceful, idyllic arrangements in which natives lived in close communion with nature. More than not, they were cruel, violent, and constantly at war. And when we say "cruel," we use a word that in modern context applies to kicking a dog. Behavior in traditional societies before British power spread Western values makes dog-kicking seem like the work of Mother Theresa. A king of Arakan, now Burma, drank a potion brewed from 6,000 human hearts.

No one could plant a crop or dig a mine, much less build a factory, when there was no way to secure the investment or the lives of the people working at it. It took power, operating with the advantages of low costs, to prevent marauding local groups from playing havoc with trade. Such groups had done exactly that through most of history, ambushing the caravan and burning the crops. They would have even more gladly flooded the mine, chopped down telegraph poles, and uprooted the railroad tracks.

For the world economy to rise above the stage of local trade and exchange required bringing this land piracy under control. Great Britain did when it rose to predominant power, or "hegemony."

So when the London stock market cheered the results of the battle of Omdurman, more was involved than the strength of Egyptian shares. The whole underpinning of world finance, investment, and trade rested upon arrangements forged by British power.

From the defeat of Napolean in 1815 through World War I, Britain was the leading industrial power in Europe, and thus the world. From this position of strength, Britain sponsored the development of economic infrastructure and industry on a global scale. Indeed, the institutions of world trade were built upon the strong shoulders of British power. The British navy kept the lanes of commerce open, stamping out piracy, opening borders to commerce, protecting international investments, and collecting foreign debts. And that is not all. Sterling was the world's reserve currency. Capital flows around the globe were tied to a gold standard regulated and supported by the Bank of England.

The British sponsored the development of rules to protect international investment. Britain was the champion of open borders and free trade. These liberal doctrines were plausible fits with British interests. So long as British goods were incomparably superior to those produced by anyone else, English industrialists had nothing to lose if all consumers had a free choice that free trade implied. As Joseph Schumpeter shrewdly observed:

The superiority of England's industry in 1840 was unchallengeable for the calculable future. And this superiority had everything to gain from cheaper raw materials and foodstuffs. These were no delusions. . . .

Time and again, the British forced other nations to adopt free trade. In 1838, Britain forced a treaty on Turkey that dramatically slashed tariffs and lowered internal barriers to trade throughout the Ottoman Empire. In 1839, Britain went to war with China over trade. As William Jardine of the famous China trading firm, Jardine Matheson, wrote:

> Nor indeed should our valuable commerce and revenue both in India and Great Britain be permitted to remain subject to a caprice, which a few gunboats laid alongside this city would overrule by the discharge of a few mortars. . . . The result of a war with the Chinese could not be doubted.*

Unfortunately for the Chinese, they did doubt the result. Twice. The British also forced free trade upon the Portuguese Empire, obliging the government in Lisbon to abolish slavery in its African colonies. Innumerable reforms in many countries, including those in Latin America, were undertaken for "the Englishman to see." The reason this was a matter of care was not merely that the British controlled a large portion of the world's investment capital. But the British also had the power to force favorable outcomes. In the century before 1914, Britain intervened with military force forty times in Latin America alone. Most of these actions were taken to halt spreading violence or protect investments against local efforts to confiscate them without compensation.

The world's policeman and banker, Britain provided massive outflows of capital that helped reduce the severity of recessions in other countries. As philosopher George Santayana rather enthusiastically described the Pax Britannica, "Not since the heroic days of Greece has the world had such a sweet, just, boyish master. It will be a black day for the human race when scientific blackguards, conspirators and fanatics manage to supplant him."

The British paid the costs of these activities, including being a lender of last resort, out of their huge share of world manufacturing output and trade. From the defeat of Napolean in 1815, England was rich. English

---

* Headrick, "The Tools of Imperialism: Technology and Expansion of European Colonial Empires in the Nineteenth Century, *Journal of Modern History*: 51, June 1979, p. 44.

industry was far ahead of that in other European countries. So startling was the wealth of England that Alexis de Tocqueville wrote in 1835:

> Cross the English countryside and you will think yourself transported into the Eden of modern civilization—magnificently maintained roads, clean new houses, well-fed cattle roaming rich meadows, strong and healthy farmers, more dazzling wealth than in any country of the world, the most refined and gracious standard of the basic amenities of life to be found anywhere. . . . There is an impression of universal prosperity which seems part of the very air you breathe.''*

So long as this disparity of wealth lasted, the world system worked well. But the advantages could not last, for fundamental reasons. The very conditions that British success created helped generate prosperity all around. The richer everyone became, the less stark the relative British advantage could be. If your income is five dollars and your nearest competitor's is one, you have a five-to-one advantage. But if both your incomes grow at the same rate, next year your income would be six dollars and his two. Your advantage has shriveled to just three-to-one. This kind of arithmetic worked against Britain. In fact, matters were even more decisive because competitors starting from a lower base could grow much more rapidly than Britain could from the position of a commanding lead.

The law of compensation was at work. No advantage can be hoarded for long. Only disadvantages can last, and even they will eventually reverse. Other countries like the United States, France, Germany, Italy, and Russia copied British industrial innovations. And began to compete.

They were able to progress in a fraction of the time that it had taken Britain to reach the same level of technological development. They followed the advice immortalized by pop economist Tom Lehrer: "Plagiarize, plagiarize, why don't you use your eyes?" By copying what had already been done, they skipped many earlier steps that the British had had to slog through. New textile manufacturers outside of Britain, for example, tended to stock their factories with modern equipment, while marginal British firms continued to use yesterday's model. American and German engineers not only copied English technology, they improved on it. And came up with brand-new ideas like the light bulb.

The relative wealth of Britain dwindled steadily, while the costs and challenges it had to meet rose. This reduced British power sharply in

---

* Alexis de Tocqueville, "Memoir on Pauperism," with a new introduction by Gertrude Himmelfarb, *The Public Interest*: 70 Winter, 1983.

comparison to its capitalist competitors, even while British advantages over the noncapitalist world continued to expand.

The erosion of the British position was well disguised, however. Most observers failed to notice it all, largely because important elements of the power gap were never understood. To the educated opinion of 1898, British supremacy was more secure than it had ever been. It seemed that British military might triumphed ever more easily with every test. It was like what might happen if a champion runner turned in ever-faster performances—and won by larger margins—without realizing that athletes with whom he was *not* running were improving even faster than he. As the nineteenth century progressed, the experience of warfare was limited to campaigns at the periphery with minor powers. By the end of the century, no one serving in the military forces could have ever seen battle between major powers, only bush wars and police actions. Usually, these conflicts were quickly and easily resolved, at low cost in money and men.

So thorough was the confusion about the slipping British power advantage that enthusiasm for military force rose just as its cost effectiveness sharply declined.

This underlines a point of importance to you as an investor. It is a very rare characteristic for people to anticipate developments before they occur. Why? Because they seldom think about the deepest causes of what goes on. By concentrating on surface appearances, people can be easily misled.

This is surely what happened to students of current events at the end of the nineteenth century. The use of force appeared to be simple. And effective. So much so that jingoist sentiment was not merely put to tunes in bar songs. It came to be widely believed that the use of force to resolve disputes was far less messy and aggravating than diplomacy. Witness this editorial from the *Times* of London, praising Germany's action in seizing the Chinese port of Kiaochow. "The experiment," claimed the *Times*, "is one which we ourselves have tried on one or more occasions, with results so excellent as compared with any obtainable by diplomatic negotiation that there is reason to wonder why we do not always follow the more effectual method."*

The trouble with such thinking was not that it was far removed from pacifism, but that it failed to grasp megapolitical reality. The magic of power was not magic at all, but a peculiar coincidence that worked in limited circumstances. Where the power gap was large, pure gunboat

* *Times*, November 16, 1897.

diplomacy may indeed have been superior to "the dilatory devices" of diplomats. But the underlying technological factors that create such a power gap were rapidly fading just as experience seemed to show otherwise.

Below, we review the meandering power equation over the period of British dominance. It is a quick history, told from a megapolitical perspective. You will see that very seldom did leaders intelligently anticipate either the widening or narrowing of power gaps upon which world arrangements rested. Seldom could anyone see the profound military and economic impact of technology. This led to gaps between the revolutionary potential inherent in new technologies and the realization of that potential for good or evil.

THE MAJOR FACTORS IN THE POWER GAP

The transitory nature of British predominance, and indeed, all predominance, was masked by clear evidence of Britain's growing absolute power. What was significant was not merely the increase in the absolute firepower of British and other Western forces, but the power gap. This power gap was measured primarily against innumerable petty polities on the periphery. The power gap had four elements. As we shall see, all four were largely transitory. They were:

1. *Offensive weapons systems and technologies for which defensive counters had not been invented.* Field artillery and cannon with explosive shells, for example, made it far easier than it had ever been to raze strongholds. Walls that had once been impervious to attack could be blasted away in short order. Improved transportation and communication dramatically lowered costs for deploying force over great distances. Huge oceangoing steamers and shallow-draft, iron-bottom boats were terrifically effective in projecting power in previously inaccessible areas. Unlike the old sailing ships, gunboats could penetrate far into interior waterways, bringing with them devastating firepower. As one British officer put it, the new ships were "a 'political persuader,' with fearful instruments of speech, in an age of progress."* New medical technology also enhanced offensive capabilities by reducing fatalities from wounds and disease. Discovery of quinine as a treatment of malaria, for example, resulted in an

---

* "Tools of Imperialism," *Journal of Modern History*, June 1979, p. 244.

apparently permanent decline in costs for projection of power into Africa.

2. *Weapons that could function as offensive threats so long as opposing forces could not deploy similar weapons.* Machine guns and rapid-firing rifles, for example, brought crushing firepower to bear in battle. They gave Western armies tremendous advantages—while they were the only ones who had them. Ultimately, however, these were defensive weapons, more deadly in resisting than initiating attack. If the Dervishes had had machine guns, they could have mowed down British troops just as well—as startled commanders discovered in World War I. In the long run, rapid-fire weapons sharply increased defensive firepower. In the short run, however, they opened a decisive power gap.

3. *A conceptual and tactical gap, arising from a lag in the ability of opposing forces to adjust to revolutionary new technologies.* As we explore below, there have always been lags of decades and perhaps generations in the ability to assimilate radical innovations in technology. New weapons demand new tactics. But figuring out just what they should be takes time. Until these adjustments are made, the side with the most appropriate tactics enjoys an additional power gap—over and above anything provided by a mechanical superiority of the weapons. In the last half of the nineteenth century, the British profited to an extraordinary degree from such a conceptual gap. We pay special attention to this below, detailing how peoples who were then technically backward, such as the Chinese, found it difficult to use effectively the modern weapons they were able to acquire.

This element in the power equation should be of special interest to you as an investor. It not only helps explain changing economic conditions, it also emphasizes the crucial importance of up-to-date thinking for survival.

4. *Effort.* When there are no power gaps created by technology, the chief deciding factor is effort. The side with the most weapons and the greatest number of personnel will probably win. A nation with an advantage in wealth, as Britain had in the nineteenth century, can better afford to project power, even against unfavorable technological trends.

Obviously, we have simplified in reducing the power equation to four elements. Other factors were involved as well. But those we emphasize were of primary importance in deciding the balance of power between individual states. They combined to temporarily reduce the costs of projecting power for Britain about as far as they are ever likely to fall. We shall explore them further in the process of recounting how the power equation came to be what it was.

WHY THE OFFENSE CANNOT DOMINATE FOR LONG

If you think about it, you can see that it is unlikely that the costs of projecting power can be held down for long. If the predominant weapons system is offensive in character, it is unlikely to open more than a temporary power gap. Unless whoever first attains a new weapon can use it immediately to conquer the entire world, and that has never yet happened, other groups will come into possession of similar weapons and use them as well. Before long, they will turn the new weapon against the power that first possessed it, neutralizing the advantage. This is the natural process of compensation, the work of competition eroding any extraordinary advantage. This is why the Pentagon's frequent complaint that the Soviet Union steals U.S. weapons technology should come as no surprise. No advantages that confer power or create a power gap can be hoarded for long.

To the extent that a political power does succeed in projecting power, thus creating a more encompassing political ecology, its very success may accelerate the evaporation of its advantage. More encompassing political ecologies will make people richer, thus making it cheaper for groups at the fringes to attain the weapons they need to split themselves off. In this sense, the success in building larger units may tend to be self-negating.

DEFENSIVE DOMINANCE MAY LAST LONGER

On the other hand, megapolitical changes that make the world poorer are more likely to be self-reinforcing. As people become poorer, they cannot afford the costly weapons needed to sustain more encompassing political ecologies. So the prospect of successful offensive action declines. As borders and barriers proliferate, everyone becomes poorer. The process feeds on itself.

DEFENSE DOMINATES TODAY

For the greatest part of modern history, developments in technology have tended to make it cheaper to project power, costlier to resist. Even when the firepower of defensive weaponry began to get the better of the strictly offensive weapons, the balance was not fully tipped toward the defense. It was still costly to purchase the most effective defensive weapons, so only large political units were likely to afford them. The result was a kind of slow devolution. Beginning around World War I, the number of sovereign entities in the world began to proliferate. As the century has progressed, that trend has accelerated. Recently, a dramatic drop in cost of defensive weapons promises to create dramatic changes in political ecology.

For reasons we shall explore, there is good reason to believe that the number of governments in the world will continue to multiply. Accidents of technology are conferring a growing superiority on defensive weaponry. And the unit costs of effective defensive weapons, such as missiles, are falling almost as fast as the cost of computers or videocassette recorders. If the cost trend continues, it implies that hand-held missiles could soon be as easy to obtain as transistor radios. Such powerful defensive weapons, available to small-scale groups, could dramatically tilt the power equation in the world. Under those conditions, any airplane in the sky could be knocked down by anyone with a rational or irrational grudge anywhere within its flight pattern.

FLUCTUATIONS IN THE POWER EQUATION

Schoolbook histories give you very little idea of how the power equation has changed over the centuries. Indeed, they give you only indirect hints that there is such a thing. Yet fluctuations of megapolitics explain more of importance in the world than anything else.

For example, a major reason why the New World colonies of Britain, France, Spain, and Portugal wrested their independence in the late eighteenth and early nineteenth centuries was that the European powers at that time no longer exercised a power advantage. Whatever technological lead the colonial powers had once enjoyed had become broadly dispersed. Their weapons were no longer superior to those of the revolting colonists.

Consider the "Brown Bess," standard gun of the British infantry. It was a plain, flintlock musket of a design dating to 1690. Similar weapons were in the arsenals of all European and most non-European armies in 1800. Even many African societies, especially those on the coasts, were well armed with cheap flintlock muskets. Indeed, gunsmiths in Birmingham had grown rich making muskets for export to Africa.

In spite of its long service, the Brown Bess was an astonishingly inefficient weapon by modern standards. It was inferior in accuracy and had less than one-half the effective range of the Pennsylvania rifles with which many American troops were armed during the Revolution. As historian Daniel Headrick put it:

> "It had an official range of 200 yards but an effective one of 80, less than that of a good bow. Despite admonitions to withhold their fire until they saw the whites of their enemies' eyes, soldiers commonly shot away their weights in lead for every man they killed."*

To make matters worse, these muskets took a full minute to load and failed to fire about 40 percent of the time. In heavy rain, they would not fire at all.

Fighting under conditions of relative technical parity, Britain and other colonial powers were at a distinct disadvantage. Transportation of troops and supplies over great distances was both difficult and costly. Because the relative costs of projecting power had gone up, first the United States, then Haiti, then most of Spanish America and Brazil slipped free.

The prospects for maintaining significant institutional control over developed colonies looked so bleak that the Colonial Department of the British government was actually abolished in the late eighteenth century. Similar thinking in Paris explains why Jefferson was able to buy Louisiana so cheaply after Haitian slaves overturned their French masters.

Where the British continued to be successful in projecting power, such as in India, the reason was not superior arms technology, but superior organization. In the Mysore Wars of the late eighteenth century, some Indian forces actually had better weapons than the British. Prince Tipoo Sahib, for example, used rockets against British positions. These had twice the range of artillery and were effective. But the ragtag organization and poor discipline of Indian forces enabled the British to prevail.

* Headrick, *The Tools of Empire*, 85.

Only in the Far East and the interior regions of Asia and Africa was there a substantial technological gap in 1800. Even so, the cost of projecting power in those areas was prohibitively high as the new century opened. This was true in spite of the fact that China and Japan both had feeble navies, and armies equipped with weapons barely changed since the sixteenth century. Infantry were armed with swords, spears, bows, and blunderbusslike weapons called "gingals." The few soldiers with muskets had matchlocks. These took twice as long to load and were even more undependable than flintlocks. Chinese artillery was equally antique. Some cannon in the forts at Canton had been cast in Macau by Jesuits during the Ming dynasty. They were cemented in the walls and could not be aimed.

In spite of the inferiority of Eastern arsenals, the cost to any Western power for invading China or Japan in 1800 would have been staggering. The Far Eastern powers could be harassed along the coasts, but there was no way to penetrate inland in the numbers necessary to overpower huge armies. Transportation technology was too primitive to afford the West many advantages from superior weapons.

The technologically primitive regions of Africa were also safe from Western penetration in the early nineteenth century. The tropical Africans did not need better weapons to fend off invasion as long as mosquitoes would do the work for them. The Portuguese had tried for centuries to push their coastal enclaves in Angola and Mozambique deeper into the African heartland. They were stopped short every time by malaria. British military records from the early nineteenth century showed fatalities of 77 percent among troops stationed in West Africa. Any white troops would have suffered the same fate before quinine was invented.

COSTS OF PROJECTING POWER PLUNGE

As the nineteenth century wore on, however, the costs of projecting power fell sharply, especially for the British, who were leading the Industrial Revolution. Improvements in transportation, communication, weapons design, and even medical technology, accumulated rapidly. One after another, these innovations placed nonindustrial political systems at a widening disadvantage. Sometime around 1875, the arms gap took a quantum leap. Repeating rifles and machine guns fashioned of steel appeared. These weapons could spit out bullets at up to ten per second. A single gun could match the firepower of an entire army of a few years earlier. Such weapons were not only beyond the imagination of peoples with primitive technologies, they were also beyond all hope of competition.

Societies without an industrial capacity could no longer copy new Western weapons the way blacksmiths in Africa and Western Asia had copied and repaired crude flintlock muskets. A broken steel firing pin or a damaged barrel on a repeating rifle could not be pounded back into shape. Steel could not be worked in a village bellows. Machine tools, rolling mills, and a blast furnace were required. Not exactly the kind of technology that the Dervishes or Ndebele tribesmen were likely to have on hand.

The only way that modern industrial weapons could possibly be had was by purchase. States that were sufficiently integrated into the world economy to be aware of the need for such weapons and command their price, bought them. Leaders in Latin America, for example, were especially quick to catch on. Although Britain achieved a substantial power gap over Latin countries and did intervene with military force an average of once every two and a half years between 1820 and 1914, this gap was never so large as it was over most Asian and African polities. The greatest gaps in megapolitical power occurred where nonindustrial societies had neither the capacity nor the awareness to purchase and use modern industrial weapons.

THE AWARENESS GAP

Part of the overwhelming advantage that British and other capitalist powers enjoyed over societies at the periphery in the nineteenth and early twentieth centuries was an advantage of awareness. This, too, had a technological basis. The British communication system was far superior to anything dreamed of in the past. Using steamship, telegraph, and submarine cable, London was able to stay well informed about events everywhere. This dramatic communications advantage allowed trivial numbers of British administrators and troops to control millions of often hostile natives. Superior knowledge allowed London to rapidly deploy troops and supplies to the areas of greatest need.

By contrast, noncapitalist peoples in the nineteenth century typically had no awareness of what was going on around them, and certainly no knowledge of the larger world. Far from anticipating and responding to the challenges presented by the startling power gap with the West, leaders of most indigenous societies had no idea that the power gap existed. Headrick summarizes the situation this way:

> In fact, nineteenth-century Africans and Asians were quite isolated from one another and ignorant of what was happening in other parts of the world. Before the Opium War, the court of the Chinese emperor was misinformed about events in Canton and ignorant of the ominous developments in Britain, Burma, and Nigeria. People living along the Niger did not know where the river came from, nor where it went. Stanley encountered people in the Congo who had never before heard of firearms or white men. Throughout Africa, warriors learned from their own experience but rarely from those of their neighbors."*

The narrow horizons of backward peoples go a long way toward explaining the startling collapse of their systems. Within a few decades, innumerable traditional states disappeared. Darah, Tafilelt, Fezzan, Bornu, Barca, Gago, Bambara, Bamuk, Calam, Calabar, Boja, Machida, Caffraroa. The Kingdom of Mandinga, Sabia, the Caliphate of Sokoto, the Kingdom of Fungi. . . . The list of defunct governments, some of which sound like ingredients from a cookbook, could go on and on. Between 1800 and 1914, European powers took control over about 30 percent of the world's surface. In the process, they displaced thousands of petty powers, many of which simply crumbled away. More than 600 states were absorbed in the Indian subcontinent alone. Only the most hostile and vigorous of these technologically backward groups were in a position to militarily resist the onslaught of Western goods, people, and influences. That most of them failed so utterly testifies not only to the startling gap in military technology, but to a large failure of understanding.

In one sorry case after another, leaders like the Khalifa of the Dervishes or King Lobengule of the Ndebele sent troops on suicidal mass assaults against machine guns and other modern weapons. They could have avoided the mass murder of their followers if they had adjusted their tactics to the new reality. But they clung firmly to outdated conceptions and tactics.

IMPORTANT LESSONS

There are important lessons for you as an investor in this apparently minor detail of modern history. A lack of curiosity and forward vision

* Headrick, *The Tools of Empire*, 207.

is not unique to nineteenth century Islamic fanatics or tribal tyrants. In fact, there is less incentive to think ahead when entering an investment than when entering a battle. Nothing is more sincere than a matter of life and death. It is a safe bet that you have made investments with less care and concern than you would give to mounting a frontal assault against soldiers firing machine guns.

Strategies of investment do have some elements in common with battles, as the language of the investment reports will tell you, if you listen closely. That is why it seems natural for a reporter to say, "The bulls were massacred on Wall Street this week." That is why every issue of the *Wall Street Journal* or the *Financial Times* describes market "retreats" or "advances." That is why investors are said to "assault" a takeover "target" or "fall back" when it fails. Even if we do not consciously recognize it, our speech reveals that investment is the same kind of reality test as a battle. And the investment massacres or triumphs that sometimes occur usually happen for the same reason that the chief of the Dervishes led his followers to slaughter once upon a time on the dusty plains of Africa.

Almost all massacres occur when you are following tactics that used to work. This is just another way of saying that reality tends to change much faster than perceptions of reality. In the battle of Omdurman, the Dervishes had all the elements they needed to obtain victory. Far better knowledge of the local terrain. Superior numbers. Considerable firepower, even without the most modern equipment. Yet they were wiped out because they were hampered by an obsolete concept of reality. Their battle tactics no longer worked.

Like almost everyone else does almost all the time, the big Dervish mistake was simply to follow the practices that had made them successful. That is what wiped them out. Their tactics had always worked in the past. They had even worked against the British only a few years earlier when Dervish warriors defeated General Gordon at Khartoum in 1885. They did not realize how rapidly reality had changed in just a few years. The Dervishes could probably have prevailed by resorting to guerilla tactics, sneak attacks, and sabotage. They had all the tools needed to wage a successful campaign with those tactics. But attempting such a campaign never occurred to them at all. Instead, they were slaughtered by the thousands in mass frontal assaults against machine guns.

In investment, as in every other aspect of life, you need to know your strengths and weaknesses. In other words, you need to have a constantly improving grasp of reality. Reality does not stay put. It is in constant flux. But most of the time, people's concepts of reality are petrified. They do not change or change too little to keep abreast of new circumstances.

Consider another example like that of the Dervishes. In the dying days of the Chinese empire at the end of the last century, millions of Chinese rose in murderous protest against the domination of that country by the Western powers. This uprising, known as the Boxer Rebellion, offers clear illustrations of how important—and difficult—it is to update obsolete conceptions of reality.

At the turn of the century, China was ruled by the Empress Dowager, Tz'u Hsi. Like most rulers of most places in most times, she considered all foreign interference with her rule barbaric insolence. So she ordered the Chinese military to support efforts by the Boxers to rid China of "red-haired barbarians."

This should have been a laughingly easy matter. In the first place, the millions of Chinese enjoyed a tremendous numerical advantage. The foreigners were few in number and easy to identify. With the exception of the Japanese, they were all white. Furthermore, the foreigners had between them only 400 armed personnel—the military guards attached to the diplomatic legations at Peking.

When the Chinese military opened fire on these small groups huddled in the British legation the hope for any of the foreigners surviving would have seemed almost nil. They had few weapons, limited ammunition, little food and water. They were surrounded, and to all appearances, completely cut off from any hope of relief. Unlike the Dervishes, the Chinese military was armed with modern weapons. Rapid-firing Krupp cannon. Breech-loading rifles. Modern machine guns. The way for reinforcements was blocked by four heavily armed forts in Taku, recently rebuilt by German engineers. In addition to the forts guarding a narrow waterway only 200 yards wide, the Chinese had four brand-new destroyers recently delivered from Germany.

The Chinese had modern weapons but were incapable of using them effectively. Even more than the Dervishes, they were completely handicapped by obsolete ideas. So astonishing was the Chinese military incompetence that one of those trapped in Peking wrote in a diary, "Had we been fighting such people as the Zulus or Dervishes we should have been polished off in two or three days."* One authority reports that the Chinese intentionally aimed their firepower over the heads of

---

* Peter Fleming, *The Siege at Peking* (New York: Oxford University Press, 1984), 225.

their enemies. Allegedly, the Chinese believed that their enemies' spirits resided in the area directly above their heads and were vulnerable to fusillades fired there. Whether for this or equally fantastic reasons, the Chinese consistently fired over the heads of the foreign devils.

Two months of furious bombardments came to little. The improvised earthworks at the legations, organized by a young American mining engineer, Herbert Hoover, were not obliterated nor even breached in spite of the fact that the Chinese fired, or rather misfired, 3,000 cannon shells.

To be sure, some of the people at the legations were killed. But miraculously few under the circumstances. The Chinese had murderous intent and the most modern technology with which to fulfill their ambitions. But their mind-set was too obsolete to use the new weapons effectively. In other words, they did not have an up-to-date grasp of reality.

The Chinese, like the Dervishes, were ignominiously defeated, not because they lacked the resources to win the battles they chose to enter, but because their conceptual apparatus was out of date.

This would have been a harder concept to explain before the age of the computer. Now everyone who has had the experience of a computer understands how important software is to its proper functioning. You can have the right hardware. You can even have the right information. But unless you have the proper software or conceptual apparatus to process it effectively, computation will never be made. The thought and then the deed that could have saved the day will never occur.

BRITISH ALSO HAMPERED BY CONCEPTUAL LAGS

Adjustment to a new technology of power takes time. And the more radical the technological departure, the greater the lag in understanding is likely to be. Often, it seems that a generation or two must die out before its successors come to grips with the new reality. Time and again, events proved that the effects of new technologies had to be *experienced*. They could only rarely be understood in advance.

Not merely "barbarians" were slow to realize the real meaning of new technology. The British were dull about it too, taking many years to adapt to new weapons and improvements. The military authorities were unable to recognize the benefits of new weapons from study of their design features or even on the basis of experimental evidence. A few examples will suffice.

Wellington adamantly refused to use rockets, even though they had twice the range of early nineteenth-century artillery.

The British navy refused to build or purchase iron-bottom boats for years after they had become feasible. The iron frigate *Nemesis,* first used in battle with devastating effect in the 1839–42 war with China, was built privately by the Secret Committee of the East India Company. The leader of the effort was not an admiral, but a poet. Thomas Love Peacock, a friend of Shelley's, commissioned the ship in secrecy. The *Nemesis* actually shipped out of England under false papers.

Likewise, improvements in the technology of the gun were long ignored by British military authorities. In 1807, a Scottish clergyman, Alexander Forsyth, invented the percussion lock musket. The superiority of the percussion gun was demonstrated in tests that showed it misfired only 4.5 times per thousand attempts, rather than 411 times for the flintlock. Yet British military authorities delayed buying the new weapons until 1836 and continued using flintlocks until 1853. Nor were they quick to embrace any of the other improvements in gun design that significantly improved their range, accuracy, and speed of fire. Developments such as rifling of barrels, elongated bullets, and paper cartridges were neglected for decades before they were finally brought into military service.*

The conceptual lag that was part of the shift to new technology helped disguise its technological character. The English forgot that they too had taken generations to come to grips with the new technologies of power. They took for granted that their proficiency by the end of the nineteenth century reflected an inherent superiority. They attributed it to the "stern discipline and enthusiastic *esprit de corps* of the British army."† Or the cleverness of British officers. A corollary was that other peoples were appallingly stupid. Chinese, Japanese, Arabs, Indians, and black Africans were all lumped together as "barbarians," "savages," "fanatics," and worse. This false impression was reinforced when other peoples failed to properly use modern weapons they did lay hold of.

---

* One of Sir William Rees-Mogg's ancestors, who died a few days before the battle of Waterloo in 1815, already owned percussion cap pistols. Officers were allowed to furnish their own weapons—and often bought the most modern available. But the army itself did not.
† Headrick, *The Tools of Empire*, 123.

CONCEPTUAL GAP CLOSES

In a few cases, however, leaders of traditional societies did have forward vision. More quickly than others, they saw through to the importance of new technologies. Military innovators in Africa, like Samori Toure, fought Europeans to a standstill by employing modern weapons and guerrilla tactics. Interestingly, Samori grasped the importance of manufacturing weapons. He even sent an industrial spy to work in the French arsenal at Saint-Louis. Putting knowledge of French techniques to work, he employed hundreds of blacksmiths to produce homemade imitations of French rifles and cartridges. These were of wretched quality, but demonstrated admirable foresight. Samori was only defeated when a complete cordon around the areas he controlled cut off resupplies of foreign weapons and ammunition.

In Ethiopia, the Emperor Menelik had a better-equipped army than any fielded by an African ruler, with breech-loading rifles, machine guns, and field artillery. When an Italian army of 17,000 men invaded in 1896, it had no power gap to exploit. The Ethiopian army was "equally well equipped and even better trained."* In a battle at Aduwa, the Italians were decisively defeated.

Perhaps the best example of a forward looking response to the new technologies came from the Japanese. In Japan, the political attractiveness of modern weapons became a stimulus to industrialization. After an American show of strength forced the Tokuwgawa regime to open Japanese ports to foreign trade in 1853–4, a civil war led by younger samurai restored power to the emperor. The leaders of this movement were "deeply impressed by the West's military technology," and "they assumed their new government posts determined to sustain Japan's independence with Western weapons."† These Japanese leaders recognized, as others did not, "the unbreakable chain that led from firearms and ship to coal mines, iron foundries, and railroads; from military technology to industrialization. . . ."‡ By 1905, the Japanese literally stunned the world by convincingly defeating Russia at war.

---

* Headrick, *The Tools of Empire*, 123.
† Barton C. Hacker, "The Weapons of the West: Military Technology and Modernization in nineteenth century China and Japan" *Technology and Culture*, Volume 18, No. 1, January 1977, p. 52.
‡ Ibid.

POWER EQUATION REVERSES

The evidence was there, for those who cared to see it, that Western military superiority could be countered. The four elements of the power gap that had made it amazingly cheap for the West, and Britain in particular, to project power shriveled rapidly. The first defensive responses to new offensive capabilities began to be introduced, such as torpedoes that could sink modern ships. These were not immediately shared among peoples at the periphery, but other modern weapons were. Those of an inherently defensive thrust, like repeating rifles and machine guns, came into increasingly wide use. As the conceptual lag in the use of these weapons closed, local people began to use them ever more effectively.

Finally, the wealth of the British economy tumbled in relative terms. That raised the costs dramatically for maintaining British power in areas where it had already been established. In contrast to the situation prevailing in 1840, when the British military budget was falling as British power was being extended in unprecedented ways, the nineteenth century closed with Britain struggling under the weight of a growing military burden.

The cost of capital ships for the navy, the most important component in the exercise of British power, rose sharply as technological developments accelerated. The invention of new defensive counters, such as torpedoes, made large portions of the fleet obsolete. And practically each year brought an improvement in torpedo capabilities. Range jumped from just 220 yards in 1866 to 18,590 yards in 1913. To maintain offensive capacity required faster, more heavily armored ships with greater firepower. The costs for these vessels, with ever more complicated technology, skyrocketed. From 1884 to 1914, spending by the British navy grew almost five times, a gigantic leap in a time of falling prices. Cost factors alone showed that the paramount power of the British Empire was waning.

INSTABILITY AND DEVOLUTION

As the megapolitical conditions that had integrated the world economy eroded, the power equation reversed. This stimulated a brushfire of efforts by local elites to break free of foreign control. Revolutionary movements—with names that were strange to an English ear—sprang up in the world almost as if a bell had sounded around 1905. In that year, Sun Yat-sen founded a secret revolutionary group in China, the T'ung Mang Hui. The All-India Muslim League came in 1906. In Egypt, the Hizb al-Ummaga came in 1907. In 1908, the first nationalist group in Indonesia, the Budi Utoma, was founded. In 1910 came Tunis al-Fatat. In 1911, the Young Arab Association (al-Jamiya al-Arabiya al-Fatat). The year 1912 brought the South African National Congress. And 1913, the Viet Nam Quang Phuc Hoi, or the Association for the Restoration of Vietnam, revolutionary ancestors of the Viet Cong. The next year, of course, brought World War I, the long, bloody conflict that marked the end of British hegemony in the world.

SO WHAT?

We dwell on this because understanding the cycles of power will be crucial to you. Without this understanding, you are likely to mistake the nature of the coming world crisis, a crisis that could shake investment markets to their foundations. The crisis to come will be one of world order, like that the British faced early in this century. But it will be more acute because the megapolitical conditions today are far less favorable to economic growth than they were then.

Notice in the details of British decline several parallels that are hauntingly similar to events today:

1. A staggering increase of military cost in the face of negative technological trends
2. A war that demonstrates the inability of the dominant power to continue policing the world
3. A breakdown of the world monetary system, touching off inflation and wide fluctuations in money values
4. A startling increase of debt in the world
5. Signs of fiscal exhaustion by the dominant power, with automatic mechanisms introduced to cut spending, especially military spending
6. Allies of the dominant power refuse to contribute to the costs of maintaining order

And not yet a parallel, but we predict it will be:

7. Negotiated disarmament required by the sheer fiscal impossibility of continuing to shoulder growing burdens of military cost

As we shall see later elsewhere in this book, these are not the only parallels. But they are important ones for the moment.

In our view, it is no coincidence that World War I started when it did. The United Kingdom's share of world manufacturing output shrank from almost 32 percent in 1870 to just 14 percent in 1913. Sometime during that year, German output exceeded that of Britain for the first time. The Great War then became a test of strength between the two powers. Similar global wars had been fought in the past almost every time a hegemonic power was displaced and a new world order created. The French fought such a war against the British from 1793 to 1815. A century before that, the French had mounted a global war against Holland, from about 1689 to 1713. They succeeded in ending Dutch military power, but Great Britain entered the battle on the side of the Dutch and emerged predominant from the fighting. The United States played a similar role in aiding Britain in the first global war of the twentieth century.

Thanks to U.S. intervention, Britain emerged victorious. But it was a nominal victory only. In most respects, Britain was in an even less commanding position than it had been before the fighting began. The British share of world output had declined further. The international gold standard had collapsed. Britain no longer had the financial resources to maintain it. The pound had lost more than half of its prewar value. The British government was practically broke. In just four years, British private investors had lost the greater part of a century's accumulation of foreign investments.

Yet the demands made on Britain's declining power grew. British soldiers were the most expensive anywhere. Repeated efforts failed to persuade Britain's allies to join in relieving the expense of garrison duty. Pressed to station troops in Armenia, Prime Minister Lloyd George said, "The poor old British Empire is asked to do everything and gets not a word of thanks."*

With government spending racing out of control, the prime minister appointed a commission from outside the Parliament headed by Sir Eric Geddes to slash expenditure. This led to major cuts in the military budget. Shades of Gramm-Rudman-Hollings.

* Keith Jeffery, *The British Army and the Crisis of Empire, 1918–22* (Manchester, England: Manchester University Press, 1984), 36.

Britain was no longer rich enough to police the world. The old policy of securing international investment and free trade required deep pockets and overwhelming power. The early twenties saw the British unable to contain spreading disorder. In Ireland, Egypt, Iraq, Afghanistan, Burma, and elsewhere, the British military struggled on a hand-to-mouth basis to suppress wars and rebellions against the empire.

So severe was the narrowing of the power gap that there was no longer any question of direct action of the kind taken in the nineteenth century to defend the free flow of capital and goods. When the Bolsheviks in Russia confiscated investments across the board, Britain contemplated action but drew back from decisive steps. In fact, the power equation was such that there was little Britain could do. Churchill's repeated proposals for intervention to overturn the Communists were dismissed for reasons of cost. As Prime Minister Lloyd George put it, significant military action against the Bolshevik regime would be "the road to bankruptcy." * In other words, the Pax Britannica was over.

In short order, the world economy began to wobble. Except in North America, where World War I provided a brief impetus to growth, the following period was one of stagnation. Real income sagged. Debt skyrocketed. Trade barriers emerged everywhere. Commodity prices sagged, then collapsed. Output shriveled. International debts were repudiated right and left. A wave of bankruptcies spread across borders, with no effective lender of last resort to halt the collapse. Unemployment reached unprecedented levels. The Great Depression had arrived.

"THE PAST IS PROLOGUE"

These unhappy events had many causes, but among the deepest was the decline of the relative wealth and power of Great Britain. These changes made the world system unstable.

We believe that the timing of the last Great Depression was no coincidence. In some surprising and mysterious ways, it was the Great Depression of British decline. Many factors that contributed to the collapse of economic output, investment and trade are traceable to dwindling British power.

Today, it is no longer possible to meet challenges to Western power with "hardly any difficulty, comparatively small risk, and insignificant

---

* Jeffery, *The British Army and the Crisis of Empire*, 45.

loss." This is not because today's Islamic fanatics such as Palestinian terrorists, Colonel Qaddafi, or the Ayatollah Khomeini have more intense grievances. If anything, they are friendlier to the West than the Khalifa of the Dervishes. The Khalifa did not wear cowboy boots and watch television. But the Khalifa also did not have machine guns. He did not have helicopters. Or radios. Or plastic explosives. His notions of battle tactics were antique notions fitted to an antique technology. His troops, fierce and loyal as they were, were poorly trained in the use of firearms. Ammunition in the Sudan in 1898 was too expensive to waste firing practice rounds.

Today's terrorists are not hindered by such disadvantages. They do not turn up to fight with spears and knives and rusty muskets. Their weapons are practically as modern as they come. And they have learned how to use them. That is why "the arms of science" can no longer triumph over "barbarians." The battles against Western people, investments, and influences are no longer confined to the remote fringes of the desert. Terrorists can use their modern weapons to shoot little girls in the capital cities of Europe. And they do.

As menacing as terrorism is, however, what is at stake is not merely a matter of containing terrorists. It is a matter of economic stability. The shifting balance of power in the world is the most important hidden threat to the economy today. Power ultimately determines the organization of society. The scope of markets. The character and security of property rights. And much more. It is no exaggeration to say that power is primary. That is the unhappy fact upon which the world is organized. As W. H. Auden put it, "Without the cement of blood, it must be human, it must be innocent, no secular wall can safely stand."

Perhaps he should have added that without blood no secular wall can be knocked down. As walls go up everywhere, the result could be a devastating shift in the political ecology.

In unseen ways that most investors never suspect, the performance of markets is inevitably affected by megapolitical change on the global stage. That is what most of this book is about. We see big changes coming. Changes that will shake the geopolitical foundations upon which many of your investments rest. Changes that imply both danger and promise. Changes that will alter the conception of reality among successful human beings.

Notice that we did not say that they will change your conception of reality. And that is another lesson to be learned from the story of the Dervishes. Many people fail to understand the deeper forces at work in the world around them. They trust too much to their own experiences and think too little to anticipate events before they occur. They stick to the old ways. And follow what used to work.

That's why the Dervishes ran right at the machine guns. You, like they, can choose to cling to the old ideas to the end. That choice is up to you.

2

The Long Coincidence: American and British Power in the World Economy

*It is she alone who, at a coming time, can and probably will
wrest from us our commercial supremacy. We have no title:
I have no inclination to murmur at the prospect. If she ac-
quires it, she will make the requisition by the right of the
strongest and best. We have no more title against her than
Venice or Genoa or Holland has had against us.*
 —William Gladstone,
    prime minister of Great Britain,
    on the coming power of the United States

FORTUITOUS CIRCUMSTANCES

The transition from British hegemony in the world was hardly smooth.
It involved two world wars. Sandwiched between them was the worst
depression in modern history. Yet, as unpleasant as these events were,
they might have been even worse. The wars and depression might have
been followed by greater chaos, with far more crippling disruptions of
economies and investment than the years actually brought.

What saved matters was a coincidence, the historical equivalent of a
coin landing on its edge. For the first time, and probably the last, the
dominant power was succeeded by another speaking the same language,
with a common culture, common legal heritage, and very nearly common political and economic ideals.

When the United States succeeded Great Britain as the supreme economic and military power in the world in 1945, the shift to new arrange-

69

ments was so friendly as to be almost seamless. The result was markedly different from what might have happened had history taken a twist and made Germany, Russia, or Japan dominant instead. Old investments and debts were not repudiated in a stroke—as they so often are when one dominant power gives way to another. Far from it. British capital was welcomed in America as American capital was welcomed in Britain. New institutions, like the International Monetary Fund, the World Bank, and the new gold reserve system were, nominally at least, Anglo-American initiatives.

The very smoothness of the transition from British to American hegemony masked the perilous nature of such a change. It was like throwing a set of china into the air and having the pieces land at place settings, properly spaced, and almost unchipped and unharmed. To say the least, it was extraordinary. And it is in good measure owing to the extraordinary succession that the English-speaking democracies, almost alone in the world, have been stable over the past two centuries. France and Germany, for example, both defeated challengers to world power, have each had four or five governments in this century, and many more in the last. During this time, both Britain and the United States have enjoyed the continuity that came of the Anglo-American dominion.

Notwithstanding bouts of disruption, especially during the transitionary 1920s and 1930s, almost every investor in the English-speaking world could have prospered over the last two centuries by investing as though the world were stable—even though it was not. That would have meant losing money in some periods. But overall, thanks to this long coincidence, the investor would have made money by betting on continuity.

That may be a much riskier bet in the future.

In the much less complicated economies of the past, the decline of a hegemonic power commonly involved dramatic financial upheaval, accompanying the shift in raw military power. Often the transitions involved global wars. No such nastiness occurred between the United States and Britain. There was brief talk of war in the late 1920s, as the strains of economic crisis tried friendly relations. But nothing happened. The last conflict between the two powers was the War of 1812, unless one counts the War of Charles Griffin's Pig, a one-shot border skirmish over San Juan Island, Washington, on June 15, 1859.

On many points of potential disruption, there was almost total continuity between the arrangements enforced by American power and those established by the British. These areas of overlap included:

1. *Monetary arrangements*. The world exchange system negotiated at Bretton Woods was established with the concept of parity
between the dollar and the pound as the world's reserve currencies.
This may have been a fiction from the beginning. But if so, it was not
obvious to the treasurers of many governments in the sterling bloc.
Their mistake became unarguable only when sterling was sharply
devalued against the dollar. At that point, nations holding their reserves in sterling rather than dollars paid a sharp penalty. Sooner,
rather than later, most of the old sterling bloc members shifted their
monetary systems to orientation around the dollar.

Part of the tale of the transition between British and American
monetary dominance is told by the names of currencies. Many former
British colonies today sport as their national currency a "dollar"
rather than a "pound" they once employed.

2. *The private property regime*. Even as Britain had employed
overwhelming power in the nineteenth century to police the globe to
protect international investment, America sought to do the same. It
is important to note that U.S. power was used not only to protect
American investments. It was also employed to ensure the continuity
of British investments. Indeed, one of the most conspicuous successes among postwar efforts to ensure the safety of international
investment came when the CIA joined with British intelligence to
engineer the recovery of seized assets of the Anglo-Iranian Oil Company. (Anglo-Iranian later became British Petroleum.) When the leftist National Front regime of Iranian Premier Mohammed Mossadegh
confiscated Anglo-Iranian oil properties in 1952, the United States
joined Britain in a counterattack. U.S. help was crucial because British power at the time was too weak to reestablish the property rules
independently. The Royal Air Force did attempt to block export of
Iranian crude. Indeed, one Panamanian tanker caught trying to evade
the ban was forced to off-load its cargo in Aden. But the British
response to Mossadegh would have come to little without full U.S.
cooperation.

Unlike more recent and successful efforts at expropriation, Mossadegh acted at a time of supreme American commercial and military
hegemony. When the U.S. government and the major American oil
firms stood by the British, there were very few other potential customers. Those trading in oil purchased from Iran were treated as
dealing in stolen property. So complete was the boycott that Iranian
oil sales in 1952 and 1953 fell to just 3 percent of their previous level.
Rarely had an act of expropriation proved so futile. As the Iranian

economy sagged in the face of the boycott, Mossadegh lost support. In short order, the CIA, and British Intelligence, organized a coup that returned the Shah to power. Mossadegh was assassinated. Iranian oil concessions were renegotiated. A majority of the oil was restored to Anglo-Iranian, with a portion going to American companies, to reflect the large role that America had played in restoring the property. Almost two decades would pass before another government would attempt to expropriate an international oil concession.

3. *Free trade.* The end of World War II left the United States in a stage of industrial supremacy almost as overpowering as that enjoyed by Great Britain a century earlier. The greater part of European and Japanese industrial capacity was buried in the rubble of war. A majority of remaining output was in the United States. This gave the United States a strong incentive to allow consumers freedom of choice. Free trade meant expanded markets for U.S. goods. And it meant cheaper raw materials for those companies importing their inputs from abroad. At a time when the U.S. enjoyed a practical monopoly on capital that could be invested abroad, free trade also meant a free flow of funds, an opportunity to invest across the artificial limits set at borders. It meant freely repatriated profits. In short, free trade was, as Keynes said, an "expression of laissez-faire" in the international arena. It fit with the domestic political interests of a nation that was paramount, not only militarily but economically.

4. *International agencies.* Institutions like the World Bank, the International Monetary Fund, and the General Agreement on Tariffs and Trade were created at the joint initiative of the United States and Britain, but primarily at American cost. They provided additional backing for the trade, investment, and monetary arrangements that the United States sought to enforce internationally. These institutions took similar forms to earlier multilateral institutions created under the sponsorship of Great Britain. The most enduring of these was the Bank for International Settlements, an offshoot of the League of Nations. But the tendency to employ international or multinational authorities to enforce property rights and collect debts dated back to the nineteenth century. In 1879, for example, Egypt went broke and was effectively placed under the receivership of an international debt commission. The many world conferences at The Hague were also vague precursors to the new international agencies.

Through all of these arrangements, the United States fashioned rules of an international economic order that were in remarkable concert with those established earlier by Great Britain. There were no attempts to deprive British investors through interventions of American power. To the contrary, where the United States retained the capacity to police trade and investment rules, the British were beneficiaries almost as much as Americans. That was the case in Iran. And in Argentina, where Perón nationalized railroads and municipal transport systems, generous compensation was paid. This upheld the tradition that the British had organized in the nineteenth century of requiring full compensation for investments seized by foreign governments.

Only in the case of the Suez did the United States fail to back British efforts to preserve the security of investment. When the invasion of Egypt was recalled under American pressure, it probably marked the end of British status as a major power. Nonetheless, the United States backed efforts to secure compensation. Shareholders of the Universal Suez Canal Company received $64,400,000. This proved far better than what owners of confiscated U.S. companies were to receive two decades later when deteriorating megapolitical conditions had sharply reduced American power.

The international liberal order to which America was committed was entirely hospitable to most of the interests of the supplanted power. The preservation of British investments was very different from what might have happened had Germany and Japan won the Second World War. It was also different from what might have been expected had the Soviet Union become the overwhelming power in the world. But as we shall see, it also differed from what would have happened had no paramount power emerged.

Today, if we think about it at all, we take for granted that one predominant power succeeding another will respect the rules of international trade and investment, and extend full protection of those rules to the displaced power. But this assumes far too much. In the first place, the new hegemony might prefer an illiberal regime, of the sort the Soviet Union has foisted upon its Eastern European dependencies. This is almost inevitable, at least at the outset, when the dominant power is militarily strong but economically weak. If a weak economy allows free choice to consumers, they will choose to buy goods from someone else. This will benefit both the consumers and the world as a whole. It will not benefit the ruling elite in the dominant power. To avoid that outcome, free trade is suppressed.

In the second place, even opting for a relatively liberal policy, the new power might have sought it in a new form, hostile to the interests of the old. The European customs union sought by Imperial Germany prior to the First World War, for example, would have meant free trade within a large area, similar to today's Common Market. But the terms of this union might not have been hospitable to British trade and investment. Had Germany won the war, a greater portion of British investments would have been forfeited. More than likely, debts and obligations payable to Britain would have been repudiated with the same speed that looters will empty an appliance store in a blackout. And no doubt, the British would have suffered under the German version of the Versailles Treaty. This could have effectively wiped out the outstanding treasury securities of the United Kingdom while burdening the British with new obligations.

None of these things happened. The fact that they did not has made for one of the more fortuitous transitions ever effected in world power. This coincidence has created the false impression that the dynamics of power are far more orderly than they are. The close and deep relationship, the community of interest between the United States and the United Kingdom as Atlantic powers, speaking the same language and sharing a similar political heritage, has helped disguise the rough and disorderly character of economic life in a world where power means too much.

THE EXTRAORDINARY POWER OF
THE UNITED STATES

To make matters even more fortuitous, the United States in 1945 was not merely a military power, like the Soviet Union. The United States was paramount in every phase of economic life, leading the world in technology, financial assets, and gross output. This was more remarkable than it may seem. In the past, hegemonic powers have sometimes fallen short of dominating all phases of the world economy. Indeed, only the two great empires of the last two centuries, Britain and the United States, have come close to achieving an all-around lead. Portugal, Spain, and the Netherlands were global powers in the early modern period without clearly dominating significant aspects of the world economy. The Spaniards, for example, were a military and a financial power. But they bought most of their manufactures abroad. The same was true of Portugal. The Portuguese had a powerful navy, but a weak army. This left the Portuguese home base vulnerable to conquest by its Iberian neighbor, Spain. The Dutch, in their heyday, led the world in financial resources. But their advantage arose not so much from technology as superior organization. Thoroughly drilled Dutch armies and highly developed capital markets gave the Dutch a temporary superiority, but their economic base was ultimately too small to sustain power for long. When other European powers began to copy their military techniques, the Dutch were vulnerable to land attack across the flat plain of northern Europe. After a period of supreme power in the third and fourth decades of the seventeenth century that saw Dutch forces pushing into Brazil, Africa, North America and Asia, the Dutch fell back into a long retreat.

In short, stable supremacy is hard to come by and harder still to maintain. There is no necessity that *any* nation be clearly dominant. At times, the world economy has operated from a scaffolding built and maintained by weak hands. This made it prone to collapse. By contrast, the United States in 1945 was strong—as strong in relative terms as any nation is ever likely to be. Like Britain, it was blessed by a lucky geography. America was protected from potential adversaries by two broad oceans, a factor that made it easy to develop a sprawling continental economy. All that had stood in the way was a weak Mexico and a weaker menagerie of native tribes. By 1945, the United States had three times the population and more than thirty times the land area of Britain. Relatively, the United States was more preponderant than Britain had been in 1890. The United States controlled 56 percent of world manufacturing value added,* about 20 percent of world trade, and had relative labor productivity almost three times as great as other members of the world economy.†

COMMUNISM IN RUSSIA STRENGTHENS U.S. ADVANTAGE

Not only was America's relative productivity higher than Britain's had ever been, but the United States had another great advantage in promoting a liberal economic order: the Soviet Union. Soviet Communism divided the world, shutting off a large portion of potential investment,

---

* Robert Ballance and Stuart Sinclair, World Industry Studies: 1 *Collapse and Survival: Industry Strategies in a Changing World,* 16. (London: George Allen and Unwin, 1983)

† Robert O. Keohane, *After Hegemony: Cooperation and Discord in the World Political Economy* (Princeton, New Jersey, Princeton University Press, 1984), 36.

output, and trade. This had two important effects that strengthened U.S. power. One was to bind all the other capitalist nations to the United States. America's major competitors were made allies. This gave America much more influence than it might have had otherwise, and more than Britain had enjoyed at a comparable point. As Robert Keohane put it, "America's economic partners . . . were also its military allies; but Britain's chief trading partners had been its major military and political rivals."*

Furthermore, Communism in Russia sharply limited the development of that giant and potentially rich country. No one in 1945—nor later— worried about consumers anywhere preferring Russian manufactured products. Other than armaments, the Soviets make almost nothing that could hold its own in an open market. To put it plainly, Communism crippled Russia. It was and is like a self-inflicted wound, a shot in the foot that effectively hobbled the Soviet Union as an industrial and trading competitor. Given the advantage of a capitalist system, a continental economy like Russia's could have posed a serious threat to American leadership. But Russia became a military power only, an armament factory grafted onto a second-rate industrial system.

MISLEADING LUCK

America was not only gigantic and rich, it was lucky. And the better part of the world was lucky on that account. Accidents of history and geography gave America disproportionate power, and to all appearances, the prospect for using it to police world economic institutions for the indefinite future. However, destiny's accidents have a way of evening out. To understand how events may differ when the United States hegemony finally dissolves, as it soon seems likely to do, we must ask why the United States and Great Britain were drawn so closely together. What special circumstances marked the interrelations between these powers? And how was the United States able to prosper so greatly during the paramount period of British economic and military dominance?

The answers to these questions are not just unimportant scraps of history. They are clues to tomorrow's headlines that can be of great importance to you as an investor.

* Keohane, *After Hegemony*, 37.

Pure Coincidence

Part of the explanation of close ties between Britain and the United States was the coincidence of common language and heritage. This need not have been an irresistible impetus to alliance. After all, the United States had fought against Britain, both in the Revolution and the War of 1812. Well into the nineteenth century, American stump orators turned their Fourth of July speeches against the "crowned heads of Europe" whose "wigs and gowns," not to mention quarrels, were commonly held up in proof of the decadence of the Old World.

Several times during the century, border disputes with Canada threatened to explode into armed hostility. Anti-British feeling was popular enough in the 1840s to make the slogan, "Fifty-four Forty or Fight" a winner. Later, during the Civil War, the South hoped for and the North feared British intervention. If any issue other than slavery had appeared to divide the two sides, British intervention might have come easily. As it turned out, nothing of consequence happened. But even a slight change of circumstance could have made for much different results. Tension could have flared into an episode making for lasting bitterness.

Benign Neglect

In the actual event, Anglo-American relations greatly benefited from the low priority with which they were treated in London. Adam Smith had predicted that the new American nation "seems very likely to become one of the greatest and most formidable that was ever in the world." But a century after Smith's death, few in London seemed to take this possibility seriously. Indeed, so little attention was paid to the United States and North American affairs that before the twentieth century, no English newspaper even maintained a correspondent in the United States. And the first, G. W. Smalley, served by himself until World War I. John Hay, who was later to serve as a pro-British U.S. secretary of state, reported in 1894 from London, "If it were not so offensive, the ignorance of people over here about American politics would be very amusing." *

The few who were well informed about the dynamic growth of Amer-

* Vivian Vale, *American Peril: Challenge to Britain on the North Atlantic 1901–04* (Manchester: Manchester University Press, 1984) 2.

ica included some who treated it as a matter of alarm. Journalist W. T. Stead, for example, launched his own "Wake Up, John Bull" campaign, claiming, probably rightly, that the emergence of the United States was "the greatest political, social and commercial phenomenon of our time." * He predicted that growing American strength would mean "our ultimate reduction to the status of an English-speaking Belgium." † In the same vein, F. A. Mackenzie, in *American Invaders,* spoke in dire terms of the future. Just as Americans today deplore the invasion of foreign, and especially Japanese, products, so Mackenzie deplored the turn-of-the-century British consumer's preference for American goods:

In domestic life we have got to this: The average Briton rises in the morning from his New England sheets, he shaves with 'William's' soap and a Yankee safety razor, pulls on his Boston boots over his socks from North Carolina, fastens his Connecticut braces, slips his Waltham or Waterbury watch in his pocket, and sits down to breakfast. There he congratulates his wife on the way her Illinois straight-front corset sets off her Massachusetts blouse, and he tackles his breakfast, where he eats bread made from prairie flour (possibly doctored at the special establishment on the Lakes), tinned oysters from Baltimore, and a little Kansas City bacon, while his wife plays with a slice of Chicago ox-tongue. The children are given 'Quaker' oats. At the same time he reads his morning newspaper printed by American machines, on American paper with American ink, and, possibly, edited by a smart journalist from New York City.

He rushes out, catches the electric tram (New York) to Shepherd's Bush, where he gets a Yankee elevator to take him on to the American-fitted electric railway to the City.

At his office, of course, everything is American. He sits on a Nebraska swivel chair, before a Michigan roll-top desk, writes his letters on a Syracuse typewriter, signing them with a New York fountain pen, and drying them with a blotting-sheet from New England. The letter copies are put away in files manufactured in Grand Rapids.

At lunch time he hastily swallows some cold roast beef that comes from a Mid-West cow, flavours it with Pittsburg[h] pickels, followed by a few Delaware tinned peaches, and then soothes his mind with a couple of Virginia cigarettes.

To follow his course all day would be wearisome. But when evening

* Ibid., 9.
† Ibid., 3.

comes he seeks relaxation at the latest American musical comedy, drinks a cocktail or some California wine, and finishes up with a couple of 'little liver pills' 'made in America.'*

British consumers tended not to share this alarm. Or if they did share it, their concern never came to the point of affecting policy. The lack of British attention to the United States as a potential economic and military rival helped keep the United States from becoming an object of British strategic planning.

The Canadian Hostage and American Foreign Nonpolicy

Another factor explaining why the United States did not become an enemy of Britain was the almost total lack of U.S. policy that could come into direct conflict with British interests anywhere. Until the very end of the nineteenth century, the United States had practically no foreign policy and no military capacity to enforce such a policy. Except during the Civil War, the United States had a small army, and more important, almost no naval power outside its coasts. The United States did not need the burdens of high military expenditures. Like Japan today, America was protected cheaply, and largely by others. In America's case, the major protections were offered by two broad oceans and the Royal Navy, whose patrol in the Atlantic was quite as beneficial to the United States as its own navy would have been. For most of the nineteenth century, the United States was content to ride free on the international order provided by Britain.

Adding to this cozy bargain was the fact that Canada was more or less held hostage along a border far too sprawling to be garrisoned by the small British army. As Carroll Quigley wrote, "Thus we had security without any real effort or expense of our own and without even recognizing that it depended upon the power of other states. Even today, the past role of the British fleet and of the Canadian hostage in our nineteenth century security is largely unrecognized." †

In any event, British strategic policy was oriented in directions that did not involve the United States. Its main thrusts were: 1) to maintain freedom of the seas through the British Navy's "two-power standard," which required the British navy to be twice the size of any two navies

---

* F. A. Mackenzie, *American Invaders*, 59–61, quoted in *American Peril*, 12–13.
† Carroll Quigley, *Weapons Systems and Political Stability: A History* (Washington D.C.: University Press of America, 1983), 34.

combined; and 2) to keep Europe divided. The British feared that any power that could unite Europe, as first France and then Germany threatened to do, could lock British goods out of Europe and raise a naval force that would threaten British access to other markets.

As the German economy expanded rapidly in Europe, with the aim of establishing a Continental customs union from the Baltic to the Middle East, British opinion became alarmed. Given prevailing strategic assumptions, the British military became locked in a naval arms race with Germany.

As usual, the key to understanding this arms race was technological. The foundation of offensive power in that period—the battleship— "was without parallel as an instrument of forceful intervention over long distances."* It controlled sea-lanes and, thus, the flow of commerce in raw materials, food, and manufactured goods. An accident of geography put British home waters between Germany and the open sea. This created an impasse. The British refused to promise that they would remain neutral in the event of a war in Europe. And without such a pledge, the Germans insisted upon building a navy strong enough to fight its way into the ocean. To the British, this implied a German navy that could dictate terms to an island nation. Before airplanes reduced the military importance of naval power, such a position would have been untenable. Thus the two governments embarked on a futile and costly arms buildup.

This strategic preoccupation with Europe kept British governments involved in attempts to foil, at various turns, the French, the Russians, and the Germans. By the time that the United States, and for that matter Japan, began to develop a significant naval capacity, Britain was so embroiled with the European armaments race that it sought accommodations with both countries. The British fleet began maneuvering with the U.S. fleet. And a formal naval treaty was signed with Japan.

In any event, the question of why Britain chose to make an enemy of Germany rather than the United States was answered as it was in part because Britain was more preoccupied with the affairs of Europe than in the more distant doings in the New World. The technology of the time was such that a powerful military tied to a nearby economy on the Continent seemed more threatening than a potentially stronger and larger economy far away.

* Charles Lipson, *Standing Guard* (Berkeley: University of California Press, 1983), 148.

Common Heritage

Another part of the answer, of course, is that the common heritage of the two nations drew them together. The late nineteenth century was a time when one heard a good deal of the virtues of the "Anglo-Saxon race." Whatever sentiment this inspired was augmented by close personal ties, especially intermarriage among the elite. Winston Churchill, whose own mother was an American, proposed common citizenship between the two countries. This was not as ludicrous as a proposal for common citizenship between Britain and Germany or Britain and France might have been. A not inconsiderable part of the connection was the common liberal character of politics and economic ideals in both countries. As Lord Lothian later put it:

> The ideals of the United States, like our own, are essentially unaggressive and threaten their neighbors no harm. But Germanism, in its want of liberalism, its pride, its aggressive nationalism, is dangerous, and [Britain] feels instinctively that if it is allowed to become all-powerful it will destroy her freedom, and with it the foundation of liberty on which the Empire rests.*

A number of organizations formed to promote closer social and cultural ties between Britain and the United States, including the Anglo-American Association, the Atlantic Union, the Anglo-American League, and the Pilgrims. Naval strategist Capt. Alfred Thayer Mahan, who found a fan in President Theodore Roosevelt, proposed exploring "the possibilities of an Anglo-American Reunion"—a combination between the two powers that would exercise hegemony across the globe. In this vein, Roosevelt himself predicted, accurately as it turned out, "I think the twentieth century will be the century of men who speak English." He also bragged that together, the United States and the United Kingdom could "whip the world." †

Economic Connections

Adding to the influence of coincidence and sentiment was the fact that a great deal of British capital was invested in the United States. It came to about a third of all British foreign investment and provided as much

---

* Vale, *American Peril,* 231.
† Ibid., 6.

as a half of Britain's overseas income.* Beginning at the time of the Boer War, some American investment began to flow back the other way. Part of the explanation for the growing interdependence of U.S. and British investment was that London was the world's most highly developed capital market. By comparison, Germany had and still has only rudimentary stock markets. American investment poured into Britain for the same reason that Japanese investment comes to the United States today—it is the only capital market large enough to accommodate the cash. The importance of dealing with London for investment reasons—amplified by the convenience of dealing in a common language—contributed importantly to the growing interconnections.

Strong business and especially financial connections were amplified even further when the enormous costs of World War I exhausted British financial reserves. It was quite natural at that point for American financiers to purchase British bonds, as they had first done in the Boer War. And, of course, as the borrowing mounted, the American stake in the British victory rose.

The British Were Better Customers of America

Not only was the British capital market more highly developed, but the British percentage of world trade was far higher. Even though the German economy surpassed the British in 1913, its strength, like that of the United States, was far more internalized. The Germans conducted less trade than Britain in proportion to their total output. And several factors made it far more difficult for Americans to sell into German markets. The first of these was that Germany, more than Britain, was self-sufficient in food. The Germans had less need for the massive shipments of food from the American Midwest that were sold annually in Britain.

Secondly, in many areas, German industry was more dynamic and technically advanced than British industry. This made it more difficult for Americans to surpass German quality in sales to Germany. American steel, for example, was a major export to Britain. But cheap German steel, made with a Krupp process, was harder than American steel, and superior for many uses.

A third reason American sales in Britain were so much larger than

* Ibid., 7.

sales to Germany is so important that it deserves special attention. The United States was able to exploit the British commitment to free trade to sell goods under unequal conditions in a way that it could not have exploited Germany.

The U.S. Exploits British Free Trade

If gratitude figured in politics, which it does not, the Anglo-American alliance might simply have been a delayed repayment for the many benefits enjoyed by the United States as it industrialized at British expense. In addition to the great infusions of capital and modern technology that the United States obtained from Britain in the nineteenth century, America also exploited British trade and defense policies in much the same way that Japan is now exploiting the United States. America isolated its own industries behind high protectionist trade barriers while enjoying almost unfettered access to the free-trade system established and maintained at British cost.

The growth of trade in this system slowed considerably after 1873. Declining British power combined with industrial depression induced many countries, including Germany, to erect tariff barriers. William Menelaus, president of the British Iron and Steel Institute, gave a speech in 1875 that highlighted in a remarkably clear way the connection between increased competition, declining hegemony and protectionism. Said Menelaus:

> We have but little demand from Europe, and we seem to have lost our American market entirely. . . . We must, I think, frankly accept the position in which we are placed, and prepare to seek new markets for our produce in countries which, even if they have the will, have not yet the power to impose restrictions on our trade.*

Those nations that did have the power "to impose restrictions on our trade" increasingly did so. While the British remained powerful enough to force free trade on weak tribal despots in Africa, British power now fell far short of what would have been required to oblige the United States or Germany to maintain open markets. As the barriers grew, trade growth slowed. Not surprisingly, British exports slowed dispro-

---

* Quoted in James A. Kurth, "The Political Consequences of the Product Cycle, *International Organization*, Winter, 1979, p. 16.

portionately. The British alone maintained free and open markets. From 1873 to 1899 British exports grew at an annual rate of 1.6 percent while imports expanded at almost triple the rate—4.5 percent.* Imports from the United States made up by far the largest percentage of any country in the United Kingdom trade balance, taking 19.8 percent in the 1870s, rising to 23.9 percent in the 1890s.

U.S. exports flooded into Britain on an even more unequal basis than that on which Japan trades with the United States today. British goods and materials entering the United States during the height of the protective tariff under McKinley were subject to an average tariff rate of 57.7 percent. American goods going the other way entered Britain unencumbered by any protective tariff at all. That was a major reason American trade relations with Great Britain were far larger than those with Germany, and were destined to be so for the foreseeable future. The Germans countered American trade barriers with barriers of their own. The British did not.

It would be simplifying rather much to say that this is why the United States and Britain became allies rather than enemies in the twentieth century. But it is certainly true that by providing free access to its own markets, Britain developed much more elaborate commercial and investment ties to a rising power like the United States than would have been likely otherwise. When this was combined with affinity growing from coincidences of language and heritage, an alliance was gradually formed. As it developed, it became the foundation for what later was the smoothest and most amiable transition of power in history.

THIRTY YEARS OF CHAOS

It took many years for the Anglo-American alliance to develop fully, and even longer for world economic arrangements to be refashioned according to the terms of the new megapolitical reality. Thirty years passed between the effective collapse of British authority in World War I and the assumption of American hegemony in 1945. These were thirty of the worst years in this or any century. Thirty years of chaos, years of horrible wars and depression.

From the perspective of the time, the transitional difficulties caused

---

* Forest Capie, *Depression and Protectionism: Britain Between the Wars* (London: George Allen and Unwin, 1983), 15–16.

by the collapse of British power were desperate matters, economically and politically. The British gave way under the duress of events that threatened the very survival of the open world economy. As Andrew Gamble wrote, British liberal opinion was "forced to accept in the 1920s and 1930s that Britain could not maintain the international monetary system alone, that sterling was no longer strong enough to be the leading world currency, and that American co-operation was indispensable if an open capitalist world economy was to survive." *

THE NEXT TIME AROUND

As it happened, the world economy had a new and more vigorous champion in the United States. Thirty years of chaos was all it took to make the transition. We may not be so lucky the next time around. The only power that could potentially succeed the United States in economic strength is Japan. But such a succession would seem to be far off. The United States was already a larger economy than Britain many decades before British hegemony ended. By contrast, Japan's economy remains smaller than that of the United States. And Japan is only potentially any type of military power at all. It would take a constitutional revision and a dramatic shift in Japanese opinion to enable Japan to take on the costly burdens of military power. Even if the will to do so existed, unfavorable technological conditions are making it ever more costly for any nation to project power in the world. If these trends continue in the decades to come, the Japanese will be quite as incapable as anyone else of restoring order in a fragmenting and increasingly violent world.

The chaos that accompanied the breakdown of British power may have been only a foretaste of the future. Many of the miseries of the first half of the twentieth century were, at least in part, consequences of the power equation. When no predominant power was able or willing to sustain investment, trade, and monetary arrangements, those arrangements began to unravel. As we shall see, much of the megapolitical evidence points to more unraveling today, but without the happy prospect that someone will step forward to weave everything back together again.

---

* Andrew Gamble, *Britain in Decline* (Boston: Beacon Press, 1981), 61.

3

The End of the Pax Americana

*The Dark Ages may return, the Stone Age may now return
on the gleaming wings of science. . . .*
                                        —Winston Churchill

*The U.S. president resorted to appeals and he is begging,
cap in hand.*
                                        —Ayatollah Khomeini

To say that the world is getting more dangerous every day has been
almost a literal truth for years. The whole planet is like a metropolis
slowly but perceptibly going downhill. Police no longer patrol the bad
neighborhoods. Many who could move uptown have departed, taking
along what valuables they could. To go into once pleasant or promising
suburbs is now a matter of courage or stupidity, like a journey to a
cannibal island in the seventeenth century. Storefronts are decorated
with graffiti, their shelves almost bare. Dulled and disgruntled men
loiter at streetcorners. Children throw stones. Windows they have broken will not be fixed.

You know this place from the evening news. It is Egypt. The Philippines. Angola. Mexico. It is practically every outlying neighborhood in
the global metropolis. Pictures of its residents, like those of the poor of
an urban ghetto, are vivid and disheartening. You can see in even 30-
second clips that they are victims, enveloped by a crisis of crime and
disorder. This crisis threatens us. It is spreading steadily, like a slow
contagion that moves a block or two and peels the paint.

And make no mistake, the paint has peeled. Economies, even in the
United States and Europe, have begun falling into their foundations,
like old houses with rotten beams. They have not yet collapsed. But
here and there, flooring planks have given way. And whole structures
are getting creaky.

86

It is misleading to press metaphors too far, but there may be an unfortunate aptness about this one. Economies are showing distinct signs of decay and decline. Consider these important developments, all of which have emerged since American hegemony effectively ended:

— The collapse of the international gold reserve system of fixed exchange rates pegged to the dollar, followed by extreme monetary disorder and currency fluctuations
— A 3,400 percent increase in the expropriation of international investments
— The emergence of the OPEC cartel, resulting in an unprecedented shift of wealth away from the major industrial countries
— An explosion of debt, on the consumer, commercial, and government levels
— An international payments crisis, with underdeveloped countries owing $1 trillion
— An unbroken string of U.S. budget deficits, skyrocketing from an annual average of $6 billion in the 1960s to $200 billion in the eighties
— A sharp increase in unemployment throughout the industrial world
— A collapse of productivity growth
— An unprecedented decline in income for the average American family
— An upsurge in terrorism and violence

This parade of bad news could be a coincidence. We doubt it. We suspect it is indicative of a deeper megapolitical crisis. And we explain why in this chapter and the ones that follow.

It many ways, it is harder to gain perspective on the contemporary economy than on those in the past. Part of the reason is that you can never be sure which trends are significant. In fact, it is hard to know what the trends are, beyond the short-term market fluctuations. You can follow this hour's trades on stock or commodity markets. But twenty years may pass before the significance of a string of budget deficits or a fall in productivity growth comes into focus.

Signs of economic decay are even harder to see at the level of the individual household. There is no typical family to follow and measure. That is why most people do not know how poorly the American economy has performed since the late sixties. The paint has indeed peeled.

Billions of dollars of infrastructure have fallen into disrepair. And even more telling, the typical American family has lost income. A study by the Joint Economic Committee of Congress showed that between 1973 and 1985, the average family lost $1,724, or an average of $157 a year. Families with children were even harder hit. In 1984 dollars, their pre-tax income fell from $28,988 to $25,836, a loss of $3,152. As startling as this is, it is understated. It leaves out the effect of taxes, which have gone up, as well as the increase in the number of hours worked. Families today are working longer for their income. Far more than in the early seventies, both wives and husbands work. Income has fallen in spite of a 50 percent increase in the number of second wage-earners. And the future looks grim. American children today have a higher poverty rate than at any time since the government started collecting the statistics.

THE DYNAMICS OF DECLINE

These symptoms of decline and shriveling income had many proximate causes. But beneath them all was a deeper megapolitical cause. A crisis of waning American power. This crisis took the hostages in Iran. It killed the marines in Lebanon and placed bombs in the cafés of Europe. Earlier, it brought Vietnam to an unhappy end. It also brought the collapse of the gold reserve system, leading to wild bouts of inflation and disinflation. It touched off the upheavals in oil markets. And led to the explosion of debt, sending more capital fleeing out of some regions in South America than still remains there.

These are all symptoms of declining American power, symptoms that many investors prefer not to recognize.

Illusions

One of the fond illusions of people shielded from life's realities is that power no longer matters. It is an illusion that arises in a secure environment where order is established and taken for granted. Those who live closer to the normal dangers of human life, such as the underclass of a big city like New York, know better. They are much more the connoisseurs of power's subtleties than many who can afford to bed down in a good neighborhood. The poor know that their persons and property are up for grabs whenever they stick their necks out the door. They know that the rules of life ultimately depend upon the exercise of raw power.

Consider a matter so simple as an old lady's purse. It is hers by the rules society sets, by law and justice, and our agreement. But so what? The old lady knows that justice alone will not protect her. If she should venture out on the wrong street in Harlem she will keep her purse only so long as there is a policeman (or someone) nearby with the *power* to enforce what is right. Otherwise, the rules that apply are the rules of the bully. The thief. The mugger. They are the rules that power sets. They change as the balance of power changes.

Even so subtle a difference as the setting of the sun can tip the balance of power on the street. As shadows lengthen, power slips away from the police and over to some youth gang that will set a stiff toll on anyone passing its way. The purse that would be the old lady's if she walked outside at 5:30 will not be hers at 8:00.

Like it or not, that is reality.

It is reality not only in the marginal neighborhoods of big-city America, it is reality throughout the globe. We are living in another twilight hour in the cycle of power. In Southeast Asia. Iran. Lebanon. Latin America. Africa. The sun is setting now on the American Empire, as it once set on the British Empire. As it does, shadows fall on many formerly safe streets everywhere. The political equivalent of youth gangs, petty local powers, are reaching for their guns. They will make the rules now. Rules that are enemies of progress. Rules that are a way of saying, "Nothing may pass this way without my say-so." Rules that tax or inhibit trade. Rules that usurp and confiscate investment—the way street bullies take whatever they can get away with.

The world is, indeed, becoming more dangerous every day. As this is written, U.S. government officials had identified forty-two wars, uprisings, and civil disorders under way across the globe. Add to their list the steady proliferation of terrorist incidents. Bombings, assassinations, arson, hijackings, kidnappings and piracy are now more common against civilians than at any time in modern history. Terrorism against commercial targets is even more rampant. Attacks against U.S. companies in Latin America doubled in 1985. *Defense & Economy World Report* reported 17 bombings of pipelines in continental Europe from December 1984 through December 1985.

The trend toward growing disorder will be of great importance to you as an investor.

The Logic of Disorder

The disorder we describe is not caused by too much violence on television. Nor dietary deficiencies. Nor poor education and bad manners.

These are more symptoms than causes. They are matters that ultimately can be affected by individual choice. The unlettered can learn. The moral slouch can become upright. The drunk, if he wishes, can put aside the bottle. Social deficiencies that are the sum of individual deficiencies can be changed and cured.

Unhappily, the bad news brought into your living room every night has a deeper and more ominous cause. Apparently unconnected stories, developing in different parts of the globe, reflect a progressive erosion of world stability. This, in turn, is a product of circumstances—impersonal megapolitical forces—that are not merely a sum of individual vices and failures. To the contrary. Some of them, at least, emerge as completely unintended consequences of people behaving wisely, honorably and well. The invention of the silicon chip, for example, was a laudable achievement. But it may have contributed greatly to making the world unsafe by reducing the scale of effective weaponry. So, too, the growth of the Japanese economy reflects a job well done. But it has reduced relative American wealth, thereby contributing to instability, oil shocks, monetary disorder debt crises and more.

No one has any idea how to change and cure circumstances such as these. They are brought about by accident. Indeed, they are so accidental that their working is beyond the range of many imaginations. Some people draw blanks trying to understand unintended consequences. Something deep and hard to shake wants us to associate every outcome of importance with the intentions of someone—a man or woman of high, majestic purpose or great evil. An anonymous development of momentous importance is almost meaningless, like a drama without characters.

Nonetheless, some of history's deepest secrets, including the sources of growing instability, are anonymous work. They are factors that alter costs and rewards of behavior for hundreds of millions and even billions of people.

While it would be wrong to account everything to "circumstances of the time," it is even more misleading to ignore them. Among the more important of these currently are:

1. Trends in technology that are making it ever costlier to project persuasive force from the center to the periphery
2. The dwindling American share of world economic output, which makes it both more burdensome and less rewarding for the United States to attempt to maintain world order

3. The incapacity of any other country for the foreseeable future to take up the slack and enforce the preservation of a liberal economic order in the world

Fighting unfavorable trends from a weakened position, America finds it steadily more difficult to halt a progressive deterioration in the underpinnings of the world economy. These trends have their origin in reactions to developments of the last century. The spread of effective weapons everywhere, the technological triumph of the defense, the declining scale of weaponry, and closing conceptual gaps have all combined to change the circumstances of behavior everywhere. Add to that the important fact that the American share of world output has declined, and you have a situation like that of Atlas growing feeble while trying to stand with the world on his shoulders. He gets flabbier until previously supportable burdens are too great to bear.

In short, American power has shriveled. This has produced many stories of trouble but little understanding of trouble's deeper causes.

MISLEADING CONCLUSIONS

Consider the misleading lessons remembered from Vietnam. The failure of that unwise American effort was laid off to many causes. Bad strategy. Insufficient efforts to win "the hearts and minds" of the people. Not enough Rambos among civilian policymakers. Too much bombing. Too little bombing. Corruption in Saigon. Poor arithmetic by General Westmoreland. And so on.

The similar postmortems, with equally misleading morals, followed bulletins a decade later recounting the collapse of U.S. policy in Lebanon. The media made much of the apparent bumbling by the Reagan administration when a suicide bomber blew up a barracks, killing hundreds of marines. The criticism was deserved. The result finally achieved in Lebanon, as in Vietnam, was worse than could have been had at the outset with no intervention at all. Unfortunately, the most obvious lessons were incidental; i.e., the marine commander was lax in setting security, firepower was misdirected, overall goals were ill defined, etc. Taken together, these appear more than sufficient to explain what went wrong. For that reason, they are misleading. They mask a deeper and more important difficulty—the declining cost-effectiveness of projecting power from the center to the periphery.

It is this that is making the world unstable—and is likely to make it more so—quite apart from anything that politicians might do. Clarity of purpose and competent implementation cannot overpower the logic of deadly force. When chaos costs less, you will get more of it.

In this respect, Lebanon is merely one of many places where changing military technology is empowering local groups to overturn any arrangement they dislike. They can do this to an increasing extent because the weapons required to *project* power are becoming more costly, while defensive weapons are falling in price.

A hundred years ago, the major Western nations possessed military technologies that were relatively cheap to them but practically impossible for distant peoples to resist. As we have seen, a gunboat with a Gatling gun could conquer 1,000 square miles of Africa. Local warriors were often courageous and cunning. But they could do little, fighting with spears and muskets.

As this century progressed, the military cost differential favoring the cosmopolitan powers reversed dramatically. Putting air or naval power to work at the other end of the globe requires increasingly huge investments. Estimates of the full cost of an American aircraft carrier battle group now range as high as $20 billion. This is greater than the gross national products of many countries against which such a fleet might be sent. Yet it is well within the reach of such countries to buy Exocet missiles and similar weapons—which pose a grave threat to any fleet lying offshore. An article in *The New York Times* in 1983 quoted an expert in new weapons technology as predicting that within a decade "no warship will be able to survive on the surface of the sea."* Similarly, new hand-held missiles, simple enough to be operated by illiterates, can knock the most expensive aircraft from the sky.

It is only a matter of time until these effective antiaircraft missiles, like the new Stingers, fall in price almost as dramatically as the transistor radio or the VCR. And why not? The crucial technological element here is the emergence of ever-cheaper and more effective computer capacity. Single computer chips can now instantaneously compute data that would have challenged roomfuls of hardware only a decade ago. This improved processing capacity, along with improved optics and radar, will make for destructive missiles of ever-greater range and accuracy.

For the moment, the newest and best of these missiles are relatively

* *The New York Times*, (August 23, 1983, p.1).

expensive. But one day they will be so cheap that even the poorest groups will have them, like hand-held radios. This will add to the growing megapolitical power of small groups.

Poorer nations and movements already have a relative cost advantage on the ground. For one thing, the sheer disadvantage of numbers has turned more decisively than ever against the United States and the Western industrial countries. In 1950, these countries, including Japan, made up roughly 30 percent of the world's population. Today, the percentage has shriveled to just 15 percent. The explosion of population is occurring almost entirely among peoples who are poor. And this has consequences for the power equation.

While armies made up of wealthy citizens are easier to train because they are better educated, they are harder to motivate. Throwing oneself into battle is a task done with less regret where life is cheap and prospects are desperate. That is not the case for even the poorest American recruits. Yet even if soldiers from advanced economies were motivated to sacrifice themselves, popular opinion, led by their close relatives, would not tolerate it. A scandal was provoked 130 years ago when the British Light Brigade charged against the Russian cannons and the odds. As Tennyson put it, "Not though the soldier knew / Someone had blundered . . . Theirs not to reason why, / Theirs but to do and die." That was before recruits were signed on with the promise of education benefits and a pension—benefits that are worthless unless the recipient survives to collect them. The tens of thousands of martyrs who launch suicide attacks at Iraqi lines for the Ayatollah Khomeini or the terrorists who blew themselves up with the U.S. and French marines in Lebanon do not worry about such things. To put the same matter another way, they have far lower opportunity costs than those of any cosmopolitan soldier.

More could be said along these lines, but the point should be clear. A great many of the cost advantages that enabled the Western powers to extend their sway through the nineteenth century have disappeared. Whatever order exists today is largely an artifact of those cost advantages. As we have seen, the scope of markets was extended, in the first instance, not in calm negotiation but by force of arms. Order was imposed and jurisdictions consolidated because of the unarguable superiority of Western military technology and the great power gap it helped create over peoples at the periphery.

THE CHANGING CHARACTER OF INSTABILITY

The changing costs and rewards of raw force have therefore altered the type of disruption the world faces. When stability broke down in the first half of this century, it was due to bickering among the leading cosmopolitan powers. Britain, Germany, France, Italy, Russia, the United States, and Japan shared between them almost all the real power in the world. They controlled almost all the world's combined navies and, later, almost the whole of their air forces. The map of the world reflected this reality. The great powers and their minor European competitors, Portugal, Holland, and Belgium, had largely partitioned the globe among themselves.

The wars they spawned were macro-disorders, squabbles between major powers that could be decisively ended by military means. Indeed, the end of both world wars brought astonishingly rapid transitions in relations, as former enemies became friends and former allies split apart. Germany and Japan, for example, became American allies almost overnight in 1945. This transformation could be negotiated with relative ease because governments had changed. There was no particular animosity between the peoples, nothing that went deeper than the passions of the moment.

So long as the colonial empires lasted, those running them controlled the physical force needed to suppress indigenous commotions. Once those empires disintegrated, however, as their technological edge was lost, the outlying regions became capable of threatening order on their own. That capacity has continued to grow.

THE COLLAPSING SCALE OF EFFECTIVE WEAPONS

Over the last century, the technology of weapons systems has increasingly shifted the edge to the defense. The machine gun proved to be a powerful antidote to attack by infantry. The antiaircraft gun, and then the missile, countered the offensive threat in the skies. Across the whole range of weaponry, defensive effectiveness has grown relative to the offense. Someday, a "Star Wars" system or something similar may once again raise the scale of effective weaponry. That day has yet to arrive.

In spite of the technological dominance of the defense, which has enormously increased the costs of offensive weapons, the collapse and fragmentation of political units has proceeded rather slowly. The number of governments in the world has multiplied fourfold in this century. A significant increase, but still modest compared to the potential for devolution. It is like having a china bowl break into four pieces rather than a thousand. Such extreme fragmentation is possible. Feudalism saw the world broken into tens of thousands of petty polities.

Part of what has kept the scale of political units high have been the dual effects of improving transportation and increasing scale in weapons, even defensive weapons. Better transportation and communication have partially counteracted the impact of better defense by making it easier to project power at a distance. And until recently, the scale of all weapons systems, even the predominant defensive ones, kept increasing. This meant staggering costs for commanding the use of effective weapons, costs that could not be borne by small groups. The defense was at an advantage, but it was an advantage that only fairly large or well-financed groups could enjoy.

This helps explain the apparently stubborn bias of revolutionary groups for Communist ideology in the face of widespread evidence that Communist systems work badly. The key to this mystery is money. The Soviet Union and other Marxist states have been the largest ready sources of finance and weaponry for ambitious leaders. And they have needed it. The scale of weaponry has been so large as to make success of any military disruption unlikely without significant backing. To get that backing, revolutionaries have absorbed and mouthed the party line.

Where funds are available from sources with other ideological bents, those too become popular with daring young men ready to take up arms. It is a case of "he who pays the piper calls the tune." During the 1930s, Fascist ideology was appealing at the periphery. In those days, Fascist governments had open checkbooks. The more they spent, the more eager Fascist movements cropped up. Without outside backing, few of these groups, then or now, could have gotten over the hurdles of scale to become militarily effective.

A significant fall in the scale of predominant weapons systems would change this dramatically. It would reduce the need for local groups to find patrons for disruption. They could go it alone. This would mean fewer Marxist-Leninist slogans spray-painted on walls. The character of disruptive groups would become more local and idiosyncratic, a feature that is already apparent in the Middle East.

History has gotten ahead of itself in that region because the effective cost of arms to local groups is lower there than anywhere else. Why?

Because more sponsors are at hand to subsidize weaponry. In Lebanon, practically every valley or city neighborhood is under the armed control of a separate militia. One may be sponsored by Syria. One by Iran. Another by Libya. Exiles in Paris buy mortars for their relatives in East Beirut. The Israelis have their groups. The Saudis support the PLO. The field is glutted. This makes disruption very cheap, as it would be if the scale of weaponry were reduced.

Not incidentally, where there are so many pipers playing so many tunes, surprisingly few groups are dancing to the clumsy Soviet polka. The armed wing of the small Lebanese Communist party was attacked and destroyed by a Syrian-backed militia in 1985, and almost nothing was heard about it. Communism is a yawn in the Middle East, as it is likely to be elsewhere if the scale of weapons systems falls. We shall explore the problems of Communism in more detail later.

NO V-DAY OVER TERRORISM

Disorder today is far more threatening because of its collapsing scale. It is micro-disorder, motivated by the discontent of small groups. As the margins of American power recede at the periphery, the raw power of these groups rises. So does their ability to disrupt arrangements they do not like. They cannot be stopped, as World War II was stopped, by forcing the surrender of a large-scale network of command. There is no single chain of command that has the authority to stop terrorism. Nor can anyone negotiate a compromise to meet demands of many of the small groups now wielding military force.

A reversion to a lower scale of military technology, with increasing advantage to the defense, means a reversion to a smaller scale of political unit. It means a reversion to grievances that are local, tribal, idiosyncratic, and sectarian. Grievances that mark deeper divisions of religious belief and ethnic animosity. Grievances that in practical fact cannot be negotiated because they are hopelessly overlapping and contradictory.

When power predominates at a large scale, these contradictions are resolved, ignored, or suppressed. In a sense, some of the freedoms taken for granted in both Britain and the United States reflect traditions of compromise over the exercise of power on a large scale. When power is wielded on the micro scale, each local group has the capacity to indulge its intolerances about the beliefs, appearance or conduct of others. In Lebanon, someone who throws a bomb at a synagogue, desecrates a mosque, or shoots worshipers coming out of church will probably find protection from some militia that bears a grudge against the targets of violence. Throw a bomb at a synagogue, desecrate a mosque, or shoot worshipers coming out of church in the United States, and the police will come after you. If they cannot muster the force to bring you under control, the authorities will send in the army. This threat of overwhelming power bridges the contradictions in deeply held beliefs. People who think that God is against selling Cheez Whiz on Sundays can coexist with military dairy farmers, as well as soy curd worshipers who do not believe that Cheez Whiz should be sold at all. In short, an encompassing political unit, like industrial-strength padding, absorbs the stresses of contradictory opinion.

At a small scale, such contradictions spring into the open. No one has the power to suppress them. People who know the devil's work when it comes their way can take violent means to stop it. Since one man's sin is another's religion, you get violent impasses and contradictions without the means to resolve them. And the more the contradictory claims grow, the more impossible it becomes to restore order even by surrender. For example, to whom would capitulation in the Middle East be offered? Abu Nidal? The Hezbollah? The Jewish Defense League? The question answers itself. Any accommodation that would satisfy one small group would infuriate the next. The declining scale of military technology means that peace will be the hostage of an increasing number of restless souls.

How bad can matters get? The final level of disintegration will not be reached until there is a change in the cost trends explained above. Until then, more devolution is the result to be expected. Its progress from the disintegration of colonial empires to Lebanon and the Middle East through other areas in years to come will be one of increasing danger and vulnerability for the world economy.

ELECTRONIC FEUDALISM?

The megapolitical trend implies far more disorder than the world has experienced for centuries. If not reversed, it will bring us eventually to a kind of electronic feudalism, an environment where cheap and effective high-tech weapons will give increasing numbers of disgruntled groups a veto over almost any activity they do not like. Safety will shrivel into smaller and smaller margins. And the economy will shrivel with it.

Of course, it is always dangerous to extrapolate too far on the basis of trends. We know that. No projection is dependable as long as the principle of compensation is at work. And compensation is the most restless, workaholic principle in nature. Indeed, it is the trick by which nature keeps its accounts in balance. Every trend is suspect. Before long it will be reversed by a countertrend, and events will move back in the other direction.

Keep that truth in mind. But also remember that the longest perspective is usually the truest. The tendency of everything to reverse direction after a time applies to long-term trends as well as shorter cycles. As hard as it may be to believe, the world system has seen an extreme of peace and stability over most of the period since the battle of Waterloo. The nineteenth century was the most peaceful in history, largely, we believe, because of the overwhelming power advantages enjoyed through most of it by the British Empire.

In this century, violence has tended to reassert itself as the common condition of life. This was especially true before 1945, when violence flared during the crisis of British hegemony. The severity of war became much worse. Fatalities from fighting skyrocketed because of the increased deadliness of weapons technology. Nonetheless, war has tended to be much less common than in earlier centuries. As historian Jack Levy put it, "In all other respects, however, the twentieth century ranks below average. War has been under way about half the time, compared to 95 percent of the time in the sixteenth and seventeenth centuries and nearly 80 percent of the time in the eighteenth century; only the nineteenth century ranks lower, with war under way 40 percent of the time."*

Seen from the longer perspective, therefore, the world has been extraordinarily stable over the whole modern period from which we draw our bearings and perspective. We may now be ready to revert to a more common level of disorder. The transition from feudalism that brought Europe from a collection of petty feudal interests to the modern system of independent nation-states was marked by the Hundred Years War, a war named by an optimist. It actually lasted 116 years. The reversion to violence by small groups could be a prelude to a new kind of feudal-

* Jack S. Levy, *War in the Modern Great Power System, 1495–1975* (Lexington, Kentucky: University Press of Kentucky, 1983) 140.

ism, based on the renewed predominance of small-scale defensive military technology.

How far could the trend toward dissolution go? We have no way of knowing. We suspect that the forms of the nation-state would remain, as in Lebanon, as indeed, the form of the old Roman Empire was preserved, like an unburied mummy, through the Middle Ages. We could be slowly entering a period as violent and murky as the feudalism of old.

THE END OF THE PAX AMERICANA

There is no longer an effective guardian of world order. America is struggling to serve that role, with little more success than Britain enjoyed in the 1920s. Reagan more effectively restored appearances than his immediate predecessors, at least for a few years. But as the weapons-for-hostages deal proved, his achievements were largely a matter of appearance. The United States could decisively project power in Grenada. It cannot deter the Sandinistas. Nor stop terrorists. And no one even dreams that force would be effectively used again to prevent the confiscation of property or to insure fulfillment of contracts such as payments of debts. In spite of the trillions spent in military budgets, America has not exercised such real power for more than a decade.

The Pax Americana lasted little more than a generation, from 1945 until Vietnam. It was a short run, almost stunted compared to the century of British dominion prior to World War I. But by the time America stepped into the limelight, the camera of history was churning at high speed. Events and crises crowded in upon one another like angry commuters at rush hour. Nothing of the sort had been seen during the calm days when Britannia ruled the waves and Queen Victoria's private train was the fastest thing on earth. When the Khalifa of the Dervishes butchered hostages and tortured old women, it literally took years for the news to reach London. Today, crimes of terrorists travel, in full color, at the speed of light.

Frontier Order . . .

Like the Pax Britannica before it, the peace that America brought to the world was the peace of power, not of agreement. And it certainly was not a peace of comprehension. No swords were pounded into plowshares. It was more the peace of the Western movie, the order of the frontier, where the "peace officer," the lonely lawman of few words, saved the sodbusters from savages on the warpath, gangs of bandits, or claim-jumping ranchers and their corrupt accomplices.

The moral of the frontier movie was the moral of hegemony. It spoke to the same purpose: the need for someone in a white hat to wield force. It was a moral imbedded deeply in the American consciousness, from the Declaration of Independence forward, when Thomas Jefferson counted among the crimes of George III that of using too little force against "the inhabitants of our frontiers, the merciless Indian Savages, whose known rule of warfare is the undistinguished destruction of all ages, sexes and conditions." In the metaphor of the frontier, Indians stood for all non-Western peoples. Enterprising directors could, and sometimes did, change locales. The same stories worked with the British in India, or the Foreign Legion chasing ruthless Arabs through the sands. Whatever the setting, the meaning of the frontier drama was the same. Someone had to wield the blazing gun that alone could bring order where it was lacking.

In a telling way, the popularity of the frontier drama survived as long as American hegemony lasted. When overwhelming U.S. power died in the swamps of Vietnam, the Western movie and its variants died of the same wound. The audience could no longer stomach its costly moral. The black hats had won the draw. Pow. In the new power environment, no one wished to be reminded that the bad men, the claim jumpers, the Indians, and the Arabs were now roaming unchecked. No one, that is, except the new winners, the non-Western peoples who rooted for the Indians.

An authoritative study counted 215 incidents from1946 through 1975 when U.S. military forces were deployed to preserve world order. These were like episodes of "Gunsmoke," or serial versions of *High Noon*. During the early years after World War II, when the United States had real power, it was used effectively. Even though the international protection of private property had deteriorated dramatically by nineteenth-century standards, there were very few acts of expropriation before 1960. And only a handful before 1966.

And Frontier Disorder

Beginning about 1967, with the United States bogged down in Vietnam, its Oriental version of World War I, governments around the world realized that the actual reach of American power had declined. And they immediately moved to take advantage of it. Like lawless ranchers who suddenly saw that they could raid the sodbusters with impunity, they did. The sheriff was not exactly dead. But what came to the same thing, he was trapped and wounded far away. The result? A dramatic upsurge in the expropriation of American businesses and investments. As the tide of war turned in favor of North Vietnam, other governments reached the accurate conclusion that they need not conform to rules America was struggling to enforce.

This impression was reinforced by riots and looting that swept American cities. As smoke rose over Washington, Los Angeles, and Detroit, it seemed for a time that the American government would have its hands full controlling looting in the United States. It could hardly hope to do so abroad. So foreign elites began to help themselves to American investments. By 1973, property seizures—the international equivalent to looting—had leaped to 35 times their earlier level.* Such an astounding increase may be merely a coincidence, but we doubt it.

British investments were also swept up in these acts of political banditry. A major reason was that the British were no longer prepared to intervene militarily "even where major economic interests were at stake."† By contrast, the French maintained a strong military presence to protect their major investments in former French colonies. And they were willing to use it. As a result, relatively few French investments were expropriated. A great disproportion of the victims of property seizures were British and American investors.

OIL AND THE POWER EQUATION

The connection between these property seizures and the power equation was never brought clearly into focus at the time. What was clear was that the costs of waging the Vietnam War were ghastly. A reasonable computation by the Department of Commerce of total private American assets in underdeveloped countries put them at $68.8 billion

* Lipson, *Standing Guard*, 98.
† Waldemar A. Nielsen, *The Great Powers and Africa* (New York: Praeger, 1969), 6.

in 1974, "less than half the estimated cost of the limited war fought in Vietnam." *

Not the least of the costs of Vietnam, however, was the unequivocal demonstration it provided of how much the relative power of America had shrunk. By clarifying the true state of power in the world, it cleared away conceptual lags. As we discuss below, this set the stage for one of the most dramatic economic and investment upheavals of all time: the emergence of OPEC. It resulted in a vast transfer of wealth from the pockets of Western consumers to the governments of oil-exporting countries. The consequent inflation and increase in the value of real assets throughout the world shifted literally trillions in assets.

The rise of OPEC was a direct consequence of declining American hegemony. If not for the shriveling of U.S. power, the oil price could not have skyrocketed. As long as American and British multinational companies had proprietary control over the majority of world oil, they could halt any abrupt price increase by raising output from the vast reserve capacity in low-cost Middle Eastern wells. The property rights of these companies had to be nullified or expropriated before the price could rise.

This brings us to a point of which you should take special note as an investor. That is the phenomenon of the reversal of cause and effect in political explanations of important events. If you judged only by what you heard on television, you would probably conclude that the energy upheavals over the last two decades were due to causes that were in fact mere fantasies. In 1973, at the time of the first OPEC shock, most people would have said that the world was "running out of oil." This was true only in the most trivial sense that the world has always been "running out of oil" since the first barrel was pumped. But as the subsequent events proved beyond a doubt, fear of an imminent exhaustion of fossil fuels was pure twaddle. In fact, the only real power outage we suffered was of a very different character. It was the insufficiency of American power to continue protecting property rights in oil internationally. This was masked, as most basic facts of political economy are masked, by misleading rhetoric.

The sudden change in the arrangements governing the pumping and pricing of oil was attributed to: 1) an almost overnight discovery that oil had become scarce; and, 2) a spontaneous eruption of new principles

* Guy J. Parker, *Military Implications of a Possible World Order Crisis in the 1980s*, p. xi (a Project Air Force Report prepared for the U.S. Air Force, November 1977.

of morality and political justice that required local powers to seize any oil developments within their grasp. Such was the rhetorical flash and adornment that was draped over the underlying megapolitical reality. Most people were taken in by this rhetorical fashion show, without asking deeper questions, a mistake as silly as imagining that a tuxedo or a fancy dress was the cause of a dinner party.

Whenever a far-reaching event happens, the first question you should pose to yourself as an investor is, "Why did this event happen now, and not five years ago—or ten years from now?" If the explanation you are hearing does not at least hint at an answer, you should look beyond it to a deeper explanation that does. Usually, though not always, you will discover something that other people are overlooking, something that can give you an information advantage.

Even now, years later, we think you can still get a head start on coming developments by understanding why the oil shock emerged when it did.

CHANGING THE RULES ON OIL

The oil expropriations did not result from the sudden discovery of new principles of economic justice; far from it. They were matters of raw power. Elites in oil-producing countries saw a chance to pocket massive windfalls by abridging property rights, so they did. The arrangements they nullified were not special inventions concocted to treat foreigners badly. In most cases, American oil companies operated abroad in more or less the same way they would have done in Texas or Wyoming, investing large sums in research and discovery. Buying and developing reserves. And paying royalties under contract. These arrangements benefited the oil-producing countries—in the same way that you would be benefited if an oil company sent a geologist to your property, then dug a well, hit oil, and started pumping. You would get massive royalty checks. And the more oil that was found, the richer you would be.

In 1965, practically the same rules applied to oil pumped up in Saudi Arabia or Iran as in Texas or Wyoming—except that laws in the United States kept the domestic price higher than the world price. Within a few years, however, elites from the Middle East to Venezuela saw that they could gain great windfalls by overturning existing rules and contracts. They simply seized the property for themselves. It was as if a gang of bandits in West Texas had come to the conclusion that they could seize an oil field. Not just seize it for an hour or a day. Seize it and keep it. Seize it because neither the Texas Rangers nor any other police authority could stop them. They would then "export" the oil to New York, but not on terms set by its previous owners. Working with other bandits in other places, they could then take actions to raise the price to extortionate levels.

In practical fact, this is what happened. The actions were dignified by nationalistic speeches. But what was said applied just as well to West Texas as Saudi Arabia. "Oil is the prime asset of West Texas. We must seize all of its value for the people of West Texas. The oil companies are controlled by shareholders in New York and San Francisco. Therefore, we are seizing this oil." The logic of such statements is the logic of local advantage, a logic that generalizes to economic warfare of all against all. It is the logic of beggaring your neighbor. Carried to a conclusion, it would carry the world economy to economic disaster. Indeed, it would push us into a black hole of depression. Every little community with any power advantage to exploit would rewrite the rules of commerce in whatever rigged way happened to yield the maximum advantage for itself—for the moment. It would be like trying to play a game of cards and having the more physically ferocious players change the rules on every draw—depending on what hand they got.

What distinguished OPEC's actions from what would have been pure banditry in West Texas was nothing other than power. The U.S. government retained the power to recover seized oil properties in Texas. In many other places, it no longer did. So the international political economy shifted abruptly. As it became increasingly clear that new rules could be implemented—and there was nothing the United States, much less Britain, could do about it—peripheral governments began to nationalize and cartelize oil reserves.

Taking the lead in this orgy of expropriation were regimes that had traditionally been friendly to the United States, Saudi Arabia, and, ironically, Iran. The Shah of Iran had himself been restored to power after the Mossadegh government tried and failed to seize Anglo-Iranian Petroleum's wells. Now, in changed circumstances, he took the lead in expropriating even more valuable oil properties. The United States did not even try to stop him. And it was just as well. As Vietnam showed, and the hostage crisis later confirmed, there was little America could do. Its power had been defeated by three factors.

Why the United States Could Not Stop OPEC

The largest of these was the abrupt decline in relative U.S. military power that we have discussed extensively. In light of the other two factors described below, that power would have needed to increase in relative terms to preserve the international treatment of investment.

The two other elements in the changed megapolitical picture were increased international competition and more widespread local knowledge of the oil business. In a surprising way, both ultimately have a technological basis.

By the late sixties, the technology of petroleum engineering and marketing was sufficiently mature that it had spread widely. This inevitably led to more international competition in oil refining and marketing. When Mossadegh attempted to seize British oil properties in 1952, the seven leading companies "controlled 98% of world oil trade."* They refused to deal with Mossadegh, treating Iranian oil as stolen property. By the eve of the first oil shock, the number of oil companies with the technical capacity and expertise to market oil had mushroomed. The seven majors now controlled just 60 percent of the trade. New European, Japanese, and American firms had grown to the point where there was no hope that a boycott of available supplies would work. There were simply too many companies for that kind of cooperation, each with far more to gain by buying "stolen" oil than it could lose by encouraging further "theft." This insured that there were plenty of buyers waiting in line when expropriations occurred.

Because oil production, refining, and marketing were technologically mature businesses, much of the mystery about how they operated had disappeared. This meant that there were people in oil-producing countries who knew how to operate oil facilities—as there had not been earlier. In the 1930s, when Bolivia seized Standard Oil properties, there had been no Bolivians available who could run the confiscated wells. Consequently, production collapsed, and the confiscation came to nothing. When industries mature technologically, they become much more vulnerable to seizure.

So it was that international property rights in the oil industry were highly vulnerable. When it became clear that America could no longer enforce the old rules, those rules changed. OPEC soon managed to raise the price astronomically. The U.S. percentage of excess production

* Lipson, *Standing Guard*, 111.

capacity in oil had fallen so far that it was no longer possible for multi-national oil companies to stabilize the price by increasing output from politically secure wells. There was plenty of oil in other wells in the Middle East and elsewhere. But the local elites who had seized control saw that they could reap billions in windfalls by withholding production from the market. So they did, pocketing hundreds of billions in the process.

The Death of Anti-Communism

The fact that anti-Communist governments, like that of the Shah in Iran and the Saud family, took the lead seizing oil properties demonstrated that this was not a Marxist initiative. It was a rather more ancient and basic form of freebooting. It was an exercise in raw power. A case of "take when the taking is good." Or "do what you can get away with." The orgy of expropriations, spreading far beyond oil, marked the effective end of anti-Communist ideology among multinational companies. The reason: anti-Communism no longer served a rational economic function.

In the era before widespread expropriations, major American companies could help defend their properties by encouraging anti-Communist sentiment. This helped bring popular support for military action abroad to police the safety of investment. As Charles Lipson put it:

> By associating both social reforms and nationalism with the overthrow of world capitalism, anti-Communist ideology integrated potentially divergent economic and security interests. It fused together various private investors and suggested an identity between their interests and public economic welfare. Finally, it implied that economic interests were parallel to compelling, if broad, notions of military security.*

In short, anti-Communist ideology paid. It helped increase the costs to foreign governments for scrambling the rules of the world economy.

But once these rules were scrambled, and it became clear that America no longer had the power to prevent property seizures, anti-Communism no longer paid. As this realization set in, anti-Communism more or less disappeared from the corporate agenda. Leaders of most multinational firms with large trade and investment interests abroad—

---

* Lipson, *Standing Guard*, 108.

at least the great majority whose interests were vulnerable—quickly realized that they had more to gain by dealing with expropriating governments than they had left to lose. It was like having your car stolen and then facing the fact that loud complaints would jeopardize the chance that the thief would hire you to fix it when it broke down. Even where personal bitterness over bad treatment, perfidity, or corruption led some individuals and companies to pull out, there were always gobs of competitors hoping to profit from service and supply contracts on the newly seized properties.

The old owners, in essence, faced a Hobson's choice of acquiescing to the theft of their properties and settling for compensation short of true market value, or protesting and getting even less. In investment, more is better than less. Those who acquiesced were usually better off. They often ended up with contracts to operate their own businesses.

In any event, the prudent course in these arrangements was usually to bow to local demands and go along with any rhetorical gloss the locals put on it. That is why you hear almost nothing critical of even the most extreme forms of government economic intervention from most multinational corporations. Such pronouncements are self-defeating in the current power environment. It is one in which capital exporters and domestic investors are at a disadvantage in most areas of the world.

In such an environment, stable rules and physical safety are hard to find. This makes doing business in large markets in Eastern Europe, the Soviet Union and China far more attractive than it used to be. The erosion of property rights in the rest of the world made corporate anti-Communism a thing of the past. In the years to come, you can expect ever less criticism of those who wield power abroad. No behavior, including cannibalism, will draw a murmur of protest, if it is the work of a government holding assets or profits of the firm hostage. For example, former Liberian army commander General Thomas Quiwampa was apparently eaten by the personal guard of President Doe. No international business with assets in Liberia protested.

International property rights have deteriorated so far from the nineteenth-century standard of equal treatment—which gave all investors the same rights of private property everywhere—that no major corporation can afford to offend host governments. The terms of trade and investment are whatever the rulers of the unruly governments say they are.

WHY EVERY BUSINESS WAS NOT TAKEN

Not all investments were as vulnerable as others. And we should probably repeat here that we are not talking solely about oil. Oil expropriations were not the only property seizures. They were merely the most dramatic. American investments of all kinds were grabbed, especially fixed investments in industries with relatively mature technologies. Mining interests, for example, were ideal targets. These required staggering sums to develop. And once developed, they could not be moved or withdrawn. High-tech investments were perhaps the least vulnerable. To seize IBM, for example, would have been idiocy. A government doing so would have gotten nothing but a small inventory of soon-to-be-obsolete hardware. And what else? Perhaps a few carbon ribbons and some surplus blue suits. People who did not know computers as well as IBM, that is to say, practically everyone, would have found a takeover of an IBM office as useless as the Bolivians found Standard Oil's wells in the 1930s.

Firms with high-tech, low-scale, portable investments dependent upon foreign parts and service tended to survive best in areas of property rights instability. If companies could move their assets, or withhold needed supplies and repairs, they could not be so easily pushed around by foreign governments. More difficult-to-capture investments, such as those outside the primary product area, or those with rapidly changing technology, were more secure. Investors in those fields normally were able to continue operating their companies. But with restrictions. They survived only so long as technological conditions and the level of organizational knowledge in the local government made them indispensable.

The problem was not merely that existing investments were confiscated in whole or in part. New direct foreign investment was discouraged or subject to more limitations than those in a 30-page insurance policy. Foreign capital was often banned in "strategic" sectors. These prohibitions usually excluded participation in industries with mature technologies, from natural resource production to financial services to transport. Where investment was allowed, it was often limited to contracting with state-owned entities. In many countries, new investments were also hobbled by "phaseout" provisions requiring foreign investors to reduce their long-term holdings. In some countries, such as Argentina, private capital was prohibited from investments in urban areas. And almost everywhere, remittance of profits was subject to restrictions, including punishing taxation.

The restrictions multiplied at the very time when other economic conditions were making investment in underdeveloped areas seem more attractive. Increased prosperity in Japan and Europe had sharply raised wage rates, creating many opportunities to expand the production of goods in low-wage countries. As it turned out, only a few nations on the Pacific rim had leadership that was open to these opportunities. Korea, Hong Kong, Taiwan, and Singapore prospered by remaining hospitable to foreign investment. They were distinct exceptions. In general, the welcome mat for foreign direct investment was not only withdrawn, it was burned.

The very fact that underdeveloped economies appeared to be more attractive sites for investment had a generally perverse effect. It increased the determination of local elites to monopolize opportunities for themselves. So they did. If a new manufacturing installation—such as a steel mill—looked as though it could be profitable, it could no longer be financed by private equity investment in most Latin or African countries. It could only be built by the new nationalized steel monopoly, staffed and controlled by the local political elite and its cronies.

Where did the money come from to finance this orgy of political investment? Simple. The foreign governments borrowed from American and other Western banks. Hence, the debt crisis. Instead of direct equity holdings from American and Western companies—or, for that matter, OPEC—the flow of new investment was suddenly limited largely to borrowing. This borrowing had almost everything to do with the deteriorating megapolitical situation. It had almost nothing to do with the fact that the nations doing the borrowing were poorer than the creditors.

The results, as we now know, were disasters almost everywhere in the underdeveloped world. The state monopolies were wasteful, corrupt, and unprofitable. A country like Mexico, far better situated for prosperity than the Asian rim economies because of its long border with the United States, became a basket case. So did most of Latin America and Africa. As we shall see in the chapter on the coming debt default, the inevitable collapse of the mountain of international debt threatens the solvency of some of America's largest banks.

LOCAL "PARTNERS"

Where direct equity investment was still allowed, new regulations forced investors to bring aboard local partners, a requirement that in many cases amounted to an indirect bribe for the local elite. Indeed, most international investments outside of the leading capitalist countries in recent years have involved local "partners," mainly politically influential figures whose stake in the investment provides some slight insurance against disruption—at least as long as the current regime lasts. The Japanese, who came to multinational investment just as American properties were being seized, organized almost all their investments in underdeveloped countries on the local "partnership" basis. Only firms with the strongest technological protection have been able to make significant new, direct-equity investments on terms of 100 percent ownership and control, as IBM has done in Mexico.

A CAUTION ON MULTINATIONAL CORPORATIONS

As an investor, you should remember that multinational firms will be increasingly vulnerable as the technology involved in their operations matures. We have included a list of the major firms operating abroad, with a rough indication of the exposure of their business to political upheaval and destruction by regulation. As the Socialist government in Greece, among others, has convincingly demonstrated, a cheap and effective way to seize assets from private investors is to regulate companies into bankruptcy. They then take over the shell that is left behind. Many American firms, including some of the largest and most dynamic, will be open to significant losses if international investment conditions continue to deteriorate as we fear. Consult our list as you analyze your present portfolio. It might be prudent to make adjustments if your holdings are highly vulnerable.

POWER TURNED AGAINST PROGRESS

Remember, governments in many parts of the world will increasingly operate like street gangs. They will do anything they can get away with. Literally anything. The "10 percenters" (corrupt officials) in Africa even demand bribes to allow emergency food aid to be delivered to their own people. In many cases, the starving are victims of previous policies of the government. They starve because their leaders have set up a national seed monopoly. And then not delivered any seed. They starve because the officials who run the government fertilizer monopoly have plundered the funds to buy fertilizer. Or, having bought the fertilizer, they have proceeded to sell it abroad. And even when peasants manage to plant and harvest crops, they often cannot take them to market. In Zambia, for instance, where all crops must be sold to a state corporation, that entity frequently has no bags or other means for collecting them. As farmer John Kalabo told the *Wall Street Journal,* "There's nothing to do. We're just going to starve like this." *

The situation is hardly unique to Zambia, or to Africa. Throughout the underdeveloped world, intense and corrupt regulation of every feature of economic life is the rule. Hernando de Soto, former governor of Peru's central bank, completed a study that showed that it took 289 days to obtain all the bureaucratic permits necessary to start a small company in Peru. Along with the delay came twenty-four separate requests for bribes. For a more significant business, delays for the necessary licenses run "three to eight years." † As a result, other experts calculate that 60 percent of the work force in Peru's capital, Lima, now works illegally. Because operating within the law is so costly, tangled, and corrupt, almost every business or citizen is a plausible target for a shakedown. As the *Economist* put it, "Small businesses are daily liable to enforced closure unless they pay more bribes. The result—under any over-big government—is a Peru fit for public officials to prosper in, but nobody else." ‡

Left, Right, or center, the leaders of governments in what Theodore Roosevelt called the "waste places of the earth" reach as far as their power allows. Whether they claim to be "advancing the Revolution" or protecting the nation from communism, they seek one common objective: to control everything. Their economies are regulated, dominated, and monopolized by government. Whatever the proclaimed virtues of these arrangements, and they are justified by a long list of alibis, their common feature is government control.

The reason is obvious.

The leaders control the government. If the government controls everything, then the leaders control everything. The further power reaches into every aspect of economic life, the greater the opportunities for aggrandizement and plunder.

In some countries, with prominent examples in Africa, the analogy between the government and the street gang has become complete. Ordinary people cannot appear on the street without permits and

* *Wall Street Journal,* July 15, 1985, p. 10.
† *Economist,* July 19, p. 34.
‡ Ibid.

passes. Curfews with strict penalties regulate the times during which travel is allowed. This gives the police an unbeatable pretext for extortion. They set their watches ahead (or behind) to nab "curfew breakers." They then harass the poor "enemies of the state" into paying a suitable bribe. Those who do not (or cannot) pay are arrested or beaten. In short, the government and its agents behave the way street gangs would if their reach were extended from a neighborhood to an entire economy.

Practically any regulation or government control is a lever that can be used to pry loose bribes or "commissions." And sometimes, when the abuse of raw power is particularly acute, no pretext is needed. Political leaders baldly seize property without even pretending to operate under color of law.

Rarely seen details of just how such practices work came to light after the fall from power of longtime Philippine President Ferdinand Marcos. "If the president wants your company, what are you going to do?" That difficult question was posed to Enrique Razon in 1976. Marcos's brother-in-law, Alfredo Roumaldez, reportedly marched into Razon's office one day and demanded all the stock of Philippine Jaialai and Amusement Corporation, a company with $20 million in annual revenues. Marcos stole it the way a petty thief would steal a purse. That is how he turned a salary of less than $5,000 a year into billions in boodle.*

Under such conditions, is there any surprise that economies in many areas of the world are underperforming? No. Stagnation and decline are the results to be expected where plunder and corruption make every transaction costlier than it should be. And plunder and corruption, of course, are not random developments or acts of nature. They are consequences of the power configuration. As power has decentralized, political institutions around the world have regressed toward the forms that existed prior to colonialism. It is inconceivable that the kind of corruption endemic in the Marcos regime could have occurred while the Philippines remained a colony of the United States. During that time, the United States guaranteed a structure of law and political stability hospitable to economic development. When the United States pulled out, power devolved to grasping local elites, who turned it against the public in an orgy of theft, extortion, and even murder.

Such developments are hardly unique to the Philippines. They reflect

* _San Francisco Examiner_, March 10, 1986, p. 1.

a general tendency rooted in the logic of power itself. The rules that made most of the world hospitable to investment were the incidental inventions of the two dominant powers of the past two centuries, Britain and the United States. Both were capital-exporting countries. So the rules they enforced were organized to facilitate investment. Today, the power equation has reversed. And the rules have reversed as well. They are now rules to facilitate capital expropriation.

This is why anyone with money in Latin America, Africa, and Western Asia wants to get it out.

This is why there is a world debt crisis. As we will see later, the debt is itself a creation of the new anti-investment climate. To some extent, money from Western banks liquefied the Third World, making it possible for people there to build dollar accounts abroad.

This process, too, has yet to be carried to its logical conclusion.

Indeed, it is this anti-investment climate in many potentially promising regions of the world that helps explain takeover binges in the American stock market, especially the big buyouts of oil companies in recent years. Though it may be merely a coincidence that takeover fever erupted among the oil companies when it did, we doubt it. Tens of billions are not invested lightly. Informed executives of politically sensitive companies decided to buy reserves in the United States, even facing the prospect of lower prices, because they expected the future investment environment in the rest of the world to sour. They understand that the Reagan administration has failed to halt the decline of U.S. power. Therefore they are retreating to the center. Daniel Yergin of Cambridge Energy Research Associates put it this way: "They now see the future as much more uncertain, and the one thing you can gamble your future on is U.S. reserves."

CAPITAL IS RETREATING TOO

One of the dependable features of economics is the principle that "capital is a coward." The retreat of the oil industry within the borders of the United States reflects the same tendency that has brought hundreds of billions of flight capital to America. Annual capital inflow to the United States rose from $58 billion in 1980 to $127 billion in 1985. During that same period, capital outflow shriveled from $86 billion to just $32 billion. Allowing for statistical discrepancies, the annual net capital inflow to the United States turned by $120 billion in just six years.* This movement of investment away from the periphery to the center is so dramatic that even though total borrowing by the Third World grew by $110 billion in 1983, the net flow of funds was in the other direction. Similar numbers held true for 1984, 1985, and 1986. To continue this trend for long would imply dramatic disinvestment and a fall in living standards throughout the debtor countries. The strains that this would place upon those countries would be a further incitement to instability—like hammering an eroded outcropping with a piledriver.

Parallels with the Past

The retreat of capital from the periphery to the center has an unhappy precedent at the time of the Great Depression. In that period, deteriorating conditions in Asia, Africa, and Latin America caused capital to flow back to America and Britain. This retreat of capital accompanied the fragmentation of the world trading system. It also coincided with widespread default and repudiation of sovereign debt. This was especially true in Eastern Europe and Latin America, areas of both the greatest borrowing and the greatest interbloc rivalry between the wars. These were areas where British power was weakest.

Around the globe, the security of investment is even shakier than it was in the 1920s. American assets have been confiscated without fair compensation even by some of America's supposed allies. Here, there and everywhere, nations are busily erecting barriers to the free flow of goods, people and capital. There is nothing the United States can do about it. Today's American military is the most expensive on the globe. Like Britain's in the 1920s, it is spread thin, trying to meet commitments that daily grow more difficult. News reports, some from the very hotbeds of trouble 60 years ago, testify to the futility of American efforts to police instability. Matters are out of control. And America's allies are as reluctant to join in cooperative efforts as Britain's were then.

World monetary arrangements are plagued by the very kind of instability that brought disastrous inflation and deflation in the early part of this century. The United States no longer has the financial resources to enforce stable international monetary arrangements. That is why the Bretton Woods system of fixed exchange rates collapsed. That is why the value of major currencies fluctuates up and down like a yo-yo.

* Paul Craig Roberts, "Beneath the 'Twin Towers of Debt' " *Wall Street Journal*, December 3, 1986, p. 8.

The United States, too, has become a debtor nation. More money is owed abroad than is owing. And many of the credits on the ledger are obligations of weak, poor countries, debts that seem unlikely to be paid, just as debts owed to Britain after World War I disappeared in a wave of default.

With government spending soaring out of control in America, arithmetic is doing the same ruthless work now that it did after British hegemony had effectively collapsed in World War I. The Congress has turned to a latter-day version of the "Geddes Axe," as the Committee on National Economy was known in 1921. Gramm-Rudman-Hollings or its successor will have a similar and inevitable result. Military spending will be significantly cut. With the United States no longer able to police the world, the world will go unpoliced.

The economic effect will be approximately what you would expect in a city if police withdrew from unruly neighborhoods. Disorder will grow and become more costly. Such a dynamic is at work now. Pressure is building for major upheavals in world trade and finance—of the sort that followed, with a lag, the collapse of British supremacy early in this century. Nothing short of a revolution in military technology or the greatest upsurge of manufacturing productivity ever witnessed in America can change it.

4

The Coming Debt Default

> *A debtor nation does not love its creditor, and it is fruit-*
> *less to expect feelings of goodwill . . . towards this country*
> *[Great Britain] or towards America, if their future develop-*
> *ment is stifled for many years to come by the annual tribute*
> *which they must pay us. There will be great incentive for*
> *them to seek their friends in other directions, and any future*
> *rupture of peaceable relations will always carry with it the*
> *enormous advantage of escaping the payment of external*
> *debts. . . . The existence of great . . . debts is a menace to*
> *financial stability everywhere. . . . Entangling alliances or*
> *entangling leagues are nothing to the entanglements of cash*
> *owing.*
>
> —Lord Keynes, 1919

> *O put not your trust in princes. . . .*
>
> —Psalms 146:3

This chapter explains one of the more dramatic financial developments of your lifetime: the default of many billions of international debt. Impoverished nations owe $1 trillion they will never pay. Major American banks, the linchpins of the world financial infrastructure, have an average of 200 percent of their capital exposed in Latin America alone.

Much of that money is gone forever. Anyone who has examined the facts knows this. Yet the dead loss of hundreds of billions has seemed for years to make very little difference. Banks have continued to book higher earnings without setting aside loan loss reserves or paying much attention to the precarious plight of their assets. Like cartoon characters that walk off a cliff and stand over an abyss, quite comfortably ignoring Sir Isaac's laws, the banks have not yet tumbled. One day, they will.

116

Remember that and begin to plan around it. It is one of the least doubtful forecasts about an uncertain future you have ever read. There will be an international debt collapse. Indeed, it may even have occurred by the time you pick up this book. We hope not. If you are lucky, the crisis is yet to come. And that gives you time to prepare. The default will have a major impact, wiping away many of America's remaining assets abroad.

Default is coming. It is coming for the same reason that it always comes. Ever since the Middle Ages, the decay of power has been a leading indicator of financial upheaval. In 1339, England responded to the collapse of papal power by repudiating its debts to Italian banks. This touched off Europe's first depression.

In this ruthless world, many debtors would prefer to shirk their obligations if they can. When money is lent on security outside the creditor's control—or on no security at all—payment can usually be ensured only by threats of punishment severe enough to offset the gains of default. In the case of sovereign debt, this is only possible when the creditors enjoy a dramatic power gap over the debtors.

In the last century, debtor nations had a rude discovery when they attempted to default on loans from Western powers, especially when default appeared to be an intentional effort to defraud creditors. The military capability of Britain, France, and even some of the weaker cosmopolitan empires was so overwhelming that they could simply "repossess" countries failing to pay their debts. This is exactly what happened to Tunisia in 1857. When Tunisian revenues were no longer sufficient to pay debts owing to French and British banks, troops from those nations occupied Tunisia. They were soon joined by troops from Italy seeking protection for Italian financial interests. The three governments then set up a commission to operate the finances of the Tunisian government.

In 1879, when the Egyptian ruler, Khedive Ismail, attempted to suspend payment on his treasury bills, an International Debt Commission was installed to place Egypt into receivership. A few years later, when popular resistance led to an uprising, British troops landed, quickly defeated the Egyptian army, and stayed to insure that the debts were paid.

Those days are past. As we have seen, the military cost differential favoring the major Western powers has reversed dramatically during this century. Putting air or naval power to work to enforce austerity on bankrupt governments is almost unthinkable today, because the costs of "repossessing" any country with an appreciable debt would far exceed the stakes. That is a major reason the risk of default is growing.

THE MEGAPOLITICS OF DEBT

Most analyses of the debt crisis are naive. They start with the assumption that the proliferation of international debt is primarily a problem of finance or cash flow. This is true only in the misleading and trivial sense that money is owing. A debt crisis is only incidentally a problem of money. It is a problem of power. To understand it, you must understand its hidden megapolitical foundations.

It is no coincidence that international debt began to skyrocket in the early 1970s—precisely when waning United States hegemony was evidenced in other ways. Defeat in Vietnam, the collapse of the international monetary system, the OPEC crisis, and the proliferation of world debt were all expressions of the same underlying instability. America no longer had a sufficient predominance of power and wealth to keep the world economy functioning efficiently. So it started to break down.

For reasons we have already explored, an unhappy shift in the balance of raw power in the world gave local political authorities greater scope to gum up the works. And they did. With notable exceptions on the Pacific rim, the leaders of most underdeveloped countries used power in counterproductive ways. The "loss of organization and efficiency" that Keynes foresaw as a consequence of "the innumerable new frontiers now created between greedy, jealous, immature, and economically incomplete, nationalist States," took a direct toll on the investment climate.* The new power elites tended to exclude private investment and steer economic development into rigid, politically controlled channels. The pileup of debt was merely a follow-on consequence of the power shift, a financial hangover after a night of economic dissipation.

If the debt crisis were really a matter of disparities in cash flow, the crisis should have been much more acute immediately after World War II than in the 1970s. At that time, the United States possessed more than half of the world's wealth. The gap between the United States and its trading partners was far more pronounced in 1945 than in 1975. Yet

---

* John Maynard Keynes, "The Treaty of Peace," *Essays in Persuasion* (New York: W.W. Norton & Co. Inc., 1963), 27.

there was no debt crisis in 1945. There were acute problems arising from the devastation of war. But they did not culminate in threatening debt, as they had in the wake of World War I, or would again after Vietnam. The reason: World War I and Vietnam ended with the predominant power too weak to ensure monetary and investment stability. At the end of World War II, by contrast, the United States was at the peak of its power. As we have already seen, the United States provided monetary stability through the gold reserve system. And American military might, in conjunction with the European colonial powers, prevented grasping local elites from confiscating investment.

In other words, in 1945, the police were patrolling the dangerous neighborhoods. Given the stability this insured, investors were willing to pursue opportunities for economic growth in underdeveloped areas. Private capital flowed into Asia, Africa, and Latin America to develop mineral deposits, agriculture, and manufacturing. Compared to later times, sovereign debt was a trivial factor. Only a few closed economies, such as Argentina, developed debt problems during the 1950s. These posed no threat at all to the international monetary system.

It was only at the time of the OPEC crisis in the early 1970s that international debt began to multiply by leaps and bounds. For many, this seemed proof that the OPEC crisis caused the debt explosion. We think it may be more accurate to say that both the OPEC oil shock and the debt crisis shared a common cause. Both were triggered by the waning power of the United States. Just as the governments of oil-producing countries began to confiscate the properties of American oil companies, so other governments, formerly too weak to attack international investments, began to confiscate them left and right. As we have seen, even properties not explicitly taken were subject to heavy-handed and corrupt regulation.*

THE LOGIC OF DEFAULT

In short, an unhappy chain of cause and effect leads from the decline of the predominant power to a shattering debt crisis that wipes away many of that power's accumulated external assets. We explain this below, but first a disclaimer.

It would be an exaggeration to speak of a "pattern of economic de-

* For more details, see Charles Lipson's excellent book, *Standing Guard*.

cline" that could completely explain the gathering debt crisis. If this book were being written a thousand years from now, we could perhaps look back to review 10 or 15 episodes in which world empires had faded from the scene. We would expect each to be accompanied by a debt crisis, defeat in war, or some other traumatic manifestation of imbalance between the assets and liabilities of the once-supreme power. If so, the explanation we set forth below would carry the credibility of centuries. Today, it does not. It is merely a theory about the way the world works. We think it is a good theory and most likely true. But history has been too spare with examples to satisfy a skeptic that what we spell out must regularly happen whenever a world empire collapses. There have been only two such global systems since the Industrial Revolution—and at most two transitions—if one counts the Dutch experience in the early eighteenth century. Yet given two examples or 20, we believe that the stitching of cause and effect links the decline of the dominant power to severe dislocation of world financial arrangements. It works something like this:

Debt proliferation reflects the decay of the predominant power. An important factor here is the decay of military capacity to police the security of international investment. This leads to a breakdown of the global system, as local elites usurp property rights and impose restrictions on trade that damage the world as a whole. This happened during the last days of British dominion early in this century. And, as we have seen, the same process was repeated beginning in the late 1960s, when the expropriation of U.S. investment worldwide jumped by 3,400 percent. The deteriorating environment for investment in most areas of the world led to the substitution of external borrowings for direct equity capital.

As conditions deteriorated, lending in some ways made more sense. There were stronger international mechanisms, such as the IMF and the World Bank, to collect debt payment than to protect direct-equity investment. And the interest payments on debt are fixed, while the dividends on equity capital can collapse if profits collapse—an increasing prospect in a risky environment. Under such circumstances, money was lent abroad because it could no longer be invested. Sovereign debt became a polite, halfway station between the observance of property rights across borders and outright theft—a subtlety easily understood by any schoolchild from whom a bully has demanded a "loan" of his lunch money.

Financial strength of the dominant power is the last element of hegemony to go. Such predominance may endure for decades after other forms of predominance are lost, like a trophy of inherited wealth hung in the parlor of down-in-heels aristocrats. Amsterdam remained the world's financial capital long after the Treaty of Utrecht put an end to Dutch hegemony in 1713. The Dutch lost their sea power but continued to be bankers to the world. The same thing happened more recently in the case of Britain, which had lost much of its technological and industrial advantage by the 1880s. Nonetheless, London remained the financial capital of the world until the Great Depression of the 1930s.

Lingering financial predominance is the outcome to be expected. Investors in a recently dominant power will have built up a large stock of capital assets, both domestic and external. Except in the case of defeat in war, these assets will not have disappeared in a puff. They will be available to finance deficits on what appear to be good terms in countries that have a recent record of honoring their debts. The appeal of this lending will be all the greater because the loss of hegemony will have cut off investors from opportunities they would previously have exploited.

Where the world is suffering from major imbalances, as will be the case when megapolitical conditions are deteriorating, large-scale financial operations will be required to finance the deficits. This, too, demands the institutional participation of the fading power. Its banks and stock markets are invariably the most advanced, and probably the only ones capable of organizing financial transactions on a world scale. Furthermore, the old power's currency is likely to remain the international currency of account until its eclipse is complete and successor institutions are put in place by a new hegemonic power. This took 31 years after the outbreak of World War I. A similar or even longer lag is likely this time. Today's emerging creditor nation, Japan, is perhaps more reluctant than America was in the 1920s to take on the direct costs of policing the world system.

The surplus position of the formerly dominant power deteriorates, as weak external assets are matched against strong external liabilities. The advanced capital markets of the once-supreme power attract investment like a magnet from other areas of the globe. Money especially flows from the nearest rivals, as it did from the United States to Britain in World War I, and is doing again today from Japan to the United States. Why? The rising nations have large profits to invest because they are gaining a greater share of the world sale of tradable goods. Those profits go into the only capital markets large enough and safe enough to accommodate them—those of the once-supreme power. Since the surplus of the rising nation (or nations) is being earned at the expense of the fading power (otherwise the one would not be rising and the other falling), it is only a matter of time until the old power's external asset position deteriorates to a crisis point. Its trading rivals are increasing their proportion of investment assets in its domestic banks and markets, while the fading country is in a poor position to add solid assets abroad.

This means trouble. It is like piling ever-greater weight upon a rapidly eroding beam. Eventually, it must give way. Or, in the case of international balances, the old power's net external asset position must take a sharp turn for the worse. In 1913, Britain's "external assets were equal to nearly 150% of GNP and produced an earnings stream equal to about 7.5% of her national income."* By the early twenties, Britain's external surplus had fallen in half—sharply curtailing its capacity to continue lending internationally. The deterioration in the U.S. position has been more rapid and severe. A surplus of $147 billion in 1982 could become a trillion dollar external debt by the early nineties.

To make matters worse, many of America's external assets are of doubtful quality. Loans to countries like Mexico are carried on the books of American banks at valuations as high as 99 cents per dollar of face value. This is pure accounting fiction, a ridiculous exaggeration of the real worth of doubtful assets. When sovereign debt actually changes hands, as it sometimes does in the London market, prices paid are at steep discounts of up to 95 percent. If bank portfolios were realistically valued, the deterioration of America's financial position would be brought into sharper focus.

While many American claims on the underdeveloped countries grow more doubtful, there is no equivalent discount on liabilities owed to America's creditors. They are not doubtful at all. Ironically, much of the money lent to underdeveloped countries, especially in Latin America, made a round trip, coming back as private deposits in U.S. banks. Those deposits of Latin American flight capital or Japanese holdings of U.S. Treasury bonds are unquestionable claims that will have to be paid—on demand.

International debt expansion continues until the sovereign debtors have milked the once-dominant power to the limit. When the old power

* David S. Hale, "Paul Volcker, Benjamin Strong and Dollar Diplomacy," The Kemper Financial Services, Inc., May 1986, p. 19.

can no longer afford to supply additional capital, because its income (and payments) position has deteriorated, the long-dormant crisis comes to a head. Debtor nations, unable to borrow further and thus relieved from the last lingering motive for servicing old debt, slide into default. The once-dominant power has no recourse. It cannot invade and rescue the situation with low-cost military action, as Britain often did in the nineteenth century but no longer could by 1929. Nor in a world suffering from great imbalances can it easily organize an effective boycott of the defaulting debtors. Too many customers will be eager for business. Under such conditions, with the old power controlling only a small fraction of the world economy, its boycotts will be notable failures. In the case of the United States, that is indeed what happened as long ago as the 1960s when Castro repudiated Cuban debts to U.S. banks. The Cubans had no trouble borrowing from other banks abroad. More recently, the American boycott of Iran and the wheat and pipeline boycotts of the Soviet Union also came to little. The ailing creditor power would have to be much stronger than the United States has been in recent years to avoid taking the loss of default.

Default shrinks external assets dramatically, creating or amplifying a financial crisis. The feedback effects of default cannot be isolated from the domestic economy. Once the dynamic of default is started, "the world will go through the wringer" before it exhausts itself. Capital losses are absorbed either in the banking system or by individual investors holding defaulted bonds. The result: a severe crisis or depression as financial assets are reduced to match the deterioration of the world's potential for growth. What follows is stagnation. It could take years or decades before a new creditor power emerges with the economic resources and military capacity to safely export capital again.

That, in a nutshell, is the logical pattern of debt crises. We see little reason to doubt that this pattern is unfolding and will lead eventually to default and financial collapse. This will happen for the same reason that Dutch debts were repudiated in the eighteenth century, and many debts owed Britain fell into default in the 1930s. Sooner or later, irresistible megapolitical forces will reduce American financial power to bring it more nearly into line with diminished American industrial and military capacity. America's large stock of accumulated assets abroad will shrink to match its diminished earnings power and military strength.

That is what we expect. Admittedly, our projection is based upon theories. And theories often turn out to be applesauce. In this case, however, there are many specific developments that suggest the theories are close to the fact. We believe that they all point toward a day of reckoning on international debt:

1. The end of new net bank lending to Latin America. The net transfer to the capital-importing developing countries fell from more than $36 billion as recently as 1980 to minus $13 billion by 1984. This puts debtor countries in a negative cash flow position if they continue servicing old debt.

2. Continuing deflation of primary product prices, including oil, copper, silver, tin, food, and fibers. Sales of these commodities provide a large proportion of the export earnings of many debtors. That does not mean that the sovereign debtors cannot pay, but it makes paying unpleasant. With incomes stagnant or falling in many countries, political pressures for debt default are rising.

3. Compounding of the debt. For reasons of simple arithmetic, this increases the profit from default. The more you owe, the more you have to gain by not paying—while the costs of default remain more or less constant. An old proverb says, "You might as well be hanged for a sheep as a lamb." As that implies, there are limits to penalties. Those the United States can impose on debtor governments who default—loss of further credit and access to markets—cannot be made more severe, no matter how much money the debtors refuse to pay. Therefore, if the penalties are fixed, but the profit from default keeps rising, sooner or later, default becomes irresistibly attractive.

4. Growing barriers to sale of foreign products in U.S. markets. As of 1986, the United States was second only to France in the number of imported goods subject to nontariff barriers. In spite of talk about maintaining free trade, many restrictions limit the ability of debtor countries to sell their products and thus earn the dollars needed to pay their debts. Throughout history, the governments of creditor countries have treated debtors who pay their bills more generously than debtors who do not. Favored countries get acess to markets on easy terms and are allowed to obtain spare parts and follow-on services they need to maintain equipment they have purchased. Nations that default are usually threatened with a loss of access to markets. A number of debtor countries, especially in Latin America, have the United States as a major trading partner, so a cutoff of U.S. sales would be a sharp blow to their fortunes. But notice an important factor: The threat means nothing if the debtors lose access to markets for other reasons, such as a trade boycott or

protectionism. That is why it was no surprise when Cuba repudiated its debts in the 1960s. The United States was already boycotting the Cuban economy, so there was no loss to Cuba when it stopped paying.

Protectionism in the United States penalizes debtor countries—just as if they had defaulted—whether they have or not. That leaves less of a punishment in reserve for actual default, again lowering its costs. If you are going to be hanged anyway, you might as well steal the sheep.

5. Rapid growth of countertrade or barter arrangements that reduce the needs of the debtor countries for cash. The less cash defaulting countries need to maintain their trade, the lower the threat to them of being cut off from foreign exchange. Thus international barter arrangements encourage default. One of the chief costs of repudiation is the threat against the debtor governments that they will lose access to cash needed to keep their economies going if they fail to honor their debts. When they can barter for essential services, they simply need less cash. Therefore, the greater the number of barter arrangements the lower the cost of default.

Debt repudiation in the 1930s illustrates this logic. The movement toward repudiation was encouraged by Germany and Italy. Both countries gained substantial influence among the Mussolini-style dictatorships that flourished in Latin America during the depression. Hitler had repudiated Germany's foreign debts soon after assuming power. He encouraged the same action among Latin debtors. Germany took the lead in negotiating clearing agreements with a number of countries, including Argentina, Chile, Uruguay, and Colombia. These agreements provided the means of settling transactions without resorting to foreign exchange.

A similar trend in the world today is reducing the importance of money in trade, giving the lie to optimistic reports that the debt problem is solved. The extent of countertrade growth can be judged from the following figures: In 1976, the cash value of all countertrade was only about $18 billion. By 1982, it had risen to $592 billion.

6. Increasing strategic risks due to higher costs for projection of U.S. power and greater activity by the Soviet Union in Latin America, Africa, and Asia. According to a study conducted by the National Bureau of Economic Research, approximately one-third of the foreign bond issues floated in the United States were repudiated in the 1930s. This analysis showed that there was no significant difference

in economic conditions between countries that continued to honor their debts and those that did not.* Furthermore, as Mark Hulbert notes, many of the nations that repudiated in the thirties did so when their economic positions had actually improved.† The reason: debts were repudiated in areas of greatest interbloc rivalry. To the extent that Soviet influence expands in underdeveloped countries, as it clearly has in Central America, this increases the danger of default— in much the same way that the Germans encouraged Latin default in the period before World War II.

7. Emergence of other industrial competitors to the United States eager to sell weapons and high-technology goods to debtor countries. This means that defaulting nations will have alternative sources of supply for crucial imports. Therefore they will be less deterred by the threat of U.S. embargoes on defaulting debtors.

8. Diversification of foreign militaries away from dependence on U.S. weaponry, thus lowering the costs of default in cutting off access to American-made spare parts.

9. The effect of lower oil prices and political unrest in altering the position of Mexico, until now one of the most cooperative of the debtors.

10. Increasing strength of antidebt groups throughout the underdeveloped world, where a consensus is now developing against debt payment. It would be hard to exaggerate the fragility of many political systems in the face of falling living standards. There were approximately 50 revolutions in Latin America during the depression of the 1930s. You can expect similar upheavals if another depression emerges. Debt repudiation would no doubt be high on the list of popular demands, as is evident already in the slogans and popular pronouncements of disaffected groups.

There is no longer a doubt about whether default is coming. It has already begun. Bolivia ceased payments on its foreign debt in May 1984. Nicaragua is in default on its international debt. In July 1985, Peru's leftist President Alan García limited interest payments on the nation's foreign debt to no more than 10 percent of export earnings. Nigeria's military government has taken a similar posture. The Philip-

---

* Ilse Mintz, "Deterioration in the Quality of Foreign Bonds Issued in the United States, 1920–1930," National Bureau of Economic Reform, 1952.

† Mark Hulbert, "The Causes and Risks of Excessive Foreign Lending," *Cato*, Washington, 1983.

pines has been stalling on its payments. In other countries throughout Latin America and Africa, popular pressures to stop servicing
foreign debt are mounting.

As falling oil prices strain the international banking system and reduce cash flow for Mexico, until now the most cooperative of the Latin
debtors, the danger of general default rises. It is only a matter of time,
perhaps only a matter of months, until weak governments stop servicing
their debt, touching off a financial crisis. Indeed, the crisis may already
have begun before you read this book.

The only questions are how quickly it will unfold, and whether you
are ready for it. If you are, you could be spared some of the bitter
consequences that may befall your neighbors. If not, your savings,
investments, and even your livelihood may be overtaken by political
developments in far-off countries.

Many investors have been lulled into a sense of false assurance that
the debt crisis has been solved. Or will be solved. Many others probably
believe that there is no debt crisis at all. News about debt payment
difficulties has flared in and out of the headlines since at least 1982.
Every time alarm bells have rung, last-minute compromises and concil-
iation have patched things together again. So it may seem that the
alarms were false, like cries of "Wolf" from a mischievous shepherd
boy.

Remember, the wolf eventually turned up.

Predicting the moment when the wolf will show its toothy grin is not
easy. It could happen whenever the delicately balanced equilibrium
between the debtors and creditors is materially changed. This could be
either because the power and wealth of the United States is decreased,
or because the debtors' position has become more difficult. Any of the
following developments could do the trick:

1. A sharp economic downturn. Any collapse in demand in industrial countries would feed back into falling export sales among the
leading debtors. With less earnings to spend, this would increase the
costs of paying the debt, making default more likely.

2. An upturn in interest rates. This would increase the pain of
making payments because most international debt interest floats
higher as market rates rise.

3. A major rebound of the U.S. dollar. The costlier dollars become, the harder it is for debtor countries to secure a share of them.
This is not as important as the increase in interest rates because the

currencies of most debtor nations have fallen against the dollar for years. A sharp deterioration, however, would add to the strains. In this light, it is interesting to note the findings of a special committee of inquiry of the Brazilian Congress in 1984. The committee found that a combination of higher U.S. interest rates and a higher dollar had added $40 billion to Brazilian debt, $40 billion that could be rejected as "illegitimate." Similar reasoning will crop up everywhere if the dollar and interest rates rise in tandem again.

4. Rapid domestic growth in debtor countries. This may even destroy the delicate debt equilibrium by reducing trade surpluses in some of the leading debtor countries, such as Brazil. As George Soros has pointed out, debtor countries in the early eighties were generating a substantial trade surplus on the basis of a sharp reduction of imports and pressure to export. Any significant recovery is likely to reduce that trade surplus and will throw a further burden on their financing. If there is to be a recovery, there must be a further increase in lending. Without it, debtor countries may be tempted to repudiate debts in order to finance increased imports.

5. Political unrest in a debtor country. The leaders of unstable governments watch one another's fates with keen interest. If it appears that popular tolerance of austerity has worn thin in one country, politicians in neighboring countries will adjust their policies in the indicated direction. People not under the compulsion of force will eventually refuse to order their lives so that a great part of their output goes indefinitely to meet foreign payments.

6. Further deterioration of commodity prices. Many debtor countries derive almost all of their foreign exchange earnings from sales of raw materials that are being used in diminishing quantities by the industrial world per unit of output. If commodity prices keep sliding, or fall sharply, this will increase the likelihood of default among major exporters of those commodities.

7. A united front among debtor governments. Several times, the Cartagena Group of Latin debtor countries has discussed the possibility of uniting to demand better terms from the creditor banks. One day, these steps toward a debt cartel will culminate in decisive action. The greater the number of defaulting countries, the more likely each would be to come out unscathed.

8. An increase in trade restrictions. The worldwide upsurge of barriers to trade, beginning with the Smoot-Hawley Tariff in 1930, helped precipitate debt default in the Great Depression. Any new

import controls in the United States would be a significant advance indicator of a debt crisis. If nations cannot sell their goods to earn dollars, they cannot pay debts denominated in dollars.

9. Any striking evidence of U.S. weakness in the military, economic, or political spheres. For reasons already spelled out, weakening American hegemony is the fundamental cause of the debt crisis in the first place. Any event that raises doubt about U.S. leadership capacity could embolden debtors to unilaterally redefine the terms of their contracts. The same thing could happen if American officials even indicate strong sympathy with the plight of the debtors or suggest a "hands off" policy. The costs of default in the 1930s were reduced when President Roosevelt announced a "Good Neighbor" policy, pledging that the United States would no longer resort to gunboat diplomacy to enforce economic claims against Latin governments.

10. Mexico as a special case. It could be crucial. Why? The United States cannot afford to see Mexico go belly-up because of its long border with the United States. It would be like having an elephant die on one's doorstep. To avoid the unhappy task of cleaning up the mess, American leaders are obliged to "pull their punches" in dealing with Mexico. This means that even effective forms of retaliation that America could bring to bear against defaulting countries may not be credible threats against Mexico. If used effectively, they would sabotage America's own interests. If Mexico were Argentina, the United States could credibly promise to retaliate for debt default in the most punishing ways it could muster. Sharp trade sanctions could be imposed, including a total import embargo, a cutoff of spare parts, and more. Argentine airliners could be seized if they touched down on American soil. Even the supply of insulin for Argentine diabetics could be impounded. In short, the United States could come as close as modern conditions allow to the old and effective expedient of sending the fleet to lie offshore and blockade the coast. If the Argentine economy collapsed as a result, the chaos would be a long way away. The feedback consequences for America itself would be slight. And that is why the potential costs to the Argentines—or almost any other major debtor—for pioneering default are far greater than for the Mexicans.

THE LONGEST POKER GAME IN HISTORY

If Mexico defaults, no retaliation could be employed that actually brought the Mexican economy to its knees. A weaker, destabilized Mexico, cut off from American credits and trade, would mean unrest on the border. Mexican officials exploit this advantage in debt brinkmanship. Their American counterparts, uneasily eyeing the influx of illegal aliens, do not wish to push the Mexican government so hard that it falls down.

At the same time, officials in Washington know that any concessions obtained by Mexico will rapidly spread, undermining the security of all debt payment. So U.S. officials must actually seem to take a hard line. The result is a long-running poker game with $110 billion in chips on the table and the better part of a trillion dollars placed in side bets. As Sidney Greenstreet told Humphrey Bogart in the 1941 movie version of *The Maltese Falcon,* "That, sir, is a matter that calls for delicate judgment. In the heat of action, we may forget where our best interests lie." Through mid-1986, all the Mexican bluffs have been called, and the banks have continued to win the hands. But someday, whether because of deteriorating conditions or because new Mexican officials of more steely eye come to the table, the U.S. bluff will be called. Mexico will stop paying—or gain dramatic concessions.

Any concessions Mexico extracts through default brinkmanship will quickly spread. Why would Brazil want to pay full interest on its $100 billion debt if Mexico pays half that amount? Or nothing at all? If Mexico effectively defaults, and gets away with it, practically no other country could be obliged to pay.

With that in mind, pay special attention to the background of Mexican developments and watch the media for further news.

The Weakening Mexican Position

Contrary to the assumption of many Americans, Mexico is not a Western democracy. Its government operates the way the Mafia might, if it could seize control of a country, from top to bottom. Practically every aspect of the economy is rigidly controlled by political operatives of the Institutional Revolutionary Party, or PRI, after its Spanish initials, who use this control to squeeze money out of everyone.

Corruption is not merely an aberration in Mexico; it is glue that holds the system together. When oil wealth began to flow in the late seventies and early eighties, politicians extended their reach, and tremendous sums stuck to their fingers. Former President Jose Lopez Portillo reportedly stole hundreds of millions of dollars, not pesos, and enriched his associates on an equally grand scale. Much of the squandered money was borrowed from American banks, and then redeposited in those banks to the credit of wealthy Mexicans. Weak assets (loans) came back to the banks as rock-solid liabilities (deposits).

When Mexican President Miguel de la Madrid inherited an economy near collapse in 1982, he promised reform and an end to corruption. Among his promises was to allow clean elections. Previously, only token opposition was allowed. On rare occasions when the opposition parties won, the ballot boxes were seized and stuffed.

In the first elections after de la Madrid's term began, there really were honest counts. A number of candidates from the pro-American, free-enterprise party, known as the PAN, actually won. This inspired deep resentment within the PRI. Several of the PAN victories were declared void. In the July 1983 elections, vote fraud was resumed on a massive scale.

This fraud continued in the December 1984 mayoral elections, when overt ballot-stuffing and other forms of "alchemy" were employed to assure PRI victories. Unlike previous years, however, the ballot-stuffing touched off popular unrest. In Nadadores, an angry crowd threw a new PRI mayor into an open sewer. In Piedras Negras, one person was killed and 50 injured, including 18 policemen, as a crowd of 4,000 rioted at the swearing-in ceremony of another PRI mayor.

The PAN used to be known as the "capitalist party of the rich," with its support limited to about 10 percent of the population. Since the debt crisis, however, its anticorruption themes have gathered increasing support from the lower classes. A strong PAN candidate for governor of Chihuahua, Mexico's largest state, probably would have won a clean election in July 1986. The protest that followed included clashes with troops, blockading of bridges to the United States, hunger strikes, and even an attempt by local Catholic bishops to close churches—a threat that was only overruled by the pope himself.

Although votes can be fixed and elections stolen, the actual effect of declining popular support can put the PRI in jeopardy, just as the Argentine and Brazilian military governments were forced to turn over power even prior to elections in those countries.

The ruling party has lost much of its support over its handling of the debt crisis. With the fall in the oil price reducing Mexican revenues,

Mexico's rulers will find a default that lifts the burden of debt service increasingly attractive.

Profits from Close Calls

Because there is no clear way of identifying when the debt crisis will reach a climactic stage, there could be a number of "scares" that will shake the markets and then be brought under control. You can make money from these near-misses, especially if they result in major sell-offs of bank shares. There have already been several such episodes.

On August 11, 1982, Mexico could borrow in international markets. On August 12, it could not. The country was broke, its credit exhausted. A major bailout over the following weekend stuffed $3 billion of U.S. government cash in Mexico's pockets, saving the day, not only for the Mexican government, but for creditor banks as well. The bailout sharply raised the value of money center bank shares. Citicorp stock jumped from 22½ on August 12 to 38½ by mid-October, a gain of 71 percent. Chase Manhattan shares went from 32 on August 12 to a high of 62¼—a gain of 97 percent. Morgan Stanley gained 78 percent and Manufacturers Hanover gained 88 percent. Other banks with significant international loans enjoyed similar gains.

In May 1984, there was another close call. Rising interest rates and declining confidence in the U.S. banking system, highlighted by the Continental Illinois crisis, brought Latin American debtors once more to the brink of default. The presidents of Argentina, Brazil, Mexico, and Colombia called a meeting of debtor countries at the Colombian resort town of Cartagena. A near-panic swept through markets as repudiation appeared imminent. Ultimately, only Bolivia went into default, and the crisis abated. Again, bank shares rose and the bond markets recovered.

There have been similar, though less dramatic, market reactions, around other news of the debt crisis. In the fall of 1985, news of the "Baker Plan" to bail out the international debtors, named for U.S. Treasury Secretary James Baker, stimulated a sharp increase in the share prices of money center banks in late 1985.

No one knows whether there will be other such episodes. The next five debt crisis episodes could end calmly, with market rebounds. Or tomorrow could bring the repudiation and financial collapse that seems inevitable in the long run.

Future bailouts will probably have to dispense with the fiction, prominent in the first bailout of August 1982, that debtors are merely suffering from a "temporary liquidity squeeze." Now everyone knows that the problem is far more severe. But that does not rule out expedients that slow down the rush to default in some future crisis.

Among the possibilities:

1. A multiyear grace period for repayment of debt principal for most debtors. The grace period could possibly be linked to special "sinking funds" to retire the principal. A number of major debtors, including Brazil, have requested such treatment. As their hands strengthen, they may get it.

2. Large infusions of cash from the Japanese and Germans. The United States will seek to pressure the surplus countries to take up the slack in American lending capacity, much as the United States took up the slack for Britain in the wake of World War I. Such a development would be a major bull signal for debt in the short run. But be cautious of reports that are not linked to specific commitments of cash. The Japanese have tended to be far less cooperative with the United States than the United States was with Britain in the twenties. There are many reasons to doubt that they will play a significant role in reliquefying the bankrupt debtors.

3. Chinese accounting to allow banks to disguise their losses on bad sovereign loans. This could take a number of different forms:

a) Banks could be allowed to separately incorporate subsidiaries that would hold the old debts of bankrupt governments. These debts, in effect, would either be guaranteed by the U.S. government (possibly in conjunction with other governments) or . . .

b) A new multinational bank could be formed to buy the debts of the commercial banks. This would appear less likely, as there are already two multinational banks involved in concessionary lending, the World Bank and the International Monetary Fund. Forming a new institution would require funding large sums to capitalize it. This would not only be politically difficult in the United States; it would be even more difficult abroad. The banks of America's major capitalist allies, Japan, Germany, Britain, France, Italy, and Canada, are less exposed to the international debt crisis. For reasons we have already explored, they would be unlikely to cooperate with this type of bailout. However, it is a possibility that has been discussed in international banking circles.

c) Sovereign debts could be transformed into new instruments. They might become bonds or instruments like stock that would pay some fixed interest rate—or be tied to a major commodity price. For example, Bolivian debt might be "transformed" into commodity bonds or equity payable in terms of tin prices. Mexican debt could be tied to oil. And so on.

d) U.S. banking regulations could be changed, allowing the write-off of sovereign debt over a long period. This is always an option, because it requires no international cooperation and little in the way of direct expenditure. However, it would devastate the earnings of many of America's biggest banks.

Be alert for any of these developments. While not all would be significantly bullish, and some might even disappoint a market used to more effective bailouts, they are all steps that are more positive than outright repudiation. In this respect, they are like expedients for treating an increasingly deadly cancer, experimental therapies that may or may not produce good results.

You may be able to profit from them, to the extent that they work, by buying call options on money center bank stocks when nervousness over debt collapse or outright crises suppress price levels. As in horseshoes, there may be profits to be taken from near-misses. The time to buy the call options, however, would be when the situation looks darkest. It is then, when the cost is low, that you are most likely to have a positive payoff from betting on another postponement of the day of reckoning.

Remember, the fundamentals are negative. For all the reasons we have stated, debt default is coming. When it happens, there will not be time for you to prepare a reaction. You will not be able to get your assets back from your banker or broker if a middle-of-the-night telex from a far-off capital is delivered simultaneously to the Secretary of the Treasury, the CEOs of big banks, and other officials, announcing a moratorium on debt payments. You must be ready to act before that happens.

THE DAY THE MUSIC STOPS

The crisis could begin while your dog is tugging at the leash for a walk. Or a soft summer breeze is stirring in the curtains. It will be like any other day. The phone will ring. Bills will have to be paid. And you will hear a 20-second summary of the news: "Meanwhile, Mexican officials have suspended payments on portions of that nation's $100 billion debt. In Washington, the President told reporters that the Mexican default will not harm America's banking system. In other news, four members of a Denver Little League team were killed when a car in which they were riding was struck by a tractor trailer. . . ."

That is the way it will be. Another matter-of-fact report, wedged between news of a heart transplant and a traffic accident. When it happens, the reporters will not tell you what to do. You will have to be ready. If you are, you could get the jump on 99 percent of all investors.

What Comes After Default?

If the Mexicans and other debtors do suspend payments, everyone knows there will be a bailout. The Fed will not allow the biggest banks in the United States to collapse. But what comes next? Almost no one has focused on the consequences of the bailout. Will it be inflationary? What will it do to the economy? To the stock market? To gold prices? To interest rates and bonds?

These are difficult questions to answer. We have been chewing them over for years without coming to any very tasty conclusions. The first Mexican bailout, in August 1982, marked the start of a major bull market. Partly this was because the Fed anticipated trouble by pushing interest rates down by about four points in the two months before the crisis actually hit. When the Reagan administration finally made the political decision to bail out Mexico, everyone saw that the day of reckoning on debt would be pushed off into the future. And this realization helped fuel a bull market.

Now the future is almost here. Our guess is that future bailouts will be less bullish for stocks and the economy. Next time, we could see a direct bank bailout, not an extension of further credit to the banks' customers. The Continental Illinois bailout was a major negative. Ditto for the Ohio and Maryland S & L crises. Bank crises usually shake confidence and shift credit from productive use to simply plugging holes in balance sheets. There will be big holes to plug.

As of 1985, each of the top ten American banks was heavily exposed in Mexican debt. Eight of the ten had more than one-third of their primary capital at risk. And three had more than 50 percent. First Chicago had more than $1 billion at risk in Mexico alone, 63.7 percent of its primary capital. Bankers Trust had lent $1.3 billion, 55 percent of its capital. Manufacturers Hanover had $1.6 billion, putting just a hair less than 55 percent of its capital at risk.

We believe that the danger of debt default is sufficiently great to merit defensive steps—especially at times of major debt payment deadlines or when news of aggressive steps by debtors is first carried in the press. Here are some steps to protect yourself. Read each carefully, and identify those that are right for you:

1. Dispose of the bonds and commercial paper of money center banks and bank holding companies. Hold no uninsured financial instruments of exposed banks. Do not hold bank deposits beyond the insurable limit. And do not tie up your money in certificates of deposit.

2. Move cash reserves into Treasury bills or money funds holding only federal government debt obligations.

3. Move commercial bank deposits to banks without significant Latin exposure.

4. Diversify your currency holdings into Swiss francs, German marks, and Japanese yen. A debt default may weaken the dollar.

5. Avoid short positions in gold. The probable outcome of default will be to raise gold prices temporarily.

6. Buy long contracts on Treasury bills. You can also buy T-bill call options, making sure that you are not paying an overly large premium. A banking crisis will most likely lower interest rates.

7. If you have a commodity account, enter a spread, buying Treasury bills, and selling Eurodollars. Both are traded in units of $1 million on the IMM. You are betting that the interest rates on bank certificates of deposit will rise faster than those on Treasury bills. This spread should widen sharply in the event of default.

8. If you are a stock speculator, a riskier play on default is to sell short the S&P 100, the S&P 500 average, or the NYSE Beta Index. We expect the market to falter on news of default. This is a three-to-one bet.

9. As the crisis peaks, buy Treasury bonds and Treasury bond calls for delivery six months out. If there is an overt default, these would be strong bets to rise. All banking crises are eventually good for Treasury bonds. (In case you wonder how to identify a "peak," remember that real crises are usually whipsaw affairs. When the spread between Treasury bills and bonds stops widening, the peak of the crisis has probably been reached.)

10. You may also be able to profit from short-run fluctuations in the yield curve. In the summer of 1982, the collapse of the Mexican economy had a major impact on U.S. interest rates. So did the crisis of May 1984. Those experiences provide hints of things to come. Both resulted not only in falling interest rates, but in major widening of the "yield curve" (the measure of the difference between short-term and long-term Treasury yields). Normally, long-term interest rates are slightly higher than short rates. During the high-water days of American hegemony after World War II, it was rare for the gap between short-term Treasury rates and T-bonds to be more than a fraction of a point. Even in the volatile period since the gold link to the dollar was severed, there have been few occasions when the bill-bond spread got as high as 2.7 percentage points. During the Mexican crisis in August 1982, the difference jumped to 5 percentage points, as investors rushed to buy T-bills to protect themselves from a banking crisis. In May 1984, when Bolivia announced a moratorium, the yield curve jumped to 3.8 percentage points. The crisis that actually leads to default will probably widen the spread even further.

It is difficult to trade the spread between T-bills and T-bonds directly because the commodity contract sizes do not match, and margins are expensive. But if you have the cash to do so, you can play the spread by buying a single contract for $1 million in T-bills and selling ten $100,000 bond contracts on a spread basis. If the yield curve widens to 3.8 percent, much less 5 percent, you should make a handsome profit.

Remember to take profits the moment the yield curve begins to narrow. Treasury bond yields normally fall in the aftermath of a financial crisis.

11. Consider buying quality corporate bonds at a discount—if a crisis of default severely shakes market confidence. A severe crisis will reduce the value of even top-rated corporate bonds, at least temporarily. In the depression that began in 1929, double-A and triple-A industrial bonds survived without default, while lower-quality single-A and Baa issues included a fraction that went bad. But the value of all corporate bonds slumped, those with the lowest ratings falling the furthest. The next time the world goes through the wringer, the market would probably follow a similar, though not identical, pattern. Well-chosen corporate bonds could provide significant capital gains if you buy when pessimism is overdone.

12. If you are a commodity trader, expect default to push primary product prices down. It will dry up the flow of funds to the periphery,

leading as it did in the 1930s to sharp declines in demand. World commodity prices for some items in the thirties tumbled by as much as 70 percent. Even if the consequences are far more modest this time, the bias in primary product prices should be down.

13. If you are an aggressive investor, you could consider selling short the shares of banks with significant risk in international lending. Speculating on this type of development, like any speculation for high profit, can be risky. However, we think that the risk may be justified because other market participants are ill informed about the full dangers of default.

Remember that a bailout of the banking system, which the authorities will surely attempt in the event of a debt collapse, does not necessarily mean a bailout of bank holding companies or shareholders. Depending upon the political climate and administration at the time the music stops, there might even be a de facto nationalization of major American banks—an outcome less farfetched than it may seem. That is what happened to Continental Illinois. In a time of crisis, the government may be the only entity large enough to save the vulnerable banks.

Major banks with foreign debt risk may suffer large capital losses. A straightforward strategy for profiting from this is to sell short their shares in the stock market. Just how much do specific banks have at stake in each country? Federal regulators, along with the banks they regulate, do not want you to know. They fear that making the full details of the situation public could undermine confidence. It is not possible from available public data to determine exactly what portion of loans has been made to underdeveloped nations. Federal banking regulators and the Securities and Exchange Commission merely require banks to report loans made to a particular country when those loans exceed 1 percent of total assets. Total assets include all outstanding loans the bank has made. It is a much larger figure than actual equity. Although the information about bad foreign loans is not directly available, Veribanc, Inc. of Wakefield, Massachusetts, has attempted to construct such a list indirectly from the public record. The figures date to mid-1986.

A prime group of targets for short sales are banks identified by Veribanc as having foreign loans in excess of equity capital. These banks are listed on pp. 139–40. Foreign loans outstanding and equity capital are listed in millions of dollars. The ratio of foreign loans to equity is given in the right-hand column. Our counsel has advised us to report that inclusion of a bank on this list does not mean that it is necessarily in

Bank	City	State	Foreign Loans	Equity	Ratio
First Interstate Bank of CA	L.A.	CA	2,728,440	1,064,726	256.26
Security Pacific NB	L.A.	CA	5,311,032	1,872,714	283.60
Bank of America National Trust	S.F.	CA	24,368,000	3,980,00	612.26
Bank of California NA	S.F.	CA	665,417	212,584	313.01
Bank of Canton of CA	S.F.	CA	51,299	42,789	119.89
Oceanic Bank	S.F.	CA	13,398	10,842	123.57
Sumitomo Bank of CA	S.F.	CA	370,726	137,877	268.88
Wells Fargo Bank NA	S.F.	CA	1,875,199	1,353,565	138.54
NB of Washington	Wash.	DC	117,042	86,951	134.61
Riggs NB of Washington, DC	Wash.	DC	563,387	247,349	227.77
Miami NB	Coral Gables	FL	5,756	1,154	498.79
Eagle NB of Miami	Miami	FL	15,095	11,080	136.24
International Bank of Miami N	Miami	FL	8,331	6,065	137.36
Capital Bank	N. Bay Vil	FL	50,378	46,904	107.41
First NB in Palm Beach	Palm Beach	FL	90,912	41,837	217.30
Sunshine State Bank	S. Miami	FL	4,955	4,073	121.65
Bank of Hawaii	Honolulu	HI	336,688	242,258	138.98
Banco Di Roma (Chicago)	Chicago	IL	144,576	14,950	967.06
Chicago-Tokyo Bank	Chicago	IL	72,658	35,096	207.03
Continental IL NB & TC C	Chicago	IL	6,990,948	2,015,402	346.88
First NB of Chicago	Chicago	IL	6,560,312	1,542,086	425.42
Northern TC	Chicago	IL	589,167	362,925	162.34
Bank of New England NA	Boston	MA	407,099	296,265	137.41
First NB of Boston	Boston	MA	4,373,231	1,062,616	411.55
First NB of Maryland	Balt.	MD	269,419	213,224	126.35
Maryland NB	Balt.	MD	475,466	357,753	132.90
Comerica Bank—Detroit	Detroit	MI	396,074	369,326	107.24
Manufacturers NB	Detroit	MI	347,057	313,808	110.60
National Bank of Detroit	Detroit	MI	987,609	750,381	131.61
First NB of Minneapolis	Minn.	MN	586,239	436,179	134.40
Norwest Bank Minneapolis NA	Minn.	MN	662,512	288,991	229.25
Mercantile TC NA	St. Louis	MO	260,231	250,301	103.97
United Jersey Bank Cumberland NA	Bridgeton	NJ	19,613	9,147	214.42
Marine Midland Bank NA	Buffalo	NY	3,329,486	993,768	335.04
Long Island TC NA	Garden City	NY	101,894	95,121	107.12
Banco Central of NY	New York	NY	32,693	25,660	127.41

Bank	City	State	Foreign Loans	Equity	Ratio
Banco De Bogota TC	New York	NY	114,025	29,333	388.73
Bank Leumi TC of NY	New York	NY	253,025	116,746	216.73
Bank of New York	New York	NY	1,683,336	887,437	189.69
Bank of Tokyo TC	New York	NY	808,400	297,447	271.78
Bankers TC	New York	NY	10,677,253	2,254,590	463.58
Central NB of New York	New York	NY	10,972	8,770	125.11
Chase Manhattan Bank NA	New York	NY	29,507,280	4,454,725	662.38
Chemical Bank	New York	NY	13,815,709	2,728,051	506.43
Citibank NA	New York	NY	50,779,000	7,037,000	721.60
Daiwa Bank TC	New York	NY	198,490	73,730	269.21
European American Bk	New York	NY	1,162,193	410,951	282.81
Fuji B & TC	New York	NY	308,171	142,337	216.51
Industrial Bank Japan TC	New York	NY	290,166	155,076	187.11
Irving TC	New York	NY	5,193,541	866,415	599.43
Israel Discount Bank of NY	New York	NY	180,151	176,041	102.33
J. Henry Schroder B & TC	New York	NY	346,711	128,466	296.89
Manufacturers Hanover TC	New York	NY	19,506,329	2,767,498	704.84
Morgan Guaranty	New York	NY	19,546,871	3,468,980	563.48
National Westminster USA	New York	NY	1,097,552	554,443	197.96
Republic NB of NY	New York	NY	1,870,589	1,440,423	129.86
UBAF Arab American BK	New York	NY	656,976	106,979	614.12
UMB B & TC	New York	NY	66,608	43,428	153.38
Union Chelsea NB	New York	NY	44,107	20,273	217.57
United Orient Bank	New York	NY	18,605	5,649	329.35
Philadelphia NB	Ardmore	PA	540,511	425,529	127.02
First PA Bank NA	Bala-Cynwyd	PA	659,831	344,193	191.70
Mellon Bank (East) NA	Bala-Cynwyd	PA	425,673	270,366	157.44
Fidelity Bank NA	E Whiteland TWP	PA	409,364	313,520	130.57
Mellon Bank NA	Greensburg	PA	3,002,329	1,059,531	283.36
Pittsburgh NB	Pittsburgh	PA	607,970	530,366	114.63
TX Commerce Bank/ Brownsville	Brownsville	TX	30,575	25,273	120.98
Interfirst Bank DAL NA	Dallas	TX	668,543	445,329	150.12
Republic Bank Dallas NA	Dallas	TX	1,176,652	769,744	152.86
TX Commerce Bank NA	Houston	TX	646,210	600,247	107.66
Rainier NB	Seattle	WA	594,092	406,664	146.09
Seattle-First NB	Seattle	WA	454,041	211,005	215.18

trouble, about to fail, or even that its foreign loans are problem loans. We also note that the U.S. branches of top-flight foreign banks, like National Westminster, are much more likely to be safe in a crisis than even some American banks without large foreign exposure.

Most of these banks sell at a discount to their stated book values. This reflects a recognition by investors that the banks' assets (loans) are overstated. As the crisis develops, it will hurt bank earnings in three possible ways, baring an unvarnished bailout: 1) Banks will be forced to set aside additional sums to increase their loan loss reserves. Putting aside just 10 percent of those foreign loans that have already been rescheduled would reduce the earnings of the nine largest money center banks sharply. 2) Banks will eventually have to write off part or all of their loans to underdeveloped nations. 3) The interest income the banks record from foreign loans will be significantly reduced. Any or all of these could be very serious. In 1975, when recession was biting into bank balance sheets, Citicorp, then known as First National City Bank, lost money on all its domestic business. Walter Wriston, then president of the bank, explained all of its success by saying, "Round here, it's Jakarta that pays the checks."* When Jakarta stops paying, the banks could be in big trouble.

Be ready for it.

Whatever you do as an investor, remember that it pays to think ahead. Check your present holdings against the prospect of default. It could mean major upheavals in the investment landscape.

AFTER DEFAULT

A wholesale international debt collapse will mark the end of American financial hegemony. It will complete the logical progression toward world economic disintegration that has been under way for decades. Default is necessitated by the same process that brought down the gold reserve monetary system, fed the worldwide upsurge of investment expropriation since the late 1960s, gave us the OPEC oil shocks, terrorism, and more. Default is a consequence of the decay of American power. Someday, hundreds of billions of the debt will be effectively repudiated, wiping out much of America's remaining assets abroad.

This "write-down" of America's financial role in the world will not only have a dramatic impact upon bank earnings and bond markets, it will weaken the U.S. economy for years to come. In the 1990s and

* *Fortune*, March 1975.

beyond, the United States could be stuck in a position similar to that Britain faced after its foreign asset position turned negative at the end of World War II. The years that followed were twilight years of slow growth and decline. Successive British governments were obliged to maintain restrictive policies, as David Hale has pointed out, "in order to persuade foreign asset holders that their Pounds were secure. The City of London remained an important world financial center but not for British capital. . . ."* This produced a queer anomaly of London capital markets welcoming foreign investors with surplus savings, while domestic British investors were heavily restricted in the disposition of their funds. In effect, London became a haven for foreign capital but a straitjacket for domestic capital.

Similar pressures on the United States to maintain confidence in the dollar, in spite of a negative external asset position and massive deficits, will probably stunt growth, darkening the investment horizon for years to come. The ultimate consequences could be exchange controls, "exchange equalization taxes," and other limits on the free flow of capital.

Plan ahead to avoid being caught in the tightening net around the U.S. economy. If you are an American, you should diversify your liquid investment holdings outside the United States, to London, Switzerland, Germany, Austria or some similar foreign money center. History does not repeat itself exactly. But similar underlying megapolitical conditions do shape policies in similar ways. In the decades when Britain was haunted by the overhang of its old reserve currency obligations it was a poor place to invest. The American experience may be less glum this time around, partly because the U.S. economy has not yet been surpassed by a new dominant power—as Britain had been after World War II. But that may even make the world as a whole a worse place to invest. Pressures will be at work to retain foreign investment in America, while preventing American capital from flowing abroad.

To the extent that these tendencies prevail, default could turn back the clock, not to London of the fifties and sixties, but to the 1930s. Default would reinforce the very tendencies making for contraction of the world economy. With no new power to take the lead in exporting capital to developing countries to finance higher imports, living standards in many places could wind down. Depression at the periphery would reduce primary product prices as it fed back through monetary mechanisms to the whole of the industrialized world.

* Hale, "Volcker, Strong and Dollar Diplomacy," 20.

5

The Twilight of Communism

Things refuse to be mismanaged long. Res nolunt diu male administrari. *Though no checks to a new evil appear, the checks exist, and will appear.*

—Ralph Waldo Emerson

Headlines that told of the accident at the Chernobyl nuclear power plant marked the end of a major phase in world history. The flumes of radioactive cloud flaring from the dying reactor marked the funeral pyre of the technological base upon which Communism was founded. They told of dangerous limits of centralization met and exceeded. The consequences for the world economy and your investments could be profound.

The same hidden megapolitical forces of decentralization that broke up the European empires are doing their work on the Soviet Empire. As it becomes increasingly costly to project power, and the scale of violence in the world continues to devolve to smaller and smaller units, the Soviet Empire will inevitably crack apart. Separatist pressures from the large Islamic populations will be especially acute as ferment from nearby Iran and Afghanistan spills over borders.

All that has slowed the collapse of the Soviet Empire so far is a coincidence of history. The czars were able to conquer vast stretches of empty steppe without encountering any vigorous states in their path. Thus, the territory under Soviet dominion, unlike the Western European empires, is mainly contiguous rather than scattered throughout the globe. It has proven easier to control an adjacent territory than one separated from the home power by thousands of miles of ocean, jungles, deserts, and mountain ranges. Nonetheless, not even the Iron Curtain can hold back the forces of change. Those forces, as they grow stronger, will do to the Soviet Empire what they have done to the others. They will break it up. Indeed, states on the fringe of the Soviet orbit have already slipped away. Albania, Yugoslavia, and, more significantly, China, were all once part of the Soviet system and are now distinctly separate.

Soviet Communism, based on economic monopoly, cannot thrive or even survive in a decentralizing world where monopoly is deadly. Although they may not know it, the dilemma Marxists face today is that their system is fundamentally at odds with the technological foundation upon which modern economies are developing.

There is delicious irony in this. Marx was at his best in understanding that old political systems are driven to crisis and destruction by technological change. When innovation leads to production techniques whose potential cannot be realized within the framework of the existing order, that order breaks apart and is replaced by a new organization of society. As wrong as Marx was about many things, he was right about that. So right, indeed, that the epitaph of Communism can be written in Marxist terms. Communism is doomed to destruction by its contradictions.

These have little or nothing to do with class analysis. Indeed, Marx's famous political opinions are superfluous to his insight into the unfolding of economic history. That story is written by technology, not by the struggles between the haves and have-nots. Such struggles are not unique to any one stage of technology or civilization. They are part of the scenery of life. They take place at a different level from the flashpoints of conflict arising from technological innovation. Shifts in the character of weapons and the tools of production are the real engines of history. They alter the scale of states and empires, centralize or decentralize economic activity, antiquate old skills and discover new ones. These "gales of creative destruction," to borrow Schumpeter's phrase, not only create new wealth, they bring down old fortunes, reshuffling the ranks of the rich and the poor.*

To think of this process as primarily a class struggle is to mistake the fundamental megapolitical forces that are at work. "Classes" of people, per se, have no coherence as operating groups and little relevance to the description of historic processes. In fact, you will misunderstand the Soviet system if you analyze it in terms of proletarian power. It is better understood as a giant electric power monopoly.

---

* (Joseph A. Schumpeter, *Business Cycles: A Theoretical, Historical, and Statistical Analysis* (New York, 1939).

GOVERNMENT BY LONG ISLAND LIGHTING

The Soviet system is a transcontinental economic utility, run by a single holding company; what America would be if all business beyond the scale of a radish patch and every function of government were owned and controlled by Long Island Lighting Company (LILCO). Imagine LILCO with a secret police. Imagine a government of, for, and by Long Island Lighting—unhampered by the inconvenience of dealing with a rate commission or referring to the interests of shareholders. In the Soviet version, there are no shareholders. It is a co-op controlled entirely by the management—another feature of surpassing stupidity, as we shall see. The only route to advancement and personal success is to go to work for the company with the aim of elbowing one's way onto the board of directors or some lesser position of privilege.

In a way that may not seem obvious, the fortunes of the Soviet system parallel those of other monopolists controlling their share of the power grid. They are all being undone by technology. The long swing toward centralization has been exhausted at the leading edges of technology.

It is easy to forget that centralized power systems are not inevitable arrangements. They did not exist 150 years ago. They may not exist 50 years from now. They are institutions unique to a certain stage of technological development, one that had its roots in the nineteenth century and is already beginning to play itself out. Energy will only be provided through a central monopoly where there are scale-economies dramatic enough to offset the rigidities of centralization. Where technology does not afford such economies, many sources will provide power. Instead of monopoly, there may be hundreds or thousands or even millions of power sources—and power substitutes.

For example, in 1817, it would have been obvious lunacy to put a single monopolist in control of access to all chopped wood, coal, whale oil, and candles. The power and lighting technologies of the day were decentralized. There were few scale economies to be realized by conglomerating lots of small businesses into large ones. Instituting a Soviet-style system then to monopolize supply would have involved ruinous costs, inefficiency, and waste. As the nineteenth century wore on, however, technological development increased scale economies. Fossil fuels replaced charcoal and raw wood as a source of power for industry. Lighting fixtures using gas came into use, displacing the whale oil lamp and the candle. In short order, coal replaced wood as a fuel for heat and power. Close upon coal's trail came oil.

As these new power sources developed, mining processing and distribution took on larger scale than the operations they replaced in the old technologies. For one thing, coal and oil could not be readily found. They had to be extracted from the ground in a few select locations and transported, sometimes over great distances to points where they would ultimately be used. To manage these tasks took larger enterprises, funded for larger sums of capital.

Then came electricity. It involved scale economies that dwarfed all previous power technologies. To turn on electric lights and other appliances meant generating electricity. It was logically possible that such power might have been provided locally by thousands of different suppliers, just as wood for fuel and tallow for candles had been. But the technology of the late nineteenth century made this economically ridiculous. The unit costs of energy generated independently tended to far exceed those of energy centrally generated and distributed through a power grid. That is why centralized utilities emerged everywhere electricity came into use. This was not a matter of politics. It was technology. Centralization was dictated by the cost characteristics of the technology of the moment.

HENRY FORD, THE STEPFATHER OF COMMUNISM

Soviet Communism was the handiwork of Lenin and Marx. But it was equally the work of technological coincidence—and Henry Ford. The advent of the assembly line, the invention of a conservative midwesterner, meant dramatic increases in the scale of production. In the capitalist countries, this led to more monopoly, with trusts and cartels and fewer large firms controlling a greater portion of output. This concentration of industry occurred in almost every country as technologies and processes that raised scale economies were introduced. It was blamed on perfidious causes, but seldom on its megapolitical cause, a dramatically centralizing shift in technology. Even prewar Russia, rapidly industrializing, experienced an upsurge in the number of trusts and heavily concentrated enterprises after about 1909. The Soviets merely took this tendency toward centralization to its extreme. They tried to turn an entire continental economy into a single public utility.

So long as technological change continued to increase economic centralization, Communist systems, operating as the ultimate monopolies, could function tolerably. But like the utilities whose functions they embody, the Communist systems have run up against the limits of centralization. Communism today is in as much trouble as LILCO.

The devotion of both to nuclear power helps illustrate their problem. Nuclear power is the most centralized of all power sources. To work at all, it must be undertaken on a scale involving monumental expense and intense centralized control. Both the expense and the control have increased in recent years for fundamental reasons. The undeniable hazards of nuclear power become more complicated and costly to manage as the number of nuclear plants rises and nuclear waste proliferates. Witness Chernobyl, a mess that will cost billions to repair, not only in the USSR, but wherever nuclear power is used. At the same time, new developments in technology are undercutting the costs of the output of nuclear plants. It is becoming ever cheaper to substitute alternatives to electricity or generate it independently.

THE TECHNOLOGICAL TREND REVERSES

In Western market societies, more efficient technology in homes and factories is substituting for the use of electricity. This takes many forms: Better insulation. Tools that employ less power. Efficient appliances. Heat pumps that circulate air more efficiently. These and other advances are proceeding rapidly as new technology is brought on line, some of it applying advances in computer technology to discretely measure and control energy use.

The use of computers is also substituting for energy uses in other ways. When a network of people work together through computer links, they can greatly reduce energy use. A document transmitted by modem does not need to be transported by plane, ship, or truck. Even the individuals who work together may not need to meet face to face so often or at all, as telecommunication is substituted for transportation. These are all developments that independently displace the need for centralized power, at a fraction of the cost required to raise additional generating capacity. For example, an experiment in Austin, Texas, has shown that investments in weatherization and more efficient appliances "will save 553 megawatts of power, and will cost only one-third as much as a coal-fired plant" of comparable capacity.*

* Christopher Flavin, "Energy Conservation in the Third World," *Journal of Commerce* July 23, 1986, p. 13A.

Improved efficiency of small-scale generating systems is also making decentralized provision of electric power more attractive. Cogeneration of electricity now makes it possible for industrial plants to convert energy used in manufacturing processes into surplus electricity. In effect, ordinary industrial firms are now able to compete effectively with the central utility. Renewable energy sources will soon make such competition even more widespread. The next generations of solar cell will enable products of all kinds to function like today's pocket calculators —without plugs. They will carry their own internal mechanisms for capturing a free power source. Wherever the sun shines, people will be able to unplug the power grid. In short, the technology of energy generation is reverting to a small-scale, decentralized basis.

Communist and Third World power systems, operating on the basis of rigid monopoly, already impose huge efficiency costs because they lack the decentralized pricing mechanisms for adjusting to the new technological trends. Energy efficiency in the Soviet Union has lagged dramatically. Soviet factories, like their centrally planned counterparts in the underdeveloped world, often use twice as much energy as equivalent installations in the capitalist West. This is just one of the inefficiencies that have arisen from operating economies as overgrown electric utilities. The problem of power is a metaphor for sweeping difficulties throughout all Communist systems.

FUNDAMENTAL FLAWS

The Communist economy, in its orthodox form, is an inherently inefficient system. The nature of this inefficiency was prophetically analyzed by a Dutch economist, Prof. N. G. Pierson, in 1902. Since Pierson wrote 15 years before the first Communist system even existed, his view could not have been based on random observations. He saw a fundamental difficulty inherent in Communism itself, the problem of information. When Communists suppress price movements in a dictatorial economy, they also suppress the information needed to move scarce resources to the point of greatest need. For that reason, a Communist system uses resources inefficiently, a point that led Pierson to suggest that famine would be a problem in Communist systems. Years later, the Soviets collectivized agriculture and proved him right.

The orthodox Communist system operates as if it were a giant monopoly—a company store so huge that it encompasses an entire country. This monopoly owns practically all the factors of production. It is practically the only outlet for the sales of goods and services to the people. And the prices at which it buys and sells from its own factories and supply organs are set artificially. Items that would be expensive in a free economy are very cheap. Items that would be cheap are expensive. Most output is geared to meet quotas set by central planners.

The example of a Soviet nail factory is often cited to illustrate the difficulties of a centrally planned system. When the central planners called for the factory to produce a large number of nails, the factory manager promptly met his quota—by making nothing but tacks. To counter this, the central planners changed the quota to require output measured by weight rather than number. The factory obliged by making great quantities of railroad spikes.

Such policies have profoundly uneconomic effects because the operations of the Communist economy are on the largest possible scale. Every mistake is magnified across the entire country. There is only one competitor. As far as possible, all enterprise is organized by the single competitor—the Communist state. Even under the best of circumstances, as Pierson noted, this involves drawbacks and a loss of efficiency. Were it not for a flourishing black market and underground economy between factory managers, the Soviet system would be even more of a basket case than it is.

Soviet Military Output

That is not to say, however, that Communist systems are equally inefficient in all areas. They are at their best where there are large-scale economies, and in areas like military output, where the state is usually the only purchaser, even in capitalist systems. That is why the Soviets are much better suited to producing missiles than growing vegetables. In the United States, agricultural economists have found that the optimum farm size is about 600 acres for most crops. In Russia, and in other orthodox Communist systems, collective farms reach into the tens of thousands, and sometimes hundreds of thousands of acres. The gigantic scale of collective farming is one of the reasons Communist agricultural output has been so abysmal.

By contrast, Russian military output has been much more impressive. One reason is that military goods are most efficiently produced at a large scale. Many weapons are not really free-market products—a fact cited in a CIA report in the early eighties suggesting that in some respects, Soviet military procurement may be more efficient than that in the United States. Even in capitalist countries, the state is usually the only buyer of tanks, rockets, and so on. This leads to inefficiency that can be compounded by political pressures from a number of constituencies "to get part of the action." Hence tales of the Pentagon paying thousands of dollars for a coffeepot or hundreds of dollars for a pair of pliers. Such stories are too common for waste to be out of the ordinary.

One of the reasons that the Soviets have some incentive advantages over a free system when it comes to military output is that they can funnel their best workers, managers, and scientists into arms work at low cost. This is easy for a system where opportunities are poor in other areas. It costs little to give special treatment to the manager or scientist who is able to increase output or devise a threatening new weapon. Such a person is denied the opportunity to work in private enterprise for higher compensation. He is not making a million in the Silicon Valley. What is more, a scientist or engineer in Russia operates under the added spur of being deported to a work camp or sent to a "mental hospital" if he fails to meet crucial goals.

Needless to say, Western societies cannot utilize such incentives to promote their arms programs. For that reason, the Soviet system, inefficient as it is, is able to mount a military challenge while it crumbles in other areas.

So long as the main area of growth in the world economy was in heavy industrial goods, the Soviet system could grow and compete in areas outside of military goods. Consider steel output. Communist systems are by no means good at producing steel. In fact, steel output in Russia under the Communists did not match output under the czars until more than 20 years of Communist rule had passed. Even today, Russia must spend billions to buy high-quality specialty steel products from Italy and other Western countries. Nonetheless, the lumbering Soviet system does produce lots of slab steel, more than any other country.

The reason: There are great scale economies in steel production. The process employs lots of people doing standardized tasks. And slab steel output is much easier to centrally control and measure than is the output of something so simple as nails—as the example above makes clear. Slab steel can be weighed and its physical properties verified through chemical and other means. Workers who screw up and reduce the quality of the steel or fail to turn out as much as they should during their shifts can be threatened with Siberia. In short, technology places fewer obstacles between the Soviet system and economic output in an old-line heavy industry, with primary output, like slab steel.

The same cannot be said in new areas of technology. Computers per se individualize work. Their most valuable output is inherently hard to measure. How long should it take a programmer to solve a new problem? No one knows. That makes fear a less effective tool for mobilizing output in the new areas of technology.

What is worse, from the Soviet standpoint, is that computers become more valuable when linked together. They enable individuals to communicate large quantities of information on an almost instantaneous basis. This implies an end to the Communist party's total monopoly on information. The Soviet Union attempts to function as a complex society without a single road map or publicly available copying machine. If millions of computers were in use throughout a Communist country, it would not only mean the effective end of censorship, it would point out many instances in which the Communist system stands in the way of progress. In short, Communism is not equipped to handle the individualization of work and the decentralization of economic output that comes with the microprocessor.

Greater Profits from Small-Scale Production

Among capitalist economies, those that have grown the fastest recently —Japan and the United States—have smaller average firm size than Europe. In Japan, the average firm employs just 15 people. In the United States, firm size and factory size have been falling as computer technology has improved productivity of small businesses. Computers have decentralized the workplace and decentralized the economy. The greatest growth of jobs has been among small firms. The area of the greatest value added or profit growth has been in producing a better match of products to consumer tastes.

Whereas in the past, to increase the *value* of the shirts you sold probably meant selling more shirts and thus using more cotton fabrics and thread, along with more energy to manufacture and transport additional output, now clothing producers are increasing value by shortening production runs. Consumers will pay more for clothes that meet their particular tastes or flatter their figures. The computer has enabled Western manufacturers to accelerate the individualization of clothing. Shirts, blouses, dresses, and pants are made in every size, in every color, and with practically every "optional feature" you can imagine.

A woman with a full figure may wish to wear a low-cut blouse. If so, that is what she gets. A woman with a scar on her neck may want a high, flouncy collar. That is what she gets. A woman with arthritis may want big buttons. A special production run is made for people like her. And all of these people will pay *more* for a product individualized to their tastes than they will for the standard issue that is meant to fit everybody.

That is just another reason that Communism is falling behind. It is notorious that clothing output in Communist countries has until recently been based on the largest scale of production possible—with the result that practically everyone was wandering around in ill-fitting clothing that more or less looked alike. Think of the old pictures from *Life* magazine of the Politburo standing at attention in ill-fitting suits. Or more to the point, think of the billions of Mao jackets that must have been manufactured in China. They all looked alike. This has begun to change in recent years. But the drab sameness of Communist clothing remains as evidence that the system is at its weakest when it comes to small-scale or individualized output.

With the exception of military equipment, the terms of trade have been turning against those things that Communist systems are best able to do. The Communists can make low-quality slab steel in their gigantic factories. But in the capitalist world, the steel mills that are making money are the small-scale, specialty steel mills. Communism is horrible at competing in small-scale production and service enterprises—the fastest-growing and most profitable areas in the world economy.

To make matters worse for the Communists, their inability to compete in areas where there are falling economies to scale also deprives them of the innovations and technological advancements across the board that are being generated in the decentralized capitalist countries.

One of the more interesting and difficult theoretical questions in capitalism is what determines the size of a firm. The leading free market economists, from Adam Smith onward, have had little or nothing to say about this. Only recently have economists tried to explain why firms sometimes seem to get bigger and other times become smaller. Their conclusions are interesting. One suggestion is that monitoring of worker output is a key variable. That means that the free market will naturally make firms larger or smaller depending on what is best suited to monitor output from the technology of the moment. When you need constant management at an intensive level to be certain that workers perform efficiently, you will tend to get firms of a larger size. Small firms will not be able to compete as well, because the overhead costs of employing the intensive management will not pay with a small number of workers.

This is just a different expression of the point we have been making —that changing scale economies alters the size of institutions in which tasks are performed. The greater the economies to scale, the better suited they are to being performed by a gigantic enterprise. Since communism is the ultimate large enterprise—the state operates everything like a huge conglomerate—the Communist economy suffers when scale economies decline. Because computers bring to small firms techniques of management, communication, and finance that were formerly available only to the largest enterprises, they reduce economies to scale even in low-tech or no-tech fields.

If this theory is right, the optimum size of almost every enterprise in the world has been reduced—a development that spells trouble for the giant, old-line manufacturers in the West, but is even worse news for Communist economic systems.

DRAMATIC CHANGES AHEAD

The character of the new technology necessitates revolutionary changes in Communist systems. Without such changes, nations now dominated by Communist elites will be unable to realize their productive potential. That is why the Chinese have already begun to abandon Communism. Soon, Russia and other state Socialist systems will be obliged to follow suit, not because they wish to give up power, but because fundamental megapolitical forces necessitate change. As Communist systems are reformed, or begin to break apart, the impact upon the world economy will be profound.

These profound changes will have far different consequences than most investors imagine. If you understand them, they could help you profit in many ways.

The Economic Impact of Communism

Communism is a two-headed coin. Americans, and indeed, most investors, have only bothered to look at one side. For more than half of the twentieth century, communism has been the main threat to the security of international investment. Whenever a Communist regime has succeeded to power, it has repudiated or ignored existing debt obligations and expropriated the existing assets of international business. That is why Communism is rightly feared as an economic threat.

The other side of the coin, one that people have tended not to notice, is that the dominance of Communism in some parts of the world increases the return to investment elsewhere. In effect, Communism acts like an international "set-aside" program to reduce world output of a wide range of products and commodities. Just as acreage set-aside programs have been employed to reduce corn output in Iowa by requiring farmers to abstain from realizing the full productive potential of their land, so Communist systems suppress output practically across the board.

As a result, Western entrepreneurs, who are more free to produce optimally, get a higher price for what they make than they would if major portions of the world population were not hobbled by Communism. There is no more dramatic evidence of this than in farm output. During the time of the czar, Russia was the world's largest exporter of grains. Under Communism, Russia has been for many years one of the largest importers. Iowa has made billions because the former bread basket of the world cannot feed itself under Communist rule. Such limitations on productions are not restricted to farming.

Executives in Detroit and their blue-collar employees have lost no sleep worrying about fending off competition from Russian automobiles. The nearest thing to a car the Russians export is an imitation of an old Fiat. No American appliance producer has ever gone broke because the masses flocked to Crazy Eddie's to snatch up the latest model of Russian stereo, TV, or VCR. Russian durable-good output is too limited and of too low quality to compete effectively in most consumer markets.

Why? Because Communism has stunted Russian growth. There is no other reason Russia would not be a formidable competitor in world markets. In the early days of this century, while Russia still had a capitalist system, it showed the potential for outstripping the United States to become the largest economy in the world. Industrial output surged on all fronts. Coal production leaped 124 percent between 1900 and 1914. Iron and steel jumped 51 percent. Living standards rose markedly, helped along by dramatic increases in farm income. Increased purchasing power of farmers and new workers in the cities allowed industry to cater for the first time to a mass consumer market. To meet the pace of rapid industrial growth, Russian industry imported large quantities of capital goods, from machinery to locomotives.

Foreign Capital and Russian Growth

Much of this growth was financed by an influx of foreign capital. Even in 1900, Russian financial markets were sophisticated enough to capture this investment by creating financial instruments to suit the needs of the capital exporters of that day—the Western Europeans. This was facilitated through a modern network of 50 banks. Completing the picture was a large and growing stock market, far more advanced than anything in Japan at that time. According to *The Cambridge Economic History of Europe,* capital from abroad played an essential role in the early twentieth-century industrialization of Russia:

> Foreign investments in 1914 represented about one-third of the capital invested in the existing 2000 or so companies. The proportion reached 90 per cent in mining business, more than 40 per cent in metallurgy, 50 per cent in chemical industries, 28 per cent in textiles. Out of a total of industrial investments valued at 2 billion roubles, French capital accounted for a third, English capital for a quarter, German for 20 per cent, Belgian for 14%. The proportion of foreign capital in the banks was still higher: 42.6 per cent for the 18 chief banks taken together. . . ."*

Communism slammed the door on the influx of foreign funds. The result was stunning. Russian growth rates fell. Having deprived themselves of capital imports, the Russians had to generate capital internally or through a trade surplus.

Exploiting the Workers

Ironically, the Soviets raised most of their capital through suppressing wage rates. You should understand how they did it. The story has important implications for today's sweeping technological changes, implications you may never guess from rough-and-ready notions of "exploitation." As an investor, you should always be wary of commonly held presumptions about economic relationships. This is especially true for a topic like wages, when special pleadings and political considerations stand in the way of the truth. The truth is that whatever their intentions, employers in market societies have a devil of a time "ex-

* *The Cambridge Economic History of Europe* (Volume VI), *The Industrial Revolutions and After,* edited by M. M. Postan and H. J. Habukkuk (Cambridge; Cambridge University Press, 1966), 851.

ploiting" the workers. Indeed, this is almost impossible where workers are free to develop their talents and move from one opportunity to another.

Surprisingly, it is far more common for workers to exploit capitalists. In general, this is the function that labor unions perform. They raise wage rates above the market-clearing level. The result is that investors receive a smaller portion of the revenue of the firm than they would otherwise. This is a politically delicate issue, for obvious reasons. Everyone feels he is underpaid compared to what he would earn in a better world. Unions mobilize this common desire for more. But they are not equally successful in all fields and under any technological condition. Exploitation of the investors tends to be greatest in areas with the greatest scale economies. Large enterprises with heavy sunk costs, like steel mills, railroads, mines, and auto companies, are the easiest targets for unions to exploit. Such operations are vulnerable to sabotage, too expensive to close down, and impossible to move. For this reason, wage rates in industries with large economies to scale tend to be significantly higher than wages in decentralized industries—quite apart from whatever skills are required to do the job.

Through most of this century, as scale economies have increased, income differentials in Western societies have narrowed sharply. Essentially unskilled assembly-line workers have gained a larger share of total income at the expense of investors.

Let's think this through and see why. When scale economies are great, that not only implies heavy sunk costs, it also means that there will be fewer competitors. Fewer large firms mean that there must be many more persons employed in subordinate positions than persons at the top. Such asymmetry is inherent in the technology of the production process. The greater scale economies, the greater the concentration of industry and the fewer persons who can be their own boss. In short, there will be far more workers than capitalists. This has political consequences. In Western democracies, where governments hold power at the sufferance of public opinion, it is obvious why policies condoning unions are inevitable. Any politician who wishes to hold power must count. There will be more votes in favor of policies that allow workers to increase their incomes at the expense of investors than there will be for protecting the investors from exploitation. The investors will only be safe when megapolitical conditions make it easy for them to resist union demands.

Therefore, the existence of democratic institutions during periods when technology increases scale economies more or less guarantees that the workers will exploit the capitalists. Income will be redistributed to the less skilled, who will receive higher than market-clearing wage rates.

This helps explain many phenomena of modern life:

— It explains why unions are now faltering in Western societies, as technology is reducing scale economies.

— It explains why income differentials are widening once more, as essentially unskilled workers are obliged to find employment at market-clearing wages.

— It suggests that industries in Western countries that depend upon discretionary spending by the less educated parts of the population are unlikely to fare well in the future. Take note, and review your investment holdings.

— It also explains the totalitarian character of Communism from its earliest years forward. As a ruthless, nondemocratic state, Soviet Russia was able to effectively eliminate labor unions. No unions meant success for the transcontinental holding company known as the Communist party. Wage rates and consumer demand were suppressed. Instead of exploiting growing scale economies in the production process to gain higher wages, workers were forced to accept lower than market-clearing wages. This allowed the Communist elite to gradually accumulate capital in the absence of financial markets.

The Soviets were able to do this because of their monopoly over all jobs. They denied workers mobility and suppressed wages across the board. In short, after the Communists destroyed the Russian capital markets, the nation industrialized by exploiting the workers in a way they can never be exploited by investors in the West. As one authority points out, "In Russia in 1960 the differential between maximum and minimum incomes was something like 40:1, whereas this ratio in Western countries such as West Germany, Switzerland, the United States and England was more like 10:1 . . ."[*]

RUSSIA STUNTED BY LOSS OF CAPITAL MARKETS

If Russia had remained capitalist after 1917, its markets would undoubtedly have continued to absorb foreign investment surpluses. This would

[*] Helmut Schoeck, *Envy: A Theory of Social Behaviour,* (New York: Harcourt Brace & World, Inc., 1966), 215.

have enabled the Russian economy to grow faster than it did. Contrary to the occasionally asserted view that Russian development has been boosted by Western finance capital or bank lending, Russia has actually enjoyed only a bare chemical trace of the capital inflows it would have received with a more flexible system.

Self-imposed limits on Russian financial markets have directly limited Russian power in the world. The Soviet failure to issue tradable securities has minimized the inflow of capital, reducing the growth of the Soviet economy. Without liquid capital instruments, the Soviets have been unable to participate meaningfully in world capital markets. The second-largest economy in the world would ordinarily be a candidate to develop an international currency competition with the largest economy. The Soviets have provided utterly no challenge to the United States in this respect. Nobody wants rubles. They are practically as useless as Monopoly money.

The logical economy to replace the United States as the world's dominant financial superpower would be the one that is runner-up in total output. But because of Communism in Russia, the financial and industrial challenge to the United States has passed to the number three economy, Japan. Ironically, the absence of Soviet financial instruments that has prevented Russia from dominating world capital markets has also kept the Russian economy from profiting from the emerging dominance of the Japanese. If the Russian economy were supported by a capital market of equivalent size, some of the hundreds of billions of surplus dollars accumulated by Japan would inevitably have flowed into Russia. Probably, the proportion of funds attracted would have been roughly equivalent to the Russian share of total world capital markets. That is the pattern with the flow of Japanese investment into Europe and the United States. The bigger the stock market, the bigger its share of Japanese investment. The same pattern, by the way, was evident in the twilight of British hegemony, with the new surplus country, the United States, investing mainly in British capital markets.

COMMUNISM IN RUSSIA PRESERVES U.S. SUPREMACY

The Soviets have cut themselves off from the advantages of tradable capital instruments, leaving the United States to enjoy financial predominance longer than it would have otherwise. The American proportion of total world capital markets is dramatically higher than it would be if Russia had not destroyed its own. This has enabled the United States to attract a greater share of foreign investment, subsidizing trade and budget deficits far larger than America could otherwise support.

Such are the effects of Communism in Russia and other countries. These effects translate into a major impact upon markets. Understanding them could be very important to you as an investor, especially in the years to come, as nations now suffering under Communism begin to shake off some of its self-limiting perversities. Among the most important investment consequences are:

1. Lower world output of most agricultural commodities. Communism is bad at producing food. As a result, Communist countries have typically been heavy buyers rather than sellers of food commodities in world markets.

2. Lower consumption and demand for extractive commodities (i.e., oil, gas, coal, metals, etc.) Residents of Communist countries are poorer than they would be; therefore, they consume less and use less energy.

3. Curtailed competition in manufactured products. The retarding effect of Communism keeps the quality of most manufactured goods from the Communist system too low to pose a competitive threat in most world markets.

4. Higher profit rates in certain industries in the West. Increased competition drives profits down. If Russia or China were as able as Japan to compete in world markets, the profits of many firms in the United States and other capitalist countries would fall.

5. Higher wage rates in Western countries. Workers in the United States and other countries are paid more than they would be, on a relative basis, because they are protected from competition by Russian and Chinese workers. The Communist system holds those workers down.

6. Higher factor prices, especially higher land and property prices in Western Europe, due to sharply diminished utility of property in Eastern Europe.

7. Less protectionist pressure and more free trade in capitalist countries. Communism in some countries effectively creates internal barriers to exports of most renewable commodities and manufactured goods. Because potential output from these countries is already excluded from markets, there are fewer protectionist pressures in the remaining countries. Therefore, trade is freer than it would be. Un-

less a presently Communist country were to become economically predominant almost instantly, on a level comparable to British dominance in 1850 or American supremacy a century later, the movement away from Communism will increase protectionism.

8. A loss of potential markets for Western goods. This partially offsets the factor analyzed above. The poverty caused by Communism deprives capitalist firms of the chance to sell goods and services to major parts of the world. If the Communists had more money, many firms would profit by selling them capital and consumer goods. This would tend to reduce protectionist pressures, but probably not enough to offset the weight of expanded output in reducing prices, profits, and wage rates.

9. Reduction in the world supply of tradable financial instruments. This means more capital flowing into the United States. Higher relative demand means higher values for the dollar and U.S. financial assets, including higher relative prices for stocks attracting foreign investment.

10. Longer reign for the U.S. dollar as the world's reserve currency. Lack of investment opportunities for holders of rubles make the currency of the world's second largest economy a big zero. The result is that challenges to the trade and investment predominance of the U.S. dollar come from the currencies of smaller economies, such as Japan, West Germany, and even Switzerland. Consequently, the U.S. dollar has remained the world reserve currency, in spite of the fact that massive trade and budget deficits now make the United States the world's largest debtor. This has meant greater foreign subsidies of U.S. living standards. If Russia suddenly reopened its capital markets and issued a convertible, gold-backed ruble, the United States would lose the ability to borrow a currency, the dollar, that it can also print.

From the viewpoint of the investor, therefore, Communism is not only a menacing system that threatens investment and stability in many areas, it is also a cartel-like arrangement for suppressing output and raising the demand for securities in U.S. capital markets. Ultimately, this means that there are two destabilizing influences that Communist systems can have on the world economy. They can continue to threaten investment in the familiar way, through revolution and expropriation. They also can threaten the stability of investments simply through internal reforms that have the potential for adding dramatically to world output and the supply of tradable securities, precipitating a crisis in profits. Indeed, any significant improvement in the efficiency of Soviet agriculture would bankrupt so many farmers that it would probably do more damage to the banking system than all the expropriations and defaults of Castro and the Sandinistas combined.

Reform of such sweeping character has already begun in China. An unprecedented policy shift toward the free market is under way in that huge country. That means increased opportunity for Western sales in China. It also means increased Chinese output will be sold to the rest of the world. Reforms in prospect in the Soviet Union will be more limited than those in China, but they, too, will have a major impact.

REFORM OF COMMUNISM IS DEFLATIONARY

The Soviet Union has long played a major role in commodity markets. It is a leading buyer of so-called soft commodities, such as grains. U.S. farmers will be affected by changes in Soviet agricultural policy that may substantially reduce Soviet grain purchases. So will the communities where farmers live, along with the American banking system, and the long chain of suppliers and transport companies who presently profit from massive shipments of grain to the Soviet Union.

The Soviets are major producers and sellers of "hard" commodities extracted from the ground. The USSR is the world's second leading producer of gold. It controls the lion's share of the output of palladium, platinum, rhodium, and other strategic metals. The Soviets also lead the world in petroleum output, and they have become major players in the international sale of certain types of chemical stocks, such as processed sulfur, anhydrous ammonia, potassium chloride, and urea.

We believe that developments in China, and to a smaller extent, the USSR, could strengthen deflationary forces in the years to come. China has already moved from being a buyer to a seller of grains. Within the next few years, the disciplined Chinese labor force will be producing manufactured items for export. As this trend develops, it will place downward pressure on Western prices and wage rates. A Chinese worker will toil for an entire day for the pay that a U.S. auto worker receives in seven minutes.

As you read this chapter, it will become increasingly obvious that economic decisions in the Soviet Union and in China will have far more of an impact on U.S. markets than is commonly believed. This creates

both danger—to which you must be alert—and opportunities for profit
you should know about. We spell out some of these dangers. We also
list more than 20 ways you can profit from the twilight of Communism.
Read these sections carefully.

Before we move into specific recommendations, however, you should
understand some of the local political and economic factors that have
aggravated the crisis of Communism in Russia and China.

CHINA—THE STRATEGIC BACKGROUND

Warlords and Soviet Agents

A quick detour into history is needed to get a perspective on the economic situation in Communist China. The better you understand this,
the more significance you will see in the dramatic reversal of policy that
has lifted the Chinese from economic stagnation under Mao to achieve
the fastest growth of any country on earth in 1984. The story begins in
1920. China was then more or less a republic on the Latin American
model. (If you want to be technical, it was several republics. Governments were sitting in various cities, each claiming authority over the
whole country.)

The Manchu dynasty had been overthrown in 1911, but the attempt
to institute stable government had foundered in civil war, with warlords
of all ilks and descriptions battling one another, most distinguished by
their total lack of belief in anything except personal greed. As one
history of the period put it: "Money was more important even than
power, for power was brief, and served only to offer the best chance of
enrichment." In one province there were so many warlords collecting
taxes that by 1923, the peasants had paid taxes in advance up to 1968.

In 1920, the Soviet Union sent two agents to China to organize a
Chinese Communist party. They were a Russian, George Voitinsky,
and a man named Maring, who was Dutch. They convened a secret
meeting in Shanghai in July 1921. Among the 12 delegates to this first
meeting was Mao Tse-tung. From these beginnings, Communist agents
were directed to infiltrate as many of the rump governments as possible.
They did so with some success, but their real progress toward power
began with a split from the Nationalist forces to form the Chinese Soviet
Republic in 1927. Until then, they had been working closely with
Chiang Kai-shek, a Nationalist general trained in Russia, who later

headed the government on Taiwan. In 1927, two Nationalist Chinese divisions deserted to join Mao and a fanatical band of rural revolutionaries who set up a government in Kiangsi.

At first, the new Communist government attracted little notice because it seemed to be just another group of armed thugs.

In fact, the Reds were different. First of all, they were motivated by ideology, not a desire to steal money for their own use. They also received significant financial support, at least in the beginning, from Soviet Russia. The Far Eastern Bureau of the Comintern, then operating clandestinely from the International Concession at Shanghai, provided direct subsidies to Kiangsi from Moscow. This operation was headed by a Russian agent named Hilaire Noulans, who was eventually exposed and arrested in the 1930s, but not before he had provided the local Communist regime with critical financial support.

Killing the Landlords

The Chinese Soviet Republic operated in the Kiangsi and western Fukien provinces for seven years. In 1934, the Reds were dislodged in a massive campaign that sent them on the so-called Long-March. The full details of the intrigues and military campaigns that brought them to power in China by 1949 are not important to our story. It is significant to note, however, that from the very first days in Kiangsi, the fundamental policy of the Communist party was to immediately communize agriculture. When Red Army troops seized control of a village, the first thing they would do was kill all landlords, then systematically destroy title deeds and dig up landmarks indicating property boundaries. All land, including religious grounds and graveyards, was then "redistributed" to the peasants. Agricultural output was monopolized in a state agency that set prices at artificially low levels.

This collectivist farm policy was essentially the first feature of Chinese Communism, around which the character of the movement was fixed in its early days.

The "800"

This is noteworthy because even today, China's top leader, Deng Xiaoping, is someone who lived through that period. He is one of the few surviving members of a group known during Mao's days as the "800." They were the people who were there at the founding of the first

Communist government in 1927 and had managed to survive wars and purges to about 1960. Deng had always been in the top leadership, serving in very important posts on the Standing Committee of the Politburo. Until the time of the Cultural Revolution, Deng was general secretary of the Politburo. Other members were: Mao Tse-tung, Liu Chaoqi, Chou En-Lai, Marshal Chu Teh (original commander of the Red Armies from 1927 on), Ch'en Yun, and Marshal Lin Piao (who was murdered on the personal orders of Mao). Together these men ruled all of mainland China from 1949 on, and they held sway over portions of China from 1927.

Leftists Go Wild

Only after conquering all of the mainland, however, did the Communists gain a full latitude for implementing Marxist policies. Their first step, after killing the remaining landlords, was to seize large enterprises and place them under state control. Small private firms were not wiped out until almost a decade later. After 1958, there was increasingly ruthless collectivization of the peasantry. That was the year of the so-called Great Leap Forward in which Mao decided to shift Chinese society toward orthodox Communism. From the Cultural Revolution, through until Mao's death in 1976, the Chinese economy stagnated, suffering from the usual difficulties of Communist systems compounded by a degree of fanatic excess seldom seen elsewhere.

For all practical purposes, wages were equalized during this time under a doctrine dubbed the "Iron Pot." All output was rigidly controlled by the state. Practically all workers were paid the same wage, no matter how hard they worked, or what they produced. For reasons already explained these policies resulted in massive inefficiencies and misallocations of resources. Big industry, operating at a large scale, grew much faster than light industry and agriculture (in which smaller-scale operation is more efficient). As you would expect, this resulted in a dramatic drop-off in innovation and the application of new technology. With the economy stagnating, and income growing little or not at all, everyone lived at or near subsistence levels. Periodic famines swept the countryside, killing uncounted millions.

From the early sixties through 1978, when Deng Xiaoping came to power, average industrial wages fell, perhaps as much as 25 percent in real terms. Gross mismanagement was a real feature of practically every enterprise, with managers chosen by the Communist party for political reasons. Most of these managers made astonishingly feeble efforts to utilize inputs without wasting them. Indeed, during the time of the Cultural Revolution, all gestures at scientific management were considered capitalistic deviation. Ignorant Red Guards sought to replace management techniques with slogans. One of their favorites: "Better to have Socialist weeds than capitalist seedlings."

The attempt to substitute slogans for any form of organization or individual thought was taken to extreme lengths. More than 100 million persons were denounced by Red Guards during the Cultural Revolution. Anyone who was seen modifying the harsher or more idiotic features of Mao's orthodoxy was denounced as a capitalist. Even bureaucratic inertia became a capitalist sin in the eyes of the radical leftists. The officials who worked in the Chinese state, as opposed to the Communist party, were seen as standing in the way of full-fledged Communism. Mao's old comrades who argued for the need to maintain some formal organization of the bureaucracy were denounced along with the others. State President Liu Chaoqi was labeled the "number one party person in the party taking the capitalist road." China's present leader, Deng, was purged and denounced as public enemy number two.

When Mao died in 1976, the disgraced "capitalist roaders" who were still alive made a rapid comeback. Mao's hand-chosen successor, Hua Guofeng, was pushed aside. By 1978, Deng Xiaoping was in control. He packed the Communist Party Central Committee with 12 new members, almost all of whom had almost been purged during the Cultural Revolution. He also brought forward as China's premier Zhao Ziyang, who had been governor of Deng's native Szechuan province. With new people in place, Deng moved against Maoism.

In a crucial speech delivered in October 1979, Deputy Communist Party Leader Ye Jian Ying denounced the Cultural Revolution and other left-wing experiments as an "appalling catastrophe suffered by all of our people."

Cautious Reforms That Worked

Beginning in 1979, Deng instituted the first cautious steps toward economic reform in agriculture. Local production units began leasing plots of land to groups of families for periods of one to three years. These families were then allowed to profit from anything that they could grow in excess of their production quotas. While they were still obliged to obtain all their supplies, fertilizers, equipment, and draft animals from the state, this was a first step toward privatization. By 1980, the Sze-chuan experiments had been expanded. In every year that followed, they were expanded further. Individual families were allowed to lease the land on their own. The length of the leases increased from a maximum of three years to 15 years, and then to 30 years in some areas. Even longer leases are now being let for forestry projects and for private investments in reclamation of marginal land.

Today, Chinese farming has essentially been privatized—although there is no sale or inheritance of production rights. Most arable land has been leased by the state to individuals. Farmers are now allowed to own their own equipment and draft animals. (Over 90 percent of the draft animals in China were privately owned as of 1985.) And the peasants have been freed of the requirement of selling only to the state. Billions of dollars of farm output is now traded through private markets.

More than 25 million peasants have turned to specialty farming—raising ducks, pigs, or fish. The increases in output among the specialty households has been tremendous. Their productivity ranges as high as ten times greater than that of ordinary peasants, a fact that accounts for the terrific upsurge in output and income in rural China.

Rural income increased by more than 250 percent from 1978 through 1985. Since China is overwhelmingly a rural and agricultural society, this has meant a much-expanded market for consumer goods. Individual farmers in rural areas have been allowed to drop out of agriculture to specialize in equipment repair, transportation, and marketing. Some have even gone into construction. A peasant named Jiang Changshen, who was honored by Communist party officials in Beijing as the country's first "Socialist millionaire," made a fortune starting and operating a prefabricated concrete factory. Many former peasants have gone to work making such items as furniture, clothing, processed foods, and the like. Private restaurants and food shops have even reemerged.

The reforms in agriculture have been paralleled by a cautious opening to outside investment. At first, this was limited exclusively to overseas Chinese. The pragmatists in the Communist Party Central Committee cast this as an attempt to involve all Chinese in the reconstruction of the homeland. Later, opportunities for non-Chinese were gradually extended, although the policy continues to be one of preference in dealing with overseas Chinese. Nonetheless, concessions set in deals with foreigners of Chinese descent have ordinarily been followed by similar deals with non-Chinese. For example, hotel concessions and development projects in resort areas were first opened to private capital in Hong Kong and other Chinese communities outside the People's Republic. Then similar concessions were made available to other private capital.

Today, many multinational corporations have either struck deals with Beijing or are eagerly negotiating in hope of landing something significant. Western oil companies that were first invited to sign deals for offshore development have now been allowed to work drilling concessions on the mainland of China.

Moving Toward Capitalism

To make matters more interesting, the Chinese government has recently taken to soliciting wealthy capitalists and free-market economists of Chinese descent to set up shop in China. An agricultural economist who formerly worked for the British sugar conglomerate, Booker McConnell, was lured to China to take an important policy post. And Chinese officials have also attracted former government officials from Singapore, a strongly capitalist nation. Significant private enterprises, organized by mainland Chinese with wealthy relatives and access to capital abroad, have also begun. For example, the Shanghai Patriotic Construction Company, a private enterprise headed by MIT graduate Chen Wuqing, claims a net worth of 180 million yuan, or more than $70 million.

The crucial element in the move toward capitalism is the emergence of tradable financial instruments in China. A red-letter day in this development occurred in 1986 when the Yanzhong Industrial Company's 18,000 shareholders received a 15 percent dividend—the first dividend paid to stockholders since the Communist takeover in 1949. The Chinese have moved to create new classes of tradable financial instruments that in time will eliminate some of the self-limiting features of Communism. The Shanghai stock market has even been reopened.

Although reforms have been introduced gradually and under the camouflage of heavy Marxist rhetoric, there can be little doubt that they depart significantly from orthodox Communist principles. In fact, they are almost the opposite of the policies implemented by the Chinese Soviet Republic 50 years ago. Then, the wealthy were murdered and agriculture was collectivized. Today, land is being privatized in plots of up to 150 acres, and the new slogan is "Strive to be rich."

Hong Kong

A key element in Deng Xiaoping's program for the economic recon-struction of China is the reversion of Hong Kong to Chinese sover-eignty after 1997. All Chinese governments from the days of the emperors have considered the British presence in Hong Kong a humili-ation. The successful negotiation for the return of Hong Kong is there-fore a matter of substantial national pride. In the process of negotiating the agreement over Hong Kong, the Chinese leadership committed to preserve capitalism for at least 50 years after the British lease expires. Deng and his pragmatic associates could justify this provision to the hard-line Communists as an essential concession required to reunite the homeland. This has given rise to a new slogan, "One country, two systems."

The official Chinese interpretation is as follows:

> Deng Xiao Ping has recently reiterated that the concept had been formulated after the thorough discussion of the Third Plenary Session of the Eleventh Chinese Communist Party Central Committee at the end of 1978. It was put forward as the correct way to accomplish the peaceful settlement of the Hong Kong and Taiwan issues which were to achieve national reunification. This flexible concept shows full con-cern for the history and current conditions of these two places by guaranteeing a continuing stability and prosperity during reunification and respect for the local people's interests and customary practices. The decision not to change Hong Kong's present system for at least 50 years comes in part from the consideration that China needs that part of time to get fully modernized.

There is also an element here of the "tail wagging the dog." The need to accommodate Hong Kong as a full-fledged capitalist enclave creates a reason to institute free-market policies, first in the areas adjacent to Hong Kong and thereafter in the rest of China. In this light, it is inter-esting to note the commentary given by Chinese government publica-tions in celebration of the Sino-British agreement on Hong Kong of September 1984. Describing the reasons for Hong Kong's prosperity, a government organ wrote: "After World War II, export processing in-dustries developed rapidly, spurred on by its [Hong Kong's] ample low-wage labor force, made up of hard-working people, flexible manage-ment methods and free economic policies which favored investors."

Extension of the same policies throughout China to encourage its rapid development would essentially turn China into a capitalist country.

New steps in that direction were taken in the fall of 1984, when the Communist leadership agreed to extend its successful agricultural reforms to the urban work force. Price controls are to be phased out, and central planning is to give way to the allocation of resources by market forces.

The Chinese have gone so far into restoring a market economy that they have come under criticism from left-wing politicians and academics in the West. Some sinologists, who took a sympathetic interest in Mao's radical experiments, have been bitterly disappointed to find Deng Xiaoping turning into an Oriental version of a supply-side economist. The restlessness of the Left, both in China and abroad, has been especially provoked by occasional comments by highly placed Deng supporters, critical of Marx and the relevance of his writing to today's problems. Where these statements have been too inflammatory, Deng has been careful to see them retracted or toned down.

Leftist Power Remains

Nonetheless, it is important to remember that leftists remain powerful in the Communist party and other Chinese institutions. Their remaining strength has impeded the progress of reform to date. And it may ultimately jeopardize its success. There is a faction of conservative Communists in the Politburo who are appalled at capitalist reforms in China. They attempted to organize opposition to Deng over anti-Marxist comments in the press, as well as the favorable publicity given to rich peasants at the end of 1984.

The conservatives are also furious over the growing popularity of Western clothes and music in China. Nightclubs have opened in Beijing, where young Chinese spend their evenings, behaving in a decadent, "capitalist" fashion. If they can, the unreconstructed leftists will use resentments of the emerging rich and their "conspicuous consumption" to turn back the reforms. They have some powerful institutional allies.

The improvement in the living standards of peasants, for example, has alienated leaders of the Chinese army. Once the army found it easy to get recruits, simply by offering the promise of regular food. Today, that is no longer true. Economic opportunities outside the army are far more attractive to most young Chinese. And the army is upset for another reason. Deng has announced plans to slash the military budget and reduce the armed forces by one million men. Very few institutions anywhere like to shrink and see their budgets cut.

Also upset are the local Communist party cadres. Under Mao, they enjoyed tremendous arbitrary powers over everyone in their communities. A local cadre, usually a busybody housewife, determined who could buy scarce goods, and even where an individual worked. If a cadre did not like a marriage, the husband or wife could be sent off to a distant city. Deng has changed that by reforming the economy. The cadres don't like it. This is especially true because many of them are former Red Guards who lack any real trade or economic skill. These disgruntled cadres, now poorly paid by comparative standards, pose a threat to the continuation of reform. To help minimize this threat, Deng raised their salaries in 1985, by 100 percent to 300 percent.

The considerable remaining power of the left-wing forces in China's Communist party is a factor that magnifies the profit opportunities for speculating on China's opening to the West. The fact that the leftists are disgruntled and seek to frustrate the reforms creates an element of political risk that scares away many potential investors. If everyone knew that the reforms were universally popular and their success just a technical and economic matter, the influx of big money seeking to capitalize on these developments would be overwhelming. Chances are you would not have the opportunity to get in at the ground floor.

Today you do have that opportunity because speculating on the future of the Chinese reforms is risky. We believe that the risk is justified. The potential for profit is high. We believe that the political conditions within Chinese society have shifted sufficiently to keep the promarket pragmatists predominant for some time. Deng Xiaoping has already purged a great many of the top leftists in the Politburo and the army. The longer he survives, the more of his remaining enemies in high places will have been put out to pasture. Massive purges have already weeded out hundreds of thousands of the leftists holding party and government jobs.

Even if Deng has died by the time you read this, his demise would not necessarily spell doom for the pragmatists. The reforms have benefited tens of millions of Chinese, bringing China one of the highest growth rates in the world in the eighties. It will not be easy for even the most dedicated leftists to turn back, especially when the evolution of technology points toward gains from decentralization.

PROSPECTS FOR REFORM IN RUSSIA

The situation in the Soviet Union differs substantially from that in China. Economically, Russia has a more industrialized and advanced economy. Politically, Russia has never swung so far to the Left as China did under Mao. Consequently, there has not been the strong reaction against "leftist nonsense" that aided reformists within the Chinese Communist Party. Even today, control in the Politburo remains with the first- and second-generation Stalinists who rose through the ranks during the 1930s and 1940s to comfortable positions of affluence and power within the closed Soviet system.

Many in the West do not understand that in spite of the egalitarian rhetoric, the Communist party elite in the Soviet Union enjoys a life of unrivaled wealth and privilege. The incomes of top officials are state secrets. Nonetheless, it is known that their salaries exceed those of Western leaders. For example, during a Gorbachev visit to Britain, Mrs. Gorbachev took time out to visit Cartier's, where she plopped down an American Express card to pay for fabulously expensive diamond jewelry. When former prominent Politburo member Grigory Romanov's daughter was married, the wedding guests at a lavish banquet were served on antique plates from the State Museum that had once belonged to the czar. These priceless treasures were then smashed as the banquet ended, an extravagance that would be almost beyond the imagination of the richest Western capitalist, let alone a political leader.

The Soviet elite has been united by a desire to maintain its comfort and privilege on a level that has not been true in China. Through their most horrid excesses, the Chinese leaders have at least been sincere egalitarians. Even today, the prime minister of China is paid just $3000 per year—an amount less than Mrs. Gorbachev paid for a single pair of earrings.

The insincerity of the Soviet elite on some of the motivating points of Communist doctrine is an important feature of its conservatism. The "Nomenclatura" are smart enough to realize that a political change that dramatically improved the Soviet economy might also undercut the monopoly on privilege enjoyed by the Communist party. Their cushy positions would be threatened. They well remember that economic liberalism in Czechoslovakia, in the mid-sixties, led to an astonishingly rapid destabilization of Communist rule. If the Soviets had not sent tanks into Prague in 1967, Czechoslovakia would have been a free society within a few years, if not a few months.

The Soviet leaders will be reluctant to allow their citizens too much of an opportunity to prosper through channels that diminish Communist party control. At the same time, however, the party bosses are acutely aware that they face another destabilizing threat—the economic challenge discussed earlier. World economic conditions and technology are turning in a direction in which a centrally planned economy is least equipped to compete. The top leadership knows that it must institute some reforms and make a major effort to import Western technology. Otherwise its cozy rule might be threatened by popular discontent and an increasing economic gap with the West.

Gorbachev

It is in this context that one must understand the role of Communist party chief Mikhail Gorbachev. Gorbachev is a dedicated Communist who fully adheres to the desire of his colleagues to maintain the Communist party monopoly of privilege in the USSR. He is also dedicated to advancing Soviet power throughout the world.

Mikhail Gorbachev came to Moscow as a protege of Mikhail Suslov, who was the main Kremlin specialist in ideology for many years. Gorbachev, like Suslov, came from Stavropol. Gorbachev was introduced to Suslov by Fyodor Kulakof, another local "boy" from Stavropol. Like most Russian Communists who rise through the ranks, Gorbachev showed himself to be a willing tool of the dominant faction in the Politburo and especially of his hard-line patrons, the aging Stalinists. Gorbachev had lots of opportunities to associate with the top party brass because he had the good fortune to be stationed in a resort community whose mineral spas were much favored by the aging Kremlin leadership.

When Kulakof died in 1978, Gorbachev was elevated to take his place in the Moscow hierarchy. There he attracted the favorable notice of Yuri Andropov, then the KGB chief. Gorbachev quickly became a candidate member of the Politburo. He was elevated to full membership in 1980.

During his period of advancement, Gorbachev was hardly a principled advocate of reform. He was an eager-beaver organization man who made it clear to his superiors that he was willing to do their bidding. At the same time, he cautiously made himself known as one who was willing to experiment with incentives in the Soviet economy, especially in agriculture. It turned out that by positioning himself as a "safe" reformer, he had done well. When the grain embargo imposed by President Carter cut deeply into Soviet food stocks, Gorbachev was selected to head a reform effort that allowed greater scope for private initiative. Kremlin leaders were quite willing to believe that this limited privatization would increase food output. Nonetheless, they were not prepared to treat it as more than an emergency measure.

When President Reagan lifted the grain embargo, the production experiment was immediately scrapped. Gorbachev went along with the decision. But intelligence experts believe that he subsequently argued within the Politburo that agricultural reforms were worth the political risk because they could make the Soviet Union self-sufficient in food. Gorbachev has identified his reform ideas with those of Lenin, whose New Economic Policy of the middle 1920s involved a reprivatization of agriculture that dramatically increased output. (The present collectivist model was instituted by Stalin, beginning in 1929 in a bloody program that involved the mass murder of millions of peasants.)

There is no indication at all that Gorbachev has been in any way offended by the atrocities and the inequities of the Soviet system. Gorbachev's conservatism, however, does not mean that he will not undertake reforms now that he has consolidated power. Throughout his early career in Moscow, he lacked a regional power base of his own. He depended entirely upon the patronage of others to advance his career. Obviously, he was in no position to insist upon policies of his own pleasing.

Gorbachev emerged in a much stronger position in the final days of Chernenko and began a program of reform. He frequently scolded orthodox economic thinking, indicating that Soviet economic science had not yet "produced a developed concept of a transition to a dynamic, highly efficient economy and an improved economic mechanism." He attacked "dogmatic views that at times do a disservice," and lashed out at planners who were quick to repeat "outmoded [views] in the midst of a worsened economic and social situation."

As general secretary of the Communist party, Gorbachev has proven more willing than his predecessors to tinker with the clunky Soviet system. Along with conventional attacks upon laziness, drunkenness, and cronyism, Gorbachev shook up the important energy sector, reversing a decline in oil output. He also prevailed upon his associates to legalize private enterprise in a limited number of services.

We have no reason to believe that Gorbachev had completed his reform ambitions during his first two years in office. More is in store.

An investor can make educated guesses about what else Gorbachev has up his sleeve and how to profit from it.

We expect the following:

Agricultural Reform

Gorbachev will move cautiously to introduce more private incentives in Soviet agriculture. He will not go as far as the Chinese have gone, at least not in the foreseeable future. But he will adopt reforms for which he has argued in the past within the Politburo. He will seek to reduce Soviet dependence upon foreign markets (essentially the United States) for food. To that end, he will turn to the Hungarian model, in which approximately 12 percent of arable land is in private cultivation, but private farms yield 35 percent of total output. More than 50 percent of Hungary's vegetables and 50 percent of the hog crop are produced privately, along with most of the output of honey, fruits, geese, ducks and rabbits.

When Hungarian-style reforms are introduced in Russia, there will be special emphasis on private farming of root vegetables, such as potatoes and turnips. These crops are particularly well suited for production on private plots, where yields will improve dramatically with intensive small-scale cultivation. Food yield per acre from the cultivation of root vegetables is high. What is more, potatoes, turnips, carrots, etc., can be fed to livestock, especially to hogs. Hogs will be the favorite production animal for farming on private plots in Russia, because they require very little space. For years to come, Russia's private farmers will have very little space.

Even a small percentage of private farming in a land as massive as the Soviet Union will yield a tremendous quantity of crops. And don't forget that the fertility of Russia is much greater than Soviet officials pretend. In the days of the czars, Russia was the world's largest food exporter, sending more grains abroad than even the United States. If Gorbachev puts his reforms into place, as we believe he will over the next few years, private farming of small-scale crops will yield enough additional output to displace a large percentage of the grain now being fed to livestock in the Soviet Union. Most of this grain is corn, now being imported from the United States. In 1984, the Soviets bought $1,389,842,000 worth of U.S. corn. Sales to the Soviet Union would drop precipitously if agricultural reforms take effect.

The United States also sold $1.17 billion worth of wheat to the Soviet

Union in 1984. These sales, too, may be jeopardized in the future, although to a lesser extent. We believe that Gorbachev has no intention of tinkering with the basic collective farming structure for large-scale crops, such as wheat, at least not for the near term. And since wheat really cannot be grown efficiently in a backyard plot, it would appear that the Soviets will have to participate in the world market to make up for their shortfall for years to come. It is important to remember that even a slight improvement in the management of the collective farming system would yield a substantially increased output. U.S. intelligence experts believe that up to 20 percent of the Soviet wheat crop rots in the field or is spoiled in transit due to appalling mismanagement of the harvest. Gorbachev will not risk destabilizing the Communist party's monopoly of rule by privatizing large-scale grain farming, but he has announced a program that will eventually result in reduced Soviet imports of U.S. wheat.

Improved Discipline and Management

Gorbachev is pushing for a crackdown on slack work habits and the introduction of Western-style management in the Soviet Union. You might be surprised to know that there is not a single business school in Russia. Most managers are party hacks who have never systematically studied how to efficiently and economically utilize available resources to do the job at hand. Consequently, there is unimaginable waste in many areas of Soviet production.

Efforts to institute reforms since Gorbachev took power have gone slowly. As in China, there has been strong resistance and foot-dragging by the bureaucracy whose power was being diminished. Leonid Abalkin, of the USSR Academy of Sciences, wrote to the *Financial Times* with an apparently realistic assessment of the obstacles to reform:

> Enterprises working in the new way have displayed more efficiency, but less than expected. Many managers are none too eager to enjoy their freedom, like birds unwilling to quit an open cage. . . .
> As people in the corridors of power started to lose their customary duties, while retaining their administrative mentality, they developed a phobia of becoming unwanted. The rank-and-file, in their turn, began to realize that if they became independent, they could no longer hope to see a helping hand proffered from above to correct their blunders.

If you act strictly on instruction, you have even less rights but are less reponsible, the[y] reasoned. . . .

. . . Be that as it may, we have a working model and are willing to implement it, not by order but by economic methods alone. That way is more difficult. It demands persistence and further break-up of our old economic concepts.*

Better Russian management, if it comes to pass as we believe likely, will have many possible effects. One of the more dramatic, as far as the outside world is concerned, would be a long-term decline in the Soviet purchases of wheat as well as corn. With better management, the Soviets should be able to boost the effective yield of wheat, rye, and other grains just by bringing seed, fertilizer, and tractors in working order to the fields at planting time, and curtailing massive spoilage during the harvest. It is estimated that hundreds of thousands of tractors and combines are destroyed in the Soviet Union each year, through incompetent maintenance and mismanagement. Almost ten million tons of fertilizer in Russia is simply lost or allowed to spoil. If the Soviets marginally reduced the damage they inflict by mismanagement, they could feed themselves.

More Investment in Energy

Gorbachev is also keen to improve management in the energy sector. One of his first acts was to purge the seventy-four-year-old minister of power, Pyotr Neporozhny. For the first time since World War II, Soviet oil production fell in 1984. It fell again in 1985. But to the surprise of most experts, it revived in 1986, a turnabout that should rebound to Gorbachev's credit within the Soviet power elite.

The Soviets depend crucially upon energy and other commodity exports to earn hard currency for the purchase of Western foodstuffs and technology. That is why the accident at Chernobyl was a heavy blow. It required massive investments in cleanup and reactor safety. It also harmed the Soviet balance of trade for food. Gorbachev, as indicated above, wishes to reduce the expenditure of hard currency for food purchases so that there will be more left to modernize Soviet industry. But a drop in Soviet oil output could wipe out the expected savings on current purchases from the United States. That is why Gorbachev in-

* Financial Times, July 12, 1986, p. 7.

tends to increase the already massive internal Soviet investment in energy.

Overproduction and poor management techniques in the Soviet Union's major oil fields in Siberia have prematurely depleted those fields. To rescue this lost output, the Soviets must turn to more sophisticated secondary and tertiary recovery technology in which U.S. companies lead. The Soviets also are in the market for improved cold-weather coal mining technology. We believe that Gorbachev will attempt to negotiate the purchase of this technology from the United States and other Western countries.

Increased Mechanization of Soviet Industry

Gorbachev is also keen to step up the mechanization of Soviet industry. To do this, he will expand on a policy that has slowly been developing in recent years. He will turn to Finland, more or less as the Chinese have turned to Hong Kong.

Finland is a Scandinavian nation that borders on Sweden and Norway as well as Russia. It has about the same population as Hong Kong, but in a much larger area. The Finns are a tough, independent people who fought a bloody war with Russia just prior to World War II and then joined as allies with the Germans when Hitler invaded Russia. In the wake of the war, the Finns managed to avoid Soviet domination of their domestic politics that fell upon other countries in eastern Europe. Finland signed a treaty more or less giving the USSR a veto right over its foreign policy. But capitalism was maintained, and the Finnish economy has progressed.

Today Finnish industry is among the most mechanized in the world. And Finland is also a leader in per capita use of computers. The Finns are therefore perfectly suited to exploit Gorbachev's coming initiative to upgrade the mechanization of Soviet industry.

Talking Down Western Military Preparation

Gorbachev will continue to talk peace, smiling without showing what Soviet President Andrei Gromyko has called his "iron teeth." One of his chief virtues in the eyes of the Soviet elite is his ability to reach out to Western countries with "peace initiatives." These are designed to undermine popular support for military resolve against the Soviet Union. Gorbachev is undoubtedly more dynamic and personable than the sick and dying men who have ruled Russia in the years before he came to power. We project that he will have at least marginal success in shifting the balance of Western opinion toward disarmament. Gorbachev will be effective in urging Western populations to take a more sympathetic view of Soviet intentions. He is keen to do this because his hopes for reforming the Soviet economy depend upon relieving military spending pressures. We expect Gorbachev to work especially hard to reduce tensions in Europe. He wants European investment in the Soviet Union. It will be difficult to lure such money while Soviet conventional forces are menacing NATO countries. Expect troop reduction and other disarmament agreements.

This is all the more likely because of the fiscal exhaustion of the United States, a position equivalent to that of Britain in the wake of World War I. At that time, Britain accepted demands from foreign opinion that the size of the Royal Navy be cut. We expect steps toward disarmament today for similar reasons.

This implies more negotiations and a slower growth of military spending in the years to come, especially in the United States.

Reintroduction of Limited Private Enterprise

We have no doubt that sooner or later, but probably sooner, many of the characteristic features of the Soviet system, including state ownership of the means of production, collectivization of agriculture, and the repression of financial markets, will be abandoned. Gorbachev has already taken the first tentative step toward legalizing private enterprise by opening 27 service industries for self-employment beginning May 1, 1987. We expect other steps to follow, including private ownership of small factories before 1990. As the reforms become more far-reaching, efforts will be made to disguise their character. Large factories will probably be retained in nominal state ownership, but will be contracted out to "cooperatives" or management groups that will run them. In time, free market disciplines will play an ever-larger role in organizing the sprawling Soviet economy. To put it simply, Communism is in its twilight.

SUMMARY AND FURTHER IMPLICATIONS OF COMMUNIST POLICY SHIFTS

As we have emphasized throughout this chapter, policy changes in Communist countries will reach far beyond the borders of Russia and

China. It is quite likely that Gorbachev's attempt to talk down Western defense spending will work. And there will be a major impact upon capitalist countries because of changes in Soviet and Chinese economic output. The Chinese reforms, themselves clearly positive steps, come at a time when automation and robotics have implicitly created a world-wide oversupply of labor *at wage rates that now prevail in capitalist countries*.

It is very easy to make a case that the implications of the Chinese reform include falling wages and prices in the West. This case may be overstated because many things could intervene to prevent events from reaching their logical conclusion. But the logic of that conclusion is not in doubt. A worldwide oversupply of agricultural and industrial commodities is about to be compounded by the removal of shackles from more than a billion industrious people. The additional output they could generate would raise living standards tremendously over the globe as a whole. But living standards at the top, especially in the United States, would come down, while those of Chinese and, perhaps, Russian peasants, would rise. This would pose a stiff economic and political challenge to the United States and other advanced Western countries. Falling wage rates and lower prices would be challenged by powerful interest groups, like labor unions, that stand to lose by them. Similar strains in times past have often led to war.

Depressed Agricultural Prices

One of the more significant negative implications of Communist reforms for the U.S. economy will be on the already damaged agricultural economy. Even if the Soviets do not make major progress quickly in their agricultural sector, the Chinese have already done so. For the first time, the Chinese have a sufficient grain surplus to compete with U.S. farmers in export markets. Chinese corn has been sold to Mexico, displacing American corn. Although this is as yet a minor development, continuation of recent output gains by the Chinese could add significantly to the world food glut, driving down already depressed prices.

Over the longer period, world agricultural output should continue to rise. It is unlikely that the Chinese will again be willing to inflict as much damage upon themselves as they did during the first three decades of Communist rule. The prudent observer must assume that the Soviets will also find a way to achieve self-sufficiency in food. This should hardly be difficult, given the vast grain-growing regions in Russia, and the well-known fact that more market incentives will stimulate output.

Other things being equal, the long-term price trend of nontropical food commodities should be down. The output of tropical foods, on the other hand, like cocoa and coffee, and to a lesser extent, oranges, will be less affected by Communist agricultural reforms. Most tropical crops cannot be grown in Russia. Tropical crops are grown in China, but on a modest scale. The potential increase in output is not likely to be large in the foreseeable future. It is far more likely that improvements in staple food output in Communist countries will lead to more cash buying of tropical commodities. These tend to be luxury products, consumed in greater quantities as incomes rise. Therefore, you should expect the relative prices of tropical commodities to rise relative to staple foods in the years ahead.

The Soviets intend to move away from purchases of American grain. For reasons already analyzed, corn exports could be especially hard hit. The effect of any cutback will be felt disproportionately in Iowa, a state that grows more corn than all of Europe, Africa, and Latin America combined.

Conditions are already depressed in Iowa and other corn-growing areas. If our projections are correct, they may be even more depressed in the years to come. This argues against purchases of Iowa regional stocks or stocks of other depressed companies such as farm equipment makers, fertilizer producers, farm banks, or barge and rail lines that participate heavily in the export of grain. Review your investments with a view to reducing exposure in any position that depends for profitability on a long-term rebound in corn prices.

We suggest avoiding the following stocks until they have hit bottom and been restructured: Deere & Company (symbol DE) and Hesston Corporation (HES) are leading manufacturers of agricultural equipment. A continued slump in the Farm Belt will likely depress the sales of these firms. Several food processing firms may be hurt as well: American Maize Products (AZEA), CPC International (CPC), DEKALB Ag Research Inc. (DKLBB), Pioneer Hi-Bred (PHYB), and Staley Continental Inc. (STA). Staley is capable of grinding four hundred thousand bushels of corn *per day*. However, exports are only 9 percent of sales, and lower corn prices may actually improve operating margins. CPC, on the other hand, exports 62 percent of its finished products. Lower Soviet demand may create a pinch.

Pain for some constitutes opportunity for others. Decreased Soviet demand for grain will lead to even lower grain prices, which in turn means wider profit margins for livestock producers such as Monfort of Colorado Inc. (MNFT) and Swift Independent (SFT).

Downward Pressure on Prices and Wages

Further declines in grain prices should contribute to lower food prices in general, benefiting food processors (i.e., makers of candy bars, soft drinks, cereals, etc.) who buy farm products, and helping to hold down prices. Since food prices are a major component in the Consumer Price Index, a greater degree of monetary irresponsibility will be required to raise the all-important CPI.

To the extent that increased Chinese industrial output requires imports of raw materials and energy from abroad, there may be a slight upward pressure on oil prices and industrial commodities. On the other hand, the Soviets have earmarked tremendous capital investment to increase their output of energy and hard commodities. To the extent that the Soviets are successful, they will place selling pressure on those commodities. Therefore, it is difficult to predict what impact the developing changes in Communist economic policies will have on world energy prices and hard commodity prices.

It is clear, however, that the opening of the Chinese economy increases the market for advanced capital goods and basic consumer products in China. The Chinese are eager to have consumer electronics products, such as radios, televisions, and tape recorders, along with appliances such as refrigerators and washing machines. Sales of these items have been rising dramatically. In the first quarter of 1985, retail sales of consumer durables in China rose by 32.7 percent over the 1984 level. Television sales were up 59 percent, washing machines up 47 percent, and refrigerator sales were up an astonishing 788 percent. The opportunities for future growth are great.

To the extent that Chinese output of export goods increases, it should exert a powerful downward pressure on both prices and wage rates throughout the world. The Chinese have been seeking modern technology for their factories. As this new technology comes on line, Chinese productivity should skyrocket. Chinese labor rates are so cheap—$3 per day for the average industrial worker—that it will be impossible for workers in Western countries to compete. Workers in some U.S. industries, such as the automobile industry, are paid $3 every seven minutes. To make the competition even more impossible, the Chinese labor force is effectively nonunion. Manufacturing operations in China will not be burdened by union slowdowns, strikes, and the like.

Unless the Chinese reforms are stopped in their tracks by a return to orthodox Communism, a development we do not anticipate, it is obvious that the tendency of increased Chinese output will be to drive down wage rates in the West, while holding down prices. Western corporations will face uncomfortable alternatives to the extent Chinese output comes on line. They will have to do one of three things: go out of business, join the Chinese in joint ventures, or tremendously increase capital investment to replace human effort with robots. Already, American automobile makers have seized invitations from the Chinese. American Motors has opened a Jeep factory. GM and Chrysler are involved in active negotiations for joint ventures. Chrysler is studying a deal with the First Automobile Works in Changchun to produce Dodge Caravans in China. After production problems were mastered, the Chinese would then produce engines for use in Chrysler cars in the United States. Any fruits of such joint ventures will be many years in the making. But their implications are clear.

They point to a profit squeeze on firms in industries subject to direct competition from Chinese output. Such competition is already hurting textile manufacturers. Those in other light industries will feel the pinch as well. To avoid being harmed, steer clear of long-term investments in firms vulnerable to low-wage competition. But watch for changes in trade laws. If major protectionist measures are instituted, as we anticipate, profits in some of the besieged industries may rise.

Effects on Monetary Policy

It is difficult to know how strong the impact of increased Chinese output on the American market will be. The potential is large. But the degree it will actually be felt is yet to be seen. The following reasoning analyzes the logic of this change. We believe that the logic is correct. Whether the cause and effect it describes will be significant or imperceptible depends upon how vigorous the growth of Chinese output becomes. And, of course, even if these developments do occur, they would not happen for years to come.

An increase in output at lower prices should increase the real wealth of consumers—at least for those consumers who keep their jobs. If other factors remained constant, the domestic value of the dollar would rise. This effect is deflationary. In a political environment where there is limited downward price flexibility, as is the case in the United States and other advanced democracies, an upsurge in low-price, low-wage competition (which increases the value of money) will tend to result in unemployment. Whether this would lead eventually to an inflationary monetary policy to counteract the unemployment is hard to say. Probably it would.

But unless inflation were already roaring out of control for another reason, it seems unlikely that it should begin abruptly just because of the prospect of new low-wage competition. Indeed, higher inflation might make the competitive situation worse. Therefore, several projections can be made. If increased competition from the Chinese does contribute to suppressing wages and prices, this should tend to increase real interest rates.

Real interest rates are determined by taking nominal interest rates—like the quoted Treasury bill rate—and subtracting the rate of inflation as measured by some index like the CPI. Since lower prices, by definition, lower the CPI, that means that the real rate of return to creditors, like bond holders, would go up unless the nominal rate fell. The Fed would then have the option of easing the money supply to bring nominal interest rates down further than they could have done otherwise without producing an increase in inflation.

Our tentative conclusion, therefore, is that Russian, and especially Chinese reforms, will tend to lower most commodity prices, lower wage rates, and lower finished product prices. Unless the effect is canceled by other inflationary developments, this should tend to lower nominal interest rates, rewarding bond holders, and perhaps stimulating interest-sensitive sectors.

Those Who Will Benefit

A number of the specific firms that will directly benefit from the reforms in Russia and China are listed among the investment recommendations. If our analysis is correct, there will also be a number of industries that will benefit indirectly. They include industries not subject to foreign competition, such as retailers, and hotels. Labor-intensive industries would benefit, to the extent that wage rates were actually reduced. But such indirect benefits may never be realized if other factors intervene, such as a political reaction to exclude Chinese goods from U.S. markets.

Dangers of Reaction

You can expect a strong political reaction to further depression of farm prices and increases in Chinese output that place significant downward pressure on prices and wages. Farmers, who have been a major constituency for free trade, may abandon the pursuit of foreign sales and lobby for protection—as they did during the 1920s. Unions and exposed industries will advocate protection of jobs by imposing tariffs and other barriers to trade. In areas where they have the political power to do so, unions may seek to impose legal restrictions making it difficult to close factories or dismiss uneconomic workers similar to legislation in effect in most European democracies. Even firms whose output is not subject to foreign competition, nor likely to be, may find their operating costs increased if such labor protectionism spreads. Other things being equal, U.S. manufacturing firms with their main operations in nonunion states should be more attractive investments.

The possible increase in trade barriers will be bad for export industries, shippers, and the banking sector. Large increases in trade barriers often lead to debt default and recessions or depressions. Be alert to those dangers.

STRATEGIES FOR INVESTORS

There are at least three levels at which it is important to be aware of the ongoing developments in China and the Soviet Union. 1) You must be able to protect *yourself* against some of the far-reaching consequences of major shifts in the Chinese and Russian economies. 2) You may wish to align your investments in a way that will *benefit but not depend* upon the direction of change that we project in the major Communist economies. 3) You may want to take on an active role as a *speculator*, making investments that can return very handsome profits if the developments we forecast come to pass.

To Protect Yourself

In summary, to protect yourself:

1. Avoid investments in agricultural land, especially land best suited to grain crops.
2. Avoid investment in firms whose profit depends upon sales in Iowa and other corn-growing areas.
3. Avoid the stocks and debt instruments of banks with large exposure in midwestern agricultural loans.
4. Avoid investments in barge and shipping companies whose profits depend upon grain exports.

5. Be wary of investments in firms whose main output comes in states politically dominated by industrial unions.
6. Be wary of investments in defense industries, except in special situations, until some decisive event renews popular commitment to military buildup.
7. Monitor the evolution of capital markets in Communist countries, especially China, where reforms are already in motion. Dramatic steps that increase the world share of tradable investment instruments will reduce foreign (especially Japanese) demand for U.S. securities. This will make it more difficult for the United States to finance its deficits, suggesting downward pressure on U.S. living standards. Lower U.S. stock prices could result.

It is easy enough to avoid defense stocks or stocks in some of the other groups mentioned. But it is more difficult to move out of agricultural land or a closely held company with a customer base in the Midwest. See the chapter on real estate for further details.

COMPANIES THAT MAY BENEFIT FROM OPENING OF COMMUNIST ECONOMIES

The following companies have substantial investments in business inside China or the Soviet Union. Most, though not all, are American firms. These are well-established companies with highly liquid, easily traded shares. The fact that they are listed here does not mean that they will necessarily gain in value. The portion of their total turnover from Communist countries is still small.

UNISYS (UIS). This high-tech company has been a leader in developing business connections in China. It has already concluded a joint venture agreement with Huafeng Industrial Corporation to provide mainframe computers to the Chinese. It has another joint-venture agreement to produce microcomputers in Yunan Province.

PHILIPS (PGLOY) (Holland). One of the world's major electronics firms, Philips has had great success to date in selling consumer electronics to the Chinese. Philips's 75 percent–owned Australian subsidiary, Philips Telecommunications Manufacturing Company of Australia, has landed contracts to build and supply China with large quantities of communications equipment. Exports have increased sharply in the last four years, tripling since 1978. For further information, contact the company directly. Its address is: Clarinda Road, Clayton, Victoria 3168, Australia. A fall in the dollar will also help boost this company's earnings.

TOSHIBA (Japan). This leading Japanese office communications firm has achieved a breakthrough in developing an effective, easy-to-use Chinese-character printer. This could have a massive market in China. Toshiba has also landed contracts to sell the Chinese copiers and to provide technical assistance to Chinese firms adopting new communications technology.

OCCIDENTAL PETROLEUM (OXY). Occidental Chairman, Dr. Armand Hammer, has known every Soviet leader since Lenin. His company is as well connected in the Kremlin as any in the world. It could stand to benefit from any Soviet opening for contracting and joint-venture arrangements in oil. Occidental has also landed an important contract in China, to develop the Pingshuo coal project in Shanxi province. We advise caution in purchasing Occidental. It is a sprawling company with many difficulties, not the least of which is the fall in the price of oil.

INCHCAPE (U.K.). This British distribution and trading company does a brisk business importing Toyota cars into China. It also plays a major role in handling Chinese exports of household goods, textiles, hardware, and foods.

AMERICAN STANDARD (AST). A major American manufacturer of plumbing equipment, American Standard seems to have the inside track in reaching the potentially vast Chinese market. It has just entered a joint venture to make toilets in China. Again, caution is advised because American Standard has its troubles in the United States, where its main operations are.

INTERNATIONAL GEO SYSTEMS CORPORATION (IGC) (Vancouver). IGC has developed the Tianma program that allows typing of Chinese-character texts on ordinary word processors.

SPECULATIVE WAYS TO PROFIT

In the future, it may be practical to make direct investments in China, either by subscribing to Chinese companies, buying bonds, or investing in public shares. This is not the case now.

There are more convenient speculative vehicles available. The following shares are more thinly capitalized and less easy to trade than the more conservative ones listed in the previous section. Some are also more or less "pure plays." If the Chinese revert to Maoism, the Hong Kong shares may suffer dramatically. If, on the other hand, the Chinese opening to the West continues, as we project, these riskier shares should appreciate handsomely.

The Finnish companies listed at the end of this section represent excellent values. We list them as speculative simply because they are unknown to most investors and brokers. Their prices are not quoted in the *Wall Street Journal*. This makes them more attractive because they have been overlooked by almost everyone else. Nonetheless, they are large companies with solid earnings whose prospects would be excellent, even if our predictions about Russian plans are wrong.

BANK OF EAST ASIA, LTD. (Hong Kong). This is one of the leading "red chips" in the China trade. The Bank of East Asia is a small Hong Kong bank controlled by the Li family, ethnic Chinese with very close connections in the Chinese government.

CHEUNG KONG HOLDINGS LTD. (Hong Kong). A major Hong Kong company, with extensive interests in land and trading, this firm is headed by a Chinese. It has good connections in China and should profit handsomely if China trade continues to grow.

HONG KONG LAND (Hong Kong). A major landholder in Hong Kong, where land prices are a sensitive barometer of future economic prospects. The mushrooming value of trade with China should encourage optimism about Hong Kong Land.

SWIRE PACIFIC A (Hong Kong). One of the major "Hongs," or British trading companies in Hong Kong, Swire is still controlled by the Swire family. It enjoys a practical monopoly on China tours, and its airline should also reap growing profits from the growth of travel into China.

HONG KONG AND SHANGHAI BANK (Hong Kong). The largest bank in Hong Kong, it is often taken as a proxy for the entire Hong Kong market.

HANG SENG BANK (Hong Kong). The bank should profit from increased retail deposits and an upturn in mortgage demand for small residential accommodation.

WINSOR INDUSTRIAL CORP. (Hong Kong). Its Chairman, T. K. Ann, is very closely connected with the Bank of China. He has already worked out a joint venture company, The International Investment Co. of Hong Kong and Macao, with the Bank of China as partner. These excellent connections should yield profits in the future as China develops.

SIMPSON HOLDINGS (Australia). Simpson has a 50 percent interest in a joint venture to manufacture washing machines in China. This market has grown from annual sales of zero to 3 million machines in just four years. If China's market reforms remain in place, the potential for additional sales is staggering.

GALACTIC RESOURCES (GLC Vancouver). This Canadian mining company has been negotiating to develop potentially rich Chinese gold-bearing deposits adjacent to the Soviet border in northern China.

In recent years, Finland, Moscow's neighbor to the west, has enjoyed one of the highest and most stable growth rates in all of Europe and North America. We expect Finnish exports to the USSR to continue rising, in spite of the fall in the oil price. The oil collapse has temporarily wrecked the barter arrangements upon which much of Finnish-Soviet trade rested. The following Finnish blue-chip stocks may be good bets:

WARTSILA (Finland). A high-tech industrial conglomerate, one of the oldest and largest public companies in Finland. It produces everything from automated capital goods to ships to toilets to components for offshore drilling. Wartsila is very well connected in Moscow, where it has an office. It stands first in line to gain from Gorbachev's ambition to automate Soviet industry. That plan will mean many billions spent on Finnish equipment and mechanical engineering products. Wartsila shares are traded on both the London and Stockholm exchanges, as well as in Helsinki.

POHJOLA (Finland). The sixth-largest company in Finland is a huge insurance company that owns a substantial portion of shares in the Helsinki stock market. Therefore Pohjola is almost bound to gain from massive new projects in conjunction with Finnish companies during the next Soviet five-year plan. Informed sources report that at least eighty such joint Soviet-Finnish projects are under review in Moscow. In recent years, Pohjola's investment income has skyrocketed as exchange rules were loosened and prospects for Finnish industry improved. If Finland becomes the "Hong Kong of Russia," as we project, Pohjola will profit. This is an easy speculation, because it could pay off handsomely in the event that we are correct about the direction of change in the Soviet economy. But even if we are wrong, Pohjola should continue to earn near-monopoly profits from Finnish insurance business. Premium income is guaranteed, not only by limits on competition, but by surpluses on statutory pension and workmen's compensation income.

NOKIA (Finland). Finland's leading high-technology company with annual sales of FMK 9.4 billion. It is a leader in bank automation and has 60 percent of the British market in mobile telephones.

UNION BANK (Finland). One of Finland largest banks. It has very few foreign loans and is an excellent proxy for the entire Finnish economy.

We believe that the shares listed above represent interesting speculations. There are others that you can uncover by following the same line of reasoning that we have suggested above. By acting now, you can "get in on the ground floor" of a market development that stands to be one of the more significant of this century. Even if the Soviet Union stops well short of matching China's dramatic reforms, tens of billions of dollars will change hands.

The resulting economic feedback will give you a rare chance to earn back some of the high costs that Communism and Communist governments have imposed on you. You have surely paid many thousands in taxes to support an adequate defense against the threatened actions of Communist governments. Now you have a major chance to get some of that money back, by profiting from efforts to patch up the economic mess Communism has created in Russia and China.

Be aware that it is not wrong for you, as an investor, to anticipate and profit from these developments. Whether you follow the recommendations in this chapter or ignore them completely will have no bearing whatever on the outcome of the geopolitical struggle in the world. The only difference it will make is in determining whether you are richer or poorer. The firms we list that stand to profit from massive new contracts with Communist governments will take those contracts and make those profits—given the chance—whether you are a shareholder or not. If, and when, the Soviets take action that drives down the world price of corn, they will do so whether or not you are ready to profit by it.

What the Communists do is beyond your control. But it will have severe economic consequences—with important implications for your investments. You should prepare yourself now.

6

Monetary Instability and Megapolitics

The only thing that has driven more men mad than love is the currency question.

—Benjamin Disraeli

If you have read the newspaper at any time over the past 15 years, you should be well aware that monetary fluctuations have affected your livelihood, your investments, and practically everything you do in life. This upheaval has been measured mostly in the form of inflation. Inflation is what happens when money goes down in value relative to real assets in the economy. During the 1970s, paper money seemed to depreciate every time you turned around. Oil prices shot up, and so did prices for ordinary commodities, like sugar, copper, and soybeans. What you paid as a consumer went up as well, but not as rapidly as the price explosion in the basic commodities.

As paper money seemed to be shedding its value like a nudist shedding clothes on a summer's day, people responded. Many investors bought precious metals. A buying panic drove gold to the unheard-of price of $800 per ounce. And silver exploded to more than $50. It seemed to many that inflation would run completely out of control in the major industrial countries, as it had often done in the underdeveloped areas of the world. Seeing prices increase year after year, people began to believe that such inflation was irreversible. Practical, sober farmers borrowed great sums on the assumption that prices for wheat, corn, and soybeans could only go up. Bankers, with the best advice that money could hire, gladly lent on that premise. And not just to farmers. When oil climbed to $35 per barrel, it seemed only a matter of

190

time until it would reach $70 or $100. That is what the petroleum experts said. And experts in practically every other commodity joined them in the same chorus. They all foresaw a tight supply situation in the future and a continuous increase in prices. So banks shoveled out billions to oil companies, miners, and natural resource producers of all kinds. Many of these billions found their way to remote areas of the world to finance the budget deficits of commodity-producing countries. This was all done under the spell of inflation.

INFLATION BREEDS DEFLATION

The enchantment ended when commodity prices started to fall. Inflation, it turned out, was not an independent force, merely one of the symptoms of monetary disorder. As is usually the case when disorder reigns, a dramatic swing in one direction—toward inflation—called into play compensating forces that pulled the pendulum back the other way —toward disinflation or deflation.

Many investors find this action and reaction doubtful. The mechanism of inflation is much more obvious and easier to grasp than the compensatory forces that bring deflation. Inflation is caused by printing money. The printing of money is clearly linked to the motives of the authorities in power. It is easy to see why politicians and central bankers have incentives to expand the money supply. They can use the newly created cash to "stimulate" the economy, reward powerful constituencies, and bail out important businesses and banks threatened with failure.

On the other hand, the overt means to deflation—a *reduction* in the money supply—does not correspond with any sane political motive. It brings bankruptcy, unemployment, and ruin. For everyone it directly benefits, it harms ten of his neighbors. Deflation is the economic equivalent of time in the penitentiary. It is the correction society pays for the excesses of inflation, a penalty no authority answerable to popular opinion would ever willingly impose.

If there is no motive to deflate the currency, then deflation itself would appear to be nothing to worry about. Or so many people have concluded. They admit to disinflation—a slowdown in the rate of inflation. But they imagine deflation to be impossible.

This could be the mistake of a lifetime. It brings to mind a trenchent comment of Paul Clay, of Moody's Investors Service. Speaking on "injurious financial fallacies" on December 28, 1928, Clay observed: "First among these fallacies is the new era delusion as typified by the famous dictum, 'This is a new era. Statistics of the past don't count.' Every period of great prosperity is considered to be a new era and so much better fortified to give promise of permanence. However, each experience has been that the improvement in commercial and financial methods has ultimately been overcome by credit inflation and business rashness, resulting in another backward movement." *

In other words, inflation will breed deflation. And not because anyone necessarily wants deflation. It was true then. It will be true again. To believe otherwise implies that our ancestors as recently as the 1930s must have been ninnies to have shrunk the money supply simultaneously in many countries and thus brought on worldwide depression. Could they have been that stupid? We doubt it. The politicians and banking authorities are hardly the sole determinants of outcomes in the larger economy. Their motives at the time of the last Great Depression were not greatly different from their counterparts' today. They did not set out to create deflation. It overcame them in spite of their wishes. We shall attempt to explain why.

The analysis that follows is by no means a comprehensive discussion of the problems of money. What we offer you instead is an overview of a complicated problem, an outline you can use as an investor. We hope to uncover some of the the hidden, megapolitical foundations of monetary instability. The better you understand these connections, the better your chance of prospering as the world regresses toward disorder.

THE QUANTITY THEORY OF MONEY

Print enough money and inflation will result. No doubt about it. And if banking authorities wanted deflation—as they almost never do—they could have it by simply slashing the money supply. Remember that, if you remember nothing else.

But we advise you not to stop there.

If you wish to understand the nature of monetary disorder as an investor, you have to move beyond the mechanistic version of the quantity theory to a more sophisticated view. Experience has shown that while the money supply is key, there is no simple relationship between

* Joseph Davis, *World Between the Wars, 1919-39* (Baltimore and London: Johns Hopkins Univ. Press, 1975), 168.

the supply of money and prices. Sometimes, as in the 1920s and again during the 1980s, rapid credit inflation has not led to higher prices.

Contemporary investors who believed that "inflation was here" by looking at the money supply, went heavily into debt and suffered losses in precious metals, real estate, and other tangible investments. If they are lucky and live long enough, those investments may yet pay off when inflation reignites. But it is also possible that deflation and depression will emerge, as they unexpectedly emerged in the late twenties. To see why, we need to look beyond the obvious fact that printing money will tend to make its value fall.

Every facet of the "inflation" and "deflation" issue is complicated. To understand it, you should look beyond the money supply to the balance between financial assets (including cash, stocks, bonds, notes, insurance policies, etc.), and real assets (commodities, precious metals, tangible assets, real estate, etc.). Roughly speaking, you get inflation when financial assets fall in value relative to real assets. You get disinflation or deflation when financial assets rise relative to real assets.

CHANGES IN THE SUPPLY AND DEMAND FOR REAL GOODS

The supply of money is obviously a major variable determining the balance between financial assets and real assets. But it is not the only variable. "Inflation," popularly understood as "rising prices," will not necessarily occur just because the money supply has gone up. Other factors can change in ways that offset the effects of increases in the money supply. For example, the supply of real goods may increase rapidly. And the demand for real goods in the production process may fall for reasons that have no direct bearing on the current supply of money.

It is important to understand that the category of "real goods" is not fixed and solid like a rock or steel slab. It is more like an indeterminate gruel or a cloud formation. That is why it does not always fit well into a mechanistic equation. The very concept of an economic "good" is subjective and changing. Once upon a time, oil in the ground was a gooey nuisance. When farmers dug a well and hit crude, they would curse their bad luck and move on. Then technology changed and oil became valuable. Crude petroleum had become an economic asset where it had not been in the past.

The point we illustrate here is that the supply of real goods is a rather slippery variable that can change for many reasons. New technological processes can sharply increase the output of goods—as they did in the last two Great Depressions and are doing again today. The same effect —lower commodity prices—can also be achieved when technological innovation unexpectedly antiquates natural resources.

We think such influences have been important factors in lowering commodity prices during the 1920s and again in the 1980s. They will be bigger factors in the future, as we explain in another chapter. New production processes are reducing the use of raw materials and primary products. As demand falls, raw material prices will tend to be lower, even if the money supply increases.

POLITICAL INFLUENCES ON OUTPUT

Politics and money are always volatile in combination. Never forget that in this chemistry, politics is the more active ingredient. Be alert for political changes with an impact on output. In a society where the law said, "No one may work more than two hours a day," a short, sweet revolution could dramatically increase productivity. Even if the money supply went up under such circumstances, prices could fall. Similarly far-reaching effects can often be realized by shifts in the tax laws. In the 1920s and again in the 1980s, changes in U.S. tax codes appreciably increased supply in some areas of the economy. Political changes in other systems have reached even further. The dramatic shift away from communism in China, for example, has contributed to reduced world grain prices by sharply increasing the output of a major fraction of the world's population. As we discuss in the chapter on communism, political decisions can have a surprisingly far-reaching impact on prices everywhere by altering marginal supply and demand.

In short, everything is connected to everything else. You should not neglect to understand that the value of money is determined, in part, by nonmonetary factors that alter the supply and demand for real goods. A war or nuclear accident that wiped out large portions of world output would lead to higher prices even if the money supply were unchanged. Similarly, rapid technological or political innovation can sometimes raise the supply of real goods relative to demand, leading to lower-than-expected prices. Under certain circumstances, such as those in the 1920s and again in the 1980s, more money may not mean as much inflation as people then or now expected. Increases in the money supply may be absorbed as higher financial asset prices. This means greater value for bonds and stocks, not higher prices for goods.

We say this not because we doubt the importance of money. On the contrary, we believe it is of overwhelming importance. But we think that you should see money in terms of the whole economy, including its megapolitical foundations.

The Megapolitics of Money

In some surprising and hidden ways, monetary instability is linked to the power equation.

This is true in the first instance because the character of money itself is transformed by power. In the fragmented, small-scale economies of the past, there was little money. And what there was tended to be limited to actual physical commodities. These could sometimes be conch shells, cocoa, corn, or brightly colored feathers. Dyes and pelts and peppercorns also served the function of money. But the overwhelming money of choice was gold. It lasted. It did not rot. It could not be eaten by insects. It did not tarnish or rust. And it was more portable than giant stones, the pocket change with which some unhappy Melanesians labored. Gold could be measured and stamped into coin. It was money the miser would gladly pack away in his chest.

Gold was the money of an insecure world, a world where few promises were kept. Its value did not depend upon a promise the way the paper money of modern states does.

Peace and Paper Money

How did the transition from gold to paper money occur? Gradually. Paper money was invented long before it came into acceptance in Western economies. The Chinese used it for many centuries. It was the money of an economy that was far more centralized and peaceful than the contemporary economies of Europe. Attempts to bring paper (or leather) fiat currencies to the fragmented medieval economies of the West flopped badly. During most of English history, the predominant currency was coinage struck in silver, as indeed the name *pound sterling* suggests. Most of this coin was of very poor quality, with clipped edges and low silver content. It tended to trade by weight rather than at face value. Gold was scarce. Small quantities were minted and served as the preferred means of exchange for high-value trade.

In the seventeenth century, Britain was racked by revolution and civil war. This descent into disorder and the subsequent recovery played a major role in establishing the gold standard. In 1640, King Charles I closed the royal mint, taking all the available bullion with him. It fell to London goldsmiths to become unofficial private banks, substituting for public authorities in providing a medium of exchange. They stored gold in their vaults and lent it out; discounting bills, usually for 90 days, and issuing promises to pay. These became bank notes. The first check was a transfer of a goldsmith's payment note to a Mr. Farrington. But notice, these were not promises to pay in sterling, they were receipts for gold. When peace was restored, the government moved to recapture its monetary dominance. This required an increase in the mintage of gold coins, beginning with the 20-shilling gold known as the guinea in 1663.

A de facto gold standard emerged. By 1730, the master of the Mint wrote that "nine parts in ten, or more, of all payments in England are now made in gold."* It was still possible to pay in silver coin, which was legal tender, but most people did not because it would have ruined their reputations.

By 1816, the gold standard had become official. The British Empire effectively extended it around the globe. And as it did, it paradoxically spread belief in the pound sterling, the "brand name" that the British government put on a certain weight of gold. Paper bank notes, drafts, and discounts spread in the forms used by the British. In short, paper money became far more widely acceptable in the nineteenth century than ever before, in large measure, because of the political stability created by the British Empire.

Great Britain controlled about a quarter of the world population and an even larger fraction of world trade. From this predominant position, Britain began to exercise a determining influence over world finances. As Mancur Olson put it, Britain's "political stability and innovative banking system made it the natural place to settle accounts not only for trade with Britain but for trade among other countries as well. . . ."†

The Pax Britannica took the risk out of monetary innovations. These innovations increased the importance of credit and paper instruments as substitutes for physical settlements in gold. A long experience showed that notes and drafts issued by the Bank of England and other British banks were "as good as gold." Anyone who wished could re-

* Sir John Clapham, *A Concise Economic History of Britain* (Cambridge: Cambridge University Press, 1963), 294.
† "A Theory of the Incentives Facing Political Organizations," p. 15.

deem them in gold. In time, these gold receipts became, for all practical purposes, substitutes for gold. For a century, persons holding pound notes were able to spend and invest them freely. They were safe from losses due to repudiation, revolution, or war. Because the pound was defined as a unit of gold, and British finances were strong enough to sustain that link, holders of pound-denominated financial assets were more or less safe from inflation. From the end of the great war of the nineteenth century in 1815 to the next great war in 1914, the purchasing power of the pound actually rose.

During this period, even currencies that were ostensibly pure fiat money, like the Austrian schilling, developed a reputation for stability and value that depended indirectly upon the monetary arrangements established by the British. The schilling was not convertible directly into gold. But it was pegged to the pound. The pound was convertible into gold. So long as the pound retained its gold value, the schilling did also.

The gradual transition to greater reliance upon paper money and credit could not have gone so far or fast without megapolitical conditions that allowed power to be projected cheaply. These made possible the integration of innumerable, petty polities into more encompassing regions of trade and commerce. They made for peace over wider areas. Just as peace in China centuries earlier had paved the way for the acceptance of paper money, so world peace in the nineteenth century gave credence to the always tenuous promises of paper money. Writing about the necessary conditions of prosperity, John Stuart Mill emphasized the importance of a "long exemption . . . from military violence or arbitrary spoliation [causing] a long-standing and hereditary confidence in the safety of funds when trusted out of the owner's hands." That same confidence was necessary to allow for the monetary innovations that emerged in the nineteenth century. If the world had remained divided into small-scale, violent little fiefdoms, it is a fair bet that gold would still be the money of preference.

WANING HEGEMONY AND GOLD

The second element in the megapolitics of money is even more crucial. It explains why the world has moved away from a gold-based money. And it offers you, as an investor, the basis of understanding how the monetary system may evolve in the future.

The key to understanding this second element in the megapolitics of money is an apparent paradox. Stability makes it possible for paper and credit to become more important elements in the monetary system. But a reversion to instability does not restore a greater role for gold—at least not immediately. Chronic instability that collapses the system—as the English system collapsed in the seventeenth century—may bring gold back. Eventually. But short-term instability merely creates contractionary pressures that weakened political systems cannot sustain. To avoid gold's disciplines, they remove it from the financial system altogether.

What does this mean? It points to some unhappy conclusions for the present period that could be of overwhelming importance to you as an investor.

The international monetary system is unlikely to function for everyone's benefit except when one country controls a predominant share of monetary and economic resources. Only then will the costs of maintaining a gold-based money be distributed in a politically bearable way. Keeping such a system going entails large costs that some country must meet out of its own resources. Unless the country upon which the burden falls is rich and controls a large share of the world's economy, it will be unable or unwilling to meet these burdens. The result will be monetary instability for everyone.

Let's look more closely at the way a gold system operates and see why.

THE THERMOSTAT EFFECT

The first thing to bear in mind is that the gold system really succeeds in maintaining price stability over the long run. It does so at the cost of greater short run instability. In effect, the gold-based monetary system works like a finely tuned thermostat. It is set at 70 degrees. If the climate becomes too chilly, it turns on the heat. If it becomes too warm, the air conditioning pops on. And quickly, before the air temperature really becomes stifling or freezing. Gold avoids extreme results by cutting short the swings in one direction or the other.

In a gold-based monetary system, such as that sponsored by Great Britain in the last century, an inflationary episode will be stopped short long before it reaches the dimensions of 1970s inflation.

This occurs because the feedback mechanisms to stop inflation are more powerful and direct than under fiat money. Whenever participants in the market begin to fear inflation, they can redeem their paper money for gold. Such an exchange of paper for gold automatically reduces the money supply because paper money always circulates in greater quantity than its gold backing. In short, fear of inflation creates a rapid deflationary reaction. The thermostat turns on and the correction begins. The economy contracts.

The short-term deflationary feedback mechanisms in a gold-based monetary system prevent inflation from reaching extreme levels. But they do so at a cost. They increase the oscillations of the business cycle. By cutting inflationary booms short, gold-backed money reduces the duration of some upturns. The thermostat that turns the air conditioning on when the air temperature reaches 72 will have more oscillations than a system that only becomes effective at 110. Some critics of gold-based money treat the shorter duration of upturns as a defect. It could also be understood as a necessary and inevitable cost of ironing out extreme fluctuations of monetary instability.

During deflation, the thermostat works the other way. A nation with lower prices will experience an inflow of gold until costs rise to match conditions in countries where costs are higher. The movement toward balance is accelerated because as gold leaves nations with higher prices, their price levels are deflated. As a result, gold-based money imposes disciplines that require governments to keep their economies in balance.

Shocks to the System

It is also true that any shock to the world system, other things being equal, will increase the demand for gold. As we saw, it was the creation of unprecedented stability through the British Empire that helped make the use of paper money acceptable. A threat to stability, quite logically and naturally, changes the monetary preferences of many people who perceive it. Some will wish to hold more gold and less paper, just as they would have done if the world had never become more stable.

The effect of this shift of preferences caused by instability is exactly what occurs in reaction to an inflation excess. Paper is cashed in for gold, shrinking the money supply with contractionary consequences for the economy.

It makes little difference where in the world such shocks begin. If they are substantial enough to matter in terms of world trade, they are liable to be transmitted back to the central bank of the most powerful country. That bank is the ultimate guarantor of the gold price. If people outside its boundaries suddenly increase their demand to hold gold, for whatever reason, there is liable to be a gold drain or a contractionary increase in interest rates. Economist Allan Meltzer described the difficulties of maintaining a unilateral gold standard. His reasoning explains the burdens that tend to fall upon the predominant power in maintaining a stable money for the entire world:

> . . . [W]henever wars, revolutions, increases in inflation abroad, or other unanticipated events increase foreigners' demand for gold, the domestic stock of money falls and the home price level falls until the rise in the relative price of gold restores equilibrium in the gold market. The agreement to supply gold at a fixed price means that every unanticipated event that affects the gold market leaves its mark on real income and prices in the home country. The cost of providing the service is borne by the public in the home country.*

In this way, the strength of the dominant country is tapped in order to maintain stability worldwide. Clearly, this is a cost that even strong nations will rarely wish to bear. Its effect is like tapping a healthy body for a blood transfusion to help someone else overcome an illness. The donor may be willing to undergo such trials for the benefit of a relative or close friend. But too many transfusions would be deadly. And his willingness to endurê them would fall as his affiliation with the person at risk grew more remote.

So it is with a hegemonic power. A nation that is very rich and whose interests encompass a great part of the globe, will bear high costs for maintaining global monetary stability. But it will be unwilling to bear these costs, even if it could afford to do so, when its share of the world economy shrinks.

Rising Costs as Hegemony Declines

When a hegemonic power, like Great Britain in the nineteenth century or the U.S. after World War II, is at the peak of its power, instability will tend to be low. Wars, revolutions, and other shocks are likely to be less numerous. In an environment of calm, few people will fear

---

* * Allan H. Meltzer, "Monetary Reform in an Uncertain Environment," *Cato Journal* 3, no. 1, Spring 1983, p. 102.

holding the paper financial instruments of the predominant nation. Just as there is never a run on a bank everyone is convinced is sound, so only when a hegemonic nation's wealth and power begin to shrink does instability become an issue. This concentrates the greatest demands upon the gold resources of the nation issuing the world's reserve currency at the point where it is no longer in a position to meet them.

The result: collapse of the monetary system, followed by wide swings of inflation and deflation.

Inflation: a Symptom of Deeper Instability

In the two modern examples, first of British, then American hegemony, the role of gold in the monetary system was abandoned under duress of financial crises. In both cases, the abandonment of gold occurred after the dominant nation had begun to falter economically. Both episodes came during a war and led to monetary instability out of all proportion to the immediate past.

Britain was obliged to drop the gold standard during World War I. The costs of the fighting became so extravagant almost immediately that they could not be met under the discipline of the gold standard. The choice was stark. Stop the war, or abandon gold. The British suspended gold, formally abandoning the gold standard by legislation in 1919.

The U.S. was forced off the gold reserve system under similar circumstances during Vietnam. The U.S. stock of gold, over 620 million ounces in 1945, had fallen to less than 290 million ounces by the late sixties. Under pressures from Europe, Lyndon Johnson de-escalated the war and balanced his last budget to avert a run on gold. Nixon, however, reverted to loose fiscal policy. By 1971, the pressures on American gold stocks were once again critical. With an eye to his re-election campaign, President Nixon rejected a contraction of the U.S. economy that would have restored balance and preserved the international monetary system. On August 15, 1971, the United States abandoned gold.

Parallels with the Past

We believe that it is not a coincidence that one of the greatest depressions in history followed close on the heels of the British abandonment of gold. Nor would we be surprised if a similar episode overtook the world today. Megapolitical conditions are evolving in ways that threaten prosperity. The abandonment of gold and hence monetary instability are not isolated events. They are episodes in a pattern of deeper instability.

If our view is correct, it is a mistake to look solely at monetary aggregates to search for evidence of a coming deflation. Its causes are more complicated. There is no better evidence of this than the behavior of the U.S. money supply in the period preceding the Great Depression. If deflation were merely a follow-on consequence of a declining money stock, there never would have been a depression in the 1930s. The money supply was not contracted by the banking authorities. It collapsed due to banking failures and other shocks to the system that began while the money supply had changed very little and well within the ordinary range.

Megapolitical Crisis Preceded Money Contraction

There was little evidence of monetary deflation before the stock market crash of 1929. If anything, observers of the time were afraid that the growth of money and credit was too rapid. Economic commentaries from 1928 and 1929 are replete with warnings of "another credit-splurging spree."* There was very little worry or complaint that the money supply was growing too slowly. Between January 1928 and the third quarter of 1929, a broad measure of the money supply, M2, grew at a 0.6 percent annual rate. This was slower money growth than the 5.2 percent from the last quarter of 1926 through the end of 1927. But it had been slowed precisely to deter what New York Federal Reserve Bank governor Benjamin Strong described as "the ever-present menace of stock exchange speculation."† In any event, such a slowing of money growth was unexceptional. As two leading economists put it, "Even greater decelerations of monetary growth had happened before without causing a drastic drop in nominal income. For instance, while the growth of M2 slowed from an annual rate of 8.8 percent in the seven quarters preceding 1925:4 to a 0.5 rate in the next four quarters, the subsequent decline in nominal income between peak and trough in the 1927 recession was only 2.8 percent."‡ In other words, if a 4.6 percent-

---

* *Analyst,* August 2, 1929, pp. 203–5.
† Davis, World Between the Wars, 165.
‡ Robert J. Gordon and James A. Wilcox,"Monetary Interpretations of the Great Depression: An Evaluation and Critique," *The Great Depression Revisited* (Boston: Kluwer Nijhoff Publishing, 1981), 66.

age point deceleration of money growth touched off worldwide depression in 1929, why did not an 8.3 percentage point deceleration touch off a bigger depression in 1926?

The answer: Money aggregates are not the only important factor in the behavior of the economy. As Nobel Prize–winning economist F. A. Hayek has written, it is a mistake to attempt to "establish *direct* causal connections between the *total* quantity of money, the *general level* of all prices, and perhaps, also, the total amount of production." * You will find better clues to the origin of the depression by analyzing the way that the whole world system—and not merely the monetary system—floundered after the collapse of British hegemony during World War I. Ultimately, monetary instability has some of the same megapolitical causes as other manifestations of disorder. They are frighteningly similar to developments today.

We have isolated a few of these characteristics. Our list is not comprehensive. Other factors may have played an important role in this sequence. Bear in mind that we are oversimplifying; giving you clues to solve a mystery, not pronouncing a final finding of fact. There are too many facts to support only one interpretation. It is a matter of weighing the relative importance of a number of different influences to see how behavior was altered in ways that led to a depression. In that light, we focus on the following:

1. A political shock that raised prices in real terms, making the world poorer
2. Monetary inflation that pushed real assets prices to a premium
3. Borrowing to create surpluses
4. Deteriorating conditions lead to a retreat of capital
5. Lack of a nation strong enough to coordinate policy and serve as a lender of last resort
6. The destruction of free trade

The combination of these factors led to an economic disaster. It comprised the longterm feedback mechanism that swung the pendulum back from inflation to deflation.

Political Shock

The first stage of this disaster was World War I. We have already discussed our view that the war erupted when it did because of Britain's

* F. A. Hayek, *Prices and Production* (London: George Routledge, 1931), 4.

weakened position. Fighting began within a few months of the moment when German economic output surpassed British output for the first time. This may have been a coincidence. But we see more ominous factors at work in the timing of the war. It reflected the end of British predominance. This predominance had been so overwhelming as to preclude a "Great War" in the century following the decisive British triumph over France in 1815.

When war was unleashed again it was a political shock. An earthquake of power. It made the world poorer, raising prices in real terms. This was true for obvious reasons. Resources that might otherwise have been devoted to producing consumer goods were converted to destructive purposes. Billions went up in smoke. Millions of able-bodied men who had been working in factories, mines, and on farms were sent to the front instead. This inevitably resulted in a fall in output. There were fewer hands to do the work. Furthermore, much output was physically destroyed in the fighting. Farmers could not plant or harvest in fields where battles were raging. Great stretches of prime farmland were taken out of production, especially in eastern and Central Europe, as fighting swept over thousands of square miles. Even output that was unscathed by battle often went to waste because its owners had no way of sending it to market. Roads were torn up. Railways were mined. Bridges were knocked out. Locomotives were disabled by the fighting or commandeered to carry troops and ammunition. At sea, powerful navies made it their business to halt the trade of their enemies. Cargoes of foods, machinery, and raw materials were regularly diverted to the bottom of the ocean.

Taken together, these developments made the world poorer. Prices rose in real terms. Many commodities, especially farm products, fell into short supply. In effect, decades of technological progress in increasing output and efficiently transporting goods to market had been reversed in a few months. Even if there had been no change at all in the money supply, the shock represented by higher prices for many commodities due to the war would have served as a powerful lure to increase output. People in areas that had imported goods, suddenly cut off from access to their former supplies, had no choice but to produce substitutes. In most cases, these infant producers added long-term increases in capacity. In areas where the fighting was not under way, in North and South America and even Africa, higher commodity prices led to large increases in capacity. Farmers, for example, added dramatically to acreage under cultivation, developing idle land and planting "fence post to fence post." Existing manufacturers also increased capacity, while new ones sprang into being to take advantage of higher prices for goods put into artificial shortage by the war.

These sharp increases in capacity would later figure significantly in depressing prices as recovery from the war proceeded.

Inflation Pushes Real Asset Prices to a Premium

The tendency to invest in real assets was amplified by worldwide inflation that followed abandonment of the gold standard. This inflation continued through the mid-1920s, with floating exchange rates and depreciating currencies similar to what the world experienced in the 1970s. As inflation reduced the value of financial assets, it made investments in real assets even more attractive. For the first time since 1870, agricultural land in Britain appeared to be a paying investment. Land prices stabilized, capitalizing an expectation of further inflation to come. Oil, mines, and metal resources also shot up in value, encouraging further capacity-expanding investments everywhere.

Borrowing to Build Surpluses

Meanwhile, inflation reduced the real costs of borrowing, conveying windfalls to those already in debt. This naturally increased the attractiveness of going further into debt. So new debt proliferated throughout the world, compounding already large reparations and war debt. Higher interest rates, reflecting increased borrowing demand and the lower expected future value of money, raised the carrying costs of every investment. This had important consequences. It meant that continuing price increases or wider than ordinary operating profits were necessary to service debt.

High interest rates themselves served to discourage this. And so did the use to which much of the borrowing was devoted. In rich and poor countries alike, funds realized by borrowing were invested to increase or rebuild capacity. In other words, there was borrowing to build surpluses. Much international lending went to build capacity in fields that were competitive with America, not complementary as earlier British investment at the periphery had tended to be.

Increases in production, helped along by lower tax rates in the United States, resulted in a flood of products such as automobiles and home appliances. One analyst writing in July 1928, described the automobile industry in America as "vastly overequipped."* Similar surpluses de-

* Davis, *World Between the Wars,* 170.

veloped in housing, where construction in the midtwenties "reached by far its highest level of the twentieth century" relative to the GNP.* These surpluses were built upon credit. Construction bonds financed building of all kinds. Sales were kept churning beyond previous limits by innovations in debt finance, such as installment purchases and new home mortgages.

International cartels, 1920s versions of OPEC, were established to keep the prices of commodities high. Like OPEC, they could succeed only temporarily. Indeed, the more they raised prices, the greater the stimulus they gave to increased production. Higher prices also reduced ultimate demand by stimulating conservation (as with the emergence of the rubber reclamation industry).

Domestic and international surpluses piled up: oil, tin, rubber, copper, steel, autos, cement, leather, housing, commercial real estate, and more. Farm products were groaning in the bins by the midtwenties, when the recovery of European agriculture was complete. By 1925, the Harvard Economic Service noted "the existence of a considerable excess of capacity in many branches of industry, especially those producing basic materials or staple commodities intended for sale to ultimate consumers."†

Eventually, the limits to credit expansion had to be reached. Debt could not compound faster than income indefinitely. Misled by higher prices generated by the megapolitical shocks and inflation, people had gone deeply into debt to finance the production of growing surpluses, especially of raw materials and farm products.

A Boom in Financial Assets

The depression of commodity prices, in turn, contributed to a boom in financial assets. Stocks and bonds went up in value in the late 1920s only partly because of "speculative fever." The bigger reason was that compensatory mechanisms correcting excesses in the real economy made other avenues of investment unappealing. Nonfinancial debt as a percentage of GNP skyrocketed. As debt rose, more and more liquidity was absorbed to service it. This made the "velocity" of money decline, reducing the stimulative effect of each new dollar created by the government and reducing inflation at the same time. Since money growth was not resulting in price inflation, it was more or less inevitable that

---

* Gordon and Wilcox, "Monetary Interpretation," 78.
† Davis, *World Between the Wars*, 164–65.

financial assets should rise in value. This movement fed on itself by making other investment alternatives seem all the less attractive. No one wished to be left out of a major bull market, especially if it appeared to be the only way to make money.

The Retreat of Capital

The major stock market boom on Wall Street coincided with a virtual suspension of new international lending and retreat of capital. New money from America stopped going to Germany, Latin America, or central Europe in June 1928. All the hot money went to Wall Street instead. And much foreign money, especially English money, was also attracted by the prospect of high returns—as compared to bleak prospects elsewhere.

In sharp contrast to the prewar pattern, in which British investment had surged into remote areas of the world, under cover of effective, low-cost military power, postwar investment was defensive. This reflected the dramatic shift in megapolitical conditions we have already explained. To an investor of the time, the world looked very unstable. And appearances were not deceiving.

Evidence of disorder was abundant. Mussolini had marched on Rome in late 1922. A similar stunt organized by Hitler had failed in Germany, but without giving any assurance of stability in the future. For the first time in living memory, international investments had been confiscated. Revolutions in Russia and Mexico had not only seized individual investments, they had overturned property rights, denying the long-standing rules of international law. Both governments refused to make "full, immediate compensation." The threat that this example would extend elsewhere was too obvious to be ignored. There had been attempts at Communist revolution in Germany, Hungary, and other European countries. For a time, revolution even seemed to threaten England. The commander of the British forces, Field Marshal Sir Henry Wilson, felt obliged to withdraw troops from abroad to stand guard against "the event of Soviet government at Liverpool."* Nothing of the sort materialized in Britain itself, but elsewhere the empire was seething with rebellion. Fighting broke out in Ireland, India, Egypt, Burma, Mesopotamia, and Somaliland. These uprisings shattered the idea that investment within the empire was secure.

As we have seen, these developments were rooted in megapolitics.

* Jeffery, *British Army and Crisis of Empire,* 27.

The deterioration of conditions for investment elsewhere in the world helped concentrate speculation in American financial assets. This helped assure that the imbalance between strong and weak countries would not be corrected by movements of capital, as had been the case under the prewar gold standard.

No Lender of Last Resort

The collapse of British hegemony left no nation strong enough to coordinate policy and serve as a banker to the world. Prior to 1914, British international investment had been countercyclical. It picked up when the domestic British economy was in recession. It leveled off when domestic opportunities were more attractive. Such were the balancing effects of favorable megapolitical conditions. This all changed with World War I. After years of fluctuating exchange rates and wild inflation, Great Britain tried to restore monetary order by returning the gold standard in 1925. This failed, partly for reasons we have already suggested. Britain was no longer wealthy enough to bear the deflating consequences of operating a unilateral gold standard in an unstable world.

This failure was compounded by an unwise decision to peg gold to the pound at the prewar level of $4.86. This overvalued the pound. To compensate for all the inflation in the intervening decade would have required deflating the domestic price level by about 20 percent. British institutions were too fragile to absorb this shock. When workers in the coal industry, a major exporter, were asked to take a pay cut, the result was a traumatic general strike. In the event, it proved impossible to reduce costs enough to restore the competitiveness of British exports and discourage an outflow of capital to the United States.

With Britain unable to provide effective monetary leadership, the United States was the only candidate to fill the gap. It did not. The United States, now a major creditor, resisted British efforts to forgive all war debts. The Congress maintained high tariffs throughout the twenties while the United States was a creditor nation. This made it difficult or impossible for debtor countries to earn the dollars needed to meet their obligations. These difficulties were temporarily disguised from 1924 through 1928 by U.S. lending abroad, sparked by the Dawes loan to help Germany meet its war reparations. But when the stock market boom began and broker loan rates rose in New York, foreign lending stopped dead in its tracks. This brought nearer the day of reckoning by ensuring a liquidity crisis of foreign debtors. The alternative would have been to continue lending, thus "borrowing time" but "digging the hole deeper." Sir George Paish analyzed the situation in 1927:

America's present prosperity is built upon her capacity to sell unprecedented quantities of her products to foreign nations, and a collapse of foreign buying power would be felt from one end of the United States to the other. The great edifice of banking . . . credit will be in jeopardy. . . . So long as America is prepared to grant credit, so long can she can continue to sell, but the more credit she grants the greater will be the subsequent contraction.*

The drying up of lending produced a liquidity crisis that spread through the world trading system. This precipitated the withdrawal of English money from New York brokers' loans that figured in the dramatic drop in the stock market in the fall of 1929. The collapse in liquidity was translated into even lower commodity prices. Then, as now, inventories of unsold products were at high levels in many countries. Those especially affected were sugar, coffee, wheat, rice, cotton, silk, wool, leather, rubber, tea, tin, and copper.† As economist Charles Kindleberger wrote, "Buyers needed financing; when they could not get it they were unable to buy, or bought only at lower prices. Coffee fell from an average of 22½¢ a pound in September 1929 to 15½¢ in December; rubber from 20.10¢ per pound to 16.06¢, tin from 45.38¢ per pound to 39.79¢."‡ All this happened while money aggregates remained practically unchanged. The situation was aggravated further when the 1929–30 growing season produced bumper crops of renewable commodities, preventing price recoveries and contributing further to the collapse of commodity cartels.

Later, when these difficulties translated into the banking system, there was no lender of last resort to effectively bail out bankrupt debtors across borders. When Creditanstalt failed in Austria, the Bank of England stepped in with emergency help. But it was too little, too late to keep the international liquidity crisis from growing to a crisis of insolvency.

* Davis, *World Between the Wars,* 177.
† Ibid, 236.
‡ Charles P. Kindleberger, *Keynesianism Vs. Monetarism* (London: George Allen and Unwin, 1985), 269.

The Destruction of Free Trade

The breakdown of commodity prices because of oversupply and liquidity difficulties in 1929 was greatly amplified by U.S. moves toward protectionism. The prevailing U.S. policy at the time was a long step away from the ideal of free trade even before Smoot-Hawley. Average tariffs on goods entering America were at or above the high 1913 level, thanks to the Fordney-McCumber Tariff Act of 1922. In spite of these high tariff barriers, however, domestic producers were suffering. Competitors around the world continued to market more goods than could be sold at a profit at prevailing prices. As the twenties wore on and protectionist pressures became more acute, they led to political efforts in Congress to shore up beleaguered local interests. The Smoot-Hawley Tariff Act became like a Christmas tree ornamented with provisions designed to protect and enrich practically every industry that was strong enough to be noticed. The effective rate of duty on imports was increased by almost 50 percent.

Black Tuesday, October 24, 1929, the day the stock market collapsed, was also the day Herbert Hoover indicated that he would sign Smoot-Hawley. We doubt that this was a coincidence. Anyone who sold on news that this tariff bill would become law correctly anticipated its effect.

Be alert to similar bad news today. Passage of new protectionist legislation could mean the downfall of the stock market, widespread debt default, and a business contraction of the sort that has not been seen since the 1930s. Watch for it.

The many protectionist provisions of Smoot-Hawley were like mosquitoes spreading malaria. Once the liquidity bug had bitten, they assured that it would quickly spread everywhere. The United States at the time used 40 percent of the world's primary goods output. Curtailment of U.S. buying abroad was a blow to weak foreign economies. Responding to the credit and trade freeze, foreign commodity producers, including even the Soviet Union, began dumping items from coal to timber. They also retaliated by imposing barriers to imports from the United States. This reduced foreign buying of all U.S. goods, especially farm products. As Allan Meltzer has pointed out, U.S. exports of food fell by 66 percent between 1929 and 1933.[*] Customers who could not

---

[*] Allan H. Meltzer, "Monetary and Other Explanations of the Start of the Great Depression," *Journal of Monetary Economics* 2, 1976, p. 460.

sell could not buy. As the process of contraction fed on itself, the world economy wound down, with trade flows falling from year to year. Ironically, producer groups that had pushed for tariffs, especially farmers, found their incomes much diminished.

The Money Supply Contracts

As heavily indebted producers came to the end of the line, a process being repeated today, small farm banks started to fail in the U.S. By October 1930, a banking crisis was under way. Banks coming under question were obliged to dump securities to build cash. This impaired the value of securities they held, as well as those held by other banks. As Friedman and Schwartz put it in *A Monetary History of the United States:*

> Banks had to dump their assets on the market which inevitably forced a decline in the market value of those assets and hence of the remaining assets they held. The impairment in the market value of assets held by banks was the most important source of impairment of capital leading to bank suspensions, rather than the default of specific loans or of specific bond issues.*

As one bank after another failed, the money supply imploded, producing at long remove the deflationary feedback that was so quickly and less painfully generated by operations of the gold standard in the heyday of British hegemony.

The mechanism of monetary deflation worked in at least three ways. None was related to an overt decision by monetary authorities to "cut the money supply." Firstly, deposits vanished when banks failed, turning the leverage of fractional reserve banking inside out. Secondly, banking uncertainties increased the demand to hold currency. Money held outside the banking system could not contribute to credit expansion. Hence every dollar withdrawn from a bank contributed to monetary contraction. Thirdly, all the commotion reduced the demand for loans. The credit system could not expand the money supply if no one wished to borrow.

This last effect is worth looking at more closely. It occurred for a

---

* M. Friedman and A. J. Schwartz, *A Monetary History of the United States, 1867–1960* (Princeton, New Jersey: Princeton University Press for National Bureau of Economic Research, 1963), 355.

number of reasons. Among them: Falling prices encouraged rational buyers to postpone purchases. Why buy now when the price will be lower next week? And lower still next month? Further, deflation raised real interest rates sharply. This made most investments in productive capacity losing propositions. They could not match the real returns on government securities. It also meant that borrowing to purchase durable goods, like automobiles and housing, was far more costly than usual. Allan Meltzer put it succinctly, "With real returns to short-term government securities between 6 percent and 13 percent in 1930–32, the gain from postponing purchases, and lending or purchasing securities instead of borrowing to purchase durables, was high by any historical standard."* Consequently, borrowing dried up.

The prime rate and other nominal interest rates fell as the money supply contracted, producing the peculiar circumstance of deflation at a time when the Federal Reserve Board, by the account of its chief economist, had "embarked on a policy of easy money which it pursued through the depression."†

More could be said about the course of deflation and depression in the 1930s. We touch on these issues in other chapters. But it should be clear that the contraction began and fed on itself without an overt reduction in the money supply. Only later did the money supply implode as debtors in a disordered world proved unable to meet their obligations. This was all part of a slow-motion response to the monetary excesses and instability beginning in 1914. Inflation led to deflation, in a much more painful and roundabout way than the short, brief contractions involved in a true gold standard. Such a standard did not operate in the 1920s because Britain no longer had the wealth to maintain it. And the United States, the only nation that might have had the capacity to make it work, failed to take up the slack. Perhaps America, large as it was, remained insufficiently predominant to form economic policies with the aim of promoting general world stability and progress rather than local parochial interests, such as those that triumphed with the passage of Smoot-Hawley. In any event, there are clear lessons for today.

---

* Gordon and Wilcox, "Monetarist Interpretations," 157.
† Quoted in George D. Green, "The Ideological Origins of the Revolution in American Financial Policies," in Karl Brunner, ed., *The Great Depression Revisited*, p. 230).

OMINOUS PARALLELS

If you have been reading imaginatively, you have already noticed many parallels between the onset of deflation in 1929 and developments today. Indeed, we spelled out a short list in the first chapter. Having developed our argument more fully, we can now add to it in interesting ways.

1. Both periods begin with the twilight of an imperial power challenged in war.
2. Experiencing sharp declines in their portions of world wealth, both countries are forced to abandon gold.
3. In both cases, monetary inflation pushes real assets prices to a premium.
4. The onset of inflation, in both cases, is compounded by a political shock that raises prices in real terms, making the world poorer.
5. Both shocks, World War I and the OPEC price increase, are far-reaching enough to require a decade or more of economic adjustment. (Of the two, World War I was by far the greater shock. But the importance of the oil shock in raising costs in a more complex world economy was also great.)
6. Money growth is reduced to more modest rates.
7. In both cases, the real shock generates capacity-building investments, especially in primary product production.
8. In both periods, there is a major increase in debt internationally as well as in the dominant country.
9. Widespread disorder challenges the predominant power, undermining the security of investment. This leads to a retreat of private capital from many areas of the world. In the 1980s, this withdrawal of investment into the United States has become, as it was in the 1920s, a major factor straining world flows.
10. In the late teens and twenties and again in the seventies and eighties, wide currency fluctuations confuse the terms of trade.
11. In both the twenties and eighties, tax incentives encourage increases in capacity.
12. About a decade after the initial shock, commodity prices weaken.
13. The farm sector collapses, but both in the midtwenties and again in the mideighties, the damage seems to be contained.
14. Mining in both periods goes into depression.

15. The velocity of money declines as debt expands dramatically as percentage of nominal GNP.

16. Long-term interest rates unexpectedly fall—leading to a deterioration of bank balance sheets as the stronger borrowers turn directly to bond markets to raise cash, leaving banks with the weaker customers.

17. Long rates fall even lower than the discount rate. This inverted yield curve happens first in 1927, thirteen years after the initial shock. The pattern is repeated briefly in 1986, also thirteen years after the shock.

18. Oil prices decline sharply in both periods.

19. Net foreign lending is sharply curtailed. In the 1980s, this cutoff has not been as stark as the abrupt halt in June 1928.

20. The fluctuations of currency exchange bring the dollar to high levels, with calls from Europe to "dissociate world credit and world prices from the deflationary influences" of the strong U.S. currency.

21. In both periods, a mounting trade deficit presses U.S. manufacturers.

22. Protectionist sentiment grows.

23. There is a rapid buildup of illiquid and overvalued loans on the balance sheets of banks, with farm and real estate problems figuring prominently. (In the 1980s, banks are additionally burdened by foreign loans to weak governments and unprecedented off-balance sheet liabilities,* such as credit guarantees, futures commitments and standby letters of credit.)

24. Commodity cartels collapse.

25. A soaring stock market encourages optimism, in spite of unexpectedly weak business performance.

26. Financial scandals occur in both periods, as the increased returns on financial assets encourage widespread speculation.

27. Highly leveraged buying of shares on margin (the twenties) or futures (the eighties) creates conditions for tumultuous market swings.

The parallels between the situation today and the period preceding the last depression grow more haunting as events unfold. The banking

---

* "Off-balance sheet liabilities" are obligations of banks, which do not appear on balance sheets under current accounting rules primarily because they are contingent. A credit guarantee, for example, is not recognized on the balance sheet until it is triggered and the commitment is paid.

system is creaky. Consumer debt is skyrocketing while income stagnates. Commodity prices remain weak. Farmers are broke. Real estate is overbuilt. Impoverished countries, overwhelmed by a trillion-dollar debt, are making angry noises. Here, there, and everywhere, it is getting harder and harder for people to live beyond their means. And to top it off, we have seen an uncharacteristic and ominous flattening of the yield curve because of a collapse of long rates.

A flattened yield curve is an omen of bad economic news. When the yield curve flattens it is usually because short rates have risen. Recession is the usual result. Only one other time has the yield curve flattened because of collapse in long-term rates. That was in 1927. The result was depression.

CAN DEFLATION BE AVOIDED?

Of course, none of this means that a depression will happen. For all the overlaps and parallels between circumstances in the late 1980s and those in the late 1920s, there are many differences. Some of these may be telling. For example, the fact that exchange rates are relatively freer today may tilt the system toward an inflationary blowout rather than a deflationary implosion. Another major difference today is that government spending constitutes a larger percentage of economies than it did in the 1930s. Government spending is seldom cut, however dire the financial straits of the moment. In the Keynesian view, this provides a certain crutch to help keep the economy limping along. Perhaps that crutch can be used to trip up a deflation in the making. Government employees, welfare dependents, and the better-connected paving contractors will still get their checks. They will still spend at the local grocer. And the grocer will occasionally take his children out to see *Friday the Thirteenth, Part IX* at the local cinema. This will not mean galloping prosperity, but it could mean something—probably that the system is more biased toward runaway inflation than deflation as a way of liquidating debt.

Or, if you choose, you could look at matters just the other way around and come to the same conclusion. The sharp growth of government spending may turn out to be a depressing rather than stimulating factor, but in a way that biases the system toward monetary inflation. Budget deficits in the United States and many other countries are now so large that they may effectively preclude moves to expand demand through more spending or tax cuts. Relative fiscal restraint may be required by the sheer magnitude of deficits. In effect, there is no reserve capacity. Governments are broke, more broke than they ever were in the thirties. Those who expect inflation are right to point out that all that stands between governments and the abyss is the printing press.

Those who argue against the likelihood of deflation sometimes have good arguments. They may prove to be right. We know that today's circumstances are not identical to those in the thirties. Furthermore, even if the historical circumstances were identical, and they are far from that, the outcome could be different—in the same way that sports teams pitted together have different scores from one game to the next. Much depends upon factors that cannot be predicted: personal performance, leadership, luck, and even the weather. Perhaps the authorities have indeed learned enough to counter or avoid the contractionary feedback mechanisms set in motion by inflation and instability. Perhaps the Federal Reserve can prevent the fall of income anywhere from turning a liquidity difficulty into debt default and insolvency that shrinks the money supply.

That said, it is too simple to imagine that just because government can print unlimited amounts of money that there are no limits to inflation. Or that deflation is impossible.

BAILING OUT A BANKRUPT WORLD?

It is commonly assumed the Federal Reserve System would never allow illiquidity of a major debtor to become an insolvency crisis and contract the money supply. Complacency on that score is stunning considering that in other respects the danger of rapid deflation is more acute than it was in 1929. Why? Look no further than the geometric growth of the $700 billion interbank lending market. Each day U.S. banks are involved in interlocking transactions that total as much as $700 billion. This is the banking equivalent of having hundreds of trapeze artists swinging through the air—to what everyone hopes will be a safe landing. If even one bank failed to make good its commitments, the whole criss-crossing show could come tumbling to the ground. This means that a liquidity crisis and a loss of confidence could contract credit almost instantly—on a far wider scale than in the past.

All the big banks depend upon large, uninsured deposits, many on an overnight basis, to fund a major portion of loans they have already made. Before its collapse Continental Illinois was raising $8 billion in overnight money each day. When rumors spread about nonperforming loans, confidence was lost. A significant portion of the bank's deposits vanished within a few days. The crisis was contained at great cost and never spread into the interbank payments system. Worse things could yet happen. Much worse. A loss of confidence in a major money center bank, or a default in the interbank market—perhaps from a foreign bank —could bring the whole Big Top down in a heap. The result: instant deflation. The banking crisis that took months or years to develop in the last depression literally could happen overnight.

OFF-BALANCE SHEET LIABILITIES

Another trip point for a banking crisis is found in the massive buildup of off-balance sheet liabilities among the big banks. What are off-balance sheet liabilities? They are contingent liabilities of banks that do not appear in their ordinary accounting of assets and liabilities. These include unused loan commitments, standby letters of credit, swaps, and futures commitments. All are potential claims upon the banks that have not yet been triggered. As of 1986, the top seven U.S. banks, Citicorp, BankAmerica, Chase Manhattan, J. P. Morgan, Bankers Trust, Chemical Bank, and Manufacturers Hanover, had between them about *$1 trillion* of off-balance sheet liabilities. Citicorp alone had about $260 billion—a sum that exceeded the bank's total assets by $93 billion. BankAmerica's off-balance sheet liabilities came to $197 billion, including a staggering $49 billion in unused loan commitments.

In principle, at least, the customers of these banks could exercise their rights to draw upon them at any time. Many corporate borrowers, for example, have turned to the money markets to borrow directly, while retaining standby facilities with banks. So long as cash is flowing freely and interest rates are falling, the arrangement works. But what happens when, for whatever reason, the corporations are unable to obtain needed cash by selling bonds directly? Answer: The borrowers turn around and draw upon their backup facilities at the big banks. As banking expert Geoffrey Bell put it, "It follows that in the event of a major panic, banks could suddenly find themselves faced with a flood of demands for borrowings potentially leading to a liquidity crisis." *

* "Back to the Breadline with Electronic Speed," *(Euromoney,* Sept. 1986, Geoffrey Bell, p. 127).

IF A LIQUIDITY CRISIS HIT . . .

To avoid such an outcome, everyone assumes that the Fed would bail out any major bank threatened with failure, printing whatever money was necessary in the process. This promise appears to be ironclad. But think again. It is a promise about the beginning of a crisis, a promise that has deterrent effect. By assuring everyone that a bailout is inevitable, government policy has undoubtedly calmed fears that might have escalated into a banking crisis. If a crisis appeared on the doorstep tomorrow morning, bailout would be the first response of the authorities. No doubt about it. But that does not mean that bailout would be the response to successive crises or a chronic insolvency of major debtors.

Just because a government has the capacity to print unlimited bundles of cash does not mean that it can do so without cost. As it happens, significant inflation is very costly. There is a point where the costs of successive bailouts would exceed their benefits. Otherwise, the stark logical implication is that all the world's debts would eventually be payable by the Federal Reserve. Anyone in the interlocking web of debt who failed to pay anyone who owed enough money to shake the interbank lending market would have to be covered. His liabilities would become liabilities of the U.S. government. In effect, the Fed would be promising to pay every bad debt from Poznan to Patagonia—a promise that could only be redeemed by truly ruinous inflation. It seems unlikely that America in its twilight of power would shoulder such a burden. Let us look more closely and see why.

"SERIOUS" COUNTRIES CANNOT AFFORD SERIOUS INFLATION

The same practical considerations that checked the compounding of inflation in the 1970s militate against boundless inflation now to bail out truly insolvent debtors. The key elements in the compounding costs of inflation are interest and exchange rates.

The late President de Gaulle of France once dismissed Brazil as "not a serious country" because of its runaway inflation rate. Putting aside the haughtiness in de Gaulle's view, it rested upon a distinction of substance. Without exception, those countries that experienced runaway inflation in recent years were not those whose currencies are freely convertible internationally or figure in any important way in world finance. They were all countries with immature capital markets whose own trade is carried on and financed largely in dollars or other convertible currency.

It is not a coincidence that only internationally unimportant currencies have been destroyed by runaway inflation, not those that really matter. The reason is that there are more complete negative feedback effects in major industrial countries. As a result, the economic costs, and ultimately the political costs, of running more than a marginal inflation are ruinous. The French Socialists found this when they came to power in 1981. The value of the franc plummeted by 30 percent on foreign exchange markets. Since France is a major international economy that must *import* as well as export great quantities of commodities and services, French industry was hit hard by a major increase in the prices of its raw materials, especially oil. Interest rates, especially long-term rates, shot up. This shriveled the capital available for investment. The profit margins on French industry fell to a rate below the carrying costs of money. Profitability waned, unemployment skyrocketed.

Having seen a prospect of economic collapse, the Socialist government of President Mitterand opted for an about-face in policy. Brakes were slammed on money growth. Disinflation and austerity took the place of inflation. And the French economy actually performed better. It was not enough to save the Socialists from an electoral defeat, but they polled a far better result than their standing in public opinion surveys at the time of their inflationary policies would have indicated.

What was true of France has been true for every major international trading nation. Any country with a significant capital market would incur steep costs for running a protracted or ruinous inflation. That does not mean such inflation is impossible, but it does suggest a caution to the complacent view that runaway inflation is inevitable. As we have said, interest and exchange rates are key factors in the feedback mechanism. With hundreds of billions of dollars scatting across the globe at the speed of light each day, the economic and political consequences to any major industrial nation of indulging in protracted inflation are likely to be staggering. As inflation rises, the exchange value of currency tumbles. Inflation also kindles a jump in interest rates, especially long-term rates. High interest rates are a deflationary force, contracting the economy. As interest rates rise, the value of financial assets falls. A bond yielding 5 percent that is worth $100,000 without inflation is worth just $50,000 if inflationary expectations scare rates to 10 percent. So just a little bit of inflation can result in staggering losses in any society where there is a significant capital market that functions in relative freedom.

DAMAGE CONTAINMENT, NOT WILD REFLATION

It is unlikely that the Federal Reserve would undertake to push inflation to its logical limit in a crisis. To the contrary, it might be at pains to avoid the appearance that ruinous inflation was at hand. Such a posture would minimize damage to the domestic economy. If the central bank appeared bent on printing money and spreading it around like confetti, hundreds of billions of dollars would flee the country at the speed of light. Foreign holders of Treasury debt would dump it on the market to avoid large foreign exchange and capital losses. Interest rates would skyrocket. Investment would stop dead in its tracks. And so would much economic activity. In short, most of the grief that an inflationary bailout is meant to avoid would happen anyway.

That being so, it would be more rational for the Fed to attempt to contain any crisis, while stabilizing the money aggregates as well as possible. That is what the Fed attempted in the Great Depression. It undertook "an easy money policy." In the event, money was not easy enough to prevent deflation. The Fed today would probably be more aggressive. But it is a mistake to think that it is easy for the authorities to control the money supply. It would be more accurate to say that they can "manipulate" the supply of money. When much of the money is brought into being by borrowing they can depend upon the voracious government to do lots of that. But individuals and corporations may not wish to borrow as much as the central bank would predict.

The amount of "money" the banks create out of reserves can vary significantly, depending upon market conditions. During the early 1960s, the banks created only about $25 of "money" out of each new dollar of reserves the Fed pumped into the banking system. During the inflationary seventies, the amount of new "money" created skyrocketed, as banks employed innovative new instruments, like repurchase agreements and certificates of deposit, to create more liquidity from each dollar of reserves. By 1984, the growth of M3—a broad measure of the money supply—peaked relative to reserves. In that year, each dollar of reserves created $75 of M3. By 1986, each dollar of reserves was creating just $70 of "money." Why? As Ed Hyman at C. J. Lawrence has pointed out, disinflation began to make innovative vehicles riskier. Banks therefore drew back from creating more money out of the reserves created by the central bank.

In short, even in a fiat system, the cause and effect of market reaction alter the effective supply of "money." In a severe crisis, the flight to safety would be pronounced. Cash would flow out of banks and into Treasury obligations. Loan demand would tumble. If the real economy were winding down, it might be difficult to expand credit fast enough to maintain nominal demand—without risking more damage by touching off an inflationary scare. Remember, it is impossible to have a negative discount rate. The banks cannot pay customers to take money away. Yet unless they do, even the lowest nominal rates could be forbiddingly high in real terms. And the higher they are, the more the economy winds down.

Furthermore, there is an ominous arithmetic about the compounding of debt. As James Grant points out, debt has skyrocketed so much that the ratio of credit growth to increase in the Gross National Product jumped from 114 percent in 1981 to 335 percent in 1986. This means that $3.35 in debt accompanied every dollar in increased economic activity. If the interest rate averaged 8 percent, the related cost of money would be $0.33. Thirty-three percent of every dollar of added economic activity would go directly to paying off interest, without paying any principal.

Even if interest rates were to fall sharply in a crisis, the compounding of debt clearly has outer limits, limits that we had already begun to approach in 1986. Contrary to expectations, therefore, we could see a deflationary crisis sometime well before the crack of doom.

DEPRESSION MAY START IN JAPAN

It may even be that the next depression will begin not in the United States, but Japan. Sixty years ago, America was the world's largest economy but not a predominant power in organizing the world system. America was the power of the future, as Japan clearly is today. The Japanese stock market has sold at much higher multiples than the American for years. Today, observers talk of the "Japanese economic miracle" as they spoke of the "American economic miracle" in the 1920s. The rapid fall of oil prices, combined with the appreciation of the yen, had already brought deflation to Japan in 1986. It is not impossible that events in Japan may contribute importantly to the onset of depression. Watch for a collapse of the Japanese market or some other trauma that could send shock waves around the world.

Another potential trigger point for depression could be geological. An earthquake in Japan could be the most dangerous thing that could happen to the world economy. Unlike Britain and the United States during their heydays as capital exporters, Japan is exceedingly vulnerable to natural disaster. The rumblings that hit Tokyo in late November 1986 should serve as a reminder that another great Tokyo earthquake could strike at any moment. Tokyo was last hit by a major quake in 1923. A similar disturbance today would devastate the most valuable real estate developments in the world—posing a grave threat to economies everywhere, including the American economy. Why? Because insurance companies would be obliged to liquidate hundreds of billions of bonds and other assets in order to pay claims on a major Japanese disaster. This rush to liquidate assets would mean a major upsurge of interest rates in the U.S. and around the globe. It could be the trigger of a recession or even a depression. If you hear a news bulletin reporting a major Japanese earthquake, this will be one of the clearest signals possible of higher interest rates and an economic downturn. Go to the phone immediately and tell your broker to sell bonds and stocks.

EXPECTATIONS MATTER

We discuss other facets of the inflation/deflation controversy in other chapters. Before leaving the subject, however, we want to focus on an issue of major importance to you as an investor.

Some day, the instability that is both cause and consequence of disorder will lead to an economic crisis. No one can now say precisely what form this crisis will take. Nor how it will be set off. It could mean runaway inflation. It could mean deflation.

If inflation is the outcome, the prices of real assets would rise. Owning precious metals such as gold, silver, or platinum could prove to be a shrewd hedge. Many people think so. And that is why precious metal prices have remained high during the 1980s, even as registered inflation tumbled.

CONCEPTUAL LAGS

People simply did not believe that disinflation (or deflation) was for real. Similarly, massive inflation would convey windfalls to debtors. The trend line of debt rising faster than income suggests that many individuals and institutions are expecting their real debt burdens to be lightened by the depreciation of money. They could be right. But if they are wrong, they could be very wrong. Ironically, the persistence of this inflation-hedging behavior as inflation has declined actually increases the prospect of deflation.

The reason is that "an inflation watch" by many market participants makes any gesture toward reflation more dangerous. It raises interest rates and threatens to send the currency into a free fall. In a case where "easy money" was required to fend off deflation, a market reacting as if inflation had arrived would cancel much of the stimulus and reassert contractionary forces.

The irony is that inflation is only likely to recur when the debate between those expecting runaway inflation and those expecting deflation is finally won by the deflationists. Only then will inflationary expectations fall too far. The authorities will be able then to expand the money supply without touching off panic. So they will, and inflation will come roaring back.

Unfortunately, the expectation that inflation is soon to renew is not likely to shift except under the prodding of painful experience. Conceptual lags are involved. Even the smartest people have "limited information processing abilities." Consequently, we are all insensitive to changing abstract relationships in our environment.

That is why investors get fixed on a certain strategy, like holding gold to protect themselves from inflation, or buying farmland "because they are not making any more of it." And there they sit. The world changes. And they lose money with a strategy that no longer applies. It is as if someone were bundled in thick clothes to protect himself against a blizzard—and never took them off as the season changed. If he sweated long enough, of course, he might become comfortable again. But such behavior is far from shrewd.

AFTER THE NEXT CRISIS

If deflation does come, it will signify a failure on the part of authorities to reliquefy the international financial system—in part because of negative market reactions to evidence of new inflation. In that sense, deflation will highlight the inherent instability of fiat money in a disordered world. The unfavorable megapolitical conditions that brought the abandonment of gold and fluctuating currencies will take a higher toll.

If the crisis becomes deep enough, to the point where even accountants are having phantasmagoric visions, the governments of the world may be obliged to do something right. Perhaps under Japanese leadership, they may turn to gold for help in doing what they were unable to do themselves—control the value of money in a world run mad.

When currencies are unconnected to anything more stable than still other fiat currencies, it may be too difficult to reflate in ways that do not involve unacceptable economic costs. It is all but impossible to simultaneously devalue floating fiat currencies against commodities without raising interest rates to forbidding levels. And higher interest rates, as we have seen, paradoxically, are deflationary. They turn the very fear of inflation into a self-correcting recipe for still more deflation.

The British gold standard and the American gold reserve system of fixed exchange rates both had their drawbacks. However, they had one clear advantage. They provided an easy mechanism for increasing liquidity throughout the entire international monetary system—a devaluation against gold. Such devaluations could capitalize expectations of future inflation in a higher gold price rather than decapitalizing most other investments through higher real interest rates.

It is therefore our prediction that the long-run instability of money will eventually have to be corrected through a return to gold. Such a reform may be years away. It will probably happen only after a crisis. We think it is more likely that the return to gold will happen as a general act of governments attempting to solve a deflation than as a desperate measure to correct a hyperinflation. Either is possible. But if the economy should fall into the abyss of deflation, a remonetization of gold may prove to be the "politically practical" solution—in a way that gold did not seem politically practical during the inflation of the 1970s.

To put the matter another way, governments are more likely to turn to gold when gold promises to help the authorities do something they need to do rather than when gold promises to keep governments in check. In deflation, gold offers governments hope for lifting sagging economies. In inflation, gold promises contraction and pain, keeping runaway governments in check.

We may be wrong, but we feel that monetary instability is merely a reflection of a deeper megapolitical instability; that a crisis of inflation leads inevitably to deflationary crisis; and that these crises are unlikely to be set right until monetary stability is restored with gold. It may take many years before the crisis can be resolved. Perhaps it must await the emergence of full-blown Japanese hegemony, a resolution that may be delayed until after the turn of the century. Perhaps a more cooperative solution can be patched together earlier, possibly coordinated through the International Monetary Fund or the World Bank. At this point we can only guess.

If gold is remonetized at a high price to reliquefy a deflated world economy, it is almost a political certainty that many governments will institute a windfall profits tax on gold owners. They may go further and confiscate gold as the United States did during the Great Depression. Therefore, holding more than trivial amounts of gold as a hedge against deflation may be futile, unless you can afford to store it in a safe location, such as in Switzerland. The shrewd investor should take note and be prepared.

7

Cycles of Progress and Decline

*Cycles are not, like tonsils, separable things that might be
treated by themselves, but are, like the beat of the heart, of
the essence of the organism that displays them.*
                                            —Joseph Schumpeter

From the time of the Greeks, thoughtful people have brooded about the
cycles of human affairs, cycles with origins in the whimsy of the gods
or in the stars. Plato tells us in the *Politicus* of a cosmic cycle. His is
only one of many cyclical processions of rise and decline, death and
rebirth, that chart the ups and downs of human life. The authors of the
American Constitution believed that the destiny of nations was governed by long-term cycles of growth and decay. Their cycles had their
origins in the effects of material circumstance in altering character and
morals. They believed that good times tended to make people slack and
soft. The cycle they perceived moved from liberty to prosperity to
waste and corruption, and ultimately to despotism. Having sunk as low
as they could sink, under the boot of a tyrant, people would then gradually rediscover the virtues of freedom, and begin the cycle of rebirth.
As Enlightenment philosopher Adam Ferguson put it, "Where there are
no longer any profits to corrupt, or fears to deter, the charm of dominion is broken, and the naked slave, as awake from a dream, is aston-
ished to find he is free. . . . When human nature appears in the utmost
state of corruption, it has actually begun to reform."*

What goes down must come up. This is said easily, for usually it is
true. However long the intervals between the peak of prosperity and
the nadir of depression, each downfall has been the foundation of a new
deliverance. Even the long downhill slide during which the Roman

---

* Adam Ferguson, *An Essay on the History of Civil Society* (Dublin: Boulter Grier-
son, Printer to King, 1767), 414–15.

world sank into the Dark Ages was not a single collapse, but a series of collapses marked by intervals of renewal and recovery. We can expect no less today, even if our gloomiest fears come true. Wherever ingenuity is given half a chance, the vicissitudes of human affairs assure that dreams of a better life will become a reality for some, though not for all. The investor wise enough to realize the way the world works has a greater chance to profit from whatever cyclical events the years actually bring, from the short-term business cycle to the long-wave depression.

MEGAPOLITICAL CONDITIONS
AS THEY ARE—AND MAY BE

We have tried to isolate some of the hidden causes of current cycles. If you have read this far, you know that we have come to some unhappy conclusions about the role of raw power in the world and the way it alters the prospects for prosperity. We have demonstrated some interesting linkages of cause and effect, covering a wide range of areas, from investment security to trade policy to monetary stability. To the extent that our view is correct, much of the patterns of boom and bust in the nineteenth and twentieth centuries reflects the waxing and waning of the British Empire and its successor as the champion of a free-market economy, the United States.

By isolating the megapolitical factors that determine the current dynamics of power in the world, we have made a bit of sense out of madness. But we have not told the whole story. And we never will. There is a long succession of causes for the cycles of boom and bust, causes whose ultimate interconnections we can only guess.

In this chapter, we round off our analysis of the hidden lessons of megapolitics by looking more closely at technological change as it may affect economic performance, especially American economic performance. This is important not only because technology has direct economic impact upon the business cycle, but also because today's technological breakthrough will lay the foundation for tomorrow's megapolitical reality.

THE REACH OF TECHNOLOGY

The direct economic consequences of technology in creating patterns of boom and bust would be important even if the meanderings of power were stilled. They would be important, though in different ways, even if there were no national boundaries in the world. In their essence, these are sources of fluctuation that would not be resolved even if investment in all corners were magically safe, with complete monetary stability and a free and open market for goods. In other words, even if the fickleness of government and laws were ended, there would still be cycles, though undoubtedly far less dramatic and dangerous ones.

The factors that determine the way that power is used in the world are in large measure technological. By examining the technological innovation, you can see the broad outlines of megapolitical changes to come. We are now at a point where even murky forward vision could pay great dividends. The technological revolutions to come could be more far-reaching than those that swept the world in 1820 or again in the late nineteenth and early twentieth centuries. Anyone who had understood the technological underpinnings of power in those times and tried to apply that understanding in a systematic way might have learned much that would have ultimately been useful.

More Implications of Technology

In the following pages, we consider how technological innovation now under way may contribute to deflationary pressures. We analyze the meaning of the product cycle for your investments and assess the mixed prospects for an American economic renaissance. Extrapolating from past examples of technological change, we suggest how individual sectors of the economy may be destabilized by the transition to new ways of doing things.

The technological revolutions now under way may offer the ultimate incentive for you to focus your energies on becoming a skilled investor. Within your lifetime or that of your children, persons without sufficient means to protect and support themselves may become economically superfluous. Indeed, they could become even more useless than the slaves of ancient times, who at the darkest moments of bad luck could at least command the means to survive so long as hard labor was in demand. Someday, technology may antiquate even that security. With nothing to offer and no way of making a living, people without capital could be truly dispensable in a violent world.

In this chapter, we offer ideas about how to comprehend and survive what could be the most profound restructuring of life in all the ages of human existence.

Be warned that our treatment of technology's role in patterns of boom and bust passes rather too easily over many issues of controversy. We are not limiting ourselves to points we can prove to standards of academic acceptability. We are trying to develop a forward view of potentially world-historic economic upheaval. This chapter, therefore, is like a warning map for an earthquake. It may go too far in warning you away from points of danger. As events unfold, you can adjust your plans to fit the facts, forgiving our errors in the spirit in which they are written, as good-faith efforts of informed guesswork.

Product Cycles and Innovation

Many students of the business cycle have argued that innovation, especially technological innovation, plays a role in altering growth rates. Joseph Schumpeter, for example, argued that innovations tend to appear in clusters, facilitated by the work of entrepreneurs. He saw four phases of a cycle: prosperity, recession, depression, and recovery. The boom begins, according the Schumpeter, with the innovations of entrepreneurs. Demand from new businesses increases prices of the means of production, including labor. This has a negative impact upon old businesses. They find that their costs have risen, but their market shares decline because of competition from new enterprises. As consumer preferences shift to products incorporating the innovations, demand falls away from the old products. Prices fall. The boom is over.

As the immediate impact of the innovations is absorbed, markets become saturated. The innovating entrepreneurs repay their debts, but there are no comparably attractive investment opportunities, so credit demand begins to fall. The market consolidates the new businesses, as some of them falter. Depression sets in. According to Schumpeter, the depression stage is not only inevitable but useful and creative. It reestablishes the economy's equilibrium, by forcing adjustments and spreading new technical and management procedures. The groundwork laid during the depression encourages innovations that appear in the next stage of recovery.

A similar theory of boom and bust based upon innovation has been advanced by Gerhard Mensch, who distinguished between "inventions," the scientific breakthrough upon which products are based, and "innovations," the actual introduction of a new product or process into the economy. Mensch emphasizes the lengthy time lags that often separate the invention of a new product and its appearance as a basic innovation. For example, Mensch points out that fluorescent lighting was invented in 1852 but did not become economically significant until the upturn from the last Great Depression in the 1930s. At that time, it was brought into production as one in a cluster of innovations.

These theories are obviously richer and more complicated than described here. But even in their skeletal form, you can see that they partially account for the impact of technological innovation on the business cycle. They suggest a mechanism by which innovation helps revolutionize the economy. We believe that the investor can learn much of value by carrying this line of reasoning further. Among our conclusions:

1. Technological innovation is a major factor antiquating old investment as well as stimulating new waves of growth. (The more sweeping the innovation the more severe the dislocation.)

2. Technology defines natural resources. Although there has been a tendency for this definition to remain fairly stable over the last century, it may be less stable now that the economy is adopting innovations based upon recent scientific advances. As an investor, you can no longer stake your capital upon old conceptions of what natural resources and real assets are.

3. Many of the new-wave technologies appear to be deflationary in that they sharply reduce the use of primary products in the economy, as well as reduce the scale of enterprise.

4. New technologies will dramatically reduce the number of man-hours of human labor in many products and services, contributing to significant transitional unemployment.

5. The emergence of new technologies of smaller scale implies increasing scope for market forces, and wider income differentials, as well as problems of dislocation as large institutions are broken up.

6. The falling scale of enterprise implies less long-term investment, faster growth among private companies, and greater lending to government or generally lower interest rates.

7. The workings of the product cycle imply that any gains to an economy making significant innovations will be short-lived. This creates the need for continuing innovations. Over the long run, the predominant economy is hindered in its ability to innovate by the burdens of added cost it tends to bear for military expenditures and subsidization of others.

8. The U.S. government, pressed by economic stagnation, will intervene with policies to benefit specific sectors or industries. We spell

out policy paths that the United States may take and give you ideas about how different policies will alter the prospects for revival of America's waning economy.

9. If historic patterns are repeated, odds against American revival are high, but declining scale economies and aspects of the innovation peculiar to the Information Revolution may improve U.S. prospects.

10. Although improvements in productivity could yield large increases in living standards over time, income may be less equally distributed in the immediate future. Barring a major war or a catastrophic spread of AIDS, physical labor will tend to become less valuable. And so long as scale economies decline, they will reduce the capacity of unions to "exploit the capitalists."

11. Ultimately, molecular technology could transcend the business cycle, antiquating most of the existing industrial base, and opening an Aladdin's lamp of promising and fearful possibilities.

"Creative Destruction"

Like most things in life, technological innovation usually involves marginal adjustments rather than big leaps. The transition from this year's model of Toyota to the next probably won't take your breath away. It involves a change of decimal points in a long, evolutionary equation. It does not involve change with a factor of ten. The same can be said of most innovation. The next "new, improved" formula for Tide may, indeed, make for "whiter whites and brighter brights." But you may be unable to see the difference in a load washed with the new formula.

This is not always the case. Some innovations really are sweeping changes from the past, as the Khalifa of the Dervishes found when his followers were decimated by the new machine guns of the British Camel Corps. The transition from one product or process to another may involve radically new ways of doing things rather than merely marginal improvements on the old. The automobile was not a hardier breed of horse. It was something altogether new. The transition from the horse to the automobile was a revolution.

The more radical technological innovation is, and the more rapidly it occurs, the more likely that it will unleash Schumpeter's "gales of creative destruction." New products and processes can lead to striking shifts in buying patterns. They can alter demand between commodities, revise the value of investments, and make a general hash out of the expectations upon which credit and cash flow have been projected.

Given the leverage involved in the modern banking system, even small deviations in cash flow or asset value can make the difference between a mere liquidity squeeze and insolvency. When the real economy diverges too far from the notional economy of money and credit, this can make for a painful, deflationary transition, no matter how promising the long-term beneficial effects of an innovation may be.

For example, there is no doubt that the improvement in the speed and capacity of communication and transportation systems in the late nineteenth century contributed much to higher living standards. But it is equally clear that the short-run effects were deflationary. From 1870 to 1900 the cost of shipping bulk cargo on a steamship fell by 90 percent. Not only did costs plummet, the speed and dependability of shipping dramatically improved. For the first time, goods could be sent across the ocean on a timetable, no longer at the mercy of the wind and the wave. Simultaneously, a widening network of railroads was sharply reducing the cost of inland haulage. The fall in inland transportation costs was "on the order of twenty-to-one, principally between 1860 and 1880."*

This revolution in transportation costs made possible a striking increase in the volume of commodities of all kinds that could be economically shipped. The advent of the telegraph supplemented the improvements in transportation by making possible almost instantaneous transmission of information. Merchants and producers could tell where in the world they could get the highest prices for their goods. The result: a dramatic upsurge of competition worldwide. Cargoes that no one could have dreamed of shipping in 1860 suddenly spilled over the whole globe.

The advent of swift and cheap haulage overturned locational patterns in commerce everywhere. The advantages that high-cost producers had long enjoyed in nearby markets were wiped out—for all but a few perishable products. Low-cost producers drew on other productivity-enhancing innovations, such as the McCormick reaper, to flood markets with greater quantities of commodities from far-flung sources than ever before. The result: Prices tumbled across the globe. Producers who could not lower their costs, from farmers to textile producers to iron makers, suffered as prices fell. Many were driven out of business. Land values, especially in England, tumbled. Nominal wages fell on a broad front. There was massive unemployment in most European countries,

* Headrick, *The Tools of Empire,* 189.

a factor that contributed to the late nineteenth-century stampede of immigrants to the United States. Indeed, the word *unemployment* first came to people's lips during the 1880s as observers were pressed to explain the upsurge of persons looking unsuccessfully for work. Previously, the problem of unemployment was too minor to merit a term in the language.

So sweeping were the deflationary effects on wages and prices from the introduction of railroads that they often precipitated political unrest. To cite a late but dramatic example, the 1911 revolution that overturned the Chinese emperor began as an uprising of the carters and carriers guild in Szechuan Province. Violent rioting broke out in the spring of that year to protest plans for a railroad linking the province with the rest of China. As proposed by the imperial court, the project was to cut across mountain ranges that had long posed a hurdle to commerce. The ultimate benefits of such a rail link were indisputable. A nineteenth-century train advocate had calculated that even a slow train hauling 50 tons could do the work of 13,333 porters, a great improvement. However, to coolies whose only livelihood consisted of carrying loads on their backs, progress was a fearful thing. "Revolutionary technology" is not merely a figure of speech.

At least part of the explanation for the downturn in growth rates among Western economies beginning in 1873 and lasting into the late 1890s is paradoxically attributable to the dazzling improvements in productivity. These innovations involved fundamental rather than marginal changes. They obviously stimulated far more gains than losses. Indeed, they laid the foundations of major new industries that grew to maturity in the twentieth century. But the transformations really did involve "gales of creative destruction." They wiped away old businesses and subjected many others to intense competition that lowered profits. And, of course, this upsurge of competition is precisely what began to undermine the predominance of the British economy, leading to adverse political changes, such as protectionist measures to close the world trading system.

Competition and the Product Cycle

There is an obvious logical reason the decline of a predominant power is associated with falling profits and depression. It is a matter of competition. There is more of it when the once-supreme country has lost its overpowering lead in output. Economists tell us that profit rates fall as competition intensifies. In a steady state of equilibrium, profits would be zero. This seldom happens outside of textbooks because the real world is in flux. Lightning strikes. Tastes shift. Innovations in products and new means of doing things keep markets in a whirl of uncertainty. Nonetheless, there is a strong tendency for profits to fall as competition intensifies. Profits would sink to disagreeably low levels were it not for the development of new technologies and new industries that increase output and offer new products to consumers.

Over the centuries there have been a number of leading industries that dominated the economies of the richest countries, beginning with the textile industry in Great Britain. That industry, like those that followed it to predominance, evolved through what Raymond Vernon has termed "the product cycle." This is a cycle of four phases:

1. *Innovation and growth.* The new product is introduced into the home market, and its sales grow.

2. *The export phase.* Demand in the home market is saturated and producers begin to export to other markets. Export efforts tend to be focused first on countries where income and tastes are most similar to the domestic market. As demand in those countries is saturated, the export effort is redirected to countries with lower income and more dissimilar tastes.

3. *The spread of manufacturing.* Manufacturers begin to export not only their products but their production. Investment goes first to areas where the factors of production most resemble those in the home country. Thereafter, production is shifted to countries where the factors of production are less similar. As output moves abroad, production in the home country tapers off.

4. *Coals coming back to Newcastle.* Eventually, the product begins to be imported into the home country from more recent manufacturers. The process continues with the import of the product into the other countries where it was introduced early on. The new exporters capture an increasing share of the market. In response to surplus capacity, output in the original home market and among early competitors drops.*

* See Raymond Vernon, *Sovereignty at Bay: The Multinational Spread of U.S. Enterprises,* (New York: Basic Books, 1971); Robert Gilpin, *U.S. Power and the Multinational Corporation* (New York: Basic Books, 1975); and James A. Kurth, "The Political Consequences of the Product Cycle," *International Organization,* Winter 1979.

Not every industry has followed this pattern exactly. Nonetheless, it fairly describes the evolution of a number of important industries, from textiles through iron and steel to automobiles and consumer electronics. It probably even tells the story of the Cabbage Patch Doll, the difference being that the Cabbage Patch Doll is a cheap product, easy to make, and with a short life. The cycle for such a product may be a matter of months rather than decades. The cheaper the product and the less fixed capital required to produce it, the shorter the product cycle will tend to be.

In any event, the story of the product cycle is the story of competition doing its work. The economy that first mothers an industry is destined to see its advantage erode. By implication, the leading economy, with a broad overall edge in many industries, is destined to fall back relative to its competitors. If a free flow of goods and capital is maintained, investment will migrate to other countries, where costs will be lower and opportunities greater. This will lead to surplus capacity for the world as a whole. Since capacity in the pioneering country will tend to be costlier, output in that country will bear the brunt of adjustment. It will be pared back while low-cost producers remain in business. In time, the once-supreme economy will find itself importing significant quantities of goods it formerly exported.

The outline of the product cycle largely summarizes the history of America's smokestack industries. And no industry provides a clearer example than automobiles. During the 40 years from the end of World War II, U.S. auto production shrank from more than 75 percent of total world output to about 20 percent. By 1980, imports as a percentage of the U.S. market had exploded to more than 100 times their 1950 level.

This matters. Although by 1986 microelectronics had surpassed automobiles as the largest sector of the U.S. economy, U.S. economic growth still tracks auto sales more closely than any other industry.

WHAT NEXT FOR THE AMERICAN ECONOMY?

An important question for you as an investor is whether computers or some other innovative industry will fill the gap left by the demise of smokestack industries. Unless new innovations provide for a dramatic spurt of growth, past patterns suggest that the United States will sink further and further from economic supremacy. Can innovation, such as in high-technology industries, arrest this trend? The answer to this question is critical. It will not only help determine the performance of stock markets, it will also likely decide whether the world investment climate and trading system can be stabilized or whether conditions will continue to regress.

What Is the Evidence?

There are arguments on both sides. There is no doubt that the United States has been the world leader in computers since World War II. (The British had the lead but failed to follow through.) However, the U.S. advantage is unstable. Advances in computer technology in recent years have so sharply reduced costs that they have accelerated the workings of the product cycle. For most computer hardware, it is now reckoned to be about two-and-a-half years.

The cost trend for computers is just the opposite of an industry like motor vehicles. Start-up costs were trivial in that industry's early days, when companies sprouted in buggy and bicycle shops. As the assembly line took hold, however, and the automobile evolved, capital costs have steadily risen. They are still rising. From 1975 to 1980, fixed capital per vehicle for American manufacturers rose by about 65 percent. In contrast, the early computer companies were gigantic undertakings. Apple could not have been started in a garage much earlier than it was, or it would have had to be a garage large enough to house a fleet of trucks. Early computers were that big. And they were also expensive. A principal reason the British did not exploit the mechanical computer designed by Charles Babbage was its dazzling cost. When the U.S. government built military computers during World War II, it was one of the few customers in the world rich enough to afford them. But as everyone knows, the costs of computers have collapsed. Systems with a computational capacity that would have cost millions a few years ago can now be had for less than a thousand dollars.

This cost trend militates against the ability of the U.S. to sustain a long-term lead as a maker of computer hardware. Indeed, as the proliferation of IBM clones suggests, certain types of computers may soon trade as commodities. As in the case with most other commodities, high-cost American producers will be at a disadvantage. Therefore, it is reasonable to expect that the falling scale of production costs will accelerate the product cycle in computers. When it is cheaper to compete, more people do it. And more competition will drive down prices and profits more quickly. In other words, American firms will have to innovate faster and faster to stay in the same place. And even that place is unsustainable.

Where the U.S. Stands Today

The case for optimism about future American economic competitiveness cannot be based upon a simple projection from trade figures during the first half of the 1980s. Historically, there has been a strong correlation between rapid growth of a new industry and strong growth of exports. U.S. exports are strong in some areas of high technology. But strength in those areas falls short of making up for declines in areas where the bulk of trade takes place. The U.S. has lost its competitive advantage in most areas of manufacturing and the output of commodities. In 1986, even American farm imports exceeded the value of exports. Many manufacturers, farmers, and other raw material producers have been clamoring for protection because they are no longer able to compete successfully in world markets. Dollar devaluation and growing nontariff barriers have done little to improve their position.

A good gauge of the decline of the U.S. trading position has been the trend in the U.S. trade balance compared to that of Japan. While Japanese competitiveness has improved, U.S. exports have been running at about half the level of imports. Notwithstanding the many negotiations and agreements meant to reduce America's trade deficit with the rest of the world, the United States has continued to lag. Meanwhile, the Japanese have employed a variety of expedients to reduce their trade surplus. Yet in spite of the political gymnastics on both sides, Japanese imports from America appear to have fallen during the 1980s. Total Japanese imports from all countries dropped by 7 percent (from $140 to $130 billion annually) over a six-year period while Japanese exports shot up by 35 percent.

In short, high technology has not as yet filled the gap left by the rapid decline of autos and other smokestack industries in the United States. Nor does it seem likely to do so anytime soon. Historical patterns are not encouraging.

A Dwindling Capacity to Innovate

For a predominant economy like the United States to maintain its overall lead, it must pioneer new innovations as rapidly as its lead in the old industries is lost. This is not always easy. A major reason is the added burden of cost its industry and citizens bear for trying to police the whole world. That added burden of unproductive government expenditure, especially for military purposes, tends to raise costs and create institutional rigidities that reduce its capacity to make the most of emerging opportunities.

We believe that it is no coincidence that every transition of economic predominance going back centuries has involved the rise of a new power enjoying much lower taxes than the one it displaced. The nations rising to positions of clear manufacturing supremacy all did so at times when they enjoyed the advantages of cheap defense. This was true as far back as the sixteenth century, when Spain was taxed into bankruptcy. Historian Jan de Vries described it this way:

> The weakness of Spain's economy became obvious at the peak of her international power under Philip II. The costs of his foreign policy as measured in tax revenues and manpower combined with a pattern of controls and privileges in the domestic economy to hobble the productive sectors while bloating such consuming interests as the nobility, the church, and the bureaucracy.*

Although taxes were tripled between 1556 and 1577, revenues fell further and further short of balancing the budget. Then, as now, technological trends were rapidly escalating the costs of projecting power. As military spending soared, so did the deficits. By 1600, 40 percent of the Spanish budget was consumed by payments on the national debt.

As Spain sank in bankruptcy, the Dutch economy emerged as the center of innovation. Textiles, brewing, bleaching, ceramics, paint making, sugar refining, and shipbuilding—among other industries—all spurted ahead. Advances in shipbuilding were particularly important because they contributed to lower military costs. By harnessing industrial windmills to power mechanical saws, the Dutch were able to build more ships of greater capacity more rapidly and cheaply than anyone else. Their low-cost ships gave them an obvious advantage in projecting power at sea. On land, the Dutch also came up with innovations that gave them a brief cost advantage. Maurice of Nassau, Prince of Orange, introduced engineering, the drill, and coordinated fire to Dutch armies. This gave them the ability to outmaneuver and outfight much larger forces. Unhappily for the Dutch, however, other nations rapidly copied

---

* Jan de Vries, *The Economy of Europe in an Age of Crisis, 1600–1750* (Cambridge, 1976), 27.

these techniques and pressed them on land. As the costs of Dutch defense rose, the economy faltered. De Vries put it succinctly:

> Increased costs, particularly in the last third of the seventeenth century, robbed Dutch trade of its dynamism. As the costs of defense forced taxes up, the high costs of urban living forced up wages. . . . And as so often happens in societies when new conditions threaten their leadership, an inflexibility permeated Dutch institutions.*

As we have seen, the same pattern repeated itself in the case of Great Britain. As an island nation, Britain escaped from the costly burdens of maintaining a sprawling land army of the sort that cannibalized the resources of its continental European competitors. Later, when Britain was able to make a successful transition from dominance in textiles to dominance in iron, its advantages were extended because of the coincidence that a lead in metallurgy allowed British defense costs to fall. By contrast, when technological dispersal raised the British defense budget, the British economy began to decline. As the costs of spending to police the globe rose dramatically, the British fell behind in innovating new industries.

Again, when the United States emerged as an industrial power in the late nineteenth century, it did so at a time of low defense costs. As we have seen, America was largely protected by two broad oceans and the British Navy. U.S. military spending and taxes were low. During its period of industrial takeoff, the U.S. exploited Britain, in much the same way that Europe and Japan exploit the U.S. today.

The recent predominance of Japanese manufacturers provides still another indication that a leading economy, burdened by high military costs and high taxes, is not likely to be a leader in innovation. The Japanese have avoided the high dead-weight costs of defense through their alliance with the United States. This has enabled them to enjoy a low tax burden, freeing resources and talent to make products for sale in consumer markets. It is particularly notable that the Japanese have devoted only a bare chemical trace of their total research and development expenditures on defense, while military R & D consumes a large portion of U.S. effort. For example, in 1983, the last year for which we have figures, Japan spent 0.3 percent as opposed to 28.1 percent for the United States. Among major capitalist countries, only the United King-

---

* De Vries, *Economy of Europe*, 123.

dom spent more, 29.2 percent. Part of the imperial legacy seems to be high military spending and low growth.*

Some readers may think it strange that we associate greater military spending with economic decline inasmuch as we have emphasized the important organizing role of predominant power in allowing the world economy to function. What we are now saying is not a contradiction. Ours is not an argument that a nation ought to go for broke in order to maximize its capacity to project power. On the contrary, our argument is a very different one. It is only when one nation's costs for projecting power are low that the perverse impact of power in the world is likely to be minimized. When the superior economy can employ power cheaply, it can knock down barriers to trade, reorganize political institutions to reduce their drag upon the economy, and police the security of investment internationally. When the military costs for the predominant power are high and rising, this is an indication that the megapolitical conditions for optimum growth have passed. Unless some new invention miraculously reduces military costs, the leading nation will falter under its heavy burden.

PRODUCT CYCLES AND STOCK MARKETS

It would be a striking departure from past patterns if the United States were to make a successful transition as the innovator of the next major product cycles. Unless policy reform and technological breakthroughs provide for lower military costs and lower taxes, the United States is likely to follow in the footsteps of its predecessors. You may see a repetition of the British experience. British science and engineering often laid the foundation of inventions that became major industries. But after the late nineteenth century, British companies could not make the best of these inventions. Early leads in fields like computers, radio, television, pharmaceuticals, and jet engines were quickly lost as industry in other nations more vigorously developed these new products.

The weak British efforts at innovation have been reflected in the performance of stock prices during this century. The London Stock Exchange is now trading at a capitalization about 25 times its 1900 level. By contrast, the New York Stock Exchange is now about 225 times its 1900 level.

* Ian Davidson, "Tonic That Failed to Give a Lift," *Financial Times,* September 29, 1986, p. 17.

Not surprisingly, the greatest growth of U.S. shares came during the period of American economic supremacy—from the end of the Second World War through 1970. The U.S. market did not even surpass the capitalization of the London market until the devaluation of the pound in 1949. But when the U.S. market spurted ahead, it left the British market far behind. The London market stagnated, and the pound was devalued a number of times. In a sense, the great upsurge of U.S. capital gains reflected the product cycle innovations in which Americans surpassed their British competitors as world leaders.

An implication for the future is that American stock prices will tend to grow less rapidly than those of foreign markets. This is exactly what has happened over the last 15 years. Compound returns in Japan have averaged 19 percent per year, more than twice the U.S. rate of 9 percent. In the midsixties, the Dow Jones Average of industrial stocks and the Nikkei Stock Market Index of Japanese shares were both trading at about 1,000. By 1986, the Dow had yet to reach 2,000, while the Nikkei had shot up to about 19,000. While the two markets are not organized on the same basis, so the capitalization of the Japanese market is overstated in American terms, the comparative growth of the two reflects the vigor of the two economies.

Capital values in other markets may continue to increase relative to the American market for three reasons: 1) A rise in the value of foreign investment is likely to reflect the shift of output away from the U.S. as product cycles do their work. 2) To the extent that Japan and other foreign competitors with lower taxes and costs are better able to innovate new products, their capital markets will tend to grow more rapidly, as they have done since 1970. 3) To the extent that protectionism and a breakdown of the world system encourage foreign companies to set up factories in the United States, an increasing share of American production will be foreign-owned. Honda may now be a domestic auto company, but if you wish to profit by its growth in market share, you will have to invest in Tokyo.

This is a major reason shrewd investors will look to invest internationally, in spite of the increasing disorder in the world. Well-chosen foreign investments stand to grow more rapidly as American predominance fades. Some foreign shares are listed on exchanges in the United States. You can purchase many shares of other foreign companies in the form of American Depository Receipts, or ADRs. The list of ADRs is far larger than you might imagine judging from the coverage of foreign shares in the American financial press.

There are many ways of investing internationally, most of them inconvenient. To succeed, you must devote large amounts of time and attention, cultivate adequate sources of information, and locate a skilled broker to help you. And at this point, you have only begun. You have to account for currency fluctuations and the thinness of trading in most foreign markets. The capitalization of the entire Italian stock market is roughly equal to the market value of IBM. The Italian bourse gained 130 percent in 1985, far better than IBM. But you could not trade the whole Italian market the same way you trade IBM. To cite another example, the Austrian stock market gained 174 percent in 1985, making it the best performer in the world in U.S. dollar terms. That brought the whole value of the Austrian market to just $4 billion—in the range of the U.S. market for penny shares.

To avoid the difficulties of personally trading in such markets, many investors turn to mutual funds. The authors, in conjunction with Global Asset Management in London, are organizing such a fund that invests anywhere in the world where it spots a profit opportunity. This is not a single-country fund. Such funds are vulnerable to wild price swings. The Cross Market Opportunity Fund will diversify risk by investing in a number of different situations in many countries (including the United States). By watching events closely, the Fund will attempt to pull back from markets that are weakening and jump into the ones that are strengthening. The Fund will be guided by the same type of short-term investment analysis that has made our newsletter, *Strategic Investment,* successful. Of course, we cannot guarantee that the Cross Market Opportunity Fund will perform as well as *Strategic Investment*'s published portfolios. Past results do not guarantee future performance. But we believe that our analysis of the world economy is sound. To the extent that we are right the Cross Market Opportunity Fund should do well. If our approach interests you, we tell in the back of the book how to send for a prospectus in order to obtain more complete information about the Cross Market Opportunity Fund.

We believe that the evolution of the product cycle helps explain the fact that not once since 1970 has the U.S. stock market been the top performer in the world. But another factor is the gigantic size of the U.S. securities market. In 1985, the value of U.S. stocks was almost half the total value of securities in the entire world. Probabilities alone are against the U.S. markets outperforming all of the smaller, more volatile ones. But none of the major foreign markets always outperforms the United States, nor is it likely to. The question is what the general, long-term trend will be.

PATHS AMERICA MAY TAKE

We have already outlined many of the factors that could bear on the future performance of the American economy, some of them negative. But it would be too simple to suppose that America must follow the pattern of other predominant nations that slipped into decline. Much depends upon the domestic political response. Among the possibilities:

1. More of the same—for as long as possible. This is the path that would appear to assure an unhappy ending—for all the reasons described so far. An economy hampered by high costs that can find no way to cut those costs as its product base erodes will revive only by accident.

2. A policy of negotiated disarmament and minimal but systematic cost containment, along the lines followed by the British after World War I. This is a not unlikely outcome. Unfortunately, as in the case of Britain, it may be insufficient response to improve economic prospects. And it might weaken still further the underpinnings of the world trading system. The aerospace industry and defense contractors in general would suffer disproportionately, for obvious reasons.

3. Sweeping cost reduction, involving actual cuts of government spending, lowered entitlements, low wage growth, and greater investment in productive capacity to improve U.S. competitiveness. To work, such an effort would have to be accompanied by institutional reform, such as reform of the legal system to lower transaction costs. Few efforts of this sort have yet succeeded politically, although there are occasional hints that sweeping reform is not impossible. Deregulation of U.S. communication and transportation systems and the 1986 Tax Reform are prime examples.*

4. Reversion to full-blown protectionism to prop up fading industries with tariffs and quotas. Such a policy is a likely follow-on to the failure of options one or two. It would damage truly multinational

---

* It is also possible that these examples reflect changing megapolitical conditions that shifted the balance of power within industries rather than a triumph of resolve to restore vitality to a high-cost system. See possibility number five.

firms and the international banks, for reasons we have already explored. Old-line industries, such as autos, steel, textiles, and others subject to competition in tradable goods would tend to suffer less or be actual winners—though the stock market as a whole should tumble—as it did at the news of Smoot-Hawley in 1929.*

"Those Who Can, Will Not, and Those Who Will, Cannot"

To summarize the first four possibilities, if historic analogies apply, it is unlikely that America will successfully innovate new products and processes to the degree necessary to compensate for fading performance in the old. The costs of attempting to police the world are gigantic and growing. The U.S. fiscal deficit is far worse than Britain's or Holland's ever was. To find a comparable instance of fiscal decay for a leading nation you have to return to the example of Spain in the declining years of the sixteenth century. Efforts at reform in the United States that would lower costs are hampered by institutional rigidity of the sort that defeated reform efforts at the court of Philip II.† In the end, those who had the power to take the sweeping steps necessary to make the economy hospitable to innovation were precisely those with the largest incentives not to do so. In every case, from Spain, through Holland, to Great Britain and now the United States, rising military costs have been driven by megapolitical trends. To have radically cut military spending in the context of prevailing arrangements would have been to saw away the support upon which far-reaching networks of power and commerce rested. That might have been preferable to what the years actually brought. But persons with the nearest access to the levers of power, who tend to benefit most from the status quo, are usually reluctant to undertake reforms whose first effects would be to whack their own pocketbooks. Therefore, the investor who governs his decisions on the basis of probabilities should expect the United States to follow the same

* For a different interpretation of the range of policy responses facing the United States, see James Kurth, "The Political Consequences of the Product Cycle," *International Organization*, Winter 1979, pp. 2–3.

† Author James Davidson has worked with others in an attempt to enact a constitutional amendment to restrict deficits and limit federal spending. Although this effort has come close to success, groups opposed to decisive cost-cutting have prevailed in every showdown. As historian Jan de Vries commented on the crisis in sixteenth-century Spain: "One observer remarking on the frustration of every reform proposal lamented that 'those who can, will not, and those who will, cannot.' " (De Vries, *Economy of Europe.*)

downward path as its predecessors at the pinnacle of the world economy.

"The Economy Grows at Night, While the Politicians Sleep"

There is, however, another possibility:

5. Sheer, blind luck may govern the destiny of America. It is possible, if not yet likely, that new technology can do for America what politicians and other guardians of the status quo lack the stomach to do—deflate costs and overturn institutional impediments to innovation. This is like being faced with a necessity to tear down an old factory in order to accommodate new processes, yet being unable to make the decision. If everything took its normal course, the old factory would stand till it rotted. But—presto—while the powers that be are dithering over some inconsequential decision, like whether to repaint, an earthquake comes along and knocks the whole thing down. What needed doing has been done, but not through any conscious choice. Roughly speaking, that is the hope for America's competitive revival. It involves not a revolution in political will, but revolutionary changes in megapolitical conditions. Such luck never befell America's predecessors at the pinnacle of the world economy. If it happens this time, it will be because of a rare coincidence of factors unique to this stage of technological innovation. We focus particularly on declining scale economies in the production process and aspects of innovation peculiar to the Information Revolution. As the speed of technological change accelerates, they may help reduce the otherwise formidable impediments to an American renaissance.

CONSEQUENCES OF DECLINING SCALE ECONOMIES

If scale economies continue to decrease, as they are now decreasing in many industries, this could play a major role in improving the American economy's ability to create new leading sectors. It could give a greater scope to market forces and alter the structure of investment in ways you will want to understand. Some of these we have already analyzed, so we will only summarize them here. Others need more explanation. The implications of changing scale economics stretch to many areas of investment importance. They can also help explain some of the puzzles of twentieth-century politics, such as the irony that the two leading international champions of free-market economics, Great Britain and the United States, have transformed their domestic economies in ways that depart decisively from the free market. To the extent that new technologies decentralize economic organization, you may now see more market-controlled outcomes. This implies a greater flexibility and therefore fewer obstacles to innovation.

There is no easy and precise way of measuring the scale of economic operations in the way that the price of soybeans or pork bellies can be tracked on a moment-to-moment basis. The optimal scale and organizational format for any process are always matters of question and experimentation. It is rare that anyone knows just how large a business should be. This is true even of the persons who run it. They always feel that their operation is too small. Their ideal is monopoly. Since that is also the ideal of all their competitors, many must be disappointed. The process of competition and the political process interact to determine the optimal scale of operations. This optimal scale varies from industry to industry, according to the technology of its production process. As technology changes, the scale of some enterprises rises while that of others falls.

In the last two centuries, the general tendency has been for the size of enterprise to grow ever larger—from the family firm to the public stock company to the multinational corporation. If this trend toward ever-greater scale of enterprise were to continue to its ultimate extreme, it would require the entire world to be folded into a single holding company. In effect, this is what some Marxists advocate and expect. They believe that they speak with history's voice in proposing a *reductio ad absurdum*—a one-world Communist state. We see the trend reversing and moving the other way.

New technologies such as the computer have made it possible for small business to attain efficiencies that were previously available only to the largest companies. This implies a reduction in firm size. It also individualizes work, loosening many of the technical strictures on employment that are features of the mass production enterprise. Whereas heavy fixed investment in the smokestack industries meant centralized control and highly structured employment of great numbers in a few firms, the new technology decentralizes. It lowers capital requirements, making it possible for many firms to employ a few people under more flexible conditions. As Robert Resek, director of economic and business research at the University of Illinois, put it, "Increasingly, the optimum-sized plant, rather than having 10,000 workers, will have 100."*

Wider Income Gaps

A declining scale of production increases the role of market forces in the setting of wages and prices. In our analysis of communism, we saw how declining scale economies are incompatible with centralized organization of economic life. We have also explored some of the connections between scale economies and the determination of wages. We saw that industries with high fixed costs tend to be characterized by nonmarket wage rates, otherwise known as "exploitation of the capitalists by the workers."

A falling scale of operations changes the underlying megapolitical reality in a way that allows investors to resist this exploitation. Falling scale means an increase in competition, lower sunk costs for resisting strikes, and footloose industry. In any market with many small competitors, no employer can afford to pay workers a wage that much exceeds the market clearing rate. Smaller scale therefore implies that wage rates will be increasingly set on an economic rather than political basis.†

Middle Managers Superfluous

Another important characteristic of declining scale is to eliminate middle-management positions. Smaller operations require fewer layers of bureaucracy between the top management and the floor worker. As the scale of industrial operations falls, many middle management jobs will be eliminated along with well-paid jobs for low-skill production labor.

During the 1970s, 19 million new jobs were created in the United

---

* "Midwest Factories in Throes of Change," *Journal of Commerce,* September 25, 1986, p. 7A.

† Just how high that wage could or should be has been a matter for delicate judgment and debate. Some economists believe that it is beneficial to an employer to pay premium wages. This may well be true if premium wages reduce absenteeism and improve morale, thus leading to a higher-quality product. Nonetheless, the advantages of higher morale and lower job turnover will be far less in some fields than others. It will be lowest where the production process itself demands fewer judgments of the work force, mistakes are less costly, and output is easier to regulate by supervision than by incentives.

States. Practically none of this job growth occurred in companies operating on the largest scale—the Fortune 500 firms. More than 70 percent of new jobs were in small firms employing fewer than 100 people. The other growth in employment came in government. This trend seems to have accelerated during the eighties. Major corporations have been curtailing employment, paring operations, and divesting subsidiaries. Meanwhile, small enterprises have been multiplying at a rate of approximately 600,000 per year. Many persons who lost unionized jobs in large-scale smokestack industries were rehired at lower wages by businesses operating at a small scale. These firms have been largely successful in fending off union efforts to leverage above-market wages by political action. As a result, income gaps are widening. In 1984, the top fifth of households in the United States received 42.3 percent of all after-tax income. This was the highest percentage since the Census Bureau started gathering the data. As one would expect if our analysis is correct, persons in the middle of the income distribution are receiving a smaller share of the total. The reason: a combination of fewer high-paying blue-collar jobs and wider profits for investors and entrepreneurs.

Higher Profits for Small Business

For fundamental reasons, union strength is largely confined to declining mass-production industries. Not only will it be increasingly costly to preserve jobs in these industries in the years to come, but the approach of risk avoidance that is appropriate to gain support of production workers is contrary to the interests of entrepreneurs and many employees of small business. The chief reason is that range of uncertainty in the lifetime income of entrepreneurs is much broader than that of union members.

Because this uncertainty has increased in an upward range, welfare state programs that aim to reduce uncertainty and narrow the income distribution have less political appeal, not more, in spite of the slowdown in wage growth for workers. This is just the opposite of the case in small business 50 years ago. Then, most small firms were mom-and-pop operations whose "best case success" was fixed at a point not much different from that of factory workers. Simplifying greatly, one could say that small firms fell into two categories: businesses that did not lend themselves to scale economies, like laundries, restaurants, and funeral parlors, and small enterprises in fields that did offer possibilities for profit from larger-scale operation, such as drugs, groceries, apparel, and department stores. Those in the first of these categories enjoyed, at best, modest upward prospects with sometimes large downside risks. Those in the second were clearly threatened by competition that they were unlikely to match. Almost all the variability in their income prospects was downward.

The New Deal or the European welfare state had something to offer these people—a respite from competition. In the U.S., the Democratic Party profited particularly by placing a greater part of the income distribution on a nonmarket basis. Legislated restrictions on supermarket chains, department stores, and other discounters, such as the Robinson-Patman Act, slowed down the realization of market efficiencies. In the process, they redistributed income toward large numbers of small-business people.

The promise of inhibiting the market will appeal less to today's optimistic entrepreneur. Therefore, he is far less likely to be part of a coalition with production workers with whose interests his now conflict. With technology on his side, the entrepreneur is outcompeting big business. Even in low-tech or no-tech fields, individuals have made great successes of small firms, launched with small capital investments, and exploiting opportunities in a decentralized marketplace. In many widely publicized cases, owners of start-up companies have become really rich. For others hoping to imitate this success, the range of uncertainty in their income prospects has expanded in an upward direction. People will take greater risk for greater reward. Throttling the competitive process to make life more certain would deprive these entrepreneurs of potential gains. Therefore, a more severe downturn would be required than in the past to produce the same degree of anti-market restriction. And even this is not certain.

Whatever the political will, it is megapolitically impractical to throttle decentralization when technology pushes irresistibly in that direction. The sweeping 1986 tax reform in the United States can be seen as a confirmation of the triumph of decentralization and low-scale operation. The reform wiped away tax advantages, such as the investment tax credit, that had favored the large-scale enterprise with heavy sunk costs. It also made a frank accommodation with wider income gaps by reducing the top tax rate by 44 percent. This may all be a coincidence, but we doubt it. From the perspective of history, the 1986 tax law may be the institutional equivalent to repeal of the Corn Laws in nineteenth-century Britain—a watershed political triumph of persons sharing an interest organized in a radically different way from those who formerly held sway.

Enhanced Demand for Luxury Goods

Lower-scale economies and wider income differentials imply that the demand for luxury goods should grow, whether or not the new technology and innovation revitalizes the American economy. In the first instance, this is likely to be true for straightforward demographic reasons. The United States has an aging population, with the greatest population growth among relatively poor black and Hispanic minorities. As the disposable income of the elderly rises, a greater portion of it will be spent upon luxury goods. But beyond this powerful demographic trend is still another reason to expect an upsurge in luxury spending.

Historically, some of the greatest spurts of demand for luxury goods have occurred when the mantle of innovation passed from one economy to another. At such times, investors in the fading economy often have few productive opportunities to exploit. Investments in the home country tend to be unprofitable because of high costs. And it is frequently difficult or dangerous to invest in another economy where innovations do offer the promise of higher profits. In such circumstances, spending money for personal luxury is a rational choice. And it is exactly such circumstances, repeated time and again over the centuries, that account for such things as the luxurious palaces the Venetians erected along the Grand Canal and their great revels the poet imagined. "Balls and masks begun at midnight, burning / Ever to midday. . . . 'Dust and ashes, dead and done with, Venice spent what Venice earned.' "*

If Browning had lived longer, he would have seen the pattern repeat itself in England during the twentieth century. A favorite complaint of the left wing of the British Labour party is that capitalists invest their wealth in luxuries as British industry declines. To the extent that that is true, it is a rational response to deteriorating conditions. The point to bear in mind for the future is that the market for luxury goods should be strong whether or not innovation revives the U.S. economy—so long as scale economies continue to fall. This implies continued vigor for firms catering to the upscale market, and less success for firms catering to the middle of the income distribution.

* Robert Browning, "A Tocatta of Galuppi."

Men's wits have of late sharpened everywhere.
                                    —Seventeenth-century Italian

HIGHER SAVINGS—MORE DIFFICULT INVESTMENT

Trends that increase the share of income going to investors and increase the market for luxury goods will add to the incentive to become a better investor. Wider income differentials not only imply greater returns to business owners, they also imply a higher savings rate. The higher one's income, the greater portion of it he is likely to save. Therefore, if conditions that previously redistributed income toward the bottom are no longer operative, investors should recover a larger share of total income. Savings rates should rise. And interest rates should be lower than they would otherwise tend to be.

Normally, higher saving rates imply greater long-term capital investment. However, a feature of declining scale is to reduce capital requirements. Most of the 600,000 new businesses incorporated in America each year are self-financed private companies. This is at least a partial explanation for the declining rate of investment in the United States. The growth of the economy is among firms with low fixed costs and few specialized tools that require long-term amortization. As a result, few are publicly traded, and most of those are open to public investment only when they have achieved a larger scale of operation. To this extent, the comparison of the performance of U.S. stock markets with those abroad in recent years may underestimate the vitality of the American economy and its ability to innovate. Much of the strength of the small-business sector is not captured in stock market statistics.

The reduction of start-up costs means greater independence for enterprise, independence of government, commercial and investment banks, and even independence of public investors. One of the difficulties of taking advantage of high-tech developments as an investor is that so many of the companies that may prove to be leaders in new fields are private concerns or tiny subsidiaries of huge companies. Consequently, it is difficult to isolate effective strategies to profit directly from a potential upsurge of innovation in the United States.

Fewer Checkpoints on Innovation

Another consequence of the relative financial independence of new firms is that it is all but impossible for centralized institutions to organize cartels or inhibit experimentation for self-interested reasons. Monopoly, or even effective collusion, is impossible in a market with many small-scale competitors. This was not the case through much of the last century. The large jump in the scale of enterprise in the late nineteenth and early twentieth centuries encouraged widespread emergence of trusts and cartels. Often organized by banks and financiers, these trusts were a response to the large-scale economies inherent in industries that were then new, like steel production. Such undertakings required massive amounts of finance capital, even by the standards of the richest countries. Since they were conducted on such a large scale, they required the participation of a large portion of the banking community and a large share of available capital. Had the technology been of a smaller scale, erecting mills would not have strained financial resources, and the steel industry, among others, would have been more competitive.

Starting a new company in a large-scale industry is a formidable task. But it is all the more formidable because success often requires the participation or approval of persons with vested interests in reducing competition. When many industries in an economy are characterized by a large and rising scale, this tends to increase the natural resistance to new techniques. Since the cooperation of more persons in more institutions is required, would-be innovators face more checkpoints where their work can be frustrated.

Consider, for example, the saga of Preston Tucker, whose Tucker Corporation promised American consumers "the first completely new car in 50 years." That was in 1948. Auto buffs were enthusiastic about the quality and performance of the Tucker car. Said *Car and Driver,* "It combined race-car engineering, aircraft aerodynamics, and innovative safety features. . . ."* Nonetheless, only fifty-one Tuckers were built. Why? Auto expert Michael Jordon offers this explanation: "Powerful men in the federal government attempted to break Tucker's lease on the assembly plant. Then the Securities and Exchange Commission decided to investigate his dealer franchise; and in June 1948, the bottom dropped out of Tucker stock as a result." † The SEC brought an indictment against Tucker and colleagues for mail fraud and securities violations. Ultimately, he was cleared of all charges, but his attempt to build a new auto company in the United States had been effectively

* Michael Jordon, "Buried Alive," *Car and Driver,* October 1986, p. 89.
† Ibid.

squashed. When Preston Tucker died a few years later, he was putting together a firm to build low-cost cars in Brazil.

Whether the Tucker Corporation could have succeeded without the powerful political opposition it faced is impossible to say. It is clear, however, that such shenanigans are more difficult with much of the current wave of technology. Start-up costs are so low that crucial breakthroughs may be the work of hackers fiddling around in a basement or professors working at home on the weekends. To the extent that this is true, it improves the prospects for innovation in U.S. industry.

SMALLER SCALE MEANS LESS SEVERE DEPRESSION?

In light of our analysis and historical experience, it is not an exaggeration to conclude that monopoly tends to be a feature of enterprises whose technology entails large-scale economies. They are usually characterized by intense unionization, politically determined wage rates, and limited downward flexibility of both wages and prices. In short, enterprises of larger scale tend to be less flexible. Sometimes they are stiff to the point of petrification. Such characteristics are precisely those that make for more severe trouble during downturns. When economies cannot adjust to increased competition or falling demand by lowering prices, there is only one alternative: falling sales. This leads to falling output and unemployment.

In this light, it is not surprising that the most recent Great Depression beginning in 1929 was characterized by more severe declines in output and greater unemployment than similar episodes in the nineteenth century, when the scale of enterprise was smaller. The last depression was the one in which the operation of business was on the largest scale and the impediments to downward price movements were the most severe. By contrast, even though the money supply and prices fell more sharply in the depression of the 1840s than in the first Great Depression in this century, there was practically no unemployment in the earlier episode. Adjusting for falling prices, real consumption increased by 21 percent between 1839 and 1843. And the real gross national product, which tumbled 30 percent between 1929 and 1933, actually rose by 16 percent in the earlier depression.

Economic historian Peter Temin put the comparison in perspective:

The economic contraction that started in 1929 was the worst in history. Historians have compared it with the downturns of the 1840's and the 1890's, but the comparison serves only to show the severity of the later movement. In the nineteenth-century depressions, there were banking panics, deflation, and bankruptcy, in various proportions. But there is no parallel to the underutilization of economic resources—to the underemployment of labor and other resources—in the 1930s.

The value of goods and services in America fell by almost half in the early 1930's. Correcting for the fall in prices, the fall in the quantity of production fell by approximately one-third. Unemployment rose to include one-quarter of the work force. And investment stopped almost completely. It was the most extensive breakdown of the economy in history.*

We think that the small scale of early nineteenth-century enterprise may have helped to limit the damage of economic contraction by encouraging flexibility. To the extent that this is true, America's next depression may be less severe than one would suppose, judging solely by the decline of American predominance and the strains it places upon the whole world economy.

Another implication is that the impact of a recession or depression will be more severe in industries with the largest scale. But be cautious in applying this to your investments. The ripple effects from the contraction of huge enterprises will swamp many small-scale firms without the resources to finance long, wide swings in cash flow.

A LAGGED ADVANTAGE IN INFORMATION

Another element to consider in weighing America's ability to innovate is the fact that many new advances involve information and knowledge substituting for industrial processes. America may have a distinct advantage here. (And, ironically, Britain too may be in a position to recover some of its lost vitality.) A recently supreme power tends to have superior scientific research capacity because of its better developed institutions of learning. As we have indicated, the British, during their decline, were the authors of many of their competitors' best ideas. As

* Peter Temin, *Did Monetary Forces Cause the Great Depression?* (New York: W.W. Norton, 1976), xi. Also see Mancur Olson, *The Rise and Decline of Nations* (New Haven, Yale, 1982), chapter 7.

one observer put it, "Britain remained the source of innumerable technological breakthroughs, but it was the United States and Germany that took these ideas and transformed them into commercial products." *

For many years after British predominance faded, British educational institutions continued to turn out more highly qualified scientists and other professionals than could be effectively utilized in the moribund domestic economy. Britain's educational system is still superb, better in some ways than America's.† However, during the transitions involving industrial product cycles up until a few years ago, scientific and informational advantages were not in themselves enough to stimulate rapid growth. When Britain's foreign investment account fell into deficit after World War II, and pressures on the pound forced a slow growth policy, the result was a "Brain Drain."

If a comparable Brain Drain became evident in the United States, it would be a strong confirming signal that America was not likely to realize the potential of new technological innovation. The new place to invest would probably be wherever the scientists, engineers, and other talented people were fleeing. Currently, no such Brain Drain exists. In fact, there seems to be a sustained inflow of able foreigners to the United States, provoked in part by deteriorating conditions elsewhere. Unless this effect is offset by the growing numbers of foreigners who take their higher education in the United States and then return to other countries, the fundamental American position might not be as glum as other indicators suggest.

Unlike the problem facing Britain during its decline, when its scientists were turning out good ideas at a time of generally increasing scale economies, the American economy is lucky to be the leader in science when information itself is substituting for capital and raw materials in the production process. It is therefore possible that an American renaissance can be founded upon the upsurge in information technologies. We don't know. And neither does anyone else. It is impossible to tell at the theoretical level. The historical analogies are against it. And America, like Britain before it, shows disturbing signs of lagging in the utilization

---

* Albert Bergesen, *Crises in the World-System*, Volume 6, Political Economy of the World System Annuals (Beverly Hills: Sage Publications, 1983), 14.

† For example, there is little doubt that the one-fifth of British children who are educated in nonstate schools are taught to a higher standard than all but a small percentage of American children. British schools maintain higher standards and tougher discipline, and this tells in the outcome. Further, while British universities teach a far smaller portion of the population than their counterparts in the United States, they are first-caliber institutions, especially Oxford and Cambridge.

of some of its better ideas, like robotics, in which the Japanese have surged to the lead. On the other hand, America has a formidable number of talented scientists and entrepreneurs. The areas of greatest economic promise are precisely areas of American strength, where start-up costs are often low, and barriers to innovation seem to be falling.

Perhaps America can be the exception to the rule that nations that have slipped from economic predominance continue to slip for some considerable time. Perhaps the cycle of American predominance, decline, and recovery can be superimposed upon the other cycles that matter: the longer megapolitical cycle of costs for projecting power, and the short-term business cycle. If so, not only America, but Britain, too, may grow more vigorously than most indicators suggest by exploiting their brain power in information technologies. Only time will tell.

MAJOR BREAKTHROUGHS ON THE HORIZON

Some of the breakthroughs on the horizon could be so revolutionary as to confer a "first past the post" benefit to those who pioneer them. In the words of Eric Drexler, "The hand that rocks the AI [artificial intelligence] cradle may well rule the world."*

The potential for truly revolutionary technological innovation is greater today than at any time in history. Depending upon the order and auspices under which these breakthroughs occur, they could either open an era of great prosperity, or lead to conditions so frightening for the great majority of people that to describe them without first offering adequate background would be to appear to talk nonsense.

We believe it is crucial for you to understand that the world is once again poised at the threshold of sweeping technological change. We are about to experience transformations of life based upon twentieth-century science. Innovations that are already in the marketplace or soon will be promise to have a strikingly deflationary impact. And before this is even fully understood or absorbed, markets may be jolted by still more dazzling innovations arising from the ultimate industrial revolution, molecular technology. As we shall see, this technology could antiquate almost the whole of existing production. Its possibilities are mind-numbing.

* K. Eric Drexler, *Engines of Creation* (New York: Anchor Press/Doubleday, 1986), 76.

Technology Defines Raw Materials

Ever since the Industrial Revolution, most technological progress has resulted directly or indirectly in the increased use of primary products —the whole range of commodities from metals to renewable foods and fibers. As output and wealth have risen, the demand for commodities has risen as well. Even innovations that involved efficiencies, like improvements that reduced the weight of auto engines, have tended paradoxically to increase the total demand for the commodities involved by lowering unit costs. The amount of metal in any given car might have gone down, for example, but more cars have been sold. Since steel and aluminum were essential ingredients in all cars, total consumption of metal in automobiles continued to go up. From 1950 to 1980, world auto production increased fourfold.

Commodities are the most basic of real assets, but their ultimate usefulness is a function of technology. As we indicated in the previous chapter, the category of real assets is subject to revision as the technology of the production process changes. It so happens that most of the effects of innovation over the past two centuries have increased the demand for commodities of all types and thus increased the stock of real assets. When the Industrial Revolution began with the spinning jennies and the hand-made tools of textile factories of England in the eighteenth century, a great many things that have since become valuable were not assets at all. They were not assets because they were not useful. Petroleum is the classic example. To have had oil on your land in 1786 was a liability. It was just a gooey mess. Then technology changed. By 1886, when new technology had transformed production, people who owned the once-depised petroleum had great assets. When the Burmah Oil Company of Britain began pumping commercially in that year, it bought 48,000 barrels of oil from 24 families who owned fields at Yenangyaung. "Yenangyaung" means "the creek of the stinking waters."

The Decline of Natural Resources

While pots and pans are 80% raw materials and automobiles 40% raw materials, an integrated circuit is less than 2% raw materials.

—George Gilder

Now, new technologies are pointing toward truly significant displacement of raw materials. People are finding ways of increasing value-added or profit in the economy, without using real assets. They are substituting information for basic commodities.

This revolution in processes and techniques is spreading across a broad front. Let us give you just a few examples. Consider fiber optics. Fiber-optic cable enables the telephone company to transmit more messages on a single line than could have been handled with every line in the world about 50 years ago. The new cable is not only capable of much more, it requires less maintenance. The basic raw material component of the fiber-optic cable is sand. Cheap, plentiful sand. As telephone companies replace their old copper wire with the new sand-based technologies, they will soon be one of the biggest sources of copper being dumped on a glutted market.

There are many other ways in which the primary product inputs for major uses will decline either in absolute terms or by dollar value as information-based technologies employing sand and other cheap inputs substitute for the old, expensive commodities.

Techniques in advanced ceramics, for example, should soon make it possible to dispense with many uses of steel and other metals. Ceramics will also substitute to an increasing degree for the use of metals in electronic, optical, and structural applications. Advanced ceramics are harder than steel, even harder than diamonds. They are high-temperature-resistant and invulnerable to chemicals. Commercial applications have lagged, apparently because of the lack of qualified personnel to engineer the applications that are scientifically possible today. High-temperature-resistant ceramic turbochargers, for example, will be perfected within a few years. They will eliminate the need for a cooling system and at the same time significantly increase the life of engines. If the optimists about ceramic technology are right, the force of competition will oblige the major industrial users of metals to adopt advanced ceramics. This trend can only accelerate with time, as engineers increase the plasticity of advanced ceramics and improve techniques for employing ceramic parts in mass production. Not only steel producers, but machine tool producers specializing in metallurgy will suffer.

Another area where digital processing of information is displacing the use of a primary metal is in photography. Videocassette recorders have already replaced silver-based film for home use. It is only a matter of time until good substitutes for silver-based film are developed for still shots. One of the main uses for silver is in film, a factor that points to weak silver prices for years to come.

New super plastics and polymers will also replace wood and metal in all kinds of applications. Some of these new plastics are so strong that they are the preferred substance for constructing bulletproof vests. Before long, they will replace steel in automobile springs, and they may compete with ceramics to replace steel in engine blocks. DuPont has a new plastic, Arylon, that will substitute for flat-rolled steel, replacing metals in many uses, from automobiles to electronics. Another firm, Polimotor Research, is working to develop a plastic engine.

The greater efficiency of new lighter materials and computer-monitored energy uses has allowed tremendous reductions in the demand for fossil fuels. In the mideighties the world was using less oil than it did at the time of the OPEC oil shock in 1973. Improvements in the technology of renewable energy sources, like wind, wave, and solar, will continue the trend to lower growth in demand for conventional sources of energy.

A big problem for electric utilities will be finding ways to sell their excess generating capacity. In 1986, excess capacity was greater than ever before, a sobering reminder that even experts who spend full time thinking about an industry, in this case utility economists, tend to be blind to the consequences of changing technology. They anticipated ever-higher demand for electricity as the economy grew. And they bet billions on that proposition, building huge generating plants, many of them nuclear-powered. They failed to see that technology would sharply curtail power usage for many applications.

They also failed to understand the implications of a declining scale of operation for their business. Even though most utilities do not compete with one another directly, the increasingly footloose nature of industry is making them more competitive than before. Customers demanding large amounts of electricity are no longer as captive as they used to be. Utilities are therefore obliged to offer cut-rate prices to keep their customers. If they refuse, those customers can simply pick up shop and move their production to areas where costs are lower. More footloose industry means lower prices and profits for utilities. Those with large nuclear plants will be particularly vulnerable because the cost efficiency of nuclear plants is dependent upon operation at a high percentage of their rated capacity. Run only on a part-time basis, as most are today, they will turn into financial black holes. Money will be sucked in and never again see the light of day.

The decentralizing character of the new technologies is pressing utility monopolies with competition in yet another way. Cogeneration, which produces electricity as a by-product in the production of steam for industrial use, is spreading rapidly. Ironically, a silicon-chip factory in Michigan was the first to use cogeneration. This is now widespread among big companies in the United States. Cogeneration enables them not only to lower their own energy costs, but to become sellers as well as buyers of energy to the power grid. In high-cost areas, the potential profit is tremendous. In New York, for example, customers have been buying electricity at an equivalent price of from $160 to $180 per barrel of oil. If cogeneration can offer electricity at an equivalent price of $40 per barrel, the appeal is obvious.

Developments in energy efficiency will result in fewer primary products being used in the production process. Raw materials that are presently valuable assets may be less valuable as years pass and we see increasing substitution of information for raw materials in production processes.

THE INFORMATION REVOLUTION AND EMPLOYMENT

Money, said the seven sages of Greece, is the blood and soul of men and he who has none wanders dead among the living.

—Scipion de Gramont

All the changes that have occurred in the world since the first Industrial Revolution may prove to be minor and marginal compared to what could arise from the second industrial revolution—the Information Revolution. In its first hours, this revolution already allows cheap binary impulses scatting across silicon chips to displace many uses of energy and primary products. It also offers the potential for sharply reducing human labor content in a wide variety of manufactured products and services. Not only is the economy moving away from the political determination of wage rates because of enhanced competition due to decentralization, but technology is also putting downward pressure on market wage levels.

Since the first stages of the Industrial Revolution, observers have feared that an impact of technological innovation would be to eliminate jobs, costing masses of people their livelihoods. Heretofore, this has always been an alarm without cause. Jobs have been created in new and dynamic industries faster than they have been destroyed in faltering ones. Improved productivity, made possible by technological innovation, has provided the greatest part of the foundation of higher living standards.

Part of the reason for this balanced effect of innovation is that productivity growth, while large over time, has generally not been dramatic in the short run. Adjustments were gradual. There was time for the increases in wealth made possible by increased productivity to stimulate the growth of new industries outside the areas where the productivity gains themselves were concentrated. Further, until the mid-seventies, new waves of technology tended to be embodied in enterprises of ever-larger scale. By implication, the larger enterprises were likely to provide a more visible focus for new employment opportunities. To locate new jobs therefore did not require much entrepreneurial skill on the part of the worker. Nor did the jobs tend to require much skill of any other kind. As Peter Drucker points out, it is mainly social convention that obliges us to speak of most factory work as "skilled labor." Most assembly-line jobs could be learned in a week or two, even by uneducated applicants. Even now, 20 percent to 25 percent of assembly-line workers in smokestack industries are functionally illiterate and innumerate.* The low-skill requirements for employment in blue-collar work in large industrial factories eased the transitions in the past as technology evolved.

These factors are only part of a complicated picture. But taken together, they have helped contribute to comfortable economic transitions as technology and productivity advanced. Different circumstances in the next few years could produce more acute and uncomfortable transitions. Technological breakthroughs that allow for exponential increases in productivity in industries employing large numbers of people are likely to produce significant transitional unemployment. Over the long run, society will be much richer. In the short run, however, the gains could be highly concentrated. It could take time for demand to increase in other areas to absorb the additional profits of entrepreneurs and shareholders. Some of these would be likely to be first felt in an increase in savings and gains for financial assets.

Another factor that could contribute to significant transitional unemployment is the mismatch of skills required for new jobs as compared to those being wiped away by technology. Most of the well-paid good jobs in the new technology require more than trivial skills. Unlettered persons who cannot do their sums will not succeed in the new world of

---

* *Wall Street Journal*, Nov. 10, 1986, p. 36D.

information technology. It may take many years, therefore, before displaced individuals make the adjustments in their personal skills necessary to compete. Some may never make these adjustments. They may live and die as disgruntled as the carters and carriers of Szechuan when they were overtaken by technological innovation.

This is not merely a hypothetical discussion. Truly astonishing reductions of the labor content of many products will be possible with advances in automation. Such gains have already been achieved in selected fields, such as in the production and dressing of chickens and turkeys. The bird at the center of your next Thanksgiving dinner will require about 95 percent fewer man-hours to bring to market than the one 30 years ago. This is just the beginning. Some utilities and chemical factories can now operate effectively without floor workers.

This trend toward the "workerless factory" will accelerate as improvements in the technology of machine vision and artificial intelligence speed automation. Computer-integrated factories, such as those run by Allen-Bradley of Wisconsin or Frost Inc. of Walker, Michigan, are capable of operating with only a handful of employees. Yet these new automated systems produce a greater number of products of higher quality than was possible under the old factory system. Companies like Frost Inc. with automated systems can be profitable without spreading production costs over a large volume of output. Says president Chad Frost, "I can make a single part for a customer and still make a profit. Now we're into economies of scope, not scale."* One of the reasons for the profitability of "economies of scope" operations is that they do not have high fixed labor costs. The labor bill as a percentage of total costs is small. Legions of blue-collar workers have been replaced by a few well-paid technicians who seldom get their hands soiled.

The innovations that are making blue-collar jobs obsolete will also wipe away increasing numbers of white-collar jobs. Computer-based "expert systems"—a primitive form of artificial intelligence—are already able to match or excel human decision making across a wide variety of tasks. The automatic teller is merely the first expert system to displace a white-collar job. Soon, the "loan officer" may also be an expert system, approving an application for a loan to buy a car engineered by artificial intelligence and largely constructed by industrial robots. Even bureaucracy could be automated by expert systems. Ar-

* "Throes of Change: Automation Is Radical, Expensive Approach," *Journal of Commerce,* September 26, 1986, p. 6A.

tificial intelligence expert Esther Dyson estimates that "monumental amounts" of money could be saved—while providing the public with better service—simply by employing technology that now exists.* Computers can be far more efficient than people in processing routine information. Instead of shuffling papers, the government agencies of the future may be computer networks trading impulses.

BEYOND BULK TECHNOLOGY

The early installments of the information revolution provide only hints of what might be possible. Computers have helped scientists unlock the secrets of DNA, the molecular coding systems of life. Already, this has spawned a new industry, genetic engineering. Companies are altering the specifications by which living organisms are assembled and grow. The first products of this new industry, designer organisms, are coming on the market. Pest-resistant strains of tobacco and dairy hormones that dramatically increase the milk yield of cows are realities. As we discuss in the chapter on real estate, these and other "information innovations" promise to dramatically reduce the use of chemical fertilizers and pesticides, sending land prices even lower.

As food and fiber crops are redesigned, markets for many types of additives will shrivel. Food processing will be accomplished at the genetic level. Soon, you will have cereal grains with flavorings and coloring programmed in. The "Artificial Chocolate Chip-Flavored Cookie Crisps" of the future will no longer be artificial. They will grow on stalks, the fruit of a science that is at once amazing and frightening.

The boundaries of the potential of information processing are nowhere in sight. Even if they could be located in theory, they will always be invisible to the eye. Scientists in the United States and Japan have already turned beyond the attempt to program the molecules of life to even more astonishing efforts at molecular engineering. As Eric Drexler explains in *The Engines of Creation,* it may be possible in the future to adopt the techniques of genetic coding to build molecular computers. These new machines will command the power of today's most advanced supercomputers in forms so tiny that they would fit comfortably into a single human cell.

As these new "nanotechnologies" develop further, they will present

* Interview, October 12, 1986.

the potential for a change in industrial technique that would revolutionize the organization of life. They might even place the business cycle
on entirely new footing.

Today, we have macro, or bulk, production. Every industry is organized around processes that rearrange atoms on a mass scale, by subjecting them to one or more forms of wholesale manipulation, such as
chemical mixing, heating, cooling, forging, casting, sawing, sewing,
pressing, pounding, and more. Some of these are very simple techniques. Others are expensive and complicated. They all share in common the rearrangement of billions upon billions of atoms, as it were,
from the outside. For the most part, people performing these acts can
forget that atoms or molecules are involved because they deal only with
the surface properties of matter. But atoms are involved, whether the
product is an X-ray tube, an aluminum engine or a tennis racket.

By contrast, the new nanotechnologies will enable people to construct final products from "the inside out," manipulating them atom by
atom. Genetic engineering is the first commercial step in this direction.
This same type of molecular engineering can be extended to produce
nonorganic products. A genetic code is merely "a numerically-con-
trolled machine tool system" for building molecules.* Experts who
know more than we do believe that it will be possible to engineer similar
numerically controlled assemblers for building nonliving molecules.
Nobel laureate Richard Feynman spoke of "the possibility of maneuvering things atom by atom" as long ago as 1959. He said then that it is
"a development which I think cannot be avoided."† In the decades
since Feynman made his prediction, scientific developments have
brought the day of nanotechnology ever nearer. Drexler describes the
likely evolution this way:

> . . . [A]ssembler-built AI [artificial intelligence] systems will bring still
> swifter automated engineering, evolving technological ideas at a pace
> set by systems a million times faster than a human brain. The rate of
> technological advance will then quicken to a great upward leap: in a
> brief time, many areas of technology will advance to the limits set by
> natural law. . . . This transformation is a dizzying prospect. Beyond
> it, if we survive, lies a world with replicating assemblers, able to make
> whatever they are told to make, without need for human labor.‡

---

* Eric Drexler, Eris Society Convocation, Aspen, Colorado, August 1986.
† Drexler, *Engines of Creation*, 40–41.
‡ Ibid., 80–81.

In short, we are on the threshold of technological innovations that could practically duplicate Aladdin's lamp. They would antiquate almost all forms of mass production enterprise. Instead of being manufactured by bulk manipulation of billions upon billions of molecules, the tennis racket of tomorrow could be "brewed up" on command, assembled at lightning speed by molecular assemblers programmed with artificial intelligence. The same would be true of practically any product human desire can imagine. It would be possible to pour raw materials into a vat and come up with an engine whose components fit more perfectly than any assembled by human labor. And this could be done almost with no human participation. The work of centuries could be achieved by molecular machines in a matter of days or hours.

This sounds fantastic. It is.

Yet the advent of nanotechnologies may involve only relatively short steps from genetic engineering and artificial intelligences systems that are already in place. Drexler and others believe that crucial breakthroughs could be only a few decades away. They could even happen sooner. If the experts are right, you have only a short time to prepare for the most astonishing megapolitical transformation in history.

"AND FORMER TIMES ARE PASSED AWAY"

It would be silly to attempt to be overly specific about the megapolitical consequences of so far-reaching an innovation as nanotechnology. Much will depend upon the sequence of engineering breakthroughs. To a greater extent than other innovations in the past, much will even depend upon who is their actual author. So great could be the power unleashed by a nanotechnological revolution that those who are present at the creation could change the direction of history according to their own individual whim. Just as the impact of Aladdin's magic lamp was inescapably an expression of the interests, ambitions, and moral character of Aladdin, so the megapolitical consequences of nanotechnology will vary according to the desires of he who first calls forth the genii.

While we cannot pretend to the future's knowledge today, our murky crystal does show the outlines of possibilities that you should think about. Consider these merely as possibilities that seem plausible from a distance.

A first point to bear in mind is that the new technology could decisively alter the character of the economic predicament. If human beings survive at all, some of us at least will no longer be condemned to the original sentence of our maker: "By the sweat of your brow shall you earn your bread." Quite the contrary. If the potential of molecular assemblers is harnessed to the production process, the new problem will be regulating the consequences of an almost unimaginable material abundance. Those who control nanotechnology will be able to enjoy almost any product or service at command. And they will need to pay little or nothing to get it. Once they control the machine tools, the molecular assemblers, and the systems of artificial intelligence to automate engineering, final products could flow forth almost like magic.

This is not to say that scarcity will be eliminated. But the scarcity that will become the object of the greatest attention will emerge along dimensions other than those with which we are most familiar. The new scarcity will not be the scarcity of conventional products and services. Rather, it will be the scarcity of clean air and clean water, the scarcity of uncongested streets, the scarcity of beautiful open scenery, choice beach-front vistas, and mountaintop estates with commanding views. In short, all the problems that population growth unleashes will be magnified in the calculus of reward and cost as it is altered by nanotechnology. If most of life's good things became superabundant, congestion problems would be magnified dramatically in proportion to the other problems that would then be diminished. If everyone had a private jet to go wherever he pleased at his own whim, the sky would be darkened by the crisscrossing traffic.

The economics of material plenty would turn the economics of scarcity inside out. The new economics would have a negative sign. It would be the economics of exclusivity and privacy. People would aim to escape congestion, in other words, to escape other people.

This would be all the more difficult because of the likely effect of nanotechnology in stimulating dramatic breakthroughs in life extension. The advent of molecular computers and machines that would fit comfortably into a single human cell opens the door to a new type of medicine. It could be possible in the future to monitor the chemical performance of cells and preserve their vitality at the optimum levels of youth. This type of molecular engineering could extend life span to rival the biblical ages of Methuselah and the patriarchs. If such technology became widely available, the already rapid growth of world population would reach astonishing proportions. Any past problems of overcrowding would be trivial by comparison.

Nor do I doubt if the most formidable armies ever heere upon earth is a sort of soldiers who for their smallness are not visible.

—Sir William Perry

It is at this level that the most frightening aspect of the megapolitics of nanotechnologies arises. These technologies will not only make possible unprecedented material bounty, they also will allow for deadlier weapons than any the world has known before—not excluding nuclear ones. In spite of the fearful destructive power of the hydrogen bomb, it is a difficult weapon to use profitably. It is a weapon of terror that can be employed only to deter aggression. In time, it may be a weapon employed by terrorists to advance some mad purpose. But outside of a madman, no one who had the capacity to detonate such a weapon today could imagine that he was furthering a selfish purpose. The world after a war fought with hydrogen bombs would be dramatically impoverished, perhaps even incapable of supporting life as we know it.

Nanotechnological weapons, however, would have deadlier consequences without many of the costs of nuclear war upon the users. Based upon replicating assemblers, such weapons could be employed, as Drexler points out, "to cheaply tranquilize, lobotomize, or otherwise modify entire populations." [*] They could also be used to discretely kill great numbers of people. Again, we quote Drexler:

> With advanced technology, states need not control people—they could simply *discard* people. . . . States have needed people as workers because human labor has been the necessary foundation of power. What is more, genocide has been expensive and troublesome to organize and execute. Yet, in this century, totalitarian states have slaughtered their citizens by the millions. Advanced technology will make workers unnecessary and genocide easy. History suggests that totalitarian states may then eliminate people wholesale.[†]

Those initiating such a move might not even constitute a government. The scale of nanotechnologies is the ultimate in miniaturization. They are totally a function of information, automated at the molecular level. And since these weapons, like viruses, would operate invisibly, there might be no effective way to identify their source or orchestrate retal-

[*] Drexler, *Engines of Creation,* 176.
[†] Ibid.

iation. Unlike nuclear weapons, nanotechnological weapons could be purposefully used. And by almost anyone. They could be effectively controlled by a group of scientists in a university laboratory, a small company, or even a single individual who happened to pioneer a breakthrough.

Those who first control molecular engineering of replicating assemblers will have ever stronger incentives than the mundane monopolist to preserve for themselves the capabilities and power their inventions will unleash. To the extent that a stable monopoly over nanotechnologies is possible, those who control it would enjoy advantages beyond the scale of anything tallied in conventional terms. They would enjoy an almost magic source of wealth, military power, and the capacity to extend their own lives. The inequality of circumstance this suggests is comparable only to the ancient inequality between humans and the gods.

It would take us too far from our main theme to speculate further about the consequences of the coming revolution in molecular technology. But we can say one thing with assurance. Whatever else this revolution does, grim or beautiful, it will antiquate the hope of success through many conventional forms of labor.

Not just molecular technologies, but all the new technologies will place an increasing premium on living by one's wit. Unlike the old industrial technologies with their roots in the science of the nineteenth century, economies organized around the new technologies will offer little prospect for the accumulation of capital to unskilled or semiskilled labor. In short, working for a living will become much less rewarding than thinking for a living. And indeed, even many forms of thinking will be better done by machines harnessing advanced forms of artificial intelligence.

Given the radical upheaval that such an industrial revolution implies, the best prospect for survival will be to *own* the machines. It is still too early to know how one can do that. So many crucial breakthroughs are yet to be achieved that any prediction about who might make them would be rubbish. It is worth noting, however, that several leading firms are already at work on molecular engineering, including Monsanto, Upjohn and DuPont.

While no one can say what the final outcome will be, or just what shape the future will take, it is clear that those who control financial resources will be much better situated to stake a claim for survival in this new world than those without them. Those who do not own a share of the machines, or command special talent and skills, will be beggars at the door of a new world.

Progress has always left behind its bewildered stragglers. In Samburu, Kenya, there is a large park, a reserve for elephants, leopards, and crocodiles. The region had long been home to nomadic herdsmen who grazed cattle on the dusty plains. The press of population growth, encouraged in part by introduction of Western medicines, led to overgrazing. Too many cattle wiped out the ground cover. The land became a desert. Herdsmen without herds became useless. Today they cluster at the gates to Samburu Park selling a few miserable trinkets to tourists, but mostly begging. Their skills are many but superfluous. They can survive in a harsh environment with few tools. Those who move away may have a better future. Maybe. If they move far enough, fast enough, and they are clever, and the part of Kenya they reach is prospering rather than sinking like so much of the Third World, then, maybe, the onetime herdsmen may become lathe operators or carpenters, or even political flunkies. The odds are against them. The odds will be against you, too, if you bank your economic future upon superfluous skills.

In the world to come, some people in Western societies may find themselves no less abruptly antiquated than the tribesmen at Samburu. The best protection against the beggar's fate is to command resources. The best way to command resources is to be a successful investor.

ROOM FOR OPTIMISM

This is not to say, however, that there is no foundation for optimism. There is. After the transitional effects have been overcome, technological innovation promises dramatic longterm improvements in living standards. In an essay published in 1930, early in the last depression, John Maynard Keynes analyzed "Economic Possibilities for our grandchildren." He was not in the mood in which he had written "in the long run we are all dead." He wrote: "I would predict that the standard of life in the progressive countries one hundred years hence will be between four and eight times as high as it is today."

In 1930 Britain, but also in Germany or the United States, the minority were enjoying a middle-class standard of life; the large majority were poor. The proportions varied a bit from country to country, always better in the United States, but the general rule was that 20 percent were prosperous and 80 percent poor. These proportions have now almost been reversed. In the United States approaching 80 percent enjoy a middle-class standard of living; Japan and West Germany are much the same. In Britain the proportion is lower, but probably still comes to two-thirds who are reasonably prosperous, with one-third being relatively poor.

The same thing is happening between nations. Again, it depends where one sets the points of definition. But it is clear that new nations, particularly in Asia, have been joining the group of advanced countries.

Copying new industrial methods is a powerful and swift way of raising the productivity of low-cost human labor. By 2030, the end of Keynes's postulated century, China is likely to have joined the group of what he called "progressive nations." This implies a great improvement in living standards for hundreds of millions of the world's people. In 1930, perhaps 20 percent of the people in 20 percent of the world's national populations enjoyed a middle-class level of prosperity. By 2030, even if income differentials in today's leading countries are wider, a much larger proportion of the world's population may be expected to enjoy a middle-class level of prosperity.

The median estimate for world population for 2030 is 8.5 billion people. If even a quarter of them were to enjoy a favorable standard of living, that would come to greater than 2.1 billion, more than the total world population in 1930. There would still be billions of poor, but the prosperous population would clearly dominate the world's affairs. This is the positive side. By the middle of the next century, it is at least possible that the average citizen of the world will enjoy a good level of prosperity, education, health care, and expectation of life, and of personal opportunity. That prospect can still be destroyed. Let us hope it isn't.

FINALLY . . .

The first step toward investment profits is understanding. We do not pretend that our explanation of the way the world works, and will work, is more than a partial version of the truth. We are no doubt missing much. But we also doubt that it will be easy for anyone to be a successful investor while ignoring the larger lessons of megapolitics.

We have seen why prosperity and international investment are in greater jeopardy than most investors believe. We have explained why the world is almost daily becoming a more dangerous place. We have warned you of the growing danger of worldwide depression, explaining why debt default and even greater monetary chaos are likely. Using the same principles of analysis, we have told why communism is in its twilight and what this will mean to you. We have explained, too, why "the American century" is dwindling to a close, in just its fifth decade. Barring an unprecedented recovery based upon the Information Revolution, the workings of the product cycle will eventually reduce the United States, in relative terms, to a latter-day version of Spain, a once-predominant economy, beggared by uncontrollable costs and massive deficits. The burdens of exploding external debt could slow growth in America for years to come, just as the erosion of Britain's surplus hobbled growth in the declining days of the British Empire. We have explained, too, why hard times may be in store for some of the biggest multinational businesses as U.S. power wanes and the world trading system cracks apart under the pressures of economic depression. We expect trade war and protectionism with all its grim implications.

Such is the contribution of megapolitical factors to long-wave cycles of growth and decline. The factors we have identified have their origins neither in the stars, in myths, nor even in the moral fluctuations of human character. We do not doubt that such moral cycles exist and are of profound importance. But megapolitical cycles are set in motion by factors beyond the range of conscious choice: the meanderings of technological change. New tools and new ways of organizing their use can sharply alter the costs and rewards of behavior. As behavior changes, often drastically, maps are rewritten. The terms of trade and finance change. Economies grow or stagnate.

From whatever ultimate causes variations in fortune arise, the human responses to them show recurring patterns. These are patterns from which we can learn much. Call them cycles, waves, or what you will, they offer us the only real guides we have in attempting to understand the future. The low points in the cycles are always the best points to buy, the foundation points upon which new fortunes can be laid. "The best time to buy is when blood is running in the streets." This is not merely a slogan, it is a fact. However gloomy matters seem, there is usually a solution of human optimism and ingenuity than can bring you greater prosperity—if you know when to act and what action to take. In times of transition or instability, when war, famine, or simple economic distress engender pessimistic thoughts, people at the nadir of events tend to be overly pessimistic.

When the day seems darkest, when the end seems at hand, when people are literally convinced that the world itself is about to expire, that is the ultimate buying opportunity. Some of the greatest bargains ever had were obtained by ungodly optimists in the year 999, when a sizable portion of the population of Western Europe sold whatever possessions they had in fear of the Last Judgment.

Many signs now suggest that the world is heading into a period of far-reaching upheaval, a time that will test the wit and optimism of saints and sinners alike. Particular trades and industries will certainly disappear, and transitional technological unemployment will often be severe. Profitable investment in Western societies will no longer be keyed to rising mass incomes as megapolitical conditions favorable to the lower classes fade away. But new ideas will become new industries organized in new ways, allowing new millions, especially in Asia, to reach out for a prosperous standard of life and attain it.

8

The Coming Real Estate Crash

Most of the millions piled up in paper profits had melted away, many of the millions sunk in developments had been sunk for good and all, the vast inverted pyramid of credit had toppled to earth, and the lesson of the economic falsity of a scheme of land values based upon grandiose plans, preposterous expectations, and hot air had been taught in a long agony of deflation.

—Frederick Lewis Allen,
Only Yesterday: An Informed History of the 1920's

If you are like most of our readers, you have a large portion of your wealth tied up in real estate. You have probably done well, but now your gains could be in jeopardy. *Six deadly storm clouds are gathering over real estate.*

They are:

1. The fall in value of farmland; it is spreading worldwide. This has an ominous parallel in the past: The collapse of land values was a prelude to the general collapse of 1929.

2. In the United States, the greatest building binge in history has quadrupled vacancy rates, driving rents down, and increasing loan defaults and repossessions to levels unparalleled since the Great Depression.

3. Most real estate investors are used to a tax code that shelters real estate investments. But new U.S. tax rules substitute exposure for the shelter you have known. *New Alternative Minimum Tax rules could require investors to pay tax on actual cash losses.*

4. Another disaster for real estate is the weakened position of hundreds of savings and loan banks in the United States. They are broke. When their doors close, real estate will have its toe slammed.

5. There is a danger of a major crackup in the mortgage market. As 1986 began, nearly 175,000 foreclosed houses were on the books of the main government lending agencies. Even with falling interest rates, the Department of Housing and Urban Development, HUD, seemed likely to add another 40,000 foreclosed properties by the end of 1986. As defaults pile up, especially in energy-producing states, a major crisis could develop in the mortgage market, another ominous parallel with the last Great Depression.

6. In most parts of the United States, private homes and condos are selling at big premiums to their rental values. Prices are being held up by guy wire and tape—and the fear of more inflation. Suppose inflation does not come roaring back. Will buyers keep paying $200,000 for a home they could rent for $750 a month? Our bet is that they will not. With the tax advantages of ownership in jeopardy, the residential market in the United States could be more fragile than it looks.

LOOK BEYOND THE OBVIOUS

Real estate brokers will tell you that three things matter in determining whether you profit from a purchase: location, location, and location. Don't believe it. Location is important. But it would be wrong to think that prices over the long haul are determined locally. They are not. The big secret of real estate is that national and, ultimately, global forces play an important role.

You already know that monetary conditions play a big role in deciding whether real estate prices go up or down. When there is inflation, prices tend to rise. When there is deflation, they fall. As we have seen, the factors making for inflation or deflation are seldom local in scope.

As with other investments, hidden megapolitical influences play a big role in determining price movements in real estate. Technological developments and shifts of raw power from one group to another help determine how land will be used, how steeply it will be taxed, and how secure ownership will be.

For example, prime quality farmland that will yield perfectly good cotton can be had in Paraguay for a few dollars an acre—a fraction of what similar land will bring in Mississippi. What accounts for the difference? Many things, but perhaps the most important factor is stability.

Paraguay is a dictatorship. The laws there are subject to arbitrary change at any moment. This dramatically reduces the security of land ownership. Land you buy in Paraguay might be stolen by the dictator or his cronies. There would be nothing you could do about it. And even getting on the good side of the dictator might not help. As this is written, the present dictator, General Alfredo Stroessner, is an old man who has been in power since the mid-1950s. He could die at any moment. Or be overthrown. Who knows what the next government would decide to do with you or your land? Because no one can really answer that question, land values in Paraguay are a fraction of the price for similar land in Mississippi.

Megapolitical factors play an important role in determining the value of land in even the most stable and prosperous areas. As we have seen, perverse agricultural policies in Russia, China, and much of the under-developed world were made possible by megapolitical developments—changing power relations brought about by technological change. These policies have kept the price of food high. This had made farmland in Iowa worth more than it otherwise would be.

Similarly, the fall of central Europe to Communism is one of the reasons that commercial and residential real estate prices in Western Europe have grown so rapidly since World War II. When the Iron Curtain fell, it was as if a great part of the European continent had been covered by a glacial frost. Great cities like Prague, Budapest, Leipzig, Warsaw, and Danzig (Gdansk) were suddenly cut off from the commercial and cultural life of the rest of the continent. As the Berlin Wall graphically demonstrates, migration patterns were significantly altered. People who might otherwise have located their homes and businesses in central Europe were drawn instead toward the West. There was almost no reverse migration of talent and capital. While the old cosmopolitan centers of central Europe stagnated under Communism, Paris, Rome, and London became even more desirable locations than they would have been otherwise. The result: higher real estate prices.

The same effect has been at work in raising property values in the United States, especially in the international gateway cities, like New York or Miami. Whenever left-wing groups increase their strength or seem close to gaining power in any part of the globe, some of those who can afford to get out go to London or Paris. Others place a down payment on property in New York or Miami. Dictatorship and economic bungling thousands of miles away can produce a fluctuation in demand for real estate in an apparently local market. So though it may be true that location is the biggest factor in real estate, it is by no means a local matter.

EMOTION IN REAL ESTATE INVESTMENT

For many, real estate is more than an investment. It is a way of life. The authors grew up in families that believed in land. If that sounds old-fashioned, it is. Not too many centuries ago, land was practically the only form of wealth that mattered. There were no stocks or bonds to speak of. The only income-producing form of wealth was real estate. Wise parents taught their children never to sell under any conditions. Part with gold. Sell the animals. The furniture. The jewelry. Do not sell the land.

Don't Argue with Success?

This attitude is deeply embedded among Europe's landed aristocracy, and it is almost as prevalent among many Americans. Part of the dream of economic success is tied directly to images of owning property. America's national board game, Monopoly, is one in which the winners are commercial property investors—not stockholders. The player who ends up owning the railroads and utilities cannot hold a candle to the player who controls the more expensive chunks of real estate, like Boardwalk or Park Place. Of course, Monopoly is only a game. But it is a game that reflects a popular conception about wealth and how it is obtained.

Experience since World War II has tended to confirm that conception. If you look at the *Forbes* list of the 400 wealthiest persons in America, real estate holdings played a big role in the success of many. Among garden-variety millionaires, real estate holdings predominate. More people have become rich in the United States over the past 40 years by investing in real estate than anything else. This is something that real estate hustlers always point to as a means of luring in new investors.

The Trap Is Set

Prices have been going up, and profits have been large over the past four decades. This record of success colors people's expectations of the future, as it should. But don't be misled. When everyone is convinced that something can only go up and never down that precisely, then the market sets a trap. Huge amounts of investment crowd in, much of it from weak buyers, taking prices to levels that are not justified by ordinary economic calculation. Such a condition is often the prelude to a crash.

We believe that such a situation exists today in real estate. But it is a difficult idea to come to grips with—partly for emotional reasons. If your attachment to your property runs deep, if you are a landholder and not an investor, if you would give up anything to keep your property, indeed, if you do not care whether it goes up or down in value, then you should hold on and enjoy your property for what it is worth— whatever that turns out to be. But if you do not have a deep attachment to your real estate and just own it because you are interested in making money, watch out. Our work tells us that factors are coming together that could make for the biggest real estate crash since the 1930s. A series of disasters is waiting to happen.

DISASTER NO. 1: FARMLAND

Everybody knows that farmers are having a hard time. So are the people who lend to farmers. But many casual observers suppose that Congress will bail out agriculture to halt the slide in land values at present levels. We doubt it. Consider the effects of the recently passed farm bill and Federal Farm Credit System bailout. The Congress placed the full faith and credit of the government behind the debts of the Farm Credit banks. In return, the Farm Credit banks (along with the Farmers Home Administration) have tightened their accounting.

This bailout will be good for the banking system—at least in the short run. It made it easier for the farm banks to meet their huge funding needs—about $40 billion in 1985–86. With the system facing the largest annual loss in banking history—about $3 billion in 1986—that did not look easy before the bailout.

But what seems good for the banking system in the short run is not necessarily good for farmland prices. Tighter accounting means more foreclosures. It is just as if hospitals were overflowing with hopelessly ill patients who were being kept alive through a partial government subsidy—with the extra cost of the treatments threatening the hospitals with bankruptcy. In effect, the government has agreed to guarantee the debts of the hospitals—but on the quiet understanding that they "pull the plug" on the patients who are too far gone to ever recover. That is what is happening on the farm front. It is a melodrama that will take years to play out.

Stepped-Up Foreclosures Inevitable

The farm banks will "pull the plug" on thousands of farmers who are the economic equivalent of "brain dead." Those who have not paid interest on their loans for years will be foreclosed. What is the magnitude of the problem? Consider: Total farm debt at the end of 1985 was about $200 billion (official United States Department of Agriculture estimate: $198.9 billion). This excludes the household debt of farm families. Mortgages on the homes in which farmers live are also excluded from the tally.

The direct real estate portion of farm debt has apparently fallen since 1984. This is due partly to foreclosures that have already occurred. Each foreclosure reduces debt outstanding. And real estate debt has also been reduced because farmers have shifted their borrowing. Household and consumer credit card debt, as well as Commodity Credit Corporation crop loans, have increased. These loans carry lower risk than real estate loans because defaults do not ordinarily involve a risk of foreclosure. Farmers have also reduced their real estate borrowings from the federal land banks, where foreclosures were most common. They have shifted their real estate borrowings, instead, to the Farmers Home Administration, an agency that has been slower to foreclose in the recent past.

In spite of these developments—and a significant drop in the number of farmers—farm real estate debt declined by only about $2 billion—from $102.9 billion in 1984 to about $101 billion in 1985. Farmland is still heavily overborrowed. We estimate that there are about 250,000 farms in financial distress. Of that number, at least 40,000 are totally insolvent, with debts that exceed the value of their assets.

Of course, there are farmers, and then there are farmers. There are hundreds of different kinds of foods and fibers produced in America. Specialty farms tend to carry the lightest debt loads. Cash grain farms, which account for only 25 percent of total farms, carry about 33 percent of the debt. Meat animal farms and ranches carry about another third. These heavily indebted farm operations are in the greatest danger.

Foreign Sales Tumble

Grain sales, especially, are falling because of worldwide overproduction. Swollen storage bins now hold a surplus greater than an entire year's consumption needs. It is hard to sell into such a glut, especially since the number of cash buyers has declined, even as the number of sellers has increased. World exports of wheat fell by 4 percent between 1981 and 1985. World corn exports were down by 15 percent. The total value of U.S. farm exports tumbled by 41 percent between 1981 and 1985—from $44 billion to $31 billion.

Farm Income Must Decline

These numbers highlight the major threat to farmland values. Efforts to prop up farm income by raising price supports are self-defeating over the long run because they increase prices worldwide. This, in turn, increases output, shriveling the potential market for U.S. farm products. That is why the Department of Agriculture has sought to reduce government price support levels. Over the long run, this will indeed improve the competitive position of some U.S. farmers. But there is no avoiding the fact that farm incomes seem likely to continue falling.

The factors making for such a result are far beyond the reach of the U.S. government to solve. Agriculture experts realize this. To continue present policies would require a ruinous increase in government subsidies. The only alternative is to drive grain prices down. This, inevitably, will reduce the number of farmers, especially grain farmers.

Triage

There is an unspoken consensus in Washington that steps should be taken soon to begin weeding out the excess farmers. A word one hears is *triage*. It literally means "sorting according to quality." Medics in military conflicts and, more recently, African famines, have used the triage concept in allocating emergency supplies to those with the best chance of surviving. The others are cut off as hopeless.

Even many farmers who have kept their loans current are dangerously overborrowed. Further dips in land values would make them insolvent—in spite of their good payment records. The farm banks will inevitably have to cut off thousands of these farmers who have too little collateral left to support further borrowing. If they can't borrow elsewhere, such as by increasing household debt, most will be unable to remain in business. Their land, too, will come on the market.

How much selling does this imply? Lots. Our estimate is that more than 20 percent of the Farm Credit System's $74 billion in loans are bad. If the actual total is even half that number, hundreds of thousands of acres of farmland could be pushed onto the market under distress conditions. That means a steep fall in land values.

There is a real danger of a downward spiral that only a Latin-style inflation could stop. Most farmland is still selling at a premium to its yield. Land that was $5,000 an acre is down to $3,000—but it may only rent for $125. This is still a huge premium. (The same money placed in Treasury bonds in 1986 could bring almost twice as much.) We could see land values plunge enough to wipe out that premium if inflation does not come roaring back soon.

Look at what happened at the end of the nineteenth century.

Seventy Years of Falling Prices

The last bear market in land in Britain lasted (with the exception of the First World War) from 1870 to 1940—a period of seventy years. Farmland worth 100 pounds an acre in 1860 changed hands at 10 pounds an acre in 1930. The bull market that followed, raising prices in some cases as much as 500 times, lasted for forty years. If land prices peaked in the early 1980s, the start of the next bull market should not be expected until the next century.

As we have explained, the reason for the long decline was technological innovation. New crops, improved tools, and new machines, like the mechanical reaper, greatly increased farm output at the end of the nineteenth century—just as transportation costs were plunging by up to 90 percent. As we have seen, railroads and steamships opened new land to cultivation and made farmers everywhere competitors. Bulk agricultural commodities that would have cost a fortune to ship by wagon or under sail could suddenly be sent anywhere on the globe economically. In Britain, then the most advanced country, cheap foreign grain poured in. Land prices plunged. Only dairy farmers, who were still isolated from competition, were able to prosper.

New Technologies

A different kind of technological innovation could do the same thing today. We have seen great increases in crop yields over the past two decades. Why? Because of better fertilizers and seeds. Think what will happen when scientists perfect the genetic experiments now under way. You will see drought-resistant crops with the hardiness of dandelions and the nutrional value of corn. Advances in genetic engineering almost guarantee it. Scientists have already started using a bacterium invented in the laboratory that protects strawberry plants from frost. Agracetus, a joint venture between Cetus Corp. and W. R. Grace, obtained approval from the National Institutes of Health to test a genetically engineered tobacco in Wisconsin in 1986. The tobacco, invented by scientific alteration of genetic codes in DNA molecules, will be resistant to a disease known as "crown gall." Genetech and Monsanto have developed synthetic somatotrophin, a hormone that stimulates milk production. When it becomes available, it promises to sharply increase the output of dairy cattle.

As the scientists reach more deeply into their bag of tricks, they will come up with amazing, revolutionary developments. Currently, about a third of the world's potential food output is lost to diseases, insects, and weeds. The potential of biotechnology to halt that loss and expand output is staggering. Genetic engineering will create new varieties of plants and medicines that will function like no hybrids in the past. Livestock will fatten on artificial animal feed. And animal diseases will be easier to suppress because medicines that are prohibitively expensive—like interferon—will be cheap. Microorganisms, already being genetically engineered experimentally, will dramatically improve the productive capacity of marginal soils. New, hardier crops will be grown almost anywhere—even on scrubland.

Ultimately, it may be possible to produce many types of foods without growing them in the ground at all. Scientists have already experimented with brewing orange juice directly in the laboratory. Using genetic engineering, they are bypassing the tree, the limb, the blossom, and even the peel. All that is produced are the juice and the pulp. Enzyme-synthesizing processes will re-create the metabolic action of animals, making possible milk manufactured by technicians, not cows. Sanford Miller, director of the Food and Drug Administration's Center for Food Safety and Applied Nutrition, has said that such processes will make "products that are identical."* Research and development along these lines is only beginning. Every success that is achieved will tend to reduce the value of farmland.†

That is why we think that farmland could not only go down from here, it might go down and stay down for a long time. So do not buy farmland, especially prime farmland, unless you are doing it for enjoyment and not for profit.

DISASTER NO.2: COMMERCIAL GLUT

When the last depression began in 1929, farmland had already been falling in value for a number of years, and so had some other forms of real estate. Unfortunately, people who noticed this tended to believe that "local" factors were involved. Properties in rural areas were down because of depression on the farm. In Florida, where speculation had been intense in the first half of the twenties, values peaked around 1925. In spite of these sobering examples of falling real estate values, people elsewhere confidently assumed that prices in their own area could only keep rising.

We see a parallel today. You do not have to look far in America's heartland for evidence that the farm crisis is spilling over into other real estate values. Commercial real estate is already underwater in many areas simply because retailers who service farm clientele are losing business.

The problem in commercial real estate, however, is not confined to small towns and rural areas; it is getting worse in the biggest cities and their suburbs. Put simply, a lot more space has been built and rehabilitated in the first half of the 1980s than anyone can use. And the glut is getting worse. If you live in a major city, just look out the window. The skyline is probably dotted with rows of big cranes at work adding still more apartments, hotels, and office space.

Massive Increase in Space

In 1985, the value of new commercial construction in the United States was $62 billion. How much new space is that? We can only guess

---

* *The New York Times*, December 28, 1986, p. K1.

† In years to come, devotees of "natural foods" may go to out-of-the-way places to buy fruits and vegetables tainted with fertilizer and pesticide residues—evidence that they were actually grown in the ground.

because good data are hard to find, and so much depends on the average cost of construction. Experts we consulted could give local averages for certain categories of construction. But they could only guess what the national average might be.

At $225 per square foot, the new space put in place comes to more than 275 million square feet.

At $175 per square foot, it comes to almost 350 million.

The actual increase in capacity could even be higher if rehabs and lower-cost construction make up a significant part of the total. James Davidson recently rehabilitated a four-story office building in Baltimore to a fairly high standard for just $50 per square foot. If that experience is common enough to reduce the average cost for all commercial construction to $125 per square foot, the total increase during 1985 would come to almost 500 million square feet.

Another estimate put the new space under construction during the middle of 1985 at 156 million square feet. As you would expect, this is a smaller number than implied by construction figures for the whole year. *But even the smaller estimate is more than twice the amount rented out in 1984—71.2 million square feet. And 1984 was a banner year for leasing new space.* With commercial vacancy rates in urban areas of approximately 20 percent in 1986—up from just 5 percent in 1981—a desperate glut of commercial space seems to be in the making.

Lawyers Take Their Toll

Adding to the trouble has been a recent upsurge in operator's liability insurance. As juries run wild, granting multimillion-dollar awards, sometimes for trivial injuries, insurance companies have responded by hiking liability premiums—by an average of 80 percent in 1985, followed by triple-digit increases in 1986. The total value of general liability premiums in the U.S. was relatively constant at about $6 billion from 1977 through 1984. In 1985, the total of paid premiums shot up to about $11 billion. Leaps of up to 500 percent have been imposed in some areas.

Even far more modest increases can have a severe impact on profitability—so much so that many operators (especially the weakest ones) will be tempted to self-insure.

Operators who self-insure are taking big risks. If they are hit with a liability settlement, they will have to pay it out of their own pockets.

Some will be unable to. Their properties could then come on the market at fire sale prices—or be turned over to lucky winners of the lawsuits. Since the owners' acquisition costs will be almost nil, they will be able to undercut the rents of established operators.

The slow speed at which the legal system works its wonders will postpone most of the bad effects of skyrocketing liability insurance into the future. Remember, however, that even though the fuse is long, the insurance problem is yet another ticking time bomb in commercial real estate.

Another insurance issue to consider if you are an investor in commercial property is the skyrocketing cost of earthquake coverage on the West Coast. Premiums have jumped so much that most businesses in quake zones no longer carry any coverage. If you own property in such an area and cannot afford to carry earthquake insurance, you run a risk of severe damage to your investment. On the other hand, there is the logical, if grisly, prospect that a major quake would wipe out a lot of commercial space that would not be replaced. But no such quake has happened yet, and depending upon one to rescue an investment would be a sad mistake.

Discount Rents

What conclusions should you draw? The usual consequence of a great increase in capacity is a falling price, in this case, falling rents. As of 1986, rents in many cities had already fallen from 25 percent to 40 percent, in spite of gimmicks to make them seem higher than they are. The fall in rents is by no means confined to new buildings. It is hitting older buildings now rented. Some will have their current tenants lured away as soon as old leases expire. Others are finding desperate competitors willing to pay fees to break current leases. Tenants are being sought with offers of one or two years free.

For example, a businessman in Washington, D.C., was paying $25 per square foot. He was offered $22 per square foot, with one year free on a 48-month lease. His effective rent fell not to $22 but to $16.50, a 33 percent drop.

Even bigger drops are in store as the commercial glut increases. Rents will tumble, and that means tumbling property values. During the Great Depression, commercial property values fell by approximately 30 percent. In some areas of the United States, mainly the West and

Southwest, losses on foreclosures as high as 50 percent of construction costs had been registered by 1986.*

You might be tempted to think that such dramatic declines signal a bottom. Perhaps they do, but we doubt it. There are too many owners with deep pockets who have the capacity to hold on in anticipation of a market reversal. As of 1985, 49 percent of all commercial space in the United States was in the hands of developers and insurance companies. And much of the property that was not previously in strong hands, and has been repossessed, was being held by lenders reluctant to dispose of it at low prices. In most cases, values of unprofitable properties were still being carried on the books on the basis of construction costs rather than current market prices. In other words, optimism was still not deflated.

No one can confidently pick a bottom. But the bottom is often characterized by panic selling and the liquidation of unprofitable positions by the strongest holders, in this case, developers, insurance companies, and banks. It is then, when optimism is exhausted, that the foundation of a new recovery is laid. On that basis, the full measure of the commercial real estate collapse is still to come, especially in the Northeast and Mid-Atlantic regions of the United States. Given the long lags involved in realizing real estate losses, and the growing inventories of repossessed properties accumulating in the hands of lenders, the bottom is not likely to be hit until the depths of a business cycle downturn in the late 1980s.

Whatever you do, do not join a commercial partnership or tax shelter syndication unless you are absolutely convinced that it has extraordinary merit. Do not put yourself on the line to pay huge debts for a property that may never realize the income that is projected. Commercial real estate is a disaster waiting to happen.

DISASTER NO.3: LESS FAVORED TAX TREATMENT

The 1986 tax reform sharply alters favorable tax treatment that has encouraged investment in American real estate in the past. Instead of being sheltered, real estate investors could find themselves exposed to cruel taxes on actual cash losses. Let us explain.

---

* Peter Waldman and William Celis III, "Empty Buildings: Severe Deflation Hits Commercial Properties in Many Areas of the U.S.," *Wall Street Journal,* September 4, 1986.

Under the new tax law, individuals who have tax shelter investments such as real estate will be allowed to write off a declining percentage of their losses against ordinary income over a four-year period. In 1987, only 65 percent of losses will be deductible. In 1988, the deductible percentage will drop to 40 percent, then to 20 percent in 1989. In 1990, the deductible percentage will fall to just 10 percent. In 1991, if the recent law remains unchanged, no losses from passive income investments will be deductible from salary, interest, and dividend income.

This will make individual real estate deals far less attractive than under previous law. By comparison, the former law permitted investors to claim tax losses about twice their investment in many tax syndication deals. You could write off buildings considerably faster than they actually wore out, claim big interest deductions, and escape with tax-free income. Further, at the end of the day, you could sell your real estate properties and pay capital gains rates of no more than 20 percent.

All of this has changed. Depreciation has been slowed. Interest deductions will be limited and perhaps lost altogether. Where they are allowed, the reduction in rates increases the carrying costs of debt, deleveraging investments. And the elimination of the capital gains exemption means that gains from real estate will be taxed at higher rates. These changes alone should significantly reduce demand for real estate assets that do not pay an income that exceeds their carrying costs.

Alternative Minimum Tax

That is just the beginning. Another crunch comes in the new Alternative Minimum Tax (AMT). This would not directly alter the economics of any given real estate investment. But it would severely curtail your ability to deduct losses, even real losses, from ordinary income.

The AMT applies whenever it would raise the tax paid to a sum higher than would have been paid under the standard calculation. Since there is no phase-in provision, the chances are high that any advantage a taxpayer got from the phaseout of old tax-shelter deductions through 1990 will be wiped out. The AMT requires investors whose income is reduced by "tax preference items," including "passive investments" such as limited partnerships in real estate, to pay an alternative tax of 21 percent. This would keep you from benefiting from tax losses—even if the losses were real. You may have to *pay a tax on your cash losses*. So instead of sheltering your other income with fictional real estate deductions, as the previous law allowed, the new rules would go to the other extreme—subjecting American investors to penalty taxes on actual cash losses.

The exact rules are so snarled that it would take 50 pages to explain them. So we won't even try. But let us give you a few of the grisly highlights:

1. The middle-class real estate investor would be hit harder than the very rich. The AMT kicks in according to percentage of your taxable income that is offset by loss. Say there are two investors in a real estate syndication that goes sour, Daddy Warbucks and Dagwood Bumstead. Each has one unit. Each has a tax loss of $50,000. Warbucks's income is a million a year. He deducts the entire amount. No problem. Bumstead makes $75,000 a year. He has a $40,000 exemption. But beyond that, he can't deduct the loss. He'll pay the Alternative Minimum Tax of 21 percent—even if the loss was real.

To reach the threshold for tax-advantaged investment in nonresidential real estate will require greater amounts of capital and higher income. In effect, most real estate investments will either have to produce income or be "spread" against other income-producing passive investments. To take advantage of losses for one property, whether they are out-of-pocket losses or fictions of accounting, you will need another property or properties paying an equal or greater cash income. Parking lots, strangely enough, may be put much in demand by the new law. They ordinarily throw off cash and should fit the passive investment rules.

2. You will need greater financial sophistication to invest successfully in real estate. American investors will no longer be able to buy into a property or a syndication, just because the deal, standing alone, looks good. (And fewer of them will until capital values come down.) You will have to make alternative calculations of your tax liability—and that calls for the kind of financial sophistication that most middle-class investors don't have. If they did, Henry Block (of H & R Block fame) would not be as rich as he is.

3. Timing in real estate transactions will become more important than ever. You'll have to time your investments much more precisely with your total tax liabilities, and not just time the market itself. Most likely, many investors will be daunted by the snarl of calculations involved, and steer clear of investments with AMT exposure.

4. That makes real estate less attractive relative to financial assets. Among the chief reasons that small investors have preferred real

estate as a vehicle for most of their wealth is that it has seemed less risky, required less financial sophistication, and required less expert timing to make a profit. The tax law would change that dramatically. Compared to figuring out your taxes years in advance using alternative calculations, picking a stock or bond to buy is easy. And if you invest in a stock or bond under the new law, you will be able to deduct any losses outright. In a real estate or oil deal, you may not.

The lower tax rates will increase the real yields on bonds and stocks and contribute to lower interest rates that will amplify that effect, bringing even greater returns to holders of financial assets. If even a portion of the capital that has typically been compressed into real estate investments in the United States were diverted into stocks and bonds instead, this could result in impressive capital gains for at least some financial assets.

Adding to the increased attractiveness of financial over real assets is elimination of the tax distinction between long- and short-term capital gains. Elimination of this distinction increases the attractiveness of trading in liquid markets where profits can be taken instantly. This is not the case with real estate. Most real estate investments are definitely buy-and-hold investments in which a fast turnover would involve resale in a year or two. The old tax laws rewarded this strategy of immobilizing capital with low tax rates on capital gains. Until January 1, 1987, American investors paid a tax penalty of 150 percent on profits taken in less than six months. (The maximum short-term rate was 50 percent rather than 20 percent.) Now with the top rate of 28 percent applying to all gains, whatever the holding period, there is no incentive to keep capital tied up. You will pay the same tax whether you make a profit in an hour or in a decade.

The Magic of Compounding

If you had a choice of making $1,000 in an hour or in a decade, which would you choose? The answer is obvious. So here is a slightly harder question—if you had a choice of an investment that made a profit of 120 percent over six months, and a series of one-month investments that each earned a profit of 20 percent, which would you choose? If you took the profit of 120 percent, you made a mistake. If you make a 20 percent profit per month, reinvesting your gains, your profit in six months would be 199 percent, a lot better than 120 percent. The new tax laws eliminate the tax penalty on compounding short-term gains.

Henceforth, trading in liquid financial assets will be far more appealing. Not only is it possible to take profits instantly, but the transaction costs of buying or selling $100,000 worth of stock, bonds, or commodities are trivial compared to closing costs, commissions, points, and transfer taxes involved in the typical real estate transaction.

You do not have to be much of a prophet to see that more people will invest in financial assets in the future and fewer will invest in real assets.

There is more to the story, but that should give you enough to see why we think tax reform could be a major factor depressing capital values in American real estate for some time to come. It could shrink the amount of income being sheltered by real estate partnerships by billions. And it will dry up most of the incentive for many middle-class investors to buy. The prospect of higher real losses and fewer buyers means lower prices.

DISASTER NO. 4: TAPS FOR 500 S & LS

Still another difficulty facing real estate investors is the deteriorating condition of savings and loan banks that are a major source of liquidity for real estate investment. Hundreds of these banks are now insolvent, running on empty. How do they do it? They borrow short-term cash at high interest rates and keep their fingers crossed. Why are they still in business? Simple. The FSLIC, the federal agency that insures deposits, does not have the cash to board them up. In late 1986, the insurance fund was essentially broke, with a grand total of 40 cents on hand for every $100 of deposits it insured. The Ninety-ninth Congress considered a bailout proposal that could have pumped about $10 billion into the FSLIC, but adjourned in 1986 without acting.

Such a bailout would give regulators the ability to close down some of the bankrupt institutions, but probably would not solve the problem. The costs of closing insolvent S & Ls has been growing rapidly. Whereas it used to cost only about 20 cents per dollar of assets to close each bankrupt S & L, the costs of insolvencies in 1986 had risen as high as 50 cents per dollar. According to the government's own list, the problem S & Ls total almost $100 billion in assets.

Gambling with Borrowed Chips

While the regulators and politicians have dithered over what to do, the insolvent S & Ls have gained a period of grace—what you might call "gambling time"—to try to get their money back.

Since these banks (about one out of every seven S & Ls) are already broke, they literally have nothing to lose by taking high-risk plays in real estate construction loans and direct investment stakes in new projects. These high-risk investments have the regulators at the Federal Home Loan Bank Board grinding their teeth because they see the prospect of huge losses—along the lines of those that came to light in the Maryland and Ohio S & L crises.

While the Home Loan Bank Board was waiting for additional funds to bail out the FSLIC, it made a decision to begin forcing the insolvent S & Ls out of business. A 1986 regulation would prohibit the weak banks from paying higher-than-average rates of interest on "new or renewed" deposits. This means, in effect, that when their present CDs expire, the weak S & Ls will be unable to roll them over. Without the cash to fund their operations, they will have no choice but to close—leaving Washington with the problem of redeeming the insured deposits. We predict that hundreds of S & Ls will go broke.

In case there was any doubt that this action was aimed at slowing the flow of risky investments in real estate, the draft regulation also barred the insolvent thrifts from making commercial real estate loans and large construction loans without special certification.

Mortgage Scandals

Budding scandals in secondary mortgage markets show how weak this real estate debt is. First American Mortgage Company, a major mortgage banker with offices nationwide, went bankrupt in November 1985. E. F. Hutton charged that 40 percent to 60 percent of mortgages in its portfolio were delinquent or in default. This followed the EPIC Mortgage Inc. collapse, in which a billion dollars of real estate debt went into default.

Sloppy Appraisals

A big factor contributing to the collapse of many savings and loans banks, as well as EPIC, were fraudulent or exaggerated appraisals. Many EPIC properties were found to be appraised at 50 percent to 100 percent above what they could actually bring in the market. These inflated appraisals were widely used to disguise the fall in value of residential property, especially condominium units. With S & Ls often ready to offer borrowers up to 90 percent of the appraised value of property, an exaggerated appraisal on a nonrecourse loan could give a borrower the chance to walk away—cash ahead.

In 1984, when matters were far better than they would become, the Federal Home Loan Bank Board had identified "serious appraisal problems" at 359 S & Ls. Many commercial banks appear to be threatened by the same problem. This came out in the wake of the Continental Illinois bailout, when the Federal Deposit Insurance Corporation had to absorb a loss of $200 million from overvalued real estate carried on Continental books at $400 million. Appraisals were inflated by 100 percent. An in-depth study by the House Government Operations Subcommittee on Commerce, Consumer and Monetary Affairs determined that "real estate appraisal abuses seem to be a serious problem of national proportions."

The Clock Is Ticking

It is only a matter of time until the savings and loan crisis intensifies. As the weak banks go belly-up, their real estate investments will be taken over by the FSLIC or the FDIC. Someday, though not immediately, the repossessed properties will be sold to raise cash. The Home Loan Bank Board has already chartered a mongrel institution in Denver to sell off a portfolio of $3 billion in real estate investments. This portfolio will be multiplied many times over by the coming S & L bankruptcies.

The sale of these assets implies more downward pressure on real estate prices. Not only will the S & L crisis lead to forced sales, it will also dry up funds that have been helping to sustain demand. As Federal Home Loan Bank Board economist Eric I. Hemel said: "We're in for a debacle that will take a number of savings institutions and commercial banks with it." The coming bankruptcies are yet another caution that barring a significant upsurge of inflation, the bottom in real estate is still to come.

DISASTER NO. 5: HOME SWEET HOME

"Home is where the heart is." It is also where most of the investment capital of many people is kept. If you have lots of your savings tied up in the value of your home, please read this section and the next very carefully. We believe that residential real estate values in many parts of the country are shaky. They could crumble if other real estate prices break. You need to consider very carefully whether the scenario we spell out could prove to be true.

There are many sound reasons to buy and keep a home. We will take a closer took at some of them in the next section. But for the moment, let us assume that your home (or other residential property you may own) is just an investment. Assume you have no emotional attachment at all. You are just in it for the money. Are you likely to make any?

Best Investment Going?

Most real estate investors will tell you that the private home is the best investment you can make. It certainly has been a great investment for most of the postwar period. Even counting inflation, most private homes in the Western world have risen handsomely in value. Will they rise further?

Many people say they must and are banking on inflation to prove them right. Maybe inflation will come roaring back. If so, real assets like private homes should hold their value as paper money becomes worth less and less. Many economists and advisers claim that inflation is just around the corner. But we advise caution. There are many more costs and limitations upon governments seeking to inflate than many people believe.

Consider what happened to housing prices in the Great Depression. They crashed. Ironically, one of the better illustrations of what depression can do to housing values came from a man who devoted his life to warning of the dangers of inflation. The late Colonel E. C. Harwood told of having purchased an estate in Massachusetts for less than $50,000 in the 1940s. Someone had paid a million for the same property in 1928.

"Inflation Is Here"

As we have indicated throughout this volume, the parallels between what happened in the 1920s and 1980s are too obvious to be ignored. Harwood himself was an astute financial commentator in the days before the depression. Although he was a very sophisticated man, he made the same mistake that many appear to have repeated sixty years later. In the January 20, 1928, issue of the *Analyst,* Harwood wrote an article entitled "Inflation Is Here."

In essence, his argument was that inflation had to come roaring along because of the dangerous buildup of illiquid assets, especially in the banking system. Credit conditions were loosening, and he saw even sloppier conditions ahead. The man who paid a million for the $50,000 mansion was doing his part to build up illiquid assets. Unfortunately, the actual event brought deflation, not inflation. It could happen again.

Debt Buildup

One of the factors that triggered the sharp sell-off in homes after 1929 was the tremendous buildup of mortgage debt in the years immediately preceding the crash. The mushrooming of debt allowed prices to rise to a level that far outstripped the growth of income. Then, as now, a considerable portion of sales was accounted for by innovations in financing. These enabled previously disqualified buyers to come into the market by reducing the cash requirements to buy. In short, higher effective demand was possible from consumers who were no wealthier than before. Even the cleverest financing innovations, however, were limited. They could not indefinitely increase sales faster than the growth of income. The bust followed the boom.

Housing started to soften after 1927, even before the stock market crash. But matters worsened dramatically in the early thirties as the banking system came into trouble. Many mortgage loans, especially those made just prior to the depression, were of low quality. Money was lent to weak buyers who later lost their jobs and could not pay. Hence the cartoon image of mortgage banker Snideley Whiplash coming to turn the beautiful blonde and her widowed mother out into the street.

Foreclosure, however, was not the only factor or even the chief factor reducing housing values. A liquidity trap developed that made it irrational to offer new mortgages to buyers. Mortgages that continued to be paid plummeted in value as the entire credit system went into shock. With almost everyone shy of cash, banks were pressured to raise funds to meet depositor demands. They could do this only by dumping their assets, including mortgage loans. The glut of these securities coming on the market at once drove down their value. As the value of mortgage securities collapsed, lenders obviously withdrew from writing new mortgages. The need of the moment was liquidity. Mortgages were

less liquid than bonds and the other investments lenders held. Therefore, the flow of cash to finance housing purchases shriveled.

Only the most liquid, creditworthy buyers remained in the market.
Since these were only a small fraction of the public, housing prices had
to fall. And fall they did. It turned out that the bottom was a lot further
down than anyone suspected.

Prices tumbled during the Great Depression and stayed down until
after World War II.

Creative Financing, Illiquid Buyers

When interest rates went through the roof a few years ago, "creative
financing" of the sort not seen since the 1920s was rediscovered. Many
properties were purchased with "no money down." Owners took back
interest-only notes with large balloon payments. Most were short-term
debt, due in five to seven years. Without even noticing it, we had re-
created some of the same deficiencies in finance that hit housing so hard
in the depression.

Much of that "creative" debt is now coming due—and that spells big
losses for some mortgage holders. To make matters worse, second and
even third mortgages have been wrapped around sound long-term first
mortgages. S & Ls, finance companies, and banks have persuaded practically everyone to indulge in "homeowner equity loans."

It Could Happen Again

The mortgage problems mentioned earlier in this chapter are only the
beginning. We expect to see other mortgage scandals and crises coming
to light. That means increasing foreclosures and forced sales. These, in
turn, point to a drop in the value of mortgage securities. Another consequence could be tighter regulation of appraisals. That could end the
happy fiction of increasing or stable prices upon which much middle-
class buying is predicated.

It is easy to see how a crash could emerge, following a similar chain
of cause and effect to the housing crash half a century ago. Then, a
withdrawal of lenders from the mortgage market significantly reduced
the universe of potential buyers. The unraveling of "creative finance"
could do the same today. Falling prices could wipe out the equity of
many heavily indebted homeowners. Even the elimination of the "infla-

tion" premium in private homes would leave multitudes of buyers owing more than their properties are worth.

A lure into the liquidity trap has been set by the new tax laws. In spite of their special provisions to continue the deductibility of interest on homes, they will lower home values. Even in the highest brackets, the reduction of tax rates will increase the carrying costs of the $100,000 to $200,000 home by 44 percent. And, of course, the tax on the gain from sale of a home will go up by 40 percent. For homes that are not true luxury property, which most are not, there will be a tendency for capital values to drift down. Meanwhile, the very provision that seems to favor continued investments in the private home, interest deductibility, will encourage unwary owners to shift debts to their home mortgage. The home equity loan will be overloaded. The new law limits deductible mortgage debt to the original purchase price, plus the cost of home improvements (except for debts incurred to meet medical and educational expenses).

It is quite likely that the law's effect in encouraging home equity loans will be felt sooner than its long-term effect in reducing capital values. In fact, as slowly as the real estate market moves, it could be years before most investors figure out that home prices are weakening. The likely result is that private homes will be mortgaged to the hilt. Instead of taking a loan to buy a car, which will no longer be deductible, middle-class investors will borrow against their homes and pay cash for the car. This will tend to run the total indebtedness on more recently purchased properties up to the limit of their sale prices.

Before the new tax law passed, lenders were offering up to 90 percent of appraised value on private homes. They may now go higher. This is dangerous. The inflation premium on many properties is as high as 50 percent of their value—at a time of falling inflation. If home prices fall as we think they may, many heavily indebted homeowners could walk away from properties in which they have "negative equity."

The Inflation Premium

Let's look more closely at the "inflation premium" that is so much of the value of many homes.

What exactly is "inflation premium"? Simply stated, it is the value of the property that is not accounted for by its capacity to produce income (including tax benefits). Most homes are selling at a huge premium compared to their rental values. While researching this book, we found a fairly typical example, a house sold for $250,000 that would rent for $700 to $800 per month. At the time of the sale, the rent was about a third of the yield the buyer could have gotten in government bonds. True, there are tax advantages in owning, as we consider below. But tax advantages do not justify a 300 percent premium over rental values.

Many homes are simply selling for far more than the income they can yield. Unless inflation returns soon, rents will either have to go up, or home values will come down. We expect home values to come down.

Obviously, the market does not yet see matters the way we do. If it did, prices would already have tumbled. But expectations can turn quickly, especially if other real estate prices break. One of the shrewdest money people we know, who controls literally hundreds of millions in cash, put the matter in perspective by quoting a real estate ad in *The New York Times*. "Can You Believe, $500,000 for a One-Bedroom in the E. 70s?" If your expectation is that prices can only go up, you might answer, "No, let's rush out and buy." But our answer is also no. We cannot believe people will pay that kind of money for so little. One of these days, the people who paid it will wonder themselves.

Should You Sell Your Home?

This is one of the more difficult questions you can ask yourself. We cannot tell you the answer, but we'll try to make finding the answer simpler by analyzing the separate issues involved.

The first thing you need to decide is whether you really like your present home. Is it the place where you really want to live? If so, that is a very strong argument for staying put. After all, your purpose is not just to rack up profits; you want to enjoy your life.

Another important factor to consider is how much capital you have. And what percentage of it is tied up in the value of your home? If your home represents a small fraction of your total capital, you will have less at stake if its value falls.

But if your home represents practically your entire savings, and you have been planning to cash in and move to another location, then you should seriously study selling now.

In the appendix to this chapter we walk through the calculations needed to determine the costs and rewards of home ownership as an investment. Refer to that section if you have a home or you are thinking of buying.

What the Numbers Mean

Let us tell you what the figures said on a private home we mentioned earlier. It sold for $225,000. The rental value was somewhere between $8,400 and $9,600. To be conservative, we took $9,000 as the value. With government bonds yielding approximately 7.5 percent at the time of the sale, that implies an inflation premium of $105,000 in the price of the home over its rental value. It had a $50,000 mortgage at 11 percent. And it probably had not gone up in value at all over the last year.

To make figures break even under the new tax laws required a 5 percent annual gain.

With these numbers, if property values remain flat, you lose about $11,500 per year.

If the home value declines 5 percent in value, you lose more than $20,000.

If the property values drop by 25 percent, you lose almost $68,000.

Is it unrealistic to think that values could fall that much? You judge. A $68,000 operating loss in the business of homeowning would represent *a shrinkage of a little more than half of the premium in the cost of the home over its rental value.* Unless inflation reignites, there is reason to expect that the inflation premium will fall. The premiums are being held up by the illiquidity of the market and the expectation of raging inflation to come. But illiquidity can only slow the speed of market reactions. Unless the fundamental trend changes, and significant inflation returns, home prices will come down.

Condos Look Especially Weak

As we see the matter, the weakest segment of the residential housing market is that for condominium and cooperative apartments. They will be subject to every drawback facing single-family houses—and more besides. Many condos in urban areas are artifacts of rent controls on apartments. When tight controls during the inflationary seventies forced landlords into a money-losing situation, they found a way out by converting apartments into condos. They were then able to sell the apartments, usually at giant multiples of the free-market level of rent.

It is hardly surprising, given the circumstances, that many of these conversions were poorly done. Many were cobbled together in haste to avoid falling afoul of rapidly changing local laws and regulations. "Conversion controls" sharply reduced potential profits, and landlords seeing controls imposed in other urban areas were keen to complete conversions before controls hit them. Since many of the converted buildings were precisely those that had been allowed to run down because of rent controls, they tended to be sold after cosmetic face-lifts. Many had structural weaknesses, such as poor roofs or creaky boilers, and no provisions for funding major capital repairs or replacements.

Many condo associations elected to forestall increases in maintenance costs by falling back on their insurance. They would not repair the roof—perhaps because they could not afford to do so. But the association—or individual unit owners—made continuous claims for water damage due to the leaky roof. This merely postponed the day of reckoning, while nudging insurance companies toward the obvious response. They have raised premiums to reflect the high level of claims. Increases of 250 percent for 1986 over 1985 levels were common. As a result, the economic attractiveness of the condo may fall even more rapidly than for the single-family home.

In one example from New York City that recently came to our attention, a cooperative apartment that sold for $900,000 in 1985 sold in 1986 for $630,000. That was a 30 percent drop in a single year. We expect to see more such drops.

If the property you own (or are considering buying) is a condo, you should plan upon price declines in all but the most extraordinary circumstances. Generally speaking, we expect the condo to be the weakest end of the residential market.

If a large portion of your wealth is tied up in an expensive home with a large premium over its rental value, you probably should sell it. If you are thinking of buying such a home, wait. You can probably rent for the time being and buy a cheaper property when home values fall. (And if we are wrong, you will not lose very much, especially if financial assets continue to go up as fast or faster than real estate.)

We expect deflationary forces to keep short-term rates down for longer than most people think. This could provide a good opportunity for you to unload real estate properties if they make up a large percentage of your total assets. The opportunities for sale of private homes and apartments will probably be especially good—so long as interest rates remain low and the stock market stays in a bull phase. Home buyers are usually less sophisticated than purchasers of commercial real estate. If the market does start to crumble, they will probably be the last to catch on.

The Duplex

The ideas set out above apply in obvious ways to the duplex apartment. The duplex should be analyzed as a commercial investment. Again, there are four important factors to consider. They are: 1) income, 2) tax benefits, 3) capital appreciation, and 4) leverage (or debt relative to the other elements of return).

Refer to the appendix to duplicate a detailed cost/reward calculation. Or you can work out even a simpler computation. Calculate income. That is the rental value, less operating costs (including insurance). (Of course, this should be compared to opportunity costs to establish a true picture of return, as we show in our calculations on the private home.) You should probably assume higher insurance rates in the years to come, especially if interest rates decline. Lower rates reduce insurance company income, requiring them to increase premiums on money-losing coverage.

You should then analyze the return you will get—setting aside capital appreciation for the moment—at the level of debt (or leverage) you are carrying (or plan to carry).

Notice the difference in cash flow that the reduction in tax benefits under the new law involves.

When you have made these calculations, you will then be able to see what rate of capital appreciation would be needed for you to break even. The higher the rate, the less likely that your investment will be profitable.

A Way to Play a Rickety Market

If you have real estate in your blood and cannot bear to put your money elsewhere, here is an idea that might work for you—distress sales.

Check the laws for clearing titles at tax sales in your state (and surrounding state or states if you live near a border). If law and tradition allow for easy title clearance, contact the tax sale officer in the local jurisdiction. Find out: a) when and how properties are advertised for sale; b) where and when the records of liens against title can be examined; c) the interest charge payable to successful bidders by property owners in order to clear title; and d) the terms and conditions for bidding.

You should then visit your banker and discuss your plans. You need his help in two ways. 1) You may wish to operate with a letter of credit or a line of credit when you purchase the properties. 2) You may need his help in researching recent sale prices and determining a risk/reward ratio for the properties you bid on. In every locale, some publishing company specializes in compiling the details of real estate transactions. These are published in book or computer printout form and sold for high prices to professionals in the real estate and mortgage finance business. In most urban areas, bank lending policies for properties in various neighborhoods are tied to sale prices reported by these services. By consulting with your banker you can find out which company publishes these figures where you live. This will give you a lead in obtaining the latest information yourself.

If you have a friendly banker, which is perhaps another way of saying if you have a large account, you may be able to use the banker's copy. If the banker is especially friendly, he may give you suggestions of his own. These may be useful or useless, depending upon how well your banker knows real estate in your area. But it should not hurt to ask his advice.

Normally the areas of greatest reward for tax sale purchases are in old neighborhoods occupied by lower-middle-class families. These are people who may tend to forget to pay their taxes—or drag out payment until they have no choice but to pay or lose their home. Newer homes are seldom up for tax auction because mortgage holders insist upon tax payments remaining up-to-date. Many mortgages even include the tax payments within the monthly charge. Usually, it is only those who own their properties outright who have the luxury of falling behind in their property taxes.

Are you an expert on trends in lower-middle-class neighborhoods with aging populations? Probably not. But since it is there that the highest returns on tax sales are often found, you may be able to "piggyback" on your banker's knowledge, or at least get his help in finding the experts who compile and publish the crucial information.

Getting a 20-Percent Yield

With this information in hand, carefully examine the properties coming up for auction. There will be many from which to choose. We recommend that you limit your sights to about 12, at least on your first endeavor. Calculate a risk/reward ratio for each property upon which you intend to bid. Decide on a reasonable sum that the property could be worth if you actually obtain title. Pick a conservative sum. In many areas, the appraised value for tax purposes would be a good starting point, perhaps discounted by an appropriate percentage to account for falling prices or your desire to turn the property over quickly. Your banker or a local real estate broker might be able to help you calculate an appropriate discount. The property appraised at $40,000, for example, might be appropriately discounted to $35,000. Or if tax assessments are low, $45,000 to $50,000 might be more appropriate. This is something you will have to determine in your own area.

Once you have a conservative reward target, decide how much money to risk on each of your tax sale offerings. Be sure to calculate the legal costs of obtaining title. An investment of $4,000 with a prospect of obtaining title to a $40,000 piece of property could be quite attractive.

Where possible, stick to stable neighborhoods, not areas struggling through ethnic or racial transformations—unless there is reason to believe that the new residents will increase property values. For example, it has been true in the past that an influx of homosexuals into marginal neighborhoods improved resale value significantly. Homosexuals tend to have fewer children and thus higher disposable incomes. For whatever reason, they seem to spend more money on housing improvements than other groups. Therefore, an influx of homosexuals into a formerly marginal neighborhood may make it attractive for tax sale speculation. At other times, however, neighborhood instability may reduce property values.

Put in bids on choice properties with relatively clear titles. Also look at major development properties. It is typical for commercial developers in some areas to let their real estate taxes fall into arrears. They will eventually clear title in most instances, giving you a fixed rate of interest for your investment. That interest rate is as high as 20 percent in some states.

If the property owner does not step up within a year (or some specified period in your locale), you file a quit claim deed to take possession of the property. (Again, this depends upon the other claims against the property. But if you have done your research carefully, you have not bid on a property, or in an area, to which you cannot easily claim title.) This could be a way for you to earn high interest on real estate investment—and even pick up properties at distress prices.

Buying Foreclosure Properties

Another method of purchasing distressed properties is to buy from the foreclosure lists of federal agencies, such as the Veterans Administration, the FHA, and HUD. They are holding properties that they are incapable of managing and eager to part with. Contact the local offices in your area for lists of properties available.

Many banks and other mortgage lenders are also holding foreclosure properties. Call major banks in your area and ask to speak to the Real Estate Owned or REO section. You can learn several valuable things from conversations with those working in such departments. You may get a list of properties for sale at lower than retail prices. You will also get a hint of how significant the mortgage default problem in your area already is. *If bank portfolios are stuffed with properties that have come back to them, this is obviously a negative indicator for real estate prices in those areas.* Don't buy into a down market unless you do so knowingly, at a discount, and with full recognition of the risk.

9

Trading Financial Assets in an Age of Upheaval

Part I: The Principles of Investment

I don't like money, actually, but it quiets my nerves.
—Joe Louis

We have tried to make sense of a chaotic world by suggesting a new view of reality. But we have no illusions that simply thinking about the "big picture" brings easy profits. Far from it. Investing is not that simple. Even if you perfectly understood the causes of the disorder—understood them better than we can—you would still be a long step from exploiting that knowledge in financial markets. Before you can profit you must understand the principles and mechanics of modern investment. You must know which markets are open to you, what instruments are traded, and how they work. In short, you must master investment techniques.

One of the ironies of capitalist societies is that no one is taught how to be a capitalist. You can take instruction on how to do anything except how to make money. There are business schools. Law schools. Vocational schools. There is a McDonald's College, where they can teach you to flip Big Macs. Or you can learn to drive a tractor-trailer. Just respond to the advertisement on the inside of the matchbook cover. But don't look for the Famous Investors' School. There is no such thing. Most people who become successful investing learn the hard way.

You have probably discovered this for yourself. Unless you were lucky enough to learn how to invest from a patient pro—who for some

303

reason took an interest in helping you—you had to slug it out in the dark. That probably meant one of two things. Either you spent lots of hours reading poorly written tomes on investment. Or, more likely, you suffered lots of losses through mistakes you might have avoided if anyone had ever told you what to do.

Our aim in this chapter is to help you avoid painful mistakes—and give you hints that may make profitable trades even more rewarding. We want you to be a financial success. To help you on the way, we have tried to put down in concise form most of what you need to know to get started in investment. This chapter explains the principles of investment and invites you to clarify your investment goals. It tells you how successful investors utilize information and how you can adopt an "investment frame of mind." The next chapter explains the mechanics of investment, including smart money techniques that offer high-profit potential both because they are leveraged and few people use them. Finally, at the end of the book you will find a glossary of investment terms. You can refer to these definitions whenever you have a question.

Unlike many other aspects of life, markets are entirely impersonal. You have as much of an opportunity to make a profit as the next person. The market does not care what you look like, whether you are fit or lame, strong or weak. If you can place an order with a broker and your expectation about what will happen to prices is correct, you will earn a profit. There is no favoritism involved. And you do not have to resort to heavy lifting.

TAKING STOCK OF YOUR INVESTMENT NEEDS AND SKILLS

I've been rich and I've been poor. Rich is better.
—Sophie Tucker

The first step is simply to draw up an inventory of your assets and liabilities, just as if you were applying for a loan. What assets do you have now? What are your debts? How much cash do you need each month to pay your bills? Can you cut your expenses in any way or sell assets you do not need to raise additional cash for investment? Is it worth sacrificing to reach your investment goals? What are those goals? Have you set an objective you mean to reach by a specific time?

Do you wish to increase the size of your holdings by a certain amount each year? Are you building cash for a major expenditure, such as buying a house or the education of your children? Do you need income to supplement your retirement?

Are you aiming just to be comfortable? Or do you want to be really rich? And how much risk are you willing to take in order to reach your goal? These are basic questions that you should have clearly answered for yourself before you undertake an investment program.

People who do not know what they really want have a hard time getting it. In this respect, investment is no different from buying a car. You have to know *before* you buy whether you want a good ride or good gas mileage, whether the vehicle should have room for six, or be a sleek two-seater. It is the same with investment. You are much more likely to meet your investment goals if you know what they are.

Once you have set your goals and you are comfortable with them, try to distinguish between your available investment capital and your risk capital. Investment capital is any money that you can spare to invest. It does not necessarily have to be all cash. It would include the equity value of real estate, antiques, paintings, coins, etc., as well as stocks, bonds and business assets. Any wealth that you own beyond what you immediately need to live could be investment capital.

Not all of your investment capital is risk capital. Ask yourself how much of your investment capital you could afford to lose without compromising your standard of living in the future. That is pure risk capital —money you could afford to risk. In a sense, that is the most valuable money of all, because you can afford to use it freely in pursuit of high profits. If you are interested in significantly increasing your wealth, your risk capital is what you will rely on.

Another important consideration is how to treat your investments for tax purposes. If your age and circumstances allow you to contribute to tax-deferred retirement accounts, you almost certainly should. While future tax changes may alter the picture, it is probably to your advantage to have self-directed programs with a brokerage firm. Such programs enable you to accumulate income and capital gains on a tax-deferred basis.

Of course, there are some limits and disadvantages on even self-directed IRA and other retirement plans. There are vehicles for investment capital, but not for risk capital. Regulations make it difficult to undertake speculative investments in retirement accounts. You cannot trade freely, invest in commodities, uncovered options, or even undertake short sales. (All of these are explained later in this chapter.) Nonetheless, retirement accounts are excellent vehicles for holding zero-coupon bonds, mutual funds, and some kinds of stocks. If you are not as yet taking full advantage of tax-deferred retirement programs, be sure to take steps to do so.

INVESTMENT SKILLS

Almost everything in life involves skills that are partly learned and partly God-given talents. The good news about investment is that most of its skills can be learned. You do not have to be a genius to succeed in the markets. If you can do basic arithmetic or lay your hands on a pocket calculator, you have gone a long way toward mastering the computational difficulties in investment.

Experience has shown that successful investors have certain characteristics in common. Among them:

1. Successful investors know themselves.
2. They are well-informed.
3. They constantly update their expectations.
4. They respond rapidly to new information.

Let us consider these characteristics in greater depth.

A SUCCESSFUL INVESTMENT DEPENDS ON THE INVESTOR HAVING A GOOD UNDERSTANDING OF HIMSELF

"Know thyself" was the inscription over the gateway to the temple of the oracle of Delphi, and all those who seek to understand the possibilities of the future must look first at their own natures. Our own consciousness is after all the only tool we have to judge of the world, including the world of investment.

There is no doubt at all, from our experience, that people get the best results from investment policies that fit their characters, and can get very disappointing results when they run against their natures. Cautious and conservative people can get excellent results from conservative investment strategies, but more radical strategies will cause them considerable anxiety—the purpose of good investment is to let you sleep at night, not to keep you awake—and will not be successful under their management. Nothing is more surely condemned to failure than a high-risk strategy pursued by a low-risk man; he will always flinch at the point before the strategy has succeeded, and will throw away his potential gains in an attempt to leap back to the security he actually prefers.

So important is this question of temperament that it ought to determine the whole investment strategy of the individual. If you are a swinger, swing. You will buy some very bad investments from some very dubious people, but you will have fun on the way, and you may very likely pick up a few penny stocks that turn into major corporations. If your broker tells you to buy IBM for the long term, do not do it. You will get bored and walk away from IBM long before the benefits can be seen. It is not IBM you cannot trust, it is yourself. Whatever your real nature is, go for investments that match that, for those are the investments you will be able to relate to, and because you relate to them, you will have the best chance of success with them.

This is true even of the most successful investors. One of the most brilliant, and successful, investment minds in the City of London is Jacob Rothschild—the son of Lord Rothschild and the latest financial genius in an astonishingly gifted family. Everyone in the City knows that Jacob's nature is to be a dealer. He starts thinking about selling an investment the moment that he has bought it. It would not do any good Jacob Rothschild trying to turn himself into a different and more conservative type of investor, holding investments longer, and building gradually for the long term. That is the nature of his cousin Evelyn de Rothschild, the chairman of the Rothschild Bank. So different, so contrasting were their temperaments that the two could not work together, but not because either was wrong. Each Rothschild was right, but in his own way.

To be a successful investor you have to be right, but in your own way. It is not only a matter of knowing yourself. It is even more important to be yourself.

Know Your Own Temperament

In order to help you fit yourself into the categories of investment temperament, we have prepared a questionnaire that, as you will immediately see, is designed to test your personal conservative/radical risk/security ratio. We have made the questionnaire turn on three different types of American personality, associated with the great cities of Boston, New York, and Los Angeles. The Boston investor is a man who is here for the next century, who aims to have his great-grandchildren in a position where they will be able to afford the school fees to send their children to Groton. He hates undue risk because it threatens the family stability, which is his highest value.

The New Yorker is another thing again. He does not have stability as his highest value; he goes more for success, but he wants success combined with a certain type of metropolitan prestige, the success most esteemed in an old and sophisticated culture. He is prepared to take risks, but he does not hum to the refrain: "He either fears his fate too much, or his doubts are small, who fears to put it to the touch, to win or lose it all." He wants to be pretty sure that he is going to win. He is a good fellow, but he does not want to be a loser.

In Los Angeles it is different again. There the best thing would be to make a billion without ever coming in from the beach. Risks are inevitable in the leading Los Angeles businesses. High-tech has changed by $100 million or more in the last year, some up, some down. Making money is a fun game, and stability, or even risk avoidance, is not a matter of much concern. If you do win, you want to win big. Here, then, is the questionnaire, at once unscientific and informative. When you have completed it, you will at least know what city you ought to be living in.

1. Do you prefer
    (a) Mozart   (b) Gershwin   (c) The Rolling Stones

2. Would you like to live in
    (a) Boston   (b) New York   (c) Los Angeles

3. If you had your choice of car, would it be a
    (a) Mercedes   (b) Cadillac   (c) Rolls-Royce or Porsche

4. Is your personal wealth target
    (a) up to $5 million   (b) up to $20 million   (c) the Forbes Four
                                                          Hundred

5. Is your favorite sport
    (a) squash or sailing (b) golf or tennis   (c) skiing or skydiving

6. Have you been or do you expect to be married
    (a) once or not at all (b) two times   (c) three or more times

7. Is your ideal family (children)
    (a) four or more   (b) three or fewer   (c) one or none

8. Is your favorite card game
    (a) cribbage   (b) bridge   (c) poker

9. When you see Westerns do you identify with the
     (a) banker   (b) sheriff   (c) outlaw

10. Do you go to church
     (a) weekly   (b) monthly   (c) never

11. Are your favorite foreigners
     (a) British   (b) French   (c) Australians

12. Is your favorite furniture
     (1) European antique (b) Scandinavian design (c) American design

13. As a present would you prefer
     (a) a rare book   (b) a car and driver for   (c) a VCR
                          a week

14. Would you rather own a memento of
     (a) Washington   (b) Lincoln   (c) FDR, or indeed, Teddy

15. If you were born again would you prefer the year
     (a) 1850   (b) 1950   (c) 2050

16. Do your friends think you
     (a) honest   (b) successful   (c) smart

17. Do your enemies think you
     (a) dumb   (b) smooth   (c) sharp

18. To make $100 million ($1 billion if you are a Hunt) would you risk
     (a) 25% of your   (b) 75% of your wealth (c) more
         wealth

19. How much is your biggest loss in a bet
     (a) less than $50   (b) $50 to $1,000   (c) More than $1,000

20. Would you regard bankruptcy as
     (a) the final disgrace (b) a terrible setback in (c) one of the risks of the
                          life   game

21. Do you wear a necktie
     (a) always   (b) usually   (c) seldom

We do not take this questionnaire very seriously as a personality indicator. It is not designed at all to indicate how you rate in aptitude for making money. There is an entire book that proposes to do that, in nineteen extensive personality and intelligence exams. If you would really like to know how you stack up on such tests, see *The Money Test,* by Elliott Weiner and Rita Aero (Beech Tree Books, $12.95). Meanwhile, our questionnaire does offer some hints about where you fit in the risk-security spectrum. It is only fair to tell you what our profiles were. Sir William had eleven *a*'s, five *b*'s, and five *c*'s. His friends would tell you that is about right, that he is indeed basically a conservative man, but with a healthy drive for a respectable kind of achievement (25 percent of him is a New Yorker, which seems right, as his mother was born and brought up in Westchester County, on the edge of Long Island Sound). He has a capacity for taking the higher risks, but that is controlled by the generally conservative balance of his personality.

So if one lays out his personality chart as an investor, it is 50 percent conservative, 25 percent dynamic, 25 percent big risk taking. And this has given him an investment flight path, a track that is natural to him. He has never been, thank goodness, in a situation he could not control, but he has been in financial situations in which he had to sacrifice opportunity in order to keep to margins which made him comfortable. As an entrepreneur, Sir William fluctuates between a willingness to gear himself only to 20 percent, a very conservative position, up to 35 percent—still in what one might call "the New York zone." Although in any individual operation he might go higher, he would not be comfortable with a higher overall gearing than that.

Not surprisingly, James Davidson, who is younger, is more willing to take risks. Appropriately, Sir William directs the Conservative portfolio in our monthly advisory, *Strategic Investment,* while Davidson selects wild and woolly Speculative plays. More than likely, as time wears on, Davidson's Speculative picks will become less exciting. Most of us get more conservative as we get older. Psychologically we all come to live in Boston at the end.

The ideal investor does not exist. If he did, he would probably be an equal blend of conservatism, dynamism, and risk. Yet the chief purpose of all investment is to survive. At least twice a century there come crises that do, in fact, wipe out large numbers of investors. The panic of 1907, the price collapse of 1920–21, and the slump of 1929–33 all wiped out large numbers of investors in the United States. Many farmers, real estate speculators, oilmen—to name but three groups—have suffered from a similar wipeout in the 1980s. There is no way to avoid increasing the risk of wipeout if one raises the debt ratio and raises the willingness to accept risk. If investment is more highly leveraged, it will do better in the good years, but there is at least some possibility that it will disappear altogether in the bad ones.

Investment is not only for profit, it is for you. It should therefore fit your own temperament, be as aggressive as you are aggressive, as conservative as you are conservative. It should also fit your real circumstances. For some people their investments are their livelihood; for others they are their recreation. A retired person using his life's capital to provide a retirement income must primarily be concerned with security, but with security in real terms. He or she wants to live comfortably for the rest of life, whether in a cottage by the sea in England or in a condominium in Florida. Living comfortably means that the investments must show the minimum of risk.

Conservative Investment Becoming More Difficult

In the old days, when our grandfathers and great-grandfathers were alive, minimum risk meant fixed interest bonds. If you knew that the British government in the heyday of the gold standard would pay you three gold sovereigns through to eternity on every hundred gold sovereigns you lent them, then you could plan your future in complete security. Prior to 1914 that was exactly what happened—but World War I finished off the reign of the gold standard, only less completely than it finished the reign of the Romanovs in Russia, the Hohenzollerns in Germany, and the Hapsburgs in Austria. In each case inflation followed.

Since 1914 security had not meant, or has not only meant, a predictable return in terms of money, because the future value of money is itself no longer predictable. We know now what the dollar or the pound will buy. We do not know precisely what it will buy in a year's time, though our guess would be likely to be broadly correct. We are fairly confident that neither currency will gain purchasing power over the next decade, nor suffer an average inflation rate above 25 percent. That range does not tell you very much. If the dollar has an average inflation rate of 3 percent compounded for ten years, that will produce a 35 percent rise in the cost of living in the United States. If the average inflation rate is 12 percent, then the cost of living in the period will rise by 310 percent. So we do not know whether in the next ten years the dollar or the pound will lose one-quarter or three-quarters of its purchasing power.

Yet any retired person who buys and holds a ten-year bond, whether issued by a government or anyone else, is taking a gamble on that outcome, and a gamble that could reduce his expected income by three-quarters.

This can be very destructive. We have most of us known people who retired on savings that made them very comfortably off, only to find that their standard of living steadily slipped. The 12 percent rate of inflation—which could return—was the level that was reached in many countries in the 1970s. Suppose a couple retire at the age of 60 and put all their money into 30-year fixed-interest bonds. Suppose they are quite well-to-do, and that on retirement the income from these bonds is $100,000, a comfortable retirement income.

Then suppose that inflation were to average 12 percent, as it has and as it could again. When the couple were seventy, their income in real terms would be $25,000—or a little less. When they reached the age of eighty, their income would be about $6,000 in real terms, and they would be below the poverty line. If they lived to be ninety, they would have a real income of $1,500, or 1.5 percent of the real income with which they started.

Of course, we all hope that inflation will be better controlled than that. But this simple calculation shows how a not very exceptional rate of inflation can be totally destructive to fixed investments expressed in money terms.

This does not mean that the distinction between security and high-risk investment has been abolished. It does mean that the dividing line between security and risk can no longer be drawn between fixed interest and other investments. If money cannot be trusted—and it cannot—then money instruments cannot be trusted. It is necessary, therefore, to use a wider choice of investments. In a chaotic age, it is increasingly difficult to match a conservative temperament to a conservative strategy. Almost any successful investment program will have to be more aggressive and active than strategies that would have seemed risky to our grandparents.

Successful Investors Are Well Informed

It is practically impossible to be a good investor if you do not take an interest in what is going on around you. The more you know about current events that will have an impact on markets, the better you are likely to do. You also need specific information about the industries or commodities you trade. This is obvious. If you did not even know that General Motors made cars, or that soybeans are a food, you would not be likely to see profit possibilities in developments that affect GM or soybeans.

Information is always the key to making money because markets are really bets about information. If everyone had the same information and accurately computed what it meant, there would be almost no market. If everyone agreed, for example, that gold was worth $415, no more and no less, trading in gold would dwindle to practically nothing. No one would be willing to sell for $414.75, and no one would offer to buy at $415.25.

In the real world, characterized as it is by upheaval and instability, information varies tremendously. Some people think that inflation will soon skyrocket, driving gold to six hundred dollars, while others think that deflation will drag it even lower. The successful investors are those whose information points in the direction that prices will really move.

That is why successful investors are likely to spend far more time and money than others acquiring good information. Successful investors are those whose information points in the direction that prices will really move.

That is why successful investors are more likely to subscribe to investment newsletters and information services that report specialized research on market conditions.

In that light, we have an obvious prejudice to indulge in thinking that a subscription to *Strategic Investment* is a wise investment. You should probably read several other investment advisories as well. They will help you interpret events in different perspectives. We work hard to make *Strategic Investment* a superior source of investment ideas. But there are 3,000 investment letters. Some will be right when we are wrong. Follow the *Hulbert Financial Digest* for the names of other top-performing investment letters. (*Strategic Investment* is not rated by Hulbert because he wishes to avoid the appearance of favoritism. We have shareholders, directors, and researchers in common.)

Other useful information sources include broadcasts on the Financial News Network, "Wall Street Week," *The Financial Times, Barron's, Investor's Daily,* the *Wall Street Journal, The Economist,* and the *Journal of Commerce.* These are noteworthy because they often interpret events from an investment viewpoint. If you follow these new sources, they should help you adopt an "investment frame of mind."

What is an "investment frame of mind"? It is simply a habit of noticing the investment consequences of whatever developments that come to your attention. For example, the war between Iran and Iraq will someday come to an end, if it has not already done so. When the fighting stops, the news reports to that effect could suggest a number of different thoughts:

—You could think it was a good thing that the killing had stopped.

—You could wonder exactly where Iran and Iraq are.

—You could ask what would become of the Kurdish rebels fighting for autonomy from both countries.

—You could see the end of a battle dividing the Islamic world as increasing the danger of a united front against Israel.

—You could think that peace between Iran and Iraq could make it less risky to visit Paris by removing the motivation of Iranian-backed terrorists for attacking in retaliation for French arms sales to Iraq.

—You could see the end of hostilities as heralding an increase in the output of crude oil, thus implying a lower price.

These perspectives are not mutually exclusive. Except for the second, which betrays a lack of knowledge of the conflict, some or all of them could occur to you at once, without involving any contradiction whatever. Yet only the thought about the oil price is informed by an investment frame of mind.

You may think that it is something you either have or you don't. Happily, that is not true. You can choose to interpret events in any number of ways. To think more like an investor, you need only expose yourself to more investment interpretation of current events. It also helps to be an investor.

You will find that if you buy just a few shares of a certain stock or take a small commodity position, you will begin to notice and follow the respective price movements—even though you previously would have ignored them completely. That is why buying a few small investments for children or grandchildren is often an excellent way to put them on the road to thinking like investors.

Remember, thinking like an investor—always looking for the investment implications behind the news—will help you make money. Most people don't think that way. And that is just fine from your selfish perspective. Your own prospects to make money improve if other investors are overlooking possibilities that you see.

Successful Investors Are Constantly Updating Their Expectations of What Will Happen

Research published in the *Journal of Portfolio Management* concluded that successful investors were far more likely than other people to adjust their impressions of what was likely to happen in the future. Bad investors were likely to form an opinion and stick with it—no matter what happened.

In a sense, bad investors are like people who fail to update their impressions of the weather and adjust their clothing accordingly. For example, if it were very cold one year, everyone might put on long underwear, fur pants, and electric socks. The people whose mental thermostats were stuck would never change out of this costume when spring came. In effect, this is how stubborn investors behave. They still trudge around sweating during warm weather in clothing suited for a blizzard.

Consider the many people who lost money investing in gold during the years of disinflation in the first half of the 1980s. There was much evidence over this period that conditions had changed and inflation was not going to rage out of control in the way that it had in the previous five years. (It will again, someday, just as it will once again be winter again.) Yet many inflexible investors held fast to the idea that gold and precious metals prices could only go up.

Some of the blame for this, of course, rests with bad advisory services. They told readers that every fall in the gold price was a once-in-a-lifetime buying opportunity. As poor as this advice was, however, most of the blame must rest with the investors themselves. They were simply inflexible. Stubborn. Plenty of good advice was being offered along with the bad, but a sad fact of the investment advice industry is that consumers sometimes prefer bad advice—if it coincides with some fixed opinion upon which large investment stakes rest. Advisers like the authors, who correctly predicted that inflation would remain low, were not very popular. The newsletters who said buy gold as it fell were only telling some readers what they wanted to hear.

By refusing to constantly update their expectations of what was happening, these investors passed up profits—and took big losses instead.

"Don't Ask the Barber Whether You Need a Haircut"

One of the worst sources of information about the future course of inflation and the economy are firms like coin dealers or the peddlers of survivalist equipment who have a vested interest in telling you only one side of the story. For example, some coin dealers always say that gold and silver will go up because it makes no sense for you to buy their products if their prices will soon fall. By the same token, some stock and commodity brokers are prone to urge you to make many transactions because they are paid on the basis of commissions. Many of them merely push the recommendations that come over the wire from the head office. While this is not true of all brokers, many, especially in the larger firms, know very little. Look for objective sources of information that can help you accurately update your expectations.

"A Stopped Watch Is Right Twice a Day"

Similarly, don't waste your time reading investment advice that is always bullish or always bearish. Successful investors update their viewpoints constantly. It doesn't make sense to subscribe to an information source that always tells you to buy gold or always tells you to sell stocks short. In real life, the markets may go up for months or years (a bull market) and then fall for months or years (a bear market). You need flexible advice to make the best of whatever market conditions exist.

"A Conspiracy Is a Waste of Someone Else's Time"

Some observers of the economic scene devote their energy to exposing "conspiracies" of international finance. Do not pay much attention to these guys. They are so obsessed with making their political points that they don't keep a flexible attitude about the market. Even worse, they encourage you to adopt a rigid—and unprofitable—approach to investing. The evidence shows that the most successful investors are flexible and open-minded. That is not to say that they lack political views. But they are not bogged down trying to interpret events in light of a grand conspiracy theory. They are thinking instead about the implications of changing developments on the market.

HINTS FOR IMPROVING YOUR INVESTMENT PERSPECTIVE

Plagiarize. Follow Tom Lehrer's advice. "Plagiarize, plagiarize, why don't you use your eyes?" Even though we have an international economy today, more closely integrated than ever before, not all developments strike each country at the same time. You can often get hints about how some other countries will behave from what happens in countries that are leading the trend. For example, supermarkets, photocopying, and television became big industries in the United States first largely because people in the United States had higher incomes than those in other Western industrial countries. But as income has risen in other countries they, too, have adopted convenience shopping, photocopying rather than hand copying, and television viewing.

The political barriers between international markets make it possible for you to study developments likely to be repeated from one country to the next, and invest accordingly. When income rises—or falls—patterns of behavior repeat themselves. Now that U.S. per capita income is no longer the highest in the world, you will be able to gauge forthcoming developments in America from the experience of other countries. For example, the VCR craze developed first not in the United States but Japan. Undoubtedly, other new products are now catching on there that will soon be big in the United States. Watch for them. This means taking an international view. As we have emphasized throughout this book, the trends that have a major impact upon investment markets are often set in motion by events far away. Investors with blinders, whose interests stop short at borders, are shutting themselves off from most of the world's opportunities to profit.

Though history never repeats itself exactly, you can study the past for hints about what the future holds in store. As we've explained throughout this book, we believe that many difficulties that accompanied the decline of British power are likely to have parallels now that American power is waning. Make sure your investment strategies take account of these possibilities.

Learn to read the newspaper. This may sound like supercilious advice, but it is not. Seldom do you find important news on the front page, perhaps only once or twice in months. The rare exception is a bolt from the blue—a nuclear accident, an unseasonable storm, or an unexpected death. These are the dramatic discontinuities that cannot be anticipated. To find them as headlines in your morning paper is like awakening to a familiar landscape and discovering that a fully grown tree has suddenly appeared overnight. Most of the time, the headline story is much less abrupt. The tree begins as a sapling on the back pages, and it grows slowly. The typical banner story is a culmination of many small stories and obscure reports that most people never see.

The successful investor anticipates future headlines. That does not mean that you must guess exactly when gathering stories will come to a head. No one can do that. There is far too much randomness in events. But you can read the back of the newspaper, and turn to other specialized information sources, such as *Strategic Investment* or other advisory services that attempt to give you a preview of tomorrow's headlines. To really take advantage of a development as an investor, you have to act upon it before everyone else knows what is happening. You have got to read important stories first between the lines, on the back pages, in preliminary reports and short dispatches that do not command much attention. That is the news you can profit from, when it is still too boring, and uncertain for most people to notice. When you read a banner headline proclaiming, "WORLDWIDE DEPRESSION BEGAN TODAY," it is too late for you to do anything about it.

The bigger the event, the longer it takes to happen. This is the principle behind the "Cartoon Effect," the staple sight gag of the Saturday morning cartoon. Wile E. Coyote wanders off a cliff. And stands there, without any visible means of support. Eventually, just as he has begun to really enjoy his unsupportable position, he looks down, and *wooosh.*

The same things happens with economies. The bigger the event, the longer it will be postponed. The great depression of British decline took decades to emerge. The great depression of American decline may be even bigger, and therefore take even longer to appear. As an investor, you must always bear in mind that you can reason through a logical analysis much more readily than events will work it through. Folk wisdom says when you are building or renovating a house you should first estimate how long the project will take. Once you have that figure, you must then double it to make the estimate right. Follow this principle as well when you are trying to estimate when a new company will become profitable, how quickly a new technology can be developed, or when Latin debt will go into default.

In short, the role of an investor today is like that of a quack physician centuries ago, trying to take the pulse of the economy without being quite sure where the heart of the matter lies. It is a question of guesswork, prayer, and art. You must listen to every murmur, every note of sound or sense that offers even a distant clue to what the future holds. Some of these clues will be misleading or wrong. But don't be daunted. The more you understand, indeed, the more you try to understand, the less likely you are to misdiagnose or mistreat symptoms of investment distress during the upheavals to come.

REMEMBER TO LOOK AT MONETARY CLUES

Fluctuations in the various measures of money's value—the foreign exchange rate, the inflation rate, and the interest rate—have more immediate impact upon the level of economic activity and investment than any other variables.

The interest rate is particularly important. The interest rate is the price that money brings when it is rented. By the magic of arithmetic, the interest rate determines the capitalization, or value of income. You must always be aware of what is happening to interest rates because they tend to determine how much your investments are worth. For example, if you own an asset that yields an income of $10,000 a year, and the interest rate is 10 percent, your investment will be worth $100,000. If interest rates fall to 5 percent, that same investment will be capitalized at $200,000. Or more ominously, if rates go to 20 percent, the capital value of your investment will shrivel to just $50,000. For obvious reasons, it pays to know which way interest rates are headed.

Not just the interest rate, but other monetary factors are major influences upon cycles of boom and bust and thus your prosperity as an investor. Foreign exchange fluctuations alter profitability of firms across borders, raising or lowering the value of investments denominated in other currencies. Increases in the money supply tend to increase nominal GNP and, within limits, to alter the character of investment. If the printing presses are run around the clock, wild inflation will result, raising the value of real assets like gold and real estate relative to financial assets, like bonds and cash. You know this already.

DON'T LOOK ONLY WHERE THE LIGHT IS GOOD

As important as monetary influences are, they alone cannot explain why some downturns become depressions rather than recessions, nor why some upturns lead to long booms, while others are short interludes in a longer period of stagnation, as was the case for much of the world economy between 1919 and 1939. Money may well be the lifeblood of the economy, as we believe it is. But there are other factors determining the larger cycles of boom and bust—factors that are the economic equivalents of the lungs, the liver, and the marrow, factors that in their complexity also replenish or weaken the world system, making it more or less suited to long-run growth.

The clues to these other factors are far more difficult to find or measure than monetary variables. You can follow details of the interest rates, exchange values or variations in money aggregates, sometimes on a moment-by-moment basis. By contrast, the megapolitical factors that figure in triggering prosperity or decline are far more difficult to identify. If you have read this far, you know that there are few statistics kept that would capture the changing megapolitical foundations of the economy. No one can measure the shifting balance between the offense and the defense in weaponry. Decades have passed before the inherent applications of new weapons like the machine gun, much less the missile or the Strategic Defense Initiative, became clear. Similarly, many dimensions of civilian technological change are difficult to track. Years may pass before anyone knows whether a new invention will be the basis of a major economic innovation, or what its full impact will be. More years may intervene before an expert can pinpoint where shifts in employment or profitability marked the transition from one leading sector of the economy to another. Shifts in scale economies, terribly important in the long run, by their very nature are hard to measure. So they tend not to be measured. Yet if our reasoning is correct, such megapolitical factors play a crucial role in precipitating changes in institutions that help or hinder the market process.

The distribution of raw power in the world and the characteristics of technology alter the pulse of economic life as it is felt through the business cycle. Investment forecasting comes nearer to measuring the true state of things by taking these hidden factors into account.

PRACTICE UPDATING YOUR EXPECTATIONS

It is a relatively simple matter to get in the habit of updating your expectations. One way is to write out a list of questions to yourself. Here are some useful ones to ask:

1. Is the economy getting stronger or weaker? (A weak economy usually means lower interest rates and lower commodity prices.)
2. Are oil prices likely to be stronger or weaker? (Strong oil prices usually increase inflation, but lower prices mean less inflation and lower commodity prices. Less inflation is usually good for bonds.)
3. Is the Federal Reserve Board likely to meet its monetary targets, exceed them, or fall short? (When the Fed expands the money supply too fast, this tends to generate fears of inflation. To counteract these fears, the Fed sometimes tightens money, raising interest rates. Higher interest rates are bad for the stock market and bad for bonds.)

4. Is the Fed raising or lowering the discount rate? An increase in rates is often a negative for the stock market.

5. Is the Fed doing "repos"? This means that the Fed is putting money into the banking system by purchasing collateral and agreeing to sell it again later. This increases bank reserves and tends to bring rates down.

6. Is the Fed doing "reverses" or "matched sales"? If so, the Fed is draining money from the banking system by selling collateral and agreeing to buy back later. This usually pushes rates up.

7. Is the Fed buying bills? This means the Fed is adding reserves to the banking system, in effect, printing money. The increase in reserves often causes short-term rates to drop, but may cause long-term rates to rise if it scares up inflationary expectations.

8. Are interest rates likely to be higher or lower a month from now? Six months from now? A year from now?

9. What government is vulnerable to being overthrown? How would this change the flow of trade and the availability and price of raw materials?

10. What policy changes are underway in Communist countries? Is the pro-reform faction in China still dominant?

11. What is the state of U.S.-Soviet relations? Are economic pressures driving the two nations to reduce strategic weapons in the same way the British were obliged to reduce strategic weapons in the 1920s?

12. Are domestic politicians becoming more responsible or less responsible? (Responsibility tends to be deflationary while irresponsibility is inflationary.)

13. What is changing in the world that everyone takes for granted? And which, if any, of the relationships in the questions above may no longer apply in the future?

Each day, ask yourself whether there is any news that would alter your bet about how to answer the questions listed above. Write out your own questions relating to areas you are particularly interested in. This practice will come in handy to you as an investor. You have to exercise your mind to get peak performance, just as you would have to exercise your body to get a peak performance. As Aristotle said long ago, "We are what we habitually do. Excellence, then, is not an art but a habit."

Successful investors respond rapidly to new information. When you

are used to updating your expectations quickly, it becomes second nature to make investment decisions almost instantly when important new
information comes along. The more you think about it, the more obvious this is. Good investors have already been considering what it
means if oil falls or the Federal Reserve raises interest rates. They're
always watching for evidence of a change in the wind. In short, successful investors are ready to take a hint. These hints are coming our
way all the time. Robert Frost was not talking about investment, but
his point applies:

> How many apples fell on Newton's head before he took the hint!
> Nature's always hinting at us. It hints over and over again. And sud-
> denly, we take the hint.

You can be a better investor if you are ready to respond quickly to
the many "hints" that come your way.

CONSIDERING THE COMPETITION

To make profits from investments is not easy. The competition is intense. It is like trying to beat your way through traffic at rush hour. If
the normal drive time is one hour, you will be able to show up with the
pack more or less easily. But if you wish to do better than everyone
else and arrive in half the time, you will need to be a hundred times'
better driver, or indeed, a thousand times better. When everyone wants
to do the same thing, only a tiny fraction of those who try will regularly
succeed in posting better-than-average performance. To get ahead, to
outrace all the other cars on the road, involves knowing exactly where
you are going, anticipating what others will do, and having lightning-
quick reflexes to change directions the instant an obstacle, like a slow
driver in the lane ahead, deters your progress. Of course, the faster you
attempt to go, the more risks you have to take, and the greater the
danger that you will hit a fender trying to scoot past another driver or
bang into somebody in an intersection trying to beat a red light. If you
have an accident, it may take hours to clean away the debris. Trying to
outrace the general flow of traffic, you always run a higher risk of being
snared in an accident, and thus arriving well after everyone else.

It is almost impossible to shave a commute time in half if you are
traveling in the same direction as the rush of traffic. But it is easy to

travel the same distance when you are going the opposite direction. The best time to go into a city is when everyone else is going out. If you want to beat everyone to the pot of gold, you have to start early, take a different route, or, better yet, go by helicopter. Fly over the traffic jam directly to your destination.

The same is true of investment. The best time to buy is when everyone else wants to sell. That is the genius of the Rothschild insight, "the best time to buy is when blood is running in the streets." It is precisely then when competition to get assets is lowest. By the same token, you want to sell when the news is best, at a higher price when everyone else wants to buy.

"BUY WHEN THE CANNONS SOUND AND SELL THE CORNETS."

To talk about this in theory is easy. It is not so easy to make the judgments that enable you to beat the market in fact. At any given moment, the market reflects the information that is available to all the people buying and selling. This does not mean that their information is right. Right or wrong, the market reflects what its participants think.

As an investor, you can therefore look on yourself as having to beat the market despite the market's great advantages. This is like pitting an ordinary chess player against a very powerful computer. Fortunately the human mind can still get outside even the most powerful automatic system and can understand things that the automaton does not understand. At least for the moment, it is possible to beat computers in chess. It is much easier to beat the market at investment.

Investment is a matter of psychology. All good investors use psychology to the full. The market is the dial that tells everything that is happening at a particular moment, including millions of different human decisions. The investor has the unique human ability to think around, before, and behind to link different systems together, to relate. The investor has time to play with, for though the investment market exists to discount future expectations, its own horizon is a very limited one and fades into the distant fog sometimes only a few days away. If this were not the case, it would never be wise to buy when "blood is running in the streets."

It is possible to imagine a perfect market in a world other than our own, with a longtime scale, perfect information, and perfect discounting of expectations. Such a market would not prevent investors making profits, for capital would still command the rent that accrues to the man who allows someone else to use his money. In other words, if you had a dollar to invest, you could still earn the prevailing interest rate. But that is all you could earn. All profits would be equal. With perfect expectations, every investment would turn into a fixed-interest proposition, and the relationship between any two investments would merely be a matter for a calculating machine. Perfect markets do not exist in this world. The investor is always seeking to beat the market, and he uses the imperfection of the markets to do so.

How can you best understand the weaknesses of the market? To borrow a phrase from the language of psychology, the market is an idiot savant, with calculating power that is at once capable of prodigious feats and is at the same time stupid. Idiots savants, though very rare, do exist and have been carefully studied. They suffer from serious mental defects and have abnormally low IQs. Many, perhaps most of them, have had to live their lives in an institution. In spite of their low intelligence, however, they have phenomenal powers of mathematical computation. A pair of twins who live near New York were quite unable to look after themselves, but could, within a few seconds, tell what day of the week it had been or would be on any date from 1000 B.C. to A.D. 3000. Try to work out what day of the week it will be on August 1, 2084, and see how hard that is.

The computer is much the same, and the market is much the same. What it knows it knows far better than human intelligence; it can calculate much more quickly; it can handle what for the human brain would be a gross overload of inputs. Yet at the same time it knows nothing but what it knows, and it has no consciousness of what it knows or does not know. The market is certainly a variant; at any given moment it knows far more than the best-informed investor, and its expectations are automatically linked through the price mechanism to the information people possess. Yet if there is a flaw in this information, some disability from which it is suffering, the market neither knows or cares. The investor is always playing against this mechanical totalizer, always trying to do better than the sum of all the activities of all other investors. In this sense, although we speak of "beating the market," the investor is not really playing against the market at all. The market is not playing against him. It is as well content if he profits as if anyone else profits—it can neither feel its own errors nor resent them.

MARKET IMPERFECTIONS

What are the imperfections of every investment market? The first and greatest is that it is simply a dial that records what people have bought and held in terms of the prices at which they have dealt. In a sense outwitting the market is like outwitting a speedometer; easily enough done, except in terms of measuring speed—and then impossible. If you say, "The speedometer says we are traveling at 50 miles per hour, and I believe we are only doing 30," you will probably be wrong. If you say, "The speedometer says we are traveling at 50 miles an hour, but I am going to slow down to 30," you will probably be right. The market is, however, the speedometer of a system that has five billion drivers— all the population of mankind on earth. It is certainly not as clever as you are—but equally certainly you cannot control it, and the great majority of attempts to corner markets end in tears.

When Sir William was working on the *London Financial Times* in the 1950s, there was an old market reporter named Bill who used to write the market report every day on the London Stock Exchange. There were many elaborate explanations for the movements of share prices— rubber shares would fall "in expectation of a large crop in Malaya," or automobile shares would rise "in view of good sales of new models," but he had one phrase that came into his report again and again. A share would rise "because there were more sellers than buyers." Bill would maintain that this was all that one could usefully say about most market movements, and that most of the reasons given for share movements were invented after the event. We believe in Bill's law. What markets tell you is that there were more buyers than sellers, or vice versa. That is all you do know from markets, but it is, of course, a very great deal.

It follows from this that markets may provide investment opportunities whenever there is buying or selling that is not motivated by ordinary investment considerations. Normally the share markets will put a reasonable value on a share. Some of the investors will be insiders who know in detail the commercial prospects for the company; others will be specialists in the shares of that company or of that section of the market. If the shares are too low, brokers will recommend them to their clients, and investors will come in to buy. Conversely, when the shares are too high, specialist funds will start to sell, there will be few buyers, and the share price will drift down. In such circumstances there is little opportunity for the investor to profit—the market is influenced entirely by investment considerations, and knows more of the real investment considerations than he does.

Yet there is both selling and buying that is not normal investment. Sometimes a large holder needs money urgently. The original family is selling out, or a speculator is closing out a stake he has built up, or there is a general pressure on the money market. In these circumstances the price of the share will be depressed below the normal level and a buying opportunity will be created. Other buyers will, of course, come in, and given time the market will correct itself; but not immediately. Similarly, there are occasions on which what might be termed artificial buying takes place—a speculator is building up his holding, or some other company is trying to acquire control. Then the price of the shares will rise above the level that is justified by normal investment considerations. The market cares only about the relative weight of buying and selling; it neither knows nor cares what the reasons for the buying and selling are.

An even more important weakness of the market is that is takes short views. Admittedly the stock market, like any other market, takes a view as long as that of the people dealing in it. If we take, for instance, the market in works of art of the highest museum quality, that is determined by immortal institutions bidding against each other for perpetual ownership. They have no intention of reselling, ever, and in practice national museum collections are only sold as a result of war or revolution. This market is so expensive that dealers normally operate as agents rather than as principals. The prices attained in this market are therefore the result of competitive bidding to establish an ownership that is expected to last for centuries. How unlike that is the normal financial market in commodities or currencies, or particularly in stocks and shares. All these markets are dominated by short-term traders, who are primarily or solely concerned to take their profit quickly, sometimes in minutes, sometimes in days, seldom in a period longer than a few months. Even investment institutions are revalued monthly and cannot afford to carry weak stocks without their performances being damaged, and their reputation with it.

WAITING FOR THE SCREW TO TURN

In many markets, the patient investor has in this an advantage over the market participants who run with the crowd. He can set himself a length of time considerably longer than the average of the market. He can select investments with an eye to their growth over years, in disregard to the following week's share price. Indeed, he can deliberately choose to flout the current opinion of the market, buying when the market is selling and selling when the market is buying. It is his length of time peak that gives him the opportunity to take the contrary view.

The market is therefore imperfect because it is impersonal—it judges only from what has happened to it—and because it is short-term. The investor can therefore take advantage of the market by acting in a personal way, by making his own decisions and by acting on a longer-term view than the market will take. The length of time is a particularly important advantage to the investor; indeed, length of view is what makes the difference between the successful investor and the failure, the prudent employer of his capital and the gambler. The good investor thinks a lot about time. Likewise, almost all investments of quality take some time to mature. If one takes one of the great technological stocks, like IBM or Xerox, and traces back their market history, one can see a period of decades from the original technological breakthrough to the full ripeness of the investment. The more important the breakthrough, the larger the market it creates; it is development and marketing that take the time. All of us who have been investors for a long time our-selves—and Sir William has been investing for forty years—can look back and see the opportunities we missed—or perhaps took—ten, twenty, thirty years ago. It is these opportunities that have paid off a hundredfold.

COMPETITION AND COMPOUND INTEREST

Yet there are counterforces to the advantages of time. Indeed, in in-vesting one finds there are counterforces to everything. Every thrust in investment produces its own counterthrust, every action its reaction. The two most significant counterforces to time are competition and compound interest. Take competition first. It is a characteristic of a good investment that it shows a high return on capital employed, and that it is constantly expanding its market. Other entrepreneurs are at-tracted by the opportunities that have been demonstrated. Competitors spring up, and if they do nothing else they tend to bring return on capital employed down to a more normal level. Sometimes, as in Silicon Val-ley, we see leapfrogging in technological advances, with yesterday's breakthrough being overtaken by today's.

So one qualification to the advantage of a long-term investment view is the principle of regression to the mean; few investments remain outstanding indefinitely.

The second qualification is compound interest. Suppose you can invest your money at 10 percent, and that you can afford to allow it to accumulate. In seven years it will have doubled; in fourteen it will have quadrupled; in twenty-one years the factor is eight; in twenty-eight, sixteen; in thirty-five, thirty-two; in forty-two years, sixty-four. So when we say that you could have multiplied your money by fifty to a hundred times by good investment over the last forty years—and some investments have indeed multiplied by that proportion—it is not all that much better, if at all, than you could have obtained if you had been able to reinvest ten percent on a compounding basis.

Of course, compound interest is not open to the ordinary taxpayer, nor was 10 percent available in the 1940s, though nowadays it often is. But compound interest is a formidable adversary to best. Fifty years ago, in 1935, gold sold for the official price of $35 an ounce, though Americans, amazingly enough, were forbidden to hold it. It had been fixed at that price by President Roosevelt in the depths of the depression. It is, as we write, at $420 an ounce, more than ten times that value —a nice appreciation, one might think. Yet ten times only represents three-and-a-quarter doublings at compound interest. A purchaser of gold in 1935 would therefore now have enjoyed about a five percent compound interest return on gold if he had held it through to 1985. Of course, the return in terms of constant purchasing power is much smaller than that.

So the long-term investor has to overcome two antagonists: the growth of competition, which will be the greater the better his investment is; and compound interest, which will always tend to mock him with the reflection that he would have enjoyed the same or greater return in fixed monetary instruments, with low risk.

TIME AND YOU

Yet time is the investor's medium. You should play time like a sailor playing out a rope. The concepts of investment are all time-related concepts. You buy a bond. What are you buying? You are buying a fixed flow of income for a fixed period of time. You lend your money. What is the interest on the money? It is a rent for allowing someone else to use your money for a given period of time. You calculate a yield.

That is the profit earned on a share for a particular period of time. You make a sale. The success of your investment is not measured by the absolute profit, but by the profit divided by the period the investment has been held. As an investor, you hold investments over time to make money over time, and time's winged chariot must be the master of your policy.

In thinking about the time you also need to think about the reliability of prediction. There are some factors that become more predictable with length of time and others that become less predictable. What becomes more predictable are those factors that can be associated with the law of averages, for the longer the run the more strongly the law of averages will predominate. If one takes the chance of red coming up at roulette, it is entirely possible that black will come up the first time, and not unlikely (the odds are seven to one against) that black will come up the first three times. That gives one chance in seven of total failure. The odds against black coming up 1,000 times are so high as to make it virtually impossible. The longer the run the closer it is likely to match average performance.

The opposite is obviously true of the intervention of random events. The investor is more likely to be confounded by some random crisis— a war, a revolution, an earthquake, a panic—the longer he holds his investment. He is like a man playing roulette in Mexico City. If he sits at the wheel for a day, he may see a very irregular performance of the numbers coming up. If he sits there for twenty years, he will certainly see regularity in the numbers, but the chances of the casino being hit by an earthquake are also very much higher.

This can be seen in the difference between life insurance and accident insurance. Life insurance is a very safe business because the actuaries' tables do average the expectation of lives—and none of us lives forever. Accident business is uncertain because it is insurance not against a predictable average event, but against an unpredictable random event. The investor is always looking to have the averages working for him, without exposing himself to too great a risk of having the random working against him.

In all types of forecasting—politics, markets, economies, your own life—this balance between the predictability of the average and the unpredictability of the random has to be borne in mind. The very short term does not enjoy the predictability of the average, and speculation for that reason is riskier than investment. It is possible to take a rational view of the likely price movement of oil over the next six months— though one may always be wrong. One can look at factors like the state of supply, the likely demand, broader trends in world trade, the strength or weakness of OPEC, and so on. An experienced forecaster in the oil market, say, a senior executive in a large oil company, will make such forecasts with much better than random results.

On the other hand, it is not normally possible to forecast rationally the movement of the spot oil price over the next two hours, and the same executive would be hard put to beat the random forecast.

We can put these two factors together. The argument then runs like this. Investment is for profit. Superior profit is obtained by finding weaknesses in the investment market (the market itself will normally be profitable). The consistent weakness of the market is its short time scale, the result of a majority of participants in the market, including most professionals, taking a short-term speculative view. By taking a time scale longer than the market the investor, with normal skill, can outperform the market.

But the advantage of length of view is offset by competition, by compound interest, and by the interference of external random events. Predictability of average factors improves with time; predictability of random factors deteriorates with time.

This suggests a pattern to the time strategy that has, we suspect, been that of most really successful investors. It is to plan long, but to try to optimize in as short a time as possible. Let us draw what we would regard as a very normal investment curve. (See following page.)

The first year shows a doubling of the investment; the second year shows a further increase of 37.5 percent; the third year 18 percent; the fourth year, zero; and the fifth year shows a decline that steepens in the sixth. The experienced investor will obviously seek to be out and away by the end of the third year, but better than that he will try to avoid the slowing down of the later period of growth itself.

If one looks at the graph, it is in the second year that the real slow-down occurs. In the first six months of the second year the graph rises from 200 to 250, a rise of 50 points at an annual compound growth rate of 56 percent. In the second half of that year the growth takes the investment from 250 to 275, a rise of 25 points at an annual growth rate of 21 percent. The optimum selling time is probably at eighteen months, even though in the following eighteen months the investment has another 30-percent rise to its peak. From eighteen months onward this particular investment is showing signs of fatigue. The growth rate is slowing, the risks are rising. This is the basis of the nineteenth century Rothschild maxim, "Always leave a profit to the other fellow." Do not chase the last penny.

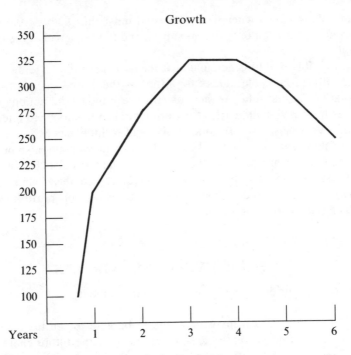

Growth

The first principle of investment is to seek profit; the second is to relate to the market; the third is to make use of time. What is the fourth principle? It is, as laid down by the great nineteenth-century economist, William Stanley Jevons: "As a general rule, it is foolish to do just what other people are doing, because there are almost sure to be too many people doing the same thing."

In recent years this has been developed as the contrarian principle, which argues that the majority is usually wrong. Jevons's formulation is, in our view, the more accurate, and applies to almost all economic activity, not just to investment. If an investor is someone who gets up early to look for mushrooms, he will not seek them in a crowd; if he is looking for good value, he will not find it where prices have already been driven up by fashion.

Most experienced investors find this out for themselves. Sir William once did an experiment for the *London Sunday Times,* in which he chose shares for two portfolios, one designed to follow fashion, the other designed to go against it. He called the two investors Mr. In and Lord Out; Mr. In represented all that was pushy and fashion-conscious in the very fashionable 1960s. Lord Out was supposed to be a crabbed old country landowner who distrusted most things about the modern world, and trusted only to real values, and to the view that the majority is usually wrong.

Sir William did his genuine best for both portfolios. He did not buy the silly fashionable stocks for Mr. In—there were a lot of dubious flotations at that time, as there usually are—and he did not buy the real duds in decaying industries for Lord Out. The results were interesting. For a year or so, Mr. In rode the wars of fashion successfully, and his portfolio went ahead of Lord Out's. But as time went on, fashion passed to new areas, and those of the earlier fashionable stocks began to fade. Of course, some had been sold. Lord Out moved ahead, and when Sir William went on to do other work, the antifashionable portfolio showed much the larger profit of the two.

FOUR INVESTMENT VIRTUES

There are four desirable qualities in an investment:

1. *Liquidity*. An investor wants to be able to sell his investment for cash if he needs the cash or his view of the future changes. He also wants to know how much cash he will get for his investment. Total liquidity is only to be found in a currency note or an immediately cashable money instrument or account. Total liquidity implies immediate cashability at a fixed price in terms of the currency being used for measurement.

2. *Reality*. Money itself is an artificial device, having no real value. Investments in property or in commodities, including gold, are real, hence the term *real* estate. If the investment is not sold, it can be used. In general, real investments are not liquid. It may take months or even years to sell your house. Gold, almost uniquely, is both real —moth does not corrupt it—and liquid—it can be exchanged almost instantaneously for money. On the other hand, gold is only useful as an investment. You cannot live in it, you cannot grow crops on it, and, as King Midas found, you cannot eat it.

3. *Yield*. Not all investors, for tax reasons, are equally concerned about income, but income is the measure of investment. Income may be expressed in current terms of dividends on an equity share or interest on a bond or bank account. It can also be found in long-term capital appreciation. The income (appreciation) on a Picasso may

only be realized when the painting is sold, but the amount by which its value appreciates each year is a nominal income. Putting capital appreciation and actual cash income together gives the true yield on the investment. Obviously the higher the better.

4. *Potential.* Also known as risk. Every investor would like to find investments more likely than average to appreciate in value. These can be of many kinds. In an inflationary period gold may appreciate in real terms—its potential is then high. A pharmaceutical company, with a new drug, may have high potential—the drug will produce a growth of earnings. A government bond may have high potential at a time when interest rates are generally expected to fall. Potential, however, is a question of the risk-reward ratio. For the conservative investor a stock of high potential may be unacceptable because of the high risk. The classic example is the mine sunk to develop ore bodies that have already been found by drilling. The potential may be much greater than the current price of the share suggests, but the risks of mining—water, breaks in the reef, and so on—have yet to be encountered. Conservative investors will accept a lower potential gain when the risk-reward ratio is favorable. Potential is, of course, a future estimate of yield.

NO IDEAL INVESTMENT

The ideal investment does not exist, for the ideal investment would combine high liquidity, reality, high current yield, and high potential yield at low risk. If there were such a thing, everyone would want it, and it would rapidly be driven to an exaggerated price, and would therefore become a bad investment. The way to create an investment policy that balances these factors is to spread one's investment over a number of different kinds of assets, which will between them provide a portfolio that does have all the investment virtues, although no individual asset will combine all of them.

Thus liquidity can be found in cash and near-cash assets. A short-dated bond is near to cash, because it will become cash in a year or two when it is redeemed and will in almost all circumstances be salable to someone who will be happy to carry it for the short period to redemption. Equity shares and gold have high liquidity in the sense that there is always a market price for them—but low liquidity in the secondary sense of knowing what that price will be. Real estate, works of art, and so on have low liquidity in both senses, but they have reality. They are therefore good assets to hold in periods when money is declining in value. Real assets tend to hold their value because they are real. Money assets obviously decline in value when money is losing its value.

DEBT

Most investors have some debts. Indeed, it is often late in life and at a relatively high level of affluence that debt is finally eliminated. Debt has been the basis of every business empire from that of the Medicis to the present day, so it is certainly nothing to be ashamed of. In an inflationary period some debt, preferably at fixed interest, is positively an advantage. But it does need prudent management.

The rules for managing debt are simple:

1. Never use debt for consumption—beyond the reasonable limit of a credit card holiday. Debt balanced against good assets is merely double-entry bookkeeping; debt balanced against a few good meals rests on thin air. Debt should be used to purchase income or to save rent. Either will help pay the interest charge.

2. Never enter a debt tunnel without having a clear plan in your own mind how you are going to get out the other end. Plan to discharge your debts, with a fallback if things go wrong, before you incur them.

3. Always honor your debts. Lenders, whether banks or other financial institutions, will relend to good borrowers.

4. Measure the interest charge against the income to discharge it. A man with a $30,000 income cannot afford a $25,000 debt charge, so he cannot afford a $200,000 house mortgage.

5. Measure the cost of your debt against the anticipated yield of the assets you are going to buy with the debt. If your debt costs 13 percent and your asset appreciates by 20 percent, you are ahead; if 10 percent, you are behind; if it falls by 10 percent, you are in some trouble. In making this calculation allow, of course, for tax on both sides.

6. Always leave yourself a little room. A man, or a corporation, at the debt ceiling is in potential trouble and has no further capacity to take opportunities that may come along.

7. Remember that debts tend to grow. What looks safe when it is incurred may seem a monster a few years later. Mismanaged debt has even eaten up billion-dollar fortunes. So caution is the watchword.

In dealing with the principles of investment, we are not trying to outline the full range of choice. However, there are certainly principles that apply to choice.

RULES OF SOUND INVESTMENT

The first relates to the basic principle of investing to suit your own capacity. Choose investments you understand and feel close to. If you are a dentist in Tampa, do buy the condominium next to your office—do not buy a hilltop farm in Vermont, six miles from the nearest road and under several feet of snow all winter. If there is any money to be made out of that property, it will not be made by you. In your own area of knowledge and experience you are strong; outside it you are weak. And remember the saying that John Carter, the famous bibliophile, first applied to collecting rare books. "It is not the early bird who gets the worm, it is the bird who knows a worm when he sees one."

The second rule may seem the opposite of that. It is that there are always opportunities somewhere. Even in the worst year some shares rise, and even in the worst years for world trade, some countries do well. The serious investor will follow his knowledge in investment, but he will always be trying to expand that knowledge, to find the investments that are going to suit next year's climate.

Remember, investment is about future profit, wherever that is to be found. Because it is about profit, in the end it always becomes a matter of realistic measurement. Because it is about the future, it will be a matter of uncertainty, an art rather than a science.

IN CONCLUSION . . .

The better part of this book has been designed to give you a perspective on changing market developments in preparation for a time of upheaval. We believe we are in a period of history when apparently small events could produce "nonlinear" results, pushing weakened systems into chaos and proving once-unquestioned assumptions wrong. To the extent that this analysis is right, the investment world may go haywire in the years to come. Among the more important implications:

—There will be increasing tendency to instability. This implies lower return from a buy-and-hold strategy. To keep ahead of a rapidly changing, unstable world, you will need to be an active investor with better, up-to-date information than most investors have heretofore employed. To be without creative ideas could be costly.

—There is a greater near-term danger of deflation than most people suspect. To counter this powerful deflationary thrust may require printing of money on a massive scale. The price of avoiding deflation may be runaway inflation. Nimble investment footwork will be required to adopt the proper defense posture.

—The higher-than-expected danger of deflation argues against taking on great amounts of debt except on a nonrecourse basis, or to purchase assets that provide a reliable source of income. Do not rely upon debt exposure to profit from inflation. Inflation will return. Someday. But we believe it is unwise to follow a strategy of putting all your eggs in one basket. The Hunt brothers piddled away one of the great fortunes in history because they were sure that inflation was coming back. Don't follow them into bankruptcy. If inflation comes back, you will know about it. You will have the opportunity to profit in commodity markets and by buying shares of heavily indebted corporations. Big issuers of junk bonds like Best Products, Cannon Group, Columbia Savings and Loan, First Executive, Integrated Resources, Lorimar-Telepictures, Minstar, Navistar, Nortek, Reliance Group, Revlon, Southland Financial, Texas Air, Triangle Industries, Turner Broadcasting, and Wickes Companies will be excellent buys —if they are still in business.

—Product cycles based on the technology of nineteenth-century science are nearing their end. The greatest profits will probably be earned in the new technologies and the proxies of the new technologies. An example of a proxy for new technology is to invest in gallium, or a gallium mining firm, such as Musto Exploration Ltd. (Canada), in the hope that gallium arsenide chips will figure importantly in coming generations of computers.

To be clear, we are not saying that no profits will be earned in oil, steel, automobiles, and the like. We are saying that the potential for profit growth in bioengineering, solar energy, or artificial intelligence far exceeds the profit potential in mature industries.

—Political arrangements based upon the technology of nineteenth-century science, such as Communism, will also come under increasing strain, implying decentralizing reforms, which we have analyzed extensively. Taken with other developments, these imply relatively lower primary product prices, especially lower prices for renewable foods and fibers.

—Communist reform may raise the relative prices of tropical commodities. Cocoa, which cannot be grown in the Soviet Union, may fare somewhat better than corn, which can be.

—You should expect slower wage growth, with labor taking a smaller share of national income and greater returns to investment. This implies higher profits for those firms making profits and capital gains for financial assets.

—You should expect lower profits for firms whose sales depend upon discretionary spending of blue-collar workers and their families. The Hammacher Schlemmers of the world will probably enjoy an easier time of it than Sears.

—The breakdown of international order will expose multinational firms to increasing dangers of direct or indirect expropriation. Check your investments against our list of the major corporations at risk.

—An international debt collapse is coming. This is bad news for the stock and debt obligations of bank holding companies.

—There could be excellent profits for holding the bonds of good makers. But watch for defaults, especially among recent issues. As deflationary forces set in, and long-term interest rates fall, investors seeking high yields tend to welcome weaker issues. If it has not done so already, the junk bond market may collapse. Hold junk bonds only if you are a skilled credit analyst who enjoys reading indentures, the fine print that accompanies a bond issue.

—Some profits will be made in farming by individuals and specialized firms, but over the long run technological development suggests that the farm sector as a whole will be depressed. This implies weak farmland prices and weak sales for firms catering to the farm community.

—You should expect a drop in the growth of world trade as a percentage of economic activity, with more protectionism all around. This will be bad for Japan and other countries with large export surpluses. Probably, this will be a negative for their stock markets. Protectionism will also be a negative for the world economy as a whole. Transport companies, such as shippers, will be hit hard, for obvious reasons.

—You should expect continued currency fluctuation. This will have a major impact upon the profitability of large firms. We include a list with suggestions on how you can profit. Over time, currency strength tends to mirror the strength of the economy. We suspect that the large overhang of debt will reduce U.S. growth relative to capital-exporting companies, at least until full-fledged protectionism takes hold.

—Don't bet on rapid long-term growth for conventional military contracting. Limit investment in defense-related industries to technology plays by buying firms that have a major role in developing new generations of technology. Rising costs in conventional defense point to scaled-back programs and slowly growing or falling budgets.

—Expect a long-term decentralization of energy supply. This implies eventual breakup of many utility monopolies and the twilight of the nuclear power industry.

—As a general rule, invest with technology, not against it. Smaller-scale firms will gain more advantages from most new technological developments. But remember, too, that small firms are less stable. They have a smaller resource base with which to protect against market shock. Therefore, investment in small-scale firms should be highly diversified. And remember, as well, that there are limits to ventured capital. The costs in pioneering some innovations of the future, such as computer-controlled highway systems, will be staggering. Although a hacker in a basement could be the person to stumble across some innovations, others will still be the property of DuPont, Monsanto, or GEC, plc. Make it your business to update your knowledge of the latest developments in technology.

—In the long term, radically decentralizing technologies could undermine the economics of the city. Most large cities are already suffering from the decline of manufacturing and the fall of the relative value of unskilled and semiskilled labor. Cities are essentially artifacts of centralization. They prospered mightily during nineteenth- and twentieth-century waves of industrial development as new technologies increased economies to scale in the production process. Now new developments are reducing scale economies, leaving cities burdened with high costs and receding resources. As the technology of terror becomes more widely dispersed, you can expect cities to be held to ransom by individuals and groups with a wide variety of grudges. Be cautious about holding long-term debt obligations of industrial cities.

—A significant upheaval in world institutional arrangements could result for the first time in almost three centuries in the passing of the mantle of predominance from English-speaking nations. If so, you should watch carefully for signs of institutional instability in Great Britain and the United States. Such instability has plagued other countries. Even Germany and France, major contenders for power and wealthy industrial countries, have had four or five governments each during the twentieth century. There is no inherent reason that the English-speaking democracies should not be prey to the same fate with the eclipse of their predominant power. From the point of view of an American or British investor, therefore, not to mention the Canadian, Australian, or New Zealand investor, the next depression may be more threatening than most people imagine.

—If past patterns apply, exchange controls are likely for the United States. Therefore, investors with large holdings should diversify internationally. Get your money out now, while you can. No major country has ever prohibited a citizen from repatriating his money when he wished to do so. Nor have exchange controls typically applied retroactively to funds moved offshore before they were activated. Therefore, the chances are high that you will increase your investment flexibility in ways that more than offset the transaction costs of parking some of your liquid funds abroad. Where? You will not go far wrong by keeping substantial funds in Switzerland, Germany, Britain, Holland, or even Austria.

—You should probably hold some gold and perhaps palladium for insurance purposes. If there is runaway inflation or dramatic instability, you will be protected to some extent by holding 5 percent of your assets in gold. Palladium will tend to benefit from the deepening crisis in South Africa. Today, that country controls almost all palladium production outside the Soviet Union. In the past, the Soviets have made vigorous efforts to manipulate the palladium market. When South Africa cracks up, you can count on further Soviet manipulation to drive the palladium price even higher. But before you invest you must check late-breaking developments to be sure you are not caught on the wrong side of the market.

—The Japanese yen may gain dramatically in value over the next three years. If the yen gains as much value as the dollar gained on the pound when the U.S. overtook Britain as the world's leading industrial power, there could be as few as 50 yen to the dollar in the not-distant future.

—Governments may turn once again to gold to reliquefy a bankrupt world in the event of widespread deflation. If so, gold prices could rise dramatically. Governments might also seek to impose penalties, windfall profit taxes, or even gold confiscation to take away the profits of gold owners. Remember, President Franklin Roosevelt confiscated gold in the United States and outlawed private ownership at the same time that he raised its price to $35 per ounce in an attempt to reliquefy the economy. Such political steps could be repeated again. Be wary. If you have large assets, you may wish to hold gold offshore, or indirectly in the form of mining shares.

These are just some of the implications of our analysis. You should question them as rigorously as you question the assumptions that they challenge. We are constantly attempting to update our understanding of how the world is tending. Chances are, by the time you read this, we shall have modified some of the thoughts listed above and come to new ones.

You should enter into the process of developing your own view, not as an exercise in pride of authorship, but because you need to work out how developments fit together. This must be an ongoing process rather than a static conclusion. Investment is a discipline that remains in constant flux.

10

Trading Financial Assets

Part II: The Mechanics of Investment

One thousand dollars left to earn interest at 8 percent a year will grow to $43 quadrillion in 400 years, but the first hundred years are the hardest.

—Sidney Homer

Most people who seek profits in financial markets never employ 90 percent of the investment techniques and instruments open to them. This is like trying to win a battle while employing only 10 percent of the available strategies. Don't unnecessarily limit your options. The more methods you have of profiting from anticipated market changes, the better able you will be to meet your objectives.

This chapter will review the mechanics of investment, from the basics to sophisticated trading strategies.

THE BASICS: GOING LONG AND SHORT

All investment profits depend upon selling something for a higher price than you pay for it. Whether you are trading stocks, bonds, warrants, commodities, options, or anything else, you want to buy low and sell high. There are two fundamental ways to do that. Only one of these is really understood by most investors. That is called going long. If you buy something first and then sell it later, that is known as taking a long position. The other method is called going short. When you go short, *you sell something first in hope of buying it later at a lower price.*

Short positions are much less popular with investors than long positions. A major reason is that so many investors really do not understand

341

how short sales work. Why this lack of understanding? There is one obvious reason. Lack of practice.

In daily life, everybody has ample practice in going long, buying things first and disposing of them later. Even people who do not think of themselves as investors have bought thousands of things that they later sold—or could have sold—from football tickets to furniture, automobiles, boats, and houses. With all that practice, it is natural when you turn to investment to first *buy* a stock, bond, or some other financial instrument, and hope to sell it later when the price has risen. In other words, it is natural to go long.

Most people get little practice in selling things first and buying them later. Auto dealers do this when they sell a car to a customer and then buy it later from the factory or another dealer for a lower price. But if you just announced to a room full of people that you had sold a car you didn't own, many of your listeners would immediately think that you had done something dishonest. This lack of practice in selling short helps explain why so many people pass up investment opportunities— when they think that the price of something will fall.

Remember, because short positions are less popular than long ones, the odds are more in your favor when you invest that way—especially in a time of deflation. You, too, can profit by selling things first and buying them later.

Of course, any technique in investment has its advantages and its drawbacks. When you sell short shares of stock, you are obliged to pay any dividends payable by the company during the period of the short sale. And you also risk a greater loss, at least theoretically, with any short sale, whether of stocks, options or commodities. When you go long, you can never lose more than the original sale price. The worst thing that can happen is that whatever you bought will fall to zero and become a total loss. On the other hand, your potential gain when you go long can be theoretically infinite. In theory, at least, a stock you bought for one penny could rise to a value higher than the national debt. In real life, of course, gains of even 200 percent or 300 percent are rare. But they do happen.

By contrast, when you sell short, you can never gain more than the sale price. And whatever you sold would have to fall to zero before your gain could be 100 percent. When selling short, it is your potential loss that is infinite. The stock or other item you sell could theoretically rise to infinity without you having a chance to replace it. (When you sell shares of stock short you must borrow them from your broker or someone else who has them.) But the practical fact is that you are not in danger of losing an infinite amount of money by selling short. Your loss or gain is usually determined by whether your market judgment is correct. You can usually make just as much money by investing on the correct assumption that the market for something will fall as you can by correctly guessing that it will rise.

FUNDAMENTAL VERSUS TECHNICAL TRADING

How do you decide when to sell and when to buy? As we explained in the introduction, if you are not inclined to trade randomly, you have only two other choices: fundamental trading and technical trading. Successful investing ordinarily involves some elements of both.

Fundamental trading is based on the assumption that you can figure out which way markets are likely to go by understanding one or more basic factors that will affect prices. Fundamental traders base their buy and sell decisions on news or analysis that they think other investors do not properly understand. For example, if you believe that unrest in Saudi Arabia will oblige the government there to start pumping more oil, you may wish to take a short position in crude oil. That is a fundamental approach to commodity trading. A fundamentalist making stock picks is not someone who holds the Bible as the sole religious authority, but an investor who looks for assets that have a value that is not accurately reflected in the price. That's just another way of saying that stock or another instrument is a bargain (or is overpriced) because other investors are overlooking some important fundamental. Factors like sales, earnings, profit margins, cash flow, and political developments affecting the firm's line of business will be important to a fundamental trader. We believe that megapolitical fundamentals are also important, as this book attests.

Technical trading is based on the assumption that you *cannot* figure out why markets will move one way or another. Technical traders believe that you can only watch the market itself for decisions about whether to buy or sell. They spend their days watching charts and trading patterns for clues about what may happen next. They do not attempt to understand *why* the prices are moving up or down.

We take a largely fundamental approach in *Strategic Investment* each month. That means we base our investment recommendations mainly on factors that we believe will affect the market. We don't spend our time poring over technical indicators or chart formations, except occasionally to time short-term trades. On the other hand, we have colleagues who do. One of the shrewdest of these is James Mayfield IV, who was selected the top commodity broker in the United States in the U.S. trading championships reported in *Barron's* in 1985. Mayfield obtained a monitored profit of 189.9 percent in just four months. He operates a technical hotline for futures trading with which we are associated, called *Goldline*.

When you invest, you will want to take technical analysis into account, especially in commodity trades. You can either subscribe to a service like *Goldline* or develop the technical indicators yourself. When you intend to make a trade, ask your broker to give you support and resistance levels for the commodity (or stock) you are considering. Most brokerage firms employ analysts to supply your broker with this technical information on a continuous basis. The support level is the price where the chartists suggest a commodity or other investment will stop falling. A resistance level is the price at which the chartists say that an item is not likely to rise further.

Remember, technical investors who trade on those concepts are relying on patterns in price movements. You will probably want to be aware that they will be tempted to take profits—or sell—when a price reaches a resistance level, and buy when it falls to a support level. Brokers should help you to stay abreast of these technical factors.

TWENTY-FIVE TRADING GUIDELINES

As you proceed in your investments, you can often keep your balance and avoid mistakes by referring to the trading guidelines of outstanding investors. We believe that these suggestions are sound and sensible ones. Most of the techniques and guidelines are not new but old. After all, the basic logic of investment will endure so long as human nature endures. Some are derived from *A Treasury of Wall Street Wisdom*, edited by Harry D. Shultz and Samuel D. Coslow (Investors' Press, 1966). Others are guidelines we follow ourselves, and are derived from the work of the shrewdest traders we know. When you read and use these guidelines bear in mind the comments of a successful man from the past named Gerald Loeb. He said, "There is no rule about anything in the stock market save perhaps one. That rule is that the key to market tops and bottoms or the key to market advances or declines will never work more than once. The lock, so to speak, is always changed." The commonsense principles that you can use to pick the lock, or cut it off altogether, may endure. Here are some that you may find useful.

1. Do not allow your investment decisions to be governed by hope. Invest on the basis of sober calculation. If you catch yourself hoping too much that an investment will work out, you are probably operating from a weak position.

2. Never risk more than 10 percent of your capital in a single trade. It is a good rule for limiting risk on speculative trades. If you never expose more than 10 percent of your account to a loss, you will be in a position to recover from any setback.

3. Always question the basic premises of every investment. Try to identify the unspoken assumptions that must hold true for you to make a profit. As the world becomes more unstable, many apparently safe assumptions will become more dicey. If you have explicitly identified these, you will be in a better position to respond and profit when the music stops.

4. No general keeps his troops fighting all the time. Do not feel obliged to constantly make trading decisions or deploy all of your capital.

5. Don't spread yourself too thin. Although it is prudent to diversify, you cannot be an expert in everything at once. Limit your investments to those in which you have a real interest and the time available to make informed decisions. Remember, every investment has a time requirement, as well as a capital requirement. Don't overstretch your time and attention.

6. Match your choice of investments to your decision-making speed. Few people are able to make snap decisions that are sound. If you are such a person, you can utilize that ability to great advantage. If you are not, you can formulate your investments to limit the requirement for split-second decision making. Trading certain futures markets, for example, can require not only constant monitoring, but very rapid decision making. Other trades, including some futures trades, can be undertaken after long contemplation and executed according to a system that has been thought out well in advance. Don't try to trade in rapidly fluctuating markets if you are not a split-second decision-maker.

7. You can sometimes key your decisions to your own or other people's tendency to err. The "contrary" approach to investment

involves taking a position opposite that taken by others. (Some investors who know their own decision-making processes well can also profitably trade by going contrary to their own first inclinations at a time of rapid market movement.) Part of the foundation of the contrarian view is the assumption that most investment decisions are wrong. This contrarian principle can often be overstated, but if understood properly, it can provide a basis for improving your trading performance. The point is not that the majority is always wrong, but rather that if pressed to decide about something at a speed that exceeds their own pace of reflection, most people will make poor decisions. As Humphrey Neill put it, "The public is not always wrong, but tends to be at the junctures of events and terminals of trends." It pays to be suspicious of the majority opinion (or sometimes, your own opinion) at just such times.

8. Always place more confidence in trades that follow the primary trend than those that buck it. No skill is more difficult than the ability to call market turns. Indeed, there is so much randomness in the short-term fluctuation of prices that it is practically impossible to make such judgments consistently accurate. Those who are best at calling major turns are artists whose hunches are wisdom, not knowledge. Once a major trend has reversed, and a new one is under way, however, you can invest with more confidence.

9. Buy the stock market when the Treasury bill rate goes below the discount rate; sell the stock market when T-bills go above the discount rate. This relationship has worked for so long that it is a matter of conviction among most professional investors.

10. Buy shares of companies that are selling at a price-earnings ratio that is less than their earnings multiplied by their growth rate.

11. The biggest buying opportunities for Treasury and top-quality bonds is during financial crises. During crises there is a flight to quality and short-term liquidity. At this point bonds fall. This puts even high-grade corporate bonds at a discount. The aftermath of a financial crisis is to weaken the economy. This tends to lower interest rates. Low interest rates are good for bonds. There is also a tendency for the Federal Reserve to buy government bonds if a crisis brings deflationary threats. T-bonds bottomed in early 1932 in the last depression, and then rose as Fed holdings of securities rose. Remember this. If our analysis is right, there should be a succession of financial crises in the future.

12. When you are looking for bargains in a falling market, buy on

the third gap down—or when the major holder has sold. A "gap" is a tool of technical analysis that arises in markets that do not trade continuously. When today's opening price is below yesterday's low or above yesterday's high, a "gap" is said to exist. Usually, three gaps down are enough to exhaust the hopes of those who have previously held the investment.

13. Another likely indicator of the bottom is when the major holder of a stock liquidates his position. A major holder is likely to be well informed. If he is ready to sell, it usually means that the good news on the horizon has been exhausted. When hope is gone you can usually look for a base to form for the beginning of another rally. Remember this. There should be many such opportunities in the years to come.

14. One month of record-breaking movement in the averages is never followed by another in succession, although the trends may be in the same direction. (Bernard Baruch)

15. After the fundamentals have turned unfavorable, the market often advances further and only technical considerations give much clue to the time of a turn. Excitement is one of the strongest evidences of weakening. (Richard Schabacher)

16. Bull markets end usually after a long period of heavy trading fails to produce a price rise worth mentioning and a moderate decline occurs with volume active. (Harold M. Gartley)

17. The end of bear markets is usually characterized by dullness.

18. In declining markets, when 80 percent of stocks are down three days in a row, a rally must be expected and should replace one-third to one-half of the distance lost. (Bernard Baruch)

19. When a market is overbought, activity goes dull on rallies and increases on declines. (William Hamilton)

20. "When in doubt, get out, and don't get in when in doubt." Beautiful alliteration, it is the wisdom of William D. Gann. It is another way of saying what we said above. You do not always have to be fully invested.

21. "Sell down to the sleeping point."

22. It is not a valid reason to hold an investment just because you bought it. In other words, cut short your mistakes.

23. Invest to make money, not to make up your losses. There is a natural tendency to gravitate toward higher-risk investments in order to recover losses quickly. Resist it. The best course for making a profit on your present trade will be the same whether your previous

trade was a profit or a loss. Losses are inevitable. When they happen, remember them for your tax return; otherwise forget them.

24. Let your winners run. Poor investors have a tendency to let their losers run in hope of recovery, while cutting short their gains.

25. Although you don't want to cut your winners short prematurely, don't aim to squeeze the last penny of profit from a position. "Always leave a profit for the other guy." This Rothschild principle is among the most important of all the rules of prudence. You will not go broke making profits.

GUARDING AGAINST INVESTMENT MISTAKES: STOP LOSSES

Every form of investment involves some risk. That risk is much higher in futures or commodity trading than in depositing your money in government securities, or investing in most stocks. On the other hand, futures trading can be much more profitable. The reason for this increased profit potential, as well as the danger, is that futures trades are highly leveraged. Leverage is the ability to control a lot of money through using just a little of your own. All leveraged situations involve risk. Although most commodity traders lose money, the ones who make money make a great deal. When you enter such trading you take a risk. The key to success is to control your risk. One way to do that is only to trade in situations when you think that a strong fundamental case exists for a market movement that has yet to take place. *Strategic Investment* gives recommendations each month in its "Speculative Strategy." As of this writing, about 75 percent of our commodity trades closed out in 1986 had been profitable, with an average gain, combining the winners with the losers, of more than $4,000 per trade.

Getting good investment guidance is only a partial help in limiting your risk. You must also limit your risk on commodity trades and speculative stock positions by entering stop losses. A stop loss is a standing order filed by your broker to close out a trade when your loss has reached a certain level. Suppose that you have purchased a contract for future delivery of 100 ounces of gold at $319 per ounce, and you want to limit your loss to $1,000. When you place your order, tell your broker that you want to enter a stop loss of $1,000. He will file an order to sell at $309 that is "good till canceled." If gold falls more than $10, the order will be triggered, and your position will be sold. Chances are good that you will be protected from losing more than $1,000.

Another form of stop loss is a trailing stop. A trailing stop is an order to close out a position whenever the price moves by a given amount in an unprofitable direction—regardless of whether it first goes up or down. Let's say you sold a 100-ounce gold contract at $327.50 with a trailing stop of $750. If the price immediately rose by $7.50 per ounce, your trailing stop would be triggered and your position would be closed out with a loss. On the other hand, suppose gold fell to $311, then rose to $318.50. Your buy order would be triggered when gold rose by $7.50 from its low. You can use trailing stops both to minimize losses and to protect profits.

Neither trailing stops nor plain stop losses are perfect. Markets do not trade continuously, and they are volatile. Even with stops there is a chance your losses will be larger than you bargain for. If you buy a 100-ounce contract on palladium at $146.80 with a $1,000 stop loss, palladium could close today at $137.60 and open tomorrow at $127.60. If that happens, you've lost more than $1000.

Some commodities markets have limit days. On these days, sell orders may not be filled because prices have moved to the limit set by the exchanges. Under such conditions, you may not be able to close out a losing investment until you've lost more than you planned. The same kinds of risks occur for short sellers on the upside. If you had sold gold at $419 with a $1,000 stop loss (an order to buy the contract back at $429), you might wake up one morning to find that the price of gold in London had suddenly been fixed at $432.

OPTIONS

It was partly to limit such risks that investment instruments known as options were developed. Options give investors the right to purchase or sell some item at a specified price within a limited period of time. Options are now available on many stocks, stock indices, commodities, and even on such exotic items as ocean freight rates. (Options on stocks trade in units of 100 shares. Options on commodities usually trade in units of a single contract.)

Options come in two types: calls and puts. An option that gives you the right to buy something at a specified price is known as a call. An option that gives you the right to sell something at a specified price within a given time is known as a put.

You can either buy or sell puts and calls. You cannot margin the purchase of puts or calls. You must pay for the options in full when you buy them. Selling (or writing) puts and calls does require you to put up margin money, unless you are selling a covered call. A covered call is one that you are backing with the underlying stock or commodity in your account. In other words, if you already own 100 shares of IBM, you can sell an option for someone to purchase those shares without posting additional margin. If market developments require you to sell the shares, your broker knows that you can produce them. By contrast, all puts are uncovered—because puts are an obligation to buy. The only way that performance on an obligation to buy can be guaranteed is by providing proof that you've got the money. That's why margins are required. In option trading, as in commodity trading, margin is merely a down payment or good faith money required by the exchange and/or your broker to guarantee that you make good on your promises. Unlike margin in stock trading, there is no need for you to pay interest on option and commodity margins. In fact, you can put up Treasury bills to cover the margins, so you can actually continue to earn interest while meeting your margin requirements.

How do options work? Let's start with a simple example. If you think the price of something will go up in the future, buy a call. Of course, you should only do this if the call has enough time remaining to allow for whatever movement you expect to take place.

If IBM is now selling at $120, and you expect it to go up by $15 within the next two months, you can buy an IBM $130 call with three months left to go. That call gives you the right to buy 100 shares of IBM stock at any time before the next three months at a price of $130 a share. Of course, you wouldn't want to exercise that right unless the price of IBM rose above $130.

Let us say you had to pay a premium of $2 for each of the 100 shares. You would then have two choices. You could actually exercise your option. You could call away the IBM shares from someone for $130. But you probably wouldn't want to do that unless the price exceeded $132 ($130 for the stock plus the other $2 you paid for the option).

The other alternative is that you could sell the option. If IBM reached $133 with a month and a half to go, the call you bought for $2 could easily sell for $5 or $6. You could then sell the call, pocketing a profit from 150 percent to 200 percent.

Obviously, you don't always make such high profits.

You can also use options in another way if you think the price of something is going to go up. You can write puts. When you write a put, you sell someone the right to force you to buy something from them within a given time. A put gives its owner the right to sell a stock or commodity to you at a given strike price within the time period during which the option is good.

Sound complicated? Many people seem to think so. But it's really rather simple. It's just that there aren't many examples in daily life that give you much practice in dealing with puts. Perhaps the closest you get as a consumer is having a money-back guarantee. When you buy diamond jewelry, for example, the jeweler may promise to buy back the diamond at whatever price you paid for it—any time within the next five years—even if the price of diamonds goes down. Of course, the jeweler doesn't think the price of diamonds will go down. In essence, he is offering you a put. A put is like a money-back guarantee, except that you don't have to own the item in the first place. It is like being able to sell the diamond to the jeweler if diamond prices fall—even if you hadn't yet bought the diamond. In other words, a **put** is just a guarantee that you can sell a stock or commodity at a certain price.

Go back to the IBM example. You think that IBM, now selling at $120, will go up in the next few months. You write a put giving someone the right to sell you IBM shares at $110 within three months. If you are right in thinking that IBM's price will rise (or even hold steady), you will make money. Let's walk through the example to see how it works.

Let's say you get $1.50 per share to write the put, not a spectacular sum of money, but still considerable. (Since there are 100 shares in each stock option, you get 100 times $1.50.) If the price of IBM goes to $130, the value of the put you wrote may fall considerably, say, to 50 cents. This means that you have made a profit. Something you sold for $1.50 you can now buy for 50 cents. You have two choices. You could buy back the put for 50 cents, making a $100 profit ($1.00 per share times 100) on each put. Or you could continue to hold the put, hoping that it will expire worthless.

Sometimes, when you write a put or call, it is better to buy the option back when it has fallen enough to give you a large profit, including commission costs. At that point, you will have gained most of the profit you could get for tying your money up for the duration of the contract. If you hold it to the end, you are always running the risk that an abrupt market swing could turn the situation against you, taking away your profit, and even handing you a loss. You have to decide whether that risk is worth giving up the last few cents of profit.

STRADDLES—PROFITING FROM A
VOLATILE MARKET

Puts and calls are also useful instruments for trading in combination. Used together, they give you a way of profiting from a flat market, or one that is highly volatile, whether or not you can guess its ultimate direction.

An option straddle is a bet on short-term market volatility. Let's suppose that you are not sure which direction the stock market will take. But you do think that it is not likely to stay at its present position. It will either go up significantly or down significantly. The option straddle gives you a way of profiting from this insight if you are correct.

How does this technique work? You simultaneously buy one or more puts and calls at the same strike price. Say the S&P 500 Futures Index is now at 280. You buy one or more 280 S&P puts. At the same time, you buy one or more 280 S&P calls. Usually when entering a straddle you will want to buy puts and calls with no more than three months to run. Why? Because you are betting on near-term volatility. If you buy options with nine months to go, you will have to pay more for them because their time premium is greater. Obviously, the more you pay for your options the less profit you will make if you are correct in thinking that the market will be volatile in the short run.

Consider this example. Suppose you buy an S&P 280 call at a price of $2 and a 280 put at the price of $1.50. Then there is a week of heavy selling, and the S&P index falls to 273. The put you bought at $1.50 is now worth at least $7. It is in the money by that amount.

At this point, you have several choices. You could do nothing and hope for the market to fall further. But you probably don't want to do this because the only reason for putting on the straddle is that you did not have confidence that the market was going to fall. The chances are as high that the market will jump back up as that it will fall further. Bearing that in mind, you should probably either close out both your put and call positions or leg out of the straddle. If you close out both positions now, you will make a profit of at least 100 percent. Your put is now worth $7 or more, and you bought it for $1.50. Remembering the price of the call at $2.00, your total cost for the trade (excluding commissions) was $3.50. If you can sell at $7 or more, you've made a whale of a profit for a week's work. The call that you bought will still be worth something, perhaps 50 cents. So you could pocket $8 or more in total revenue in closing the position. (Your in-the-money put was worth more than $7 because of the chance that the market could go down further in the months that the option has left to run.)

LEGGING OUT

You have yet another strategy, which may be the best one. That is to leg out of the straddle. Simply sell your put to lock in your profit. Keep your call. You're only giving up 50 cents by not closing out your position now. And if you were right in the first place in thinking that the market would be volatile, it may turn and go back the other way. Three weeks later, the market may have risen. The S&P index could be at 283. In that case, the call that you bought at $2 would be worth at least $3. You can then sell it, adding an additional dollar profit to your straddle position.

Of course, it is also possible that the market will not go back up. Your call position could expire worthless, reducing your overall profit on the straddle.

NONVOLATILITY SPREADS

You can also use options to register handsome profits if you are correct in thinking that the market will not be volatile. How do you do it? You write (or sell) put and call options on the S&P or some other market instrument. Say that the S&P is now at 280 and you believe that the market will remain flat, trading in a very narrow range in the next few months. You may sell one or more S&P 290 call options with a nearby expiration period. At the same time, you sell one or more S&P 270 put options. In essence, what you have sold is the right for someone to buy the S&P index from you at 290 within the expiration date—the call. You have also sold someone a put that allows him to force you to buy the S&P index at 270.

No one will do either if the market does not rise above 290 or fall below 270. So you will profit if you are correct in thinking the market won't move.

VERTICAL SPREADS

You can also use option spreads to profit if you think the market will move in one direction slowly or turn around and go the other way in a buying or selling panic. That pattern often occurs in precious metals. (Options are available on both gold and silver.)

To give an actual example, in March 1985, *Strategic Investment* recommended a vertical spread on gold that proved to be amazingly profitable. (Vertical spreads involve options with the same maturity date but different strike prices. They can be either bullish or bearish, depending on whether the higher- or lower-priced option is bought or sold.) The spread in our example was a bear-market spread because we sold the lower strike price and bought the higher. We wrote (or sold) June calls on gold at $290 and bought June $300 calls on gold.

Gold had been drifting down over previous months. The thought behind this spread was that gold would probably continue to drift, or if it didn't, it was likely to shoot up rapidly. (It would go up faster than down because it was trading near its lows, and there were many bulls waiting for the turn.) Therefore the strategy was to hold the spread so long as gold drifted down, but to buy back the short call if gold shot up by more than $5 in a single day.

On March 11, 1985, with gold selling at about $287, you could have written (or sold) June 290 gold calls at $13 per ounce. Since there are 100 ounces in each contract, this meant you could have pocketed $1,300 for each call you wrote (100 × $13 = $1,300). To buy a June 300 gold call cost $7.40 per ounce, or $740 for each contract. Therefore, anyone who placed the spread did not have to pay a penny to establish the position. He just had to put up a good faith margin. (The amount of the margin varies from broker to broker. But it could have been as little as $440—the difference between the net premium income of $560 and the $1,000 spread between the two contracts ($1,300 − $740 = $560; $1,000 − $560 = $440).

If the price of gold had continued to drift down, or even remained at $287, you could have earned a profit of $540 per contract by holding both sides of the spread until they expired on May 10. (Gold futures options expire on the second Friday of the previous calendar month.) As it turned out, however, the gold market turned abruptly—what *Strategic Investment* thought it might do. Readers were advised to buy back the short $290 calls if the price of gold rose by more than $5 per ounce in a single day. On March 11, gold rose by $8. Those who followed the advice would have bought the $290 calls back for $21.50 per ounce, or $2,150 per option. This meant a loss on the short call of $850. But this loss was more than offset by a staggering gain in the long June $300 calls. They soon traded as high as $50. One who sold at the top could have made a profit of more than $4,260 on the long calls, or $3,410 for each option spread.

Option spreads are suited to let you profit from this pattern of an abrupt breakout from a sluggish market. They are equally effective for use in the opposite circumstance—a market that is creeping up, but prone to plunge on dramatic developments. In that event, you could make the spread by writing a put at a price near the market and buying a lower-priced put at a lower strike price. For example, suppose you thought that the stock market would either continue to inch up or fall dramatically. With the NYSE Composite Futures Index trading at 129.95, you could write a put at the higher nearby price of 130, for 80 cents (times 500, for a total value of $400) and buy a put at the lower price of 128, for 15 cents (times 500, for a total cost of $75).

It would have cost you nothing to place this vertical spread. In fact, your account would have been credited with $325 for each spread you placed. If you were correct, you would make money if the market continued to inch up (both your puts would expire worthless, and you'd pocket $325 per spread) or you could make money if the market plunged (you'd have to buy back the short put at a loss on the first sign of a reversal, and then hold on to your long put for the profit).

In summary, vertical option spreads are useful but speculative trading techniques. They enable you to take both sides of a market in a way that cannot be done with a direct position in the commodity or stock itself. And they limit risk while allowing you high leverage.

In futures markets this risk can be almost unlimited, as we have seen. When options are involved, the risk is still high, but it is limited. You usually don't have to worry about losing more than you put up, except when you write puts and uncovered calls. Option spreads limit even that risk by backing a short call or put with a long call or put. A long option (call or put) is one that you own. A short option, on the other hand, is one that you have written. Since you have written the option, it is a claim against you. But if you own a call on gold at $300 when you are short a call at $290, your maximum risk is limited to $1,000 minus the net premium income you receive. You can't lose more than that unless you make a blunder in closing out one side of the spread while holding the other.

SYNTHETICS

Synthetics are combinations of options and futures contracts that give you the same market exposure as simpler positions. Sometimes it is beneficial to resort to synthetics when individual instruments are over-priced, or when unusual conditions, such as limit days, place direct buying and selling out of reach. There are six basic pairings of options and underlying instruments that produce a synthetic position:

    Long call + short put   = long futures
    Short call + long put   = short futures
    Long put   + long futures   = long call
    Short put + short futures = short call
    Long call + short futures = long put
    Short call + long futures   = short put

To give but one example of a synthetic, suppose you believe that bond prices are going to rise, but you don't want to take the risk of buying a bond futures contract. You'd like to buy a call option, but a rally is under way and September 100 call premiums are very pricey. You could walk away and pass up the chance to profit if you are right. Or you can purchase a September 100 put with a lower premium and simulta-neously buy the futures contract to create a synthetic call. Synthetics can be useful substitutes for buying calls outright because put premiums are typically lower than those for calls. If the difference is significant enough to cover the added commission of trading two instruments rather than one, you can effectively write yourself a call with a lower premium.

OPTION TRADING RULES

Unless special circumstances make for an exception, you will increase your trading profits by governing your option trades by the following rules:

    1. Understand call options that give you the right to buy at a spec-ified price, and put options that give you the right to sell at a specified price.

    2. Know the expiration date of the option you are trading. Options

on different contracts expire at different times. If you don't know the expiration date, ask your broker.

3. Understand how the options are priced. Some options, such as those on T-bonds, for example, are priced differently from the T-bond futures contract.

4. Concentrate on trading in a few markets, so you can get to know them well.

5. Study the ratio between puts and calls in markets you trade. Normally, it is not wise to buy a call when the number of calls being traded is extremely high relative to the number of puts. Buy puts when bullish sentiment is high. Buy calls when bearish sentiment is greatest.

6. Never risk more than 10 percent of your option trading capital on any one trade.

7. Set a percent loss at which you will close out your position.

8. Be prudent in taking a profit or protecting your position when you have a profit.

   a) Sell when you have doubled your investment.

   b) Another possibility: If you think that the market may continue to move your way, sell enough options to recover the cost of your original investment when the profit in your position allows it.

   c) Buy out-of-the-money puts when you hold appreciated calls, and vice versa. That way, if the market moves against you, your profit will not suddenly vanish.

   d) If the option rises rapidly and dramatically, sell it with the aim of buying it back at a lower price.

WARRANTS

Warrants are in some ways similar to options. They are long-term options that give you the right to buy stock from the company that issues them at a stated price. A warrant is traded like a stock by stockbrokers. If you wished, you could usually buy odd numbers of warrants. Unlike options, warrants are issued by the company on whose shares they are traded. They are registered with the Securities and Exchange Commission. You will find the prices of warrants quoted in the stock listings of the newspaper. Another distinguishing feature of warrants is that they are usually issued for much longer periods than the more familiar options traded on option and commodity exchanges. Warrants are good for exercise at some period that may be years in the future. Most other options expire within nine months.

FOREIGN STOCKS

Most American investors are reluctant to invest in foreign stocks. This is stupid. Opportunities for profits in foreign shares are sometimes easier to spot than in domestic stocks. *Strategic Investment* has recommended foreign shares, both in its regular portfolios and its special reports. We will continue to do so, because there is a high likelihood that some foreign stocks will be among the best candidates for large capital gains in the months and years to come.

Of course, one obstacle you may have to overcome is finding a broker who is reputable and knowledgeable enough to handle foreign stock trades. If your present broker does not make foreign stock trades, don't let him discourage you from high potential profits. Use another broker.

You will also have an increasing number of possibilities for trading foreign stock market indices on futures exchanges. These are volatile, but they can be traded without difficulty in the United States and offer geared opportunities to profit with low transaction costs. Remember, however, these trading instruments are suited best to exploiting market action when a definite trend has set in. You cannot trade a list of shares effectively when the market is drifting.

GLOSSARY OF INVESTMENT TERMS

This section contains definitions of investment terms. We've made a point of duplicating some of the explanations from the text so that it will be easier for you to review concepts. Most of the definitions are in alphabetical order.

ADR, or American Depository Receipt, is a certificate issued by an American bank, usually Morgan Guaranty Trust, Bank of New York, or Citibank, that entitles the owner to all the benefits of ownership of the equivalent share of a foreign corporation. ADRs can be traded through most brokerage firms.

ARBITRAGE consists of purchasing and selling the same item in different markets simultaneously to profit from small price differences (e.g., buying IBM in New York at $126 per share while selling it at the same moment in London for British pounds worth $126.20). Arbitrage can only be exploited by stock exchange members, who do not need to pay brokerage commissions.

RISK ARBITRAGE is another type of arbitrage which can be done by anyone. It consists of purchasing securities that are the subject of a takeover bid with the intention of holding the securities until the deal goes through. A risk arbitrageur buys stock at a price reflecting the announcement of the takeover bid, but at a discount both for the risk that the proposed deal will fall apart and the time expected to elapse before consummation of the takeover or merger. If the deal goes through, the arbitrageur makes money.

A BEAR MARKET is one in which the majority of traders believe that prices will decline. A BEAR is a seller or a pessimist. A BULL believes that the market will soon rise. A BULL MARKET is one thought to be in a broad uptrend. Investors do not always agree whether the market is currently bullish or bearish.

The BID is the highest price that a prospective buyer is willing to pay for a stock, bond, option, or commodity at a given moment. The OFFER is the lowest price at which a prospective seller is willing to sell a security or commodity. A sale only takes place when the bid and the offer meet. This occurs when a buyer is hungry and is willing to pay a little more or when a seller is a little more desperate than the prospective buyers and lowers his price. The SPREAD refers to the price differential between the bid and the offer.

For example, IBM stock might be quoted "$125.50 bid, $126.00 asked (offered), $125.75 last." This means that the last trade in IBM took place at $125.75, but buyers are only willing to pay a quarter less than that, and sellers want a quarter more. If you place a MARKET ORDER to buy IBM, you will be charged $126.00 per share. If you turn around and sell the stock right away, you will only get $125.50. Your loss of $0.50 per share is the spread. You can often get a better price in trading stocks that are listed on an exchange by placing LIMIT ORDERS (see page 364).

A BOND is a long-term debt instrument of a corporation or government. When a bond issuer takes money from the public, it exchanges an IOU called a bond for the money borrowed. A BOND INDENTURE is the legal document that details the terms under which a bond is issued: its interest rate, frequency of interest payments, maturity date, redemption rights, conversion privileges, and secured collateral. Bond prices are quoted at one-tenth of the actual price of the bond. Most bonds have a par value of $1,000. A bond trading at 84 is really selling for $840 per bond.

A CALENDAR SPREAD (also known as a HORIZONTAL SPREAD) is an options position that involves buying and selling an option on the same underlying stock or commodity at the same exercise price, but with different expiration dates.

A CALL is a type of option that grants its purchaser the right to buy 100 shares of stock (or one commodity contract) from the writer of the call at a specified price within a specified period. The price paid for an option is called the PREMIUM. E.g., if IBM is trading at $126, an owner of IBM stock might sell someone else the right to buy his stock from him at any time in the next six months at $135 per share for a premium of $7 per share. In this way, the owner of IBM stock either realizes extra income of $7 per share, without needing to sell the stock, or he can be forced to sell the stock for a total of $142 ($135 strike price plus $7 premium), which may look good to him when the stock is selling for only $126. At the end of six months, if the purchaser of the call has not exercised it, it expires worthless. The IBM owner can write another call at that point on the shares he owns. In fact, you can write a call on stock you do not even own.

This is termed NAKED WRITING and is akin to short selling and is risky. If it makes sense under certain circumstances to WRITE (sell) options, does that mean it's a bad deal to buy calls? Not necessarily. Which side you choose depends on your outlook for the likely price range of IBM stock in the next few months. The chief attraction to buying calls is that you risk a relatively small sum—in this example, $7—but your profit potential is unlimited. If IBM is trading at $165 six months from now, your right to buy the stock at $140 is clearly worth at least $25 ($165 minus $140). If the stock is trading below $140, however, you will have lost your entire premium. The amount you risk in buying options is reduced, your profit potential is high, but your risk of losing everything you invest is also high. Options require that you not only accurately predict whether a stock, commodity, or market is about to move up or down; you must also predict when. If, in our example, IBM moves up from $126 to $138 in just six months (10 percent in six months—a strong move) and then takes off, it won't do you any good as the buyer of a call.

CAPITAL GAIN OR LOSS is the tax term for profit or loss from the sale of securities, commodities, real estate, or other capital assets. Under the tax law that expired on December 31, 1986, any profit derived from a capital gain on an asset held for more than six months before sale qualified as a LONG-TERM CAPITAL GAIN and received preferential federal income tax treatment. That distinction of law was abolished in the 1986 tax reform but may be reinstated in the future.

COMMERCIAL PAPER is the term for short-term corporate debt, frequently issued in $100,000 denominations. Unlike bonds, these corporate IOUs mature within 270 days of issuance.

COMMODITY FUTURES TRADING COMMISSION is a federal agency that regulates commodity futures trading.

COMMODITIES are agricultural products (e.g., corn, wheat, pork bellies), minerals (e.g., gold, silver, palladium), raw materials, or financial instruments (e.g., Treasury bills, Treasury bonds, foreign currencies, stock indices) traded at almost a dozen different exchanges for cash or by contract specifying date and amounts for exchange at a specified future date.

COMMON STOCK is the paper issued by a public corporation to indicate a share of ownership. Common stockholders generally have the right to vote in annual proxy elections, choose a board of directors, etc., but they do not have the right to a dividend amount fixed in advance. All corporate creditors are paid off before shareholders in the event of corporate bankruptcy or liquidation. Shareholders do benefit, however, from increasing corporate earnings, unlike creditors and bondholders.

CONTRARY INVESTING is a trading philosophy based upon the assumption that the majority is usually wrong or tends to be wrong under certain conditions. CONTRARIANS advise buying when most people sell and selling when most people buy.

CONVERTIBLE BONDS are a hybrid that have some aspects of bonds and some aspects of common stock. A convertible bond pays a fixed interest rate but is convertible into stock at a prespecified price. If the stock price declines, a convertible bond will trade just like a straight bond, based on the creditworthiness of the issuing corporation and the interest rate. If the stock price rises, however, the convertible bond will eventually begin to trade like stock, based on the value of the shares into which it can be converted.

COVERED WRITING is the practice of writing a call against a stock or commodity you own in order to obtain the extra premium income. For example, if you own 400 shares of IBM and write four calls (remember, each call gives the purchaser the right to buy 100 shares of the stock from the writer) on IBM, you have engaged in covered writing. Covered writing is a conservative use of options. Contrary to popular misimpression, not all option plays are speculative. A covered option writer receives a premium up front. His only cost is limiting the gain he might otherwise have made if the stock later soars.

A DEBENTURE is a debt instrument that is backed by the general credit of the corporation but is not secured by a lien or mortgage on a particular piece of collateral.

The DISCOUNT RATE is probably more important to the American economy than the better-known prime rate. The discount rate is the interest rate at which the Federal Reserve Board lends funds to member banks. At the end of each day, some banks are temporarily short of cash. They can cover this shortfall through borrowing from the Fed. The discount rate represents an always available, relatively cheap source of money for lending institutions. The rates at which banks are willing to make loans is marked up from the discount rate. So when the Fed lowers the discount rate, interest rates in general are likely to fall, increasing economic activity. Conversely, when the Fed raises the discount rate, it makes credit more expensive, forcing interest rates upward and slowing the economy.

The EXERCISE PRICE (also known as the STRIKE PRICE) is the price at which an option or warrant can be exercised. For example, a September 70 GM call gives the buyer of that call until a specified date in September to buy 100 shares of GM stock from the writer at $70 per share. Obviously, if the stock is selling below $70 at that time, there is no point in exercising the call since you can buy the stock more cheaply on the open market. In that event, the call will expire worthless. On the other hand, if GM stock is selling for $76 in September, the call will be worth at least $6.

The EXPIRATION DATE of an option or warrant is the date on which that instrument expires. An option only gives its buyer a right to buy or sell stock for a specified period, the last day of which is known as Expiration Friday, since options always expire on a Friday.

FANNIE MAES are pools of mortgages sold by the primary lender, such as the initiating savings and loan institution, to the quasi-governmental Federal National Mortgage Association, whose credit is guaranteed by the U.S. government.

The FUNDAMENTAL approach to investment attempts to predict market movements by understanding one or more economic or political developments that should affect prices. (See TECHNICAL.)

FUTURES (also known as COMMODITIES) are contracts that carry the obligation to buy or sell either physical commodities, financial instruments, or the cash value of abstractions such as the Consumer Price Index on a specified date. Because an increasing number of contracts are traded around nonphysical items, the term *futures* has begun to supplant *commodities* as a general description.

GINNIE MAES are pools of mortgages on lower-income housing sold by the primary lender to the Government National Mortgage Association.

GNP is the abbreviation for Gross National Product, which is the total value of a country's output of goods and services. The method of calculating the GNP varies from nation to nation. For example, in the United States, housework, although essential to the maintenance of families, a home life, and outside sources of income, is not included in the calculation of the GNP. Work done by domestic workers, maids, and waitresses is included, however. The GNP is the broadest measure of the health of an economy. As productivity increases, so does the GNP. As people are laid off, the GNP declines. The GNP is commonly adjusted for inflation to avoid giving a distorted picture of the economy. Two consecutive quarters of declining GNP constitutes the formal definition of a RECESSION.

IN-THE-MONEY options are options that have intrinsic value in addition to a time premium. For example, if you own an October 30 put on Merrill Lynch, and Merrill is now selling at $28, your put is in-the-money by $2. It may be worth more than $2, because it also commands a time premium.

INVESTMENT CAPITAL is constituted by the wealth you have to invest, i.e., all your money above and beyond what you need to live. RISK CAPITAL is a fraction of your investment capital. It is the money you could afford to lose without harming your standard of living in the future. You should only devote risk capital to speculative investments.

JUNK BONDS are corporate bonds graded BB+ or lower. Such bonds offer very high yields compared to high grade corporate and government issues. They are described as junk because many indentures of companies issuing such debt indicate that without restructuring or the sale of assets, they will lack the cash to meet their obligated payments. In that sense, *junk bonds* are claims upon corporate assets. They have some of the characteristics of preferred stock.

LEGGING OUT means to exit only one side (or one "leg") of a futures or option spread. For example, if you are long T-bills and short Eurodollars, and you believe that interest rates are about to fall, you can "leg out" of your short position by buying back the Eurodollars. You are therefore left with a simple long position in T-bills.

A LIMIT ORDER is one in which you instruct your broker to take some action (buy or sell stock, option, or commodity future) only if the price of that security or commodity reaches a specified price. For example, if IBM seems a little expensive at $126, but you would like to buy some at $123 or $110 or $75, you can place an order with your broker to buy IBM if the stock trades as low as the price you specify. You must tell your broker that your order is GOOD TILL CANCELED, or it will expire automatically at the close of the trading day.

LIQUIDITY is a characteristic of an asset that indicates the relative ease with which it can be converted into cash without a significant loss of value. Thus, cash is 100 percent liquid. And Treasury bills can be readily turned into cash with no loss of value. But a real estate investment may take months or years to be converted into money without an appreciable loss.

LOAD refers to the commission, frequently 8.5 percent but often less, charged to the buyer of mutual fund shares to compensate the fund for sales commissions, promotion, and distribution costs. A NO-LOAD fund refers to a mutual fund that does not charge an initial sales fee. A LOW-LOAD fund is one that charges 1 percent to 3 percent up front. Some funds charge a REDEMPTION FEE to discourage market timers from trading in and out of the fund, which would increase its overhead (see MUTUAL FUNDS).

A LONG position is one in which the investor is betting that the stock or commodity price will go up. You are "long" stock if you own shares. The opposite of "long" is "short." (See SHORT SALE.)

LONG-TERM DEBT refers to the bonds and debentures of a corporation that are scheduled to mature more than one year from now.

LIMIT DAYS are days in which certain commodities have risen or fallen so much that further price movements are limited in order to maintain an orderly market. Limits on price swings on commodities are seldom reached, but they can be a safeguard against panic buying or selling.

M1 is the narrowest measure of the money supply. It includes currency, coins, travelers checks, and the most easily spent forms of bank money, checking accounts, and other checkable deposits. M2 includes everything in M1 plus time and savings accounts at commercial banks, net overnight repurchase agreements, net overnight Eurodollars, and money market mutual funds. M3 is broader still. It includes M2 and accounts at non-banks, credit unions and savings and loans, plus large time deposits, term repurchase agreements and Eurodollars, and institution-only money market mutual funds. Savings bonds, short-term Treasury securities, bankers acceptances and commercial paper are liquid assets sometimes under the category *L* in money supply reports.

MAINTENANCE LEVEL. If you drop below that level, either by your stocks or commodities declining sharply in value or by withdrawing too much cash from the account, your broker will send you a MARGIN CALL, which requires you to immediately put up more cash, or the broker will sell your position.

MARGIN is a complicated subject. When you buy stock, you are permitted to borrow up to half the cost of the purchase from your broker. The money borrowed is called margin. The broker charges you interest, just as a bank would. The interest rate, however, is often lower than the prime rate. This rate compares very favorably with the rates charged on credit card balances, so you may find it worthwhile to borrow against your stock and pay off some of your other loans. This is especially true in that margin interest is deductible (up to the level of your investment income) while consumer interest is not. At all times, however, the equity in your brokerage account must exceed 25 percent of the market value of the stocks in the account. This is a Federal Reserve Board requirement. Most brokers require a 30 percent or 35 percent margin.

MARGIN for COMMODITIES and OPTIONS is entirely different. When you enter into a futures transaction, whether on the long side or the short, you are required to put up a small good-faith deposit. The amount varies from contract to contract but often is as low as 5 percent or less of its value. This is why commodities are so much more highly leveraged than stocks. This means that you can make large profits from a small down payment, but it also means that you can lose not just your margin deposit, but thousands more as well. You do not have to pay interest on commodity or option margin.

MEGAPOLITICS is the study of the ultimate determinants of economic and political action. New technology alters the boundaries of the possible, changing incentives across a wide range of behavior. Far-reaching megapolitical change foreshadows changes in economic outcomes and political institutions, with impact upon investment. This book analyzes investment opportunities in terms of *megapolitics*.

MONETARISM is a theory that the quantity of money in circulation determines the price level. All economists accept this proposition to some extent. Some monetarists, however, have argued that control of the money supply is the key to practically all economic variables. This more mechanistic view of the importance of the money supply is highly controversial.

To MONETIZE debt is, in effect, to print money. When the Federal Reserve or other central banks create new money to purchase debt, they expand the money supply. This tends to reduce the value of the currency, raising prices.

MUNICIPAL BONDS are bonds issued by cities and towns to obtain the financing for major expenditures, such as sewage systems, bridges, and new roads. The interest received on municipal bonds is not subject to federal income tax. This means that although municipal bonds pay interest at a lower rate than Treasury bonds or corporate bonds, your after-tax return may be higher, depending on your income tax bracket.

Many Americans invest in MUTUAL FUNDS without even knowing it. The most common type of mutual fund today is the MONEY MARKET FUND. A mutual fund is a company that pools together the funds of thousands of investors and uses the money to buy stocks, options, bonds, or money market instruments, depending on the type of mutual fund. In this way, small investors are able to obtain professional management of their investments for a small fee. Mutual funds move up and down in price, depending on the value of the securities in the portfolio. The sales commissions charged by some mutual funds are discussed at LOAD on page 364.

NAKED WRITING refers to the practice of writing puts or calls on stock or commodities that you do not own. This is a speculative technique, since if the stock moves in the direction you do not anticipate, you may be forced to buy or sell the stock at a large loss. Naked writing of calls is similar to SHORT SELLING (see page 369).

NASDAQ is the abbreviation for the National Association of Securities Dealers Automated Quotations systems. The prices of about 4,000 stocks that are traded OVER THE COUNTER (see page 367) through this system are available from your broker throughout the trading day through a computer hookup. The 2,000 or so most heavily traded and most profitable OTC companies report each transaction as it occurs through NASDAQ's National Market System.

The NOTICE DATE is the last day on which the owner of a commodities futures contract can sell the contract. If he does not do so by this date (similar to EXPIRATION DATE; see page 362), he will be forced to accept delivery of the physical commodity. This entails shipping and storage costs, not to speak of possible embarrassment—your neighbors might not be terribly thrilled if a truck unloaded 38,000 pounds of pork bellies on your front lawn!

NONVOLATILITY SPREADS are option spreads that make money when a stock or commodity stays at the same price or in a narrow trading range. For example, if gold is selling for $315 and you think it will continue to trade in a narrow range, you can enter a nonvolatility spread. You simultaneously sell both a nearby $310 put on gold and a $320 call. If you are correct and the gold price remains flat, you will pocket premiums on both sides.

An OPTION is a contractual right to buy (a call) or sell (a put) a commodity or 100 shares of a particular stock at a specified price by a date three, six, or nine months in the future. See the discussions of CALL, PUT, SPREAD, and STRADDLE elsewhere in this glossary. For a much more complete explanation of options and options strategies, see chapter 10. Ask your broker for a free copy of a booklet prepared by the options exchanges entitled "Understanding the Risks and Uses of Listed Options."

The OVER-THE-COUNTER market refers to stocks that are not traded on a securities exchange. Instead, these stocks are bought and sold by individual securities dealers. Until recently, the OTC market had a bad reputation among investors. Today it is the fastest-growing segment of the stock market. Many large, respectable companies that could be traded on the New York Stock Exchange, such as Apple Computer, MCI Communications, and some of the largest insurance companies, have chosen to be traded over the counter.

PREFERRED STOCK is a type of stock that gives owners a "preferred" claim to a company's earnings and assets as compared with that of common stockholders. Preferred stock often pays a better dividend (and the dividend is more secure) than common stock. It often trades more like a bond than a stock.

PREMIUM refers to the price that an option buyer pays and an option writer receives for the rights conveyed by the option. The premium for a particular option constantly changes. It depends largely on how close the current market price of the stock or commodity is to the exercise price, how volatile the stock is, how much time remains until the option expires (this part of the premium is known as the TIME PREMIUM). Current interest rates also figure in setting the option premium. The higher interest rates go, the higher premiums tend to be. PREMIUM also refers to the added value that is sometimes charged in an investment, as opposed to a DISCOUNT, which is a reduction below the stated value.

The PRICE-EARNINGS RATIO of a stock is perhaps the most common measure of a stock's value. The PE ratio is calculated by dividing a stock's current price by its earnings for the most recent 12 months. The lower the price-earnings ratio, the cheaper the stock is. An average PE ratio today is approximately 10 or 12. But investors are willing to pay much higher prices for companies that are expected to grow rapidly in the next few years (high-technology and bioengineering companies, for example). In these cases, investors are paying a high price for current earnings, but what they hope is a low price relative to the company's earnings next year or a few years down the road.

A PROSPECTUS is the document that the SEC requires to be given to prospective purchasers of new stock, options, bonds, and even mutual funds. The prospectus contains very important information concerning a company's operating history, management, lines of business, competition, prospects, and includes certified financial statements. Most investors don't take the time to read the prospectus furnished to them. You could avoid some bad investing mistakes if you just take a few minutes to read this very important statement prepared by the company in which you're about to invest.

A PUT is an option that gives the buyer the right to sell the specified stock or commodity to the seller/writer of the option at a prespecified price for a certain period of time. See the discussion of CALL on page 360.

REALITY is the characteristic of an investment that has physical existence apart from the income stream or claims of ownership that it represents. A bond, for example, has no reality outside of the certificate, which may sometimes have decorative value, while a house is convincingly real.

RESISTANCE is the price level where technical traders believe that an upward price movement is likely to be halted by selling. (See SUPPORT.)

RISK ARBITRAGE—see ARBITRAGE.

RISK CAPITAL is cash you could afford to lose without reducing your standard of living.

The S&P 500 refers to STANDARD & POOR'S 500 STOCK INDEX, a widely followed market index. It is similar to the Dow Jones Industrial Average, except that this average includes the 500 stocks making up most of the total capitalization on the New York Stock Exchange. In contrast, the Dow includes only 30 blue-chip corporations. Index options are now traded on the S&P 500.

The U.S. SECURITIES AND EXCHANGE COMMISSION is the federal agency that monitors compliance with securities laws by requiring companies to make full and truthful disclosures about their businesses, by regulating stockbrokers, and by handling investor complaints.

SHORT SELLING is the practice of borrowing stock from another investor (your broker handles this for you automatically) and selling that stock, or selling a futures contract without the intention of delivering the underlying commodity, in anticipation of the price going down, and later buying it back and returning it to the person who lent it to you. It is the opposite of the normal transaction sequence, in which you first buy something and then sell it. In a short sale, you sell stock first and later buy it back. There is nothing illegal, immoral, or un-American about selling short—clearly, the market can't just go up and up every day and every year. By selling short, you can profit from a drop in the price of a particular stock or commodity.

A SPREAD is a combination of futures or options positions in which you are both the buyer and the seller of the same type of instrument on the same underlying stock or commodity, with the instruments having different exercise prices or expiration dates.

STOCK INDEX FUTURES are the most popular type of financial future. These are commodities, but unlike other commodities, no physical good changes hands. A stock index future is simply a bet on the direction of the market. You are buying, in essence, a cross section of the market. If you have large stock holdings and are worried that a decline in the market will pull your stocks down with it, you can write a call or buy a put on a market index. Stock index futures now exist (and are heavily traded) on the S&P 500 STOCK INDEX, and the Value Line Composite Stock Index. Options on the futures are available for the S&P and the NYSE indices. Your broker can provide you with an excellent free publication entitled "Listed Options on Stock Indices."

A STOP LOSS is a type of limit order that you can leave with your broker instructing him to close out your position if it moves against you by a certain amount. For example, if you buy IBM at $126, expecting it to rise to $150, you could enter a STOP LOSS at $115. If the stock dropped to that point, your broker would sell your stock, limiting your loss to $11.

A STRADDLE consists of buying or writing both a put and a call on the same stock with the options having the same exercise price and the same expiration date. A STRADDLE BUYER is betting that the price of the stock or commodity will soon break out of its trading range. A STRADDLE WRITER, on the other hand, expects little change in the price of the underlying stock or commodity during the life of the option.

A STRIKE PRICE is the price at which an option may be exercised. It is also known as the "exercise price."

SUPPORT is the price level where technical traders believe that a downward price movement is likely to be halted (see RESISTANCE).

The TECHNICAL approach to investing is taken by some traders who do not attempt to understand why prices move up and down. They take their buy and sell clues from studying movements and technical formations of price charts. (See FUNDAMENTAL.)

A TRAILING STOP is a standing order you give to your broker to close out an investment at a certain amount. In other words, it is an order to close out your position that is based on market movement and not upon a specific price. If you buy Treasury bonds at 74-11, with a trailing stop of 22/32ds, your position will be closed out whenever the bonds drop by 22/32ds. This is true whether they fall immediately, or go up to 80-1, and then fall back to 79-21.

A VERTICAL SPREAD is an options position in which you simultaneously buy and sell an option on the same stock or commodity. The options have the same expiration date (compare with a CALENDAR SPREAD; see page 360) but a different exercise price.

A WARRANT is a type of long-term option that gives you the right to buy stock directly from the company at a stated price. Unlike ordinary options, which can only be written for a maximum period of nine months, warrants can extend for years or even indefinitely. A number of warrants are traded on the New York and American Stock Exchanges; others are traded OVER THE COUNTER.

WRITING AN OPTION is the same as selling one that you do not own. The person who gives the buyer of an option the right to buy stock, currency or commodity from him (a call) or sell stock to him (a put), is known as the OPTION WRITER.

The YIELD on an investment refers to the rate of return from interest or dividends. To calculate the yield, divide the interest or dividends received in a year by its current market price. For example, if a stock sells for $30.00 and pays a quarterly dividend of $0.75, its yield is 10 percent ($3.00 divided by $30.00).

APPENDIX I

U.S. Multinationals Vulnerable to a Breakdown in World Order

Company	Foreign profits as a % of total profits	Rank by foreign sales vol.	Industry	Vulnerability	Comments
1. Aluminum Company of America	226	124	Bauxite mining; refining/smelting; aluminum	High-medium	Mining especially vulnerable; has plants in South America
2. Trans World Airlines	211	52	Air travel	Low	
3. Intel	179	147	Develops & makes components/computer systems	Low	Advanced industry; plants located in non-vulnerable countries
4. Schlumberger	110	15	Oilfield services, offshore & land drilling	Medium	Some operations in vulnerable South American & African nations
5. NL Industries	104	103	Oilfield services; manufactures chemicals	Medium	Major operations in N. America & Europe; mining properties in S. America
6. Control Data	99	66	Computer services & products	Low	Advanced industry; plants in Europe & North America

Company	Foreign profits as a % of total profits	Rank by foreign sales vol.	Industry	Vulnera-bility	Comments
7. American International	93	41	Insurance	Low	
8. Texas Eastern	88	107	Diversified energy co., incl. chemicals	Low	Canada is main country of foreign operation
9. Murphy Oil Company	85	89	Explores for & produces oil/gas	Low	Production centered on Canada
10. CBI Industries	84	97	Diversified co.—incl. oil-gas production	Medium	
11. American Family	83	139	Insurance	Low	
12. Diamond Shamrock	77	118	Oil, gas, & coal production	High-medium	Some vulnerable interests, but cutting back foreign operations
15. Castle and Cooke	76	113	Branded food products	Medium	Not a vulnerable industry but has plantations in unstable Central America
16. AMP Inc.	73	109	Electrical and engineering services	Medium-low	
17. Lafarge	73	137	Cement & related products	Low	Production largely in Canada

Company	Foreign profits as a % of total profits	Rank by foreign sales vol.	Industry	Vulnerability	Comments
18. Occidental Petroleum	68	16	Oil, gas, coal, chemicals & other products	High	Oil & gas especially vulnerable—op. under concessions incl. Libya
19. ITT Corporation	67	19	Telecommunications & electronics	Medium	
20. Halliburton	65	59	Oilfield, engin. & construction services	Medium	Main property incls. plants in Mexico & Middle East
21. Baker International	64	105	Drilling and mining products and services	Medium-low	
22. Firestone	63	73	A leading producer of tire and rubber products	Medium	Major plants located in unstable South America
23. Deere & Co.	62	86	Agricultural equipment	Medium	
24. Polaroid	61	133	Photographic equipment & sunglasses	Low	Not a vulnerable product
25. Dow Chemicals	60	11	Agricultural, pharmaceuticals, chemicals	High-medium	Processing plants in very unstable nations (incl. Iran, Libya, etc.)

Company	Foreign profits as a % of total profits	Rank by foreign sales vol.	Industry	Vulnerability	Comments
26. American Cynamid	60	67	(as Dow) coal production	Medium	Back foreign ops
27. Exxon Corporation Company	59	1	Oil, gas, coal, chemicals, ind. equipment	High-medium	Refineries in Central America. Co. withdrew from Libya in Dec. 1981
28. Mobil Corporation	58	2	Oil, gas, and chemicals; also merchandising	Medium	Refineries generally located in low-risk countries
29. Gillette	58	61	Leading producer of razors and shavers	Low	Not a vulnerable product
30. Monsanto	55	47	Chemicals, agric. products & pharmaceuticals	Medium	Not a vulnerable industry, but plants in Central & S. America
31. CPC International	54	38	Branded grocery products	Medium-low	Plants incl. 7 in Africa/Middle East & 27 in Latin America
32. Ocean drilling	54	132	Oil services and products	Medium	Largely off-shore property
33. Coca Cola	53	26	Soft drinks	Low	
34. Lubrizol	52	150	Specialty chemicals & agric. equipment	Low	Plants located in developed world

Company	Foreign profits as a % of total profits	Rank by foreign sales vol.	Industry	Vulnera-bility	Comments
35. Emhart Corporation	51	101	Hardware products, compo-nents & electrical prods.	Medium	Major facilities in U.S., but has plants in S. America, S. Africa
36. American Standard	51	82	Compo-nents, transporta-tion products	Low	Principal facili-ties in W. Eu-rope & U.S.

NB: Table includes only those U.S. companies with more than 50 percent or above foreign profits as a percentage of total operating profits

Sources: Business Week, pages 290-298, April 18, 1986
  Standard and Poor's Corporate Records, 1985/6
  Moody's Industrial Manual, 1985
  Moody's Bank and Finance Records, 1985
  Moody's Public Utility Manual, 1985
  Directories of American firms operating in foreign countries, Vol. 1, 1984

APPENDIX II

Firms That Tend to Benefit from a Falling Dollar
(and Suffer Lower Earnings When the Dollar Rises)

Pan Am
Reading & Bates
Phibro-Saloman
Schlumberger, Ltd.
International Flavors and
   Fragrances
CPC International
Parker Pen
Ocean Drilling & Exploration
Hoover
American Brands
Colgate Palmolive
Interpublic
Gillette
Dow
Lubrizol
CBI Industries
American Family
Raychem
Pfizer
NL Industries
Anderson, Clayton
ITT
Caterpillar Tractor

Schering Plough
American International Group
NCR
Boeing
F.W. Woolworth
Merck
Black & Decker
Crown Cork & Seal
Richardson Vicks
Norton
Polaroid
IBM
Emhart
Squibb
TWA
Warner Lambert
Coca-Cola
Johnson & Johnson
Unysis
Keystone International
Milloport
Eastman Kodak
Omark Industries

APPENDIX III:

INVESTING IN
BREAKTHROUGH TECHNOLOGIES

How do you invest in the new technological trends we explore in Chapter 7? Many of the pioneers in growth areas are small firms, but not all. Among fiber-optics companies, we are especially inclined toward Optelcom (OTC, symbol OPTC). *Strategic Investment* has recommended it, and we believe it has a bright future.

Among advanced ceramics firms the following bear watching: Norton is involved in a joint venture with TRW. Dow Corning is a leader in ceramics with a good deal of experience in the field. Ceradyne Incorporated, located in San Jose, California, has advanced ceramics applications. So does DuPont. Dow Chemical and the Koppers Company both have significant equity investments in ceramic companies. General Electric has a ceramics division. General Ceramics of Haskell, New Jersey, is a high-tech ceramics products company. The Garrett Turbine Engine Company is involved with the Ford Motor Company in developing ceramics for engines. Allison Gas Turbine is doing similar research for GM. In Japan, Kyocera has developed advance ceramics for applications in false teeth and to provide packages for integrated circuits. Other leading Japanese ceramic firms are Nebon Carbon, Nissan, Isuzu, Murata, and Ngk Sparkplugs. In Canada, the Lanxide Company is working with Alcan Aluminum. IBM also has its hand in the production of advanced ceramics for integrated circuits. But all of IBM's production is used internally.

Leaders in plastics research and development are primarily huge companies: Dow Chemical, GE Plastics, DuPont, Celanese Research Company, Boeing, Allied Signal, Borg-Warner, Hercules, Polimotor Research, and Imperial Chemical Industries. Among the leading Japanese firms are Mitsubishi Chemical Industries, Tejin, Toyota, Sumitomo Chemical, Toray, Ube Industries, Mitsui-Toatsu Chemical, Mitsui Petrochemical, Asahi Chemical, and Kureha. We mention these, not as buy recommendations, but as targets for your watch list. Long-term investments should be made only upon close examination of the management, cash flow, and value of the company, based upon its current share price. And the larger the company, the more important timing is. You can buy a penny share at 2 cents rather than a penny, and it will make little difference in your ultimate return. But if you buy DuPont at $80 rather than at $40, that is quite another story.

A small plastics company that may make an interesting play is AEC Incorporated (AECE). It is not a leader in advanced plastics research, but it is prominent in plastics recycling, which must be a growing business if plastics become more widely used.

Among firms standing to profit from continued improvements in energy efficiency we believe particularly in Thermo Electron (TMO). It is the leader in selling hardware for small-unit cogeneration. In the years to come, this market should expand tremendously. We also recommend that you watch Thermo's spin-off, Thermatics (THMD), a firm that has developed equipment that can apparently detect bombs more accurately than previous technology. Other firms to watch in decentralized energy production include: Billings Energy, Diamond Shamrock, Luz International, Scientific Solar Installations, and Windfarms, Ltd.

In our view, there is a great potential for growth among firms specializing in artificial intelligence and automation. All the major computer companies have at least some participation in these fields, and so do many other Fortune 500 firms. Among the small firms, many are private. But we mention them anyway because they bear watching. Firms to watch in AI are Applied Expert Systems, or APEX, Artificial Intellicorp, Automatix, Cognitive Systems, Computer Thought Corporation, Intelli Genetics, Intelligent Software, Lisp Machines, Machine Intelligence, MCC (Microelectronics & Computer Technology Corporation), Symbolics, and Teknowledge Inc.

Two small companies have made notable progress in developing speech-recognition devices that enable personal computers to "understand" spoken words. They are Kurzweil Applied Intelligence Inc. of Waltham, Massachusetts, and Dragon Systems of Newton, Massachusetts. Giants IBM, ATT, and Texas Instruments are also doing promising work in the field.

A firm that could become an important player in factory automation is Oshap Technologies. Although it is small, it has a broad international reach. It owns 90 percent of RobotiCad, Inc., 96.9 percent of Tecnomatix N.V., and 96 percent of Tecnomatix Automatisierungs Systems GmbH. American firms active in factory automation and robotics include: Autoplace, Control Data, Cincinnati Milicron, Draper Labs, GE, IBM, Prab Conveyors, Unimation, and Westinghouse.

Bio-Technology General Corporation (OTC-BTGC) and Chiron (OTC-CHIR) are two leaders in development and applications of biotechnology to life extension. Potential applications are so far-reaching that it is a reasonable speculation to place both in your portfolio.

U.S. biotechnology companies have been hampered competitively by long regulatory delays required to approve experiments. It takes seven to ten years to bring a drug to market under FDA requirements. And agricultural uses of biotechnology have been hampered by opposition from a number of federal agencies. As a result, Great Britain and Australia have taken the lead in some areas of research. Biogen, a Swiss company, has also profited by avoiding U.S. restrictions. As you would expect, there is also a tremendous research effort under way in Japan. Among the firms to watch: Advanced Genetic Sciences (AGSI), Agrigenetics, Allied Chemical, Amgen (AMEN) Applied Biosystems (ABIO), Atlantic Richfield, Biogen, California Biotechnology, Cetus (CTUS), Centocorp (CNTO), Chiron (CHIR), Ciba-Ceigy, Collaborative Genetics, Cytox, DEKALB Ag-Research, Dow Chemical, DuPont, Eli Lilly, General Mills, Genentech (GENE), Hoffman-La Roche, Immunomedics, Immunex (IMMX), Integrated Genetics, International Plant Research, Molecular Genetics (MOGN), Monsanto, Pioneer Hi-bred International, Ribi Immunochem (RIBI), Sandoz, Schering-Plough, Shell, Stauffer, and Union Carbide. Again, this is a watch list, not a buy list. Some of these firms cannot even be traded.

APPENDIX IV:

How to Calculate Your Break-Even Point in Home Ownership

You cannot make a decision to sell your house on the basis of a simple arithmetic calculation. That said, it does not hurt to know what the numbers tell you. Get out a yellow pad, your pocket calculator, and a pencil. Let's work them through.

There are really four areas—other than emotional satisfaction—to look at in calculating your return on a real estate investment. They are: 1) income, 2) tax benefits, 3) capital appreciation, and 4) leverage (or debt relative to the other elements of return).

Start with the present value of your home. How much could you get if you put it on the market now? Write that figure on the first line.

Next, figure out your home's approximate rental value. If you had to rent your home, how much could you get for it on an annual basis? Put that figure on line 2.

Figure out how much you would have to invest in long-term government bonds to make an income equal to the annual rental value of your home. To make this calculation, divide the bond yield into 100; then multiply the resulting figure by the rental value of your home. This will give you the approximate capital value of the rental income in your home. For example, if you could make $9,000 per year renting your house, and the bond yield is now 7.5 percent, you divide 100 by 7.5. The quotient is 13.33. Multiplying that number by $9,000, you get an approximate capital value of $120,000.

Enter that number on line 4.

Then subtract line 4 from line 1.

The number you come up with will be the simple *premium* or *discount* at which your home is selling above its rental value.

If the rental value of your home is *greater* than its present price (the number on line 5 is negative), you are in an unusual situation. You must be living on the San Andreas fault line or in a dry area where you cannot get fire insurance. If that does not sound like your situation, you may want to go back and check the figures again. If, after double-checking, it still seems as though your home is worth much more to rent than it is to buy, you should throw a party. The value is likely to go up.

If the present price of your home is approximately equal to its rental value, you would be taking a greater risk to sell at the moment. You would probably have to pay the same amount in rent that you now get free for living there. And you would lose the tax subsidy of ownership, plus transfer taxes, commissions, the costs of moving, headaches, etc. Unless you would be happy moving to a place that rents for much less than your current home —or you expect home values to fall significantly—you may want to stay put.

But if the figure on line 1 is much greater than line 4, your house is selling at a significant *premium* to its rental value. You should think further about selling.

1. Value of home   _____

2. Rental value of home   _____

3. 100 divided by bond yield =   _____

4. Multiply line 2 × line 3 =   _____
   (Capitalization of rent)

5. Subtract line 4 from line 1   _____
   Premium (or discount)

If line 5 is a positive number, take the calculation further. Divide line 1 by line 4 and subtract 1 to obtain the percentage premium of your home's present selling price.

6. Divide line 1 by line 4 and subtract 1   _____
   The percent premium

If the premium percentage (number on line 6) is 50 percent or greater, and more than $10,000 is at stake (number on line 5), you have a strong preliminary case for selling now. But more calculations are in order. . . .

You must consider both your equity in the value of your home and the tax advantages of ownership. On line 7 enter the total debt outstanding on all of your mortgages. Then subtract line 7 from line 1. This will give you the value of your present equity in the home. The larger this figure, the more you have to gain by cashing in.

Next multiply the number on line 8 by .1 (or the long-term government bond yield) for an approximation of the income you could get with your capital in another investment. A 10 percent annual return on financial investments is modest. You might do better or worse. *Strategic Investment*'s Conservative Portfolio has recorded about a 40 percent gain in each of the years since its inception—invested only in international bank deposits, bonds, and blue-chip stocks. Market conditions may not allow such rapid gains with conservative investments in the future. And losses are possible as well as profits. But a 10 percent return on financial assets is not unreasonable.

   7. Mortgages due   _____

   8. Subtract line 7 from line 1   _____
      Your equity

   9. Multiply by .1   × .1

  10. Your opportunity cost   (_____)

(In case you're wondering, parentheses (_____) are employed because costs are negative numbers.

Against the opportunity cost of owning, you have to consider the so-called tax subsidy. If you itemize your deductions, you get to reduce your interest cost for borrowing to finance a home by the percentage of your marginal tax bracket. That means that if you are in the 28 percent bracket, your actual interest expenses are 72 percent of what you pay to the mortgage holders. The other fraction of the cost is money that you would have paid in taxes.

On line 11 enter your annual interest cost. On line 12, multiply by .72 (or 100 minus the amount of your tax rate if it is different from 28 percent). Enter the product of these two numbers on line 13. This is your true annual interest cost.

  11. Annual interest cost   _____

  12. Multiply by .72   _____

  13. True interest cost   (_____)

Now add lines 10 and 13 together to get your annual carrying costs of owning a home. (This figure does not include property taxes, utilities, and other operating expenses.)

  14. Add lines 10 and 13   (_____)
      Your carrying costs

To know whether you are gaining anything, you have to know your annual gain from inflation in reducing the value of the mortgage—as well as the gain (or loss) in value of the home. In our opinion, home values are as likely to fall as rise. There is a possibility of negative movement in the CPI. That would increase the real cost of the mortgage and turn leverage against you.

However, even without extreme developments, many homeowners are losing money by holding their properties now. If gains in home value are nil and your interest costs are high, you may be one of them.

Multiply the mortgage value times the current inflation rate (1.5% in 1986). This will give you the simple gain from inflation (without taking interest costs into consideration).

Then add (or subtract) the annual rate of change in the value of the home. That is a number you will have to guess unless you are well informed about property values in your area. There were a few areas in the United States where home prices increased in 1985 over 1984. For example, Boston and Menlo Park, California, were said by Caldwell Banker to have posted gains. Many other areas posted losses of up to 12 percent—as reported by Caldwell Banker. We believe that there is a tendency to underestimate declines because the housing market is so illiquid. Many people will offer their homes for sale at too high a price. Their homes will not sell. But rather than lowering their price to reflect actual market demand, owners will hold out for an enthusiastic buyer. It may take many months or even years of waiting before they acknowledge the lower demand by reducing their asking price so a sale can transpire.

If you have read this far, you know that we expect any gains you may presently be realizing to be in danger. Plug in various numbers to see what would happen if we are right. What would a 10 percent decline in your home value do to your equity? A 15 percent decline? A depression-sized drop of 25 percent?

In calculating your gain from owning a house, you also have to consider the fact that you can live there rent-free. Add in the rental cost you would have to bear by living elsewhere. Put that figure on line 18.

Then add lines 16, 17, and 18 to give the current dollar benefits of owning your home.

Number from line 7 _____

15. Multiply line 7 by .02   .02
    (or the current inflation
    rate)

16. Current inflation gain   _____

17. Annual equity change   _____
    (Subtract if negative)

18. rental cost

19. Add lines 16, 17, and 18   _____

20. Add lines 14 and 19   _____

Are the benefits greater or less than the costs at present? Compare the totals on lines 14 and 19. If costs exceed the benefits by more than 25 percent, you have a very strong reason to sell. We have left out of consideration many of the real costs of operating a home, such as painting, repairs, insurance, maintenance, and other costs that are often borne by landlords when you rent. If those costs were calculated, they would reduce the benefit from owning further.

This rather tedious wrestling match with arithmetic was designed to help you bring your own bottom line more clearly into focus. However, unless you have been filling in numbers as you read, you have not seen any bottom line at all, just blanks. We urge you to spend the time to make the necessary calculations for your own situation.

AVERAGE NEW HOME PRICES

The following are the median home prices in major metropolitan areas of the United States for 1985. Data are from the United States League of Savings Institutions:

Boston $126,000

New York City $129,700

Philadelphia $69,450

Baltimore $75,157

Washington, $105,000

Raleigh/Durham $73,825

Atlanta $87,250

Miami $82,400

New Orleans $90,500

Houston $88,350

St. Louis $67,000

Detroit $61,000

Cincinnati $55,300

Pittsburgh $54,152

Chicago $87,000

Milwaukee $69,750

Dallas/Fort Worth $94,750

Oklahoma City $80,500

Salt Lake City/Ogden $66,000

Los Angeles/Long Beach $123,000

San Francisco $152,000

Portland $69,900

APPENDIX V:

Investment Products from James Dale Davidson and Sir William Rees-Mogg

STRATEGIC INVESTMENT

If you are interested in the line of analysis in this book and would like to follow investment advice that updates it on a regular basis, write for a sample copy of *Strategic Investment*. Edited by James Dale Davidson and Sir William Rees-Mogg, this monthly investment advisory provides specific stock, option, and futures recommendations. Steve Newby, one of America's most succesful analysts of small companies, makes regular portfolio recommendations. And there are occasional contributions from other leading contributors. While past results are no guarantee of future performance, the record to date has been outstanding. From the onset of publication in 1984 through the end of January 1987, *Strategic Investment* closed out 89 high-risk, Speculative trades. Fifty-two of those trades (58 percent) were profitable. The average result, combining winners with losers, was a profit of 60.55 percent. Since the average holding period was less than three months, the annualized rate of profit (noncompounded) was an astounding 252 percent. Each issue also includes exclusive intelligence bulletins that provide early warning of geopolitical developments and economic trends. The subscription price is ninety-six dollars per year.

GOLDLINE

If you are interested in trading metals, including gold, silver, platinum, palladium, and copper, Davidson and Rees-Mogg also publish *Goldline*, a twenty-four-hour hotline service, that provides technical trading advice by James J. Mayfield IV. Mayfield was selected as the top commodity broker in the United States in the 1985 trading championships reported in *Barron's*, with a monitored return of 189.9 percent in just four months. A *Goldline* subscription is $197.

Both *Strategic Investment* and *Goldline* have offices at Suite 701, Watergate Building, 2600 Virginia Avenue, N.W., Washington, D.C. 20037

CROSS MARKET OPPORTUNITY FUND

James Davidson and Sir William Rees-Mogg have started a new mutual fund to invest along the lines suggested in this book. Among the other directors are Gilbert de Botton, president of Global Asset Management in London and former president of the Rothschild Bank in Zurich; Steve Newby, one of America's leading analysts of over-the-counter stocks; and Gary Vernier, former chief of futures trading at Shell Oil.

The Cross Market Opportunity Fund is being registered with the Securities and Exchange Commission, so it will be open to American citizens. Brown Brothers, Harriman & Co. will be the custodians. The minimum investment is $1,000.

For more complete information about the Cross Market Opportunity Fund, including a description of all charges and expenses, write to The Cross Market Opportunity Fund, Advanced Information Management, Inc., P.O. Box 2798, Boston, Massachusetts 02208. Shares will be sold only by means of a prospectus which should be read carefully before you send money.

ABOUT THE AUTHORS:

James Dale Davidson and Sir William Rees-Mogg edit and publish *Strategic Investment,* one of the world's best-performing investment letters. Davidson is founder and chairman of the National Taxpayers Union and the driving force behind the Constitutional Convention to Balance the Budget. Davidson was also the founding president of the *Hulbert Financial Digest,* the authoritative financial journal that rates and analyzes the profitability of investment advice. He is a director of four corporations and a frequent television commentator. He has written for the *Wall Street Journal* and national magazines and is the author of *The Squeeze,* published by Summit in 1982.

Sir William Rees-Mogg is a financial advisor to some of the world's wealthiest investors. He was formerly editor of the *Times* of London, and vice-chairman of the British Broadcasting Corporation. In 1951, he was president of the Oxford Union. He was Visiting Fellow, Nuffield College, Oxford, from 1968 to 1972. He is now chairman of the Arts Council of Great Britain, an independent government agency with an annual budget of $200 million. Sir William is a director of General Electric Company, PLC, and Chairman of the publishing house, Sidgwick & Jackson. He is also proprietor of Pickering & Chatto, one of London's leading antiquarian booksellers. He is the author of *The Reigning Error: The Crisis of World Inflation.*